To Serve and Protect

"The United States today delivers law and order in the same socialist manner that the USSR delivered food and shoes—and with comparable results. We can do better. In his provocative yet practical book, *To Serve and Protect*, Bruce Benson shows how to harness the productive power of competition and choice to deliver police, courts, and sanctions geared to protect individuals and their rights, rather than the prerogatives of the law enforcement bureaucracy. He considers both radical and incremental reforms and chronicles the real-world benefits that have been achieved where they have been implemented. Anyone concerned with crime and justice should study these recommendations carefully."

—RANDY E. BARNETT
Professor of Law, Boston University

"Bruce Benson's book, *To Serve and Protect*, will cause readers to rethink their preconceived notions of not just what law enforcement services can be contracted out but also when government involvement is even desirable. The book is as comprehensive as it is bold, and it does not shy away from difficult questions. Benson's effort in drawing all these different sources together has done us all a great service."

—JOHN R. LOTT, JR.
Former Chief Economist, U.S. Sentencing Commission
Fellow, School of Law, University of Chicago

The Political Economy of the Austrian School Series
General Editor: Mario Rizzo, New York University

Although long associated with a deep appreciation of the free market, the Austrian School has not been fully recognized as a unique approach in analyzing the role of government in the economy. A major contribution of the Austrian School was to demonstrate, as early as 1920, the impossibility of economic calculation under socialism. Recent events in the former Soviet Union and Eastern Europe have dramatically illustrated the cogency of this argument. In more recent times and in contrast to conventional static analyses, Austrian research has been concerned with the impact of government control on entrepreneurial discovery. To what extent does the impact of such control go beyond the firm's static pricing decision and reach into the very discovery of new opportunities and hence the transmission of knowledge in society? Austrians are also concerned with the dynamics of state intervention—the degree to which one intervention induces further interventions and, conversely, the degree to which one decontrol "necessitates" further steps in the process of deregulation. Finally, the Austrian School is firmly committed to the value-freedom of economics, that is, the separation of the analysis of policy consequences from the moral and political values inherent in the *advocacy* of particular economic policies.

 The Independent Institute is a nonprofit, nonpartisan, scholarly research and educational organization that sponsors comprehensive studies on the political economy of critical social and economic problems.

The politicization of decision making in society has largely confined public debate to the narrow reconsideration of existing policies. Given the prevailing influence of partisan interests, little social innovation has occurred. In order to understand both the nature of and possible solutions to major public issues, the Independent Institute's program adheres to the highest standards of independent inquiry and is pursued regardless of prevailing political or social biases and conventions. The resulting studies are widely distributed as books and other publications, and publicly debated through numerous conference and media programs.

Through this uncommon independence, depth, and clarity, the Independent Institute pushes at the frontiers of our knowledge, redefines the debate over public issues, and fosters new and effective directions for government reform.

To Serve and Protect

*Privatization and Community
in Criminal Justice*

Bruce L. Benson

Foreword by Marvin E. Wolfgang

An Independent Institute Book

NEW YORK UNIVERSITY PRESS
New York and London

NEW YORK UNIVERSITY PRESS
New York and London

Library of Congress Cataloging-in-Publication Data
Benson, Bruce L., 1949–
To serve and protect : privatization and community in criminal
justice / Bruce L. Benson ; with a foreword by Marvin E. Wolfgang.
p.   cm. — (The political economy of the Austrian school)
"An Independent Institute book."
Includes bibliographical references and index.
ISBN 0-8147-1327-0 (cloth : acid-free paper)
1. Criminal justice, Administration of—United States. 2. Privatization—
United States. 3. Police—Contracting out—United States. 4. Corrections—
Contracting out—United States. 5. Crime prevention—United States—
Citizen participation. I. Title. II. Series.
HV9950.B49   1998
364.973—ddc21   98-19688
                         CIP

New York University Press books are printed on acid-free paper,
and their binding materials are chosen for strength and durability.

Manufactured in the United States of America

10 9 8 7 6 5 4 3 2 1

For my daughters:

May they grow up and grow old in a free society, where they are also free from both fear of crime and fear of ill-conceived government solutions to crime.

Contents

Foreword

Like most of my colleagues in criminology, and like many of my lay friends, I have been fearful about and fascinated with the prospect of privatization of prisons, or of any other aspects of the criminal justice system. Part of that hesitant concern for privatizing what has long but not always been under public domain was rooted in the scattered history of vigilantism, nineteenth-century convict labor, Georgia chain gangs, Wild West frontier gun-toting justice, corruption among cops, and bribery of legislators and judges.

Although aware of what I have felt to be an increasing encroachment by government on my personal life, I have not equated legalized usurpation of property, liberty, and responsibility with illegal acts of burglary, theft, and other criminal concepts. From a political philosophical perspective, I consider myself a blend of traditional liberal and libertarian ideas. Democratic freedom of my individual rights along with governmental security and protection through the Lockean social contract have been thoughts that guided my ship through the waters of life while allowing me to be a reasonable "captain of my fate."

Through *To Serve and Protect,* the author leads the reader to realize the extent to which the government has taken over many functions and private property rights from the individual. In a succinct, compact philosophical way, and with the logic of a trained scientist, the author makes the reader aware of the private security industry with its thousands of skilled crime-prevention experts, sophisticated microcomputers, armored trucks, alarm systems and perimeter safeguards, neighborhood watch groups, private community policing, and many other ways of coping with crime that far exceed the remedies provided by the public governmental sector.

The thrust of the theme of the chapters that follow is not a screaming attack on public law enforcement nor on the traditional prosecutorial, judicial, and correctional systems. Rather, the theme running through this volume is the strength of the complementarity that private security, victim input to prosecution, and negotiation and mediation outside of public prosecution and trial can offer to improve the efficiency and effectiveness of society's proaction and reaction to crime reduction.

My short definition of criminology, with an emphasis on the suffix that refers to knowledge, is the scientific study of crime, criminals, and society's reaction to both. The phrase "society's reaction to both" includes law enforcement, the police, prosecution, trial and judicial response, probation, prisons, and parole—what we normally refer to as corrections.

Our traditional textbooks in criminology and criminal justice describe the government's role in the management of the criminal justice system. Causes of crime, theories of crime causation, types of crime, and the history of criminal law are common features of the graduate and undergraduate education of students who seek degrees in criminology throughout the country. What is lacking, I have come to realize, is an awareness of teaching of the importance of the private, or nongovernmental, activities that exist not only in the United States but in France, Scandinavian countries, and in the most populous country in the world, the People's Republic of China.

There are many things that I and the reader of this volume will learn. There are significant differences between contracting out and true or complete privatization of aspects of the criminal justice system. The Federal Bureau of Prisons has contracted out all of its halfway house operations since 1979. Almost all aspects of corrections in publicly operated facilities including food services, counseling, industrial programs, maintenance, security, educational, and vocational training are under contract with private firms on a piecemeal basis. As chapter 6 tells, arbitration, mediation, private courts, and other less formal ways of imposing private sanctions are becoming widespread. The prosecutor's diversion programs to a private mediation program are now taking hold in the United States. My own experience over the past decade of research on crime and delinquency in the People's Republic of China has convinced me of the importance, efficiency, and effectiveness of the process of mediation. There are thousands of mediation committees in China, before and since the revolution in 1949, that rely upon Confucian principles and current political philosophy for resolving disputes and criminal behavior between offenders and their victims. Although we may think of China exercising more control over individual behavior than is done in Western societies, there is indeed more privatization of "society's reaction to crime and criminals" than, I think, we have in the West. An old Chinese proverb warns us: "In death, avoid going to hell; in life, avoid going to court." In China, negotiation, arbitration, and mediation have long been common avenues of avoiding the strict governmental approach to deterrence, reformation of the offender, reduction of recidivism, and prevention of crime.

This volume emphasizes the Cesare Beccarian notion (from his 1974 "Essay on Crime and Punishment") that it is the certainty not the severity of punishment that deters crime. Yet in the United Sates only about 39 percent of crimes reported in the National Crime Victim Survey are eventually reported to the police and end up in the Uniform Crime Reports published annually by the FBI. Under these circumstances, of one hundred crimes reported only about one or two offenders are convicted and sent to prison. The public criminal justice system must be classified as a failure system. Indeed, as the author of *To Serve and Protect* suggests, along with Jeremy Bentham, the eighteenth-century English philosopher, "criminals implicitly weigh the expected benefits of an offense against the expected costs when they are choosing to commit a crime. One potentially important cost of committing a crime is the punishment the criminal expects," or the "price" society charges for crime. If the length of a sentence is irrelevant as a deterrent, the first reaction to crime is the private citizen who should report the crime. And our citizens are not taking this step. Why? Fear of retaliation? Yes, but more likely because the public police enforcement agencies fail to respond to citizens' reporting of crime and because victims who report to our public agencies lose time, wages, and often their dignity when they become involved in the prosecutorial and judicial processes.

There is convincing evidence in chapter 6 that the high cost of cooperating with police and prosecutors leads to the development of extrajudicial processes and "self-help" procedures, or "private justice." Private justice is defined as "the localized nonstate systems of administering and sanctioning individuals accused of rule breaking or disputing."

Government law enforcement was not the norm in the original thirteen colonies. Moreover, we are told, there is a growing literature that is concluding that the frontier West in the nineteenth century was not very violent, that it "was a far more civilized, more peaceful and safer place than American society today," mostly because there was private justice that did not offend the values of democratic processes. Hence, the American West of that century was not lawless, it was "stateless." Even during the gold-mining days of mid-nineteenth-century California, miners had a strong desire for organization and law, and they established a full range of private property law including an elected *alcalde,* or justice of the peace, to act as arbitrator in mining disputes.

The Milton Eisenhower Foundation, a private outgrowth of President Johnson's National Commission on the Causes and Prevention of Violence, and of which I am Chairman of the Board, sponsored a visit of twenty-eight U.S. police commissioners and public security personnel to the Police Academy in Tokyo to learn how law enforcement functions in Japan. The result of that memorable experience helped to promote the development of what is now referred to as community policing. In the United States, private security guards and patrolmen and voluntary watch and patrol organizations do what our public police have no generally done, namely, making routine checks on buildings for residents or businesses and "watching to prevent" crime. In Japan, the public police function more like our private security. It is not surprising, therefore, that our police departments are actively supporting neighborhood watch organizations and aiding in their formation.

Not every reader of this volume will be convinced that the privatization of criminal justice is appealing. But the author makes a good argument for the advantages of freedom of choice, competition, better information, reduced costs, and the benefits of specialization in the private sector. He argues, for example, against the belief that private police are violent, indicating that fewer than 10 percent of the total private security is armed. Guardsmark, one of the largest national private security firms, we are told, armed only 3 percent of its uniformed personnel, in 1985.

The underlying philosophy of human behavior represented here is that of free will, the notion of the Classical School of Criminology from the eighteenth century, that we are free moral agents and know right from wrong. "All individuals," we are told, "should be treated as free and responsible beings as long as they live up to their responsibilities to others." "But someone, who, in the exercise of free will, intentionally violates another person's property rights through theft or violence, forfeits his own property rights (economics and civil) until justice is done."

This philosophy of free will underlies our criminal code and pursuit of punishment. But there are considerations of a broad biocultural determinism that should be considered as well. From the historical moment of our birth to the color of our eyes and hair, to the native language we speak and the gender we possess, we are persons formed by determinate forces beyond our control. Causes of crime are not simply or merely the result of freedom of choice. By the same reasoning, society's response to crime and criminals may be viewed as a function of broad determinate forces. We are required, therefore, to study the history of crime prevention, deterrence, reformation, and protection of society to ferret out the best resolutions. Privatization and restitution to victims emerge as the most viable measures, says the author of this provocative, persuasive volume.

Restitution is highlighted here. Japan is again used as an example, for most Japanese criminals admit guilt, not only to public authorities but also through intermediaries (for example, family, friend) to the victim. The admission to the victim occurs before public prosecution. In effect, the criminal bargains with the victim and offers restitution through a mediator. A similar process is traditional in the People's Republic of China. Rather than offering the prosecutor a guilty plea, the criminal satisfies the victim with a sufficient restitution.

The Occident, I believe, can learn much from the Orient about nongovernmental procedures of criminal justice. If restitution were to be the primary goal of the criminal justice system, as is suggested in chapter 9, much stronger incentives for greater victim reporting and cooperation in prosecution would occur, thus increasing the certainty of punishment and greater deterrence.

To Serve and Protect enlivens the argument that the primary costs of crime are borne by victims who are not compensated for their losses. Noncriminal taxpayers pay for all prisons as well as such indirect costs as the maintenance of the families of many criminals with welfare programs. The enormous prison population in the United State remains an untapped resource that could be employed to reduce substantially the costs to taxpayers. This is a message that is difficult to rebut.

The privatization of criminal justice from crime reporting to enforcement, mediation, prosecution, restitution, and prison management should be seriously considered, empirically evaluated, and if found to be positive, implemented. This volume is an important, logically coherent, and cogently presented advocacy of the value of more private involvement in society's proaction and reaction to crime.

> Marvin E. Wolfgang, Director
> Sellin Center for Studies in Criminology
> and Criminal Law
> University of Pennsylvania

Preface

Why the Timing Might Be Right

The 1994 congressional and gubernatorial elections suggested that the majority of U.S. citizens may no longer see big government as the solution to the problems they face. Perhaps they rightly recognize that government generally does not resolve most (any?) of the problems that citizens demand that it solve and politicians and bureaucrats claim are solvable. This may explain why they elected large numbers of Republicans—the prominent party whose candidates make the most vocal claims about recognizing government failures everywhere and wanting less government.

The 1996 reelection of President Clinton and reductions in the Republican majority of 1994 may suggest second thoughts on the part of some voters, but Clinton clearly was running on a moderate platform against a rival who is even more identified with "Washington politics as usual" than the president is; and furthermore, many Republicans do not appear to be carrying their arguments as far as they could and perhaps should. As William A. Niskanen, chairman of the Cato Institute, explains in discussing the House Republicans' "Contract with America": "The most unfortunate measure passed by the House to date is a new crime bill that maintains most of the outrageous provisions of the crime law enacted in 1994. The crime bill, which federalizes most violent crimes and increases federal spending, is wholly inconsistent with the general commitment to limited constitutional government in other parts of the contract" (1995). Although the Republican majority apparently sees failures in *almost* every area of policy where big-government tactics have been tried, many Republicans (and Democrats) continue to advocate a big-government solution to crime: the most popular recommendations for "solving the crime problem" appear to be building more prisons, mandating more punishment, getting tougher on drugs, and to a lesser degree, employing a larger public police bureaucracy! But these are simply variants on the same big-government policy themes that have been tried and have failed for at least the last three to four decades, if not much longer. The 1996 election clearly demonstrated dissatisfaction with at least part of the crime policy emanating from Washington as both California and Arizona voters chose to legalize the use of marijuana for medical purposes (in Arizona other drugs were legalized as well). Perhaps the Dole candidacy was also hurt by its illicit-drug-policy proposals, given the growing perception that the war on drugs is not working and that its costs in terms of both taxpayers' money and citizens' civil and economic liberties are enormous.

E. J. Dionne, Jr. (1994) reports that many important members of the Republican majority established in 1994 are likely to be generally skeptical of big-government remedies, so perhaps a careful and detailed articulation of the potential scope for privatization in criminal justice could have a significant policy impact now that it could not have had earlier. This possibility is reinforced by the fact that policymakers in at least some states and local jurisdictions are seriously considering avenues for privatization. Since 1980, at least twenty-five states have passed legislation to authorize contracting out for correctional services, and some have begun to consider other options as well. Among these promising developments is the William I. Koch Commission on Crime Reduction and Prevention for the State of Kansas, which in 1994 commissioned a report from me on privatization in criminal justice (Benson 1996b) in order to explore a broad range of privatization alternatives. Furthermore, even some public officials who are directly charged with crime control admit that there may be little that government can really do about the problem without much greater private-sector involvement. In Chicago, for example, the police department is attempting to implement a massive change in strategy, abandoning the traditional big-government model of policing that emphasizes random automobile patrols, rapid response, a reliance on forensic technology in after-the-crime investigations, and a focus on arrest and incarceration. The department's decision makers explain that this change is a result of the strong evidence that (1) even doubling the number of police squad cars does not significantly affect crime, (2) rapid response by police does not alter the probability of arrest (what matters is rapid reporting and cooperation by victims and witnesses), (3) information from cooperative private citizens is the key to solving crimes, but the traditional approach tends to isolate police from the citizenry and reduce private involvement rather than to create a cooperative environment, and (4) emphasis on arrests after crimes are committed and on incarceration as punishment appears to have no long-term deterrent effect (Chicago Police Department, 1993, 7–9). The Chicago Alternative Policing Strategy (CAPS) emphasizes the need for "community"—that is, private citizen—involvement in a proactive effort to prevent crime. Thus, CAPS's goals are to actively encourage and support the development of localized citizen and business groups that can cooperate in watching to prevent crime, and to take public police out of their patrol cars and rapid response system in order to put them back on the beat, in large part in order to establish cooperative relationships with private citizens in the neighborhoods and local communities of the city. The latest U.S. crime statistics, released on June 1, 1997, show crime rates dropping for the fifth year in a row, and although some Washington politicians want to claim credit, most observers recognize that Washington has had little or nothing to do with it. In fact, the sources of this continued drop are very decentralized. One factor appears to be that police officials in many of America's cities and towns are beginning to at least recognize that they cannot control crime without drawing on the private sector for significant levels of support, and as a consequence local communities all over the country are adopting innovative new approaches to policing along the lines of CAPS. But much of the change is arising from even more decentralized sources. The Tallahassee, Florida, police chief, Tom Coe, an active advocate of greater private-sector involvement in crime control, recently stated, for example, that "the police have very little to do with crime when it comes down to it. The community cannot put enough cops out there to protect everyone. You've got to empower the people to protect themselves" (Cole 1995). People are in fact protecting themselves in a wide variety of ways. They are organizing their neighbors to watch out for one another, they are buying all sorts of crime prevention and detection devices from the rapidly expanding markets for such equipment, and they are employing ever increasing numbers of private security personnel. The tremendous scope and impact of these private-sector activities is rarely recognized and clearly underappreciated by public-sector policymakers and policy analysts. Perhaps as a consequence, they have created a number of legal barriers that hamper the development of additional opportunities for people to protect themselves. What else can be done to empower the citizens to prevent crime?

Certainly programs like CAPS, which encourage organizations such as Crime Watch and create mechanisms for these organizations to comfortably interact with police, appear to be steps in the right direction, but much more can be done. Furthermore, despite a long history of disdain for private security, some police are even beginning to recognize the vital role of the private security industry. In New York, for example, the Area Police/Private Security Liaison (APPL) program was started in 1986 in order to create a better working relationship between public and private security, to share information, to identify and discuss crime trends, and to work together in order to control crime. This book provides a policy-oriented examination of the potential for and the steps required for empowering the people to develop even greater levels of private-sector involvement in criminal justice.

The perception that the time may be right for such a book is reinforced by the facts that many widely regarded "experts" on criminal justice policy are explicitly or implicitly declaring that they really do not know what government can do either. For instance, James Q. Wilson, perhaps the best reputed of all "conservative" academic commentators on crime policy, and Joan Petersillia, a highly regarded "liberal" past president of the American Society of Criminology and former director of the prestigious Criminal Justice Program at the Rand Corporation, coedited a book entitled *Crime,* drawing together leading experts from both the liberal and the conservative sides of the issue. The result should become the "most definitive source of references to the policy-oriented literature on crime and justice," according to Charles H. Logan, professor of sociology at the University of Connecticut, who reviews the book in *The Public Interest.* Logan points out that the "careful and realistic assessments of what is truly known on their respective topics" suggest that these experts are generally admitting that no one really knows what to do about crime. But he also emphasizes that "common to both liberal and conservative thinking about crime . . . is support for considerable government intervention, albeit of different sorts. . . . Missing from *Crime* is any sustained discussion of criminal justice from a libertarian or rights-based perspective. More than either liberals or conservatives, libertarians are reluctant to authorize government to try to shape behavior" (Logan 1995, 83). I have attempted in the current volume to fill the void that Logan suggests has been left by *Crime,* with an exploration of potential nongovernmental solutions to crime problems.

Others are trying to supply at least part of what is lacking as well. Academics are examining some aspects of privatization in considerable detail. Charles Logan's book *Private Prisons: Cons and Pros* (1990) and the forthcoming volume *Private Corrections: Penal Reform, Justice, and Society,* edited by Jan Brakel, are excellent examples of such focused research. Despite the fact that I work at Florida State University and therefore face considerable pressure to not say anything good about "the gators," I must also mention the important efforts of the people at the Center for Studies in Criminology and Law at the University of Florida, who are going beyond research by working with the Private Corrections Services Association to serve as a clearinghouse for research and information on private correctional services. The potential for privatization in numerous areas of criminal law is also beginning to be explored in such publications as *Privatizing the United States Justice System* (see Benson, 1992a), edited by Gary W. Bowman, Simon Hakim, and Paul Seidenstat (all from Temple University), and the Morgan O. Reynolds' (Texas A&M University) report *Using the Private Sector to Deter Crime* (1994b). Similarly, the Office of International Criminal Justice in March of 1995 sponsored a conference "Privatization in Criminal Justice: Public and Private Partnerships," directed by James Moran of the University of Illinois at Chicago (see also Moran's article "Privatizing Criminal Justice" [1995]). Thus, the idea of privatization in criminal justice appears to be gaining some credibility in the academic community as well as among some public officials. Given the mood of the electorate, the substantial number of elected Republicans who clearly want to find ways to reduce the size and scope of government, and the increasing recognition that expensive big-government crime programs are not working, the time appears to be ripe for a policy-oriented examination of the potential for and the steps required to make a wide range of possible changes that can lead to greater private-sector involvement in all aspects of the criminal justice process.

Acknowledgments

The foundation of this book was developed in a report prepared in 1994 for the Koch Commission on Crime Reduction and Prevention for the State of Kansas, entitled "Privatization in Criminal Justice." David Theroux, president of the Independent Institute, deserves special recognition and thanks in this regard, first because, as a member of the Koch Commission, he contacted me and asked me to prepare the report. He then published it as one of the Institute's *Independent Policy Reports*. Later he encouraged me to write this book, both by showing strong interest in it and by offering me an attractive contract for the finished product. Furthermore, comments and suggestions from Theroux and other people from the Koch Commission and the Independent Institute, particularly Robert Higgs, were instrumental in shaping the book's content. I also want to thank Peter Boettke, Mario Rizzo, and William Butos, editors of this series, "The Political Economy of the Austrian School," for their positive reactions to and comments on the book. Anonymous reviewers also deserve thanks for their helpful comments, as do a number of people who have served as sounding boards for my ideas or critics of various related papers (e.g., David Friedman, Randy Holcombe, Hans Herman Hoppe, John Lott, Andrew Morriss, David Rasmussen, Kevin Reffitt, Murray Rothbard, Gordon Tullock, and many of the faculty, staff, and students participating in the Institute for Humane Studies– sponsored "Liberty and Society Seminars" at which I lectured in 1995 and 1996; my apologies to anyone that I failed to mention).

This book overlaps with and builds on both ongoing and previous work. In fact, it represents one component of my primary research agenda on law and legal institutions, various parts of which have been generously supported over the years by the Independent Institute, the Earhart Foundation, the Carthage Foundation, the Pacific Research Institute, and the Institute for Humane Studies. It is a particularly important component of my overall research agenda focusing on the costs and benefits of privatization in criminal justice, however. For instance, material initially prepared for this book has been used also as the basis for portions of my papers in the *Journal of Security Administration* (1996a), the *Journal of Libertarian Studies* (1996c), and the *Madison Review* (1997c), and parts of forthcoming papers in *The Independent Review: A Journal of Political Economy* (1998b), *The Journal of Private Enterprise,* and *The Merits of Markets—Critical Issues of the Open Society* (1998d) (an Egon-Sohmen Foundation–sponsored book) are also drawn from sections of this volume. This focus has been explicitly supported by a grant from the Carthage Foundation and a Research Fellowship from the Earhart Foundation. I am very grateful to all of these foundations and institutes for their support, and especially to the Carthage and Earhart Foundations for facilitating my efforts to study and write about private-sector activities in the criminal justice arena. They freed up my time, allowing me to complete the book and its related papers much more quickly than I otherwise could have.

Since this book is part of a larger research agenda, it should not be surprising that it also draws on (and extends) material from my other published or forthcoming articles. These papers appear in *Economic Inquiry* (1994a), the *Journal of Law, Economics, and Organization* (1995a), the *Harvard Journal of Law and Public Policy* (1986b), the *Journal des Economistes et des Etudes Humaines* (1992b), the *Journal of Libertarian Studies* (1986a, 1991b, and 1994b), the *Southern Economic Journal* (1989a), *Firearms and Violence: Issues of Regulation* (1984a, a Ballinger Press book edited by Don Kates, Jr., for the Pacific Research Institute), *Privatizing the United States Justice System* (1992a, a McFarland and Company book edited by Gary Bowman, Simon Hakim, and Paul Seidenstat), *Can the Present Problems of Mature Welfare States Such as Sweden Be Solved?* (1995b, a book edited by Nils Karlson for the City University Press), the *Encyclopedia of Law and Economics* (1997a), the *New Palgrave Dictionary of Economics and the Law* (1998a), *The Voluntary City: New Directions for Urban America* (forthcoming, b, a book edited by David Beito and Peter Gordon for the Independent Institute), and *Private Corrections: Penal Reform, Justice and Society* (forthcoming, a, an Independent Institute–sponsored book edited by Jan Brakel). Parts of this book also can be traced to work I did with David W. Rasmussen, including *The Economic Anatomy of a Drug War: Criminal Justice in the Commons* (a book published by Rowman and Littlefield in 1994); articles in *The Independent Review: A Journal of Political Economy* (1996b) and *Contemporary Policy Issues* (1991); reports written for the Florida Chamber of Commerce ("Crime in Florida," 1994a) and for the Koch Crime Commission ("Illicit Drugs and Crime," published as an *Independent Policy Report,* 1996a); papers written for *The Florida Economy, 1995 Edition* (David A. Denslow, J. F. Scoggins, and Anne Shermyen, editors), and *Taxing Choice:*

The Predatory Politics of Fiscal Discrimination (1997 from Transactions Publishers and edited by William F. Shughart for the Independent Institute); and some of our coauthored work with Iljoong Kim, David Sollars, and Brent Mast, including articles in *Public Choice* (1995), the *Southern Economic Journal* (1994), and the *International Review of Law and Economics* (forthcoming). I thank Dave Rasmussen, Iljoong Kim, Dave Sollars, Brent Mast, Rowman and Littlefield, and the Florida Chamber of Commerce, as well as the editors, publishers, and sponsors of all of these journals and volumes, for their input and support on these earlier publications.

Finally and significantly, *The Enterprise of Law: Justice without the State* (Benson 1990, Pacific Research Institute for Public Policy), which explores government failure in law and the private sector's responses to that failure, is also an obvious precursor to this book. My efforts to write *The Enterprise of Law* really started me on this whole research agenda and, not surprisingly, there is some unavoidable overlap in the content and presentation. Therefore, it is especially appropriate that I thank the Pacific Research Institute for its financial and intellectual support in preparing and publishing *The Enterprise of Law*. Several people who worked at the institute while that project was under way also deserve special thanks, once again including David Theroux, who was the creative force in initiating the project, president of the institute, and who provided a great deal of advice and assistance. Thanks also to Chip Mellor, David's successor as president, and Terry Anderson, the institute's economic advisor, who together steered the book through its many reviews and revisions to its ultimate publication, as well as all of the reviewers acknowledged in the book itself (especially Randy Barnett, whose extensive and careful review almost makes him a coauthor of *The Enterprise of Law* and much of my subsequent work).

This project differs from and extends *The Enterprise of Law* in four important ways. First, this book focuses exclusively on crime and crime policy, a vital issue of the day, rather than covering broader issues (e.g., commercial law, examples of stateless legal systems) that are apparently of little immediate interest to most citizens and most policymakers. Second, it contains less of the "negative" government-failure analysis emphasized in large sections of *The Enterprise of Law*, stressing instead the potential benefits and costs of privatization alternatives. It is easy to criticize the government, but it may be more important to demonstrate that there is an attractive and viable alternative (of course, in order to fully appreciate the benefits of privatization, some discussion of the failures of the government-dominated alternative is still necessary). Third, whereas *The Enterprise of Law* emphasized efficiency issues to the virtual exclusion of other norms that can be relevant to a choice between public and private legal institutions, a broader range of potential normative objectives is considered here. Efficiency gains in crime prevention and in rehabilitating criminals through privatization are still extensively discussed, but justice for victims of crime is the primary normative objective underlying the book's recommendations. Justice for victims and efficiency in crime prevention and rehabilitation of criminals are complements, however, under the right privatized institutional arrangements, so these different normative objectives do not involve tradeoffs or imply different institutional arrangements. And fourth, though *The Enterprise of Law* ended with a discussion of what a fully privatized or "stateless" legal system might look like, it really did not have much practical policy discussion about how to go about supporting and encouraging a movement in the direction of more privatization. In contrast, this book closes by explaining and advocating a wide range of specific policy options that can lead to varying degrees of privatization.

1

Introduction

Questions about crime policy are almost inevitably stated in a fashion that immediately eliminates a huge number of potential options. The question typically asked is "What should the government do to solve the crime problem?" But there are other ways to solve problems. As Israel M. Kirzner (1997: 62) explains, for instance, entrepreneurial discovery of opportunities gradually and systematically pushes back the boundaries of ignorance, thereby driving down costs and prices while increasing both the quantity and quality of output. In the public sector's production of crime control, ignorance abounds, costs are high and rising, and both the quality and quantity of the effective output of the criminal justice system clearly have room for improvement. For instance, a massive National Advisory Commission on Criminal Justice Standards and Goals (NACCJSG) report explains:

> Over the past 25 years, this country has become the unwilling victim of a crime epidemic. The present seriousness of the disease has outstripped even the most pessimistic prognosis. Coupled with a steadily rising numerical frequency of crimes is a savage viciousness that has rendered the American public almost immune from further shock. The ten-million-plus major felonies that annually occur have seriously debilitated the quality of life in the United States.
>
> Citizens do not feel safe and, in fact, are not safe in their own homes or on their own streets. Businesses are rocked to bankruptcy by the high cost of crime committed by their own employees as well as by hordes of outsiders. Downtown areas at night are all but deserted. Large cities are viewed as jungles of criminality. (NACCJSG 1976: Introduction)

It certainly sounds as if there may be some advantage to turning the entrepreneurial discovery process loose on crime control, but instead the focus has been on government programs, as the NACCJSG report notes:

> In a valiant but vain attempt to stem this massive tide of criminality, government officials, scholars, politicians, and a vast array of other professionals have responded with plans, programs, and projects all designed to reduce crime.

One great hope was vested in increases in the numerical strength of the criminal justice system. More police, more prosecutors, more public defenders, more judges, more corrections workers, and more probation and parole officers soon swelled city, county, State, and Federal budgets but did not cause a reduction in crime.

A second approach involved upgrading the quality of the criminal justice system personnel. College education for police, training programs for prosecutors, sentencing conferences for judges, and seminars and institutes for corrections officers served to professionally upgrade criminal justice personnel but did not result in lower crime or recidivism rates. Nor did the quality of justice noticeably improve.

Technology and applied sciences were also thrown into the fray, resulting in sophisticated police communications, computer-assisted court calendar control, and a wide variety of sociologically and psychologically oriented offender-adjusted programs.

Finally, millions of dollars were used to reshape the criminal justice system through the addition of new practices and the deletion of old processes. . . . Unfortunately, although many of these programs were improvements over outdated practices, crime, the cost of crime, the damages from crime, and the fear of crime continued to increase. (NACCJSG 1976: Introduction)

Despite the overwhelming focus on government strategies to control crime, it has been recognized for some time now that private-sector entrepreneurs can discover better ways to reduce crime.

The Privatization Challenge

Perhaps surprisingly, the preceding quotations are from a *1976* report, which also anticipates some of the suggestions made here by concluding that

One massive resource, filled with significant numbers of personnel, armed with a wide array of technology, and directed by professionals who have spent their entire adult lifetimes learning how to prevent and reduce crime, has not been tapped by governments in the fight against criminality. The private security industry, with over one million workers, sophisticated alarm systems and perimeter safeguards, armored trucks, sophisticated mini-computers, and thousands of highly skilled crime prevention experts, offers a potential for coping with crime that can not be equalled by any other remedy or approach.

The application of the resources, technology, skills, and knowledge of the private security industry presents the best hope available for protecting the citizen who has witnessed his defenses against crime shrink to a level which leaves him virtually unprotected.

Underutilized by police, all but ignored by prosecutors and the judiciary, and unknown to corrections officials, the private security professional may be the only person in this society who has the knowledge to effectively prevent crime.

Not represented on the boards or staffs of State Planning Agencies, rarely used by municipal or county planners, only infrequently consulted by elected officials, these members of a six-billion-dollar-a-year industry have crime prevention answers desperately needed by homes, schools, businesses, neighborhoods and communities. (NACCJSG 1976: Introduction)

Even though this 1976 report provides a clear recognition of the growing crime problem and the failure of government programs to stem this growth, for the most part, it had no impact on crime policy. Thus, the 1985 Hallcrest Report on private security for the National Institute of Justice (NIJ) begins in a very similar fashion, noting that government units have continued to pour ever increasing amounts of taxpayer dollars into the public-sector criminal justice system as new plans, programs, and projects are hatched by politicians and public officials, but "neither local, State, nor Federal resources had seriously affected the problem of crime" (Cunningham and Taylor 1985: 1). Furthermore, "conspicuously absent from police-based crime prevention programs . . . is the input of the private security industry. . . . There appears to be little cooperation between public law enforcement and private security" (3).

The private security industry actually is only one component of the still largely unrecognized private-sector involvement in crime control. Voluntary participation in neighborhood or tenant watches and patrols is increasingly widespread, for instance. Moreover, "growing numbers of Americans have undertaken self-help measures to protect themselves" (Cunningham and Taylor 1985: 2). This includes more than just the allocation of personal time and effort to security concerns, however. More and more citizens are buying firearms for personal protection, and burglar alarms are being installed and locks improved. Citizens are barring their windows, learning self-defense, carrying whistles and other noisemakers, and buying self-protection devices. It is more true today than it was in 1976 that "there is virtually no aspect of society that is not in one way or another affected by private security" (NACCJSG 1977: xix).

The private sector's role in criminal justice goes even beyond protection and security. Large amounts of complementary inputs from private citizens are necessary for the public sector's crime control efforts to be effective. Victims' statements are particularly important in the public sector's crime control process, for instance (McDonald 1977; Benson 1994a, 1996c). As McDonald (1977: 301) observes, a huge portion of all crimes that come to the attention of police are those reported by victims. Very few arrests for property or violent crimes result from police-initiated investigations or actions. Furthermore, without the prospect of cooperation by victims or witnesses in providing testimony, a very substantial portion of the violent and property criminals that are arrested would never be successfully prosecuted. Even when a conviction arises through plea bargaining, the threat of such testimony is a primary source of the prosecution's bargaining strength. Clearly, successful production of the commonly shared benefits of crime control such as deterrence requires that a private-sector investment be made in providing these victim and witness inputs. That is, private-citizen input is necessary to public-sector crime control, but the costs of providing that input are borne by the individual private citizens themselves, not by the government (i.e., taxpayers in general).

Private inputs to successful prosecution go even further. Prosecution cannot occur if the accused offender flees after being arrested. Some offenders are held in jail until trial, but jail space is far too limited to hold them all, and besides, constitutional protection of due process includes a requirement to allow for bail. Therefore, many must be released. The most effective way to assure their return for prosecution, compared to the alternative of supervision by the public-sector pretrial release bureaucracy, is the private bail bonding system (Monks 1986; Reynolds 1994b).

The private sector can provide more than crime prevention and inputs to successful public arrests and prosecution. If we look to history, we find that rather than the emphasis on government inputs to and dominance over crime control that we see today, the norm is complete or nearly complete private production of policing, prosecution, and punishment (Cunningham and Taylor 1985: 41; Cardenas 1986; Benson 1990: 21–30, 43–77; 1992b; 1994a; McCrie 1992; Reynolds 1994b). Public police forces did not develop until the middle of the nineteenth century in the United States and Great Britain, and crime victims served as prosecutors in England until almost the turn of the century. Publicly financed and operated prisons are also a relatively recent development, arising in England near the end of the eighteenth century and in the United States even later. Historically, privately imposed sanctions such as ostracism have provided powerful incentives to obey the law (Anderson and Hill 1979; Benson 1989a, 1989b, 1990, 1991a, 1991b, 1992b, 1994a, 1997a, 1998e; Friedman 1979; Solvason 1992, 1993; Morriss 1997).

The historical reality of crime policy is that public provision of criminal justice is a recent social experiment that has not worked as predicted. The increasing role of private-security that we see today is actually a return to historical practices rather than something new, although private-sector institutions and technologies have changed dramatically as entrepreneurs have discovered new ways to deliver the desired protection. Furthermore, "private justice" in the form of sanctions imposed by businesses (e.g., job reassignment, restitution agreements, firing employees who steal from the firm) and neighborhoods (e.g., social ostracism) is once again being substituted for public-sector criminal prosecution. One survey indicates that nearly half of all business security managers investigate and resolve employee thefts within the business organization without ever reporting the crime (see, e.g, Cunningham and Taylor 1985: 11).

The suggestion made above that public officials have continued to ignore the potential benefits of increased private-sector involvement in criminal justice is a bit strong. Many police departments now encourage citizen crime prevention programs that they disparaged as vigilantism not too many years ago: by 1985 more than 90 percent of the nation's police and sheriff departments had formal relationships with citizens' groups such as Crime Watch (Cunningham and Taylor 1985: 2). In Chicago, for instance, the police department is implementing a massive change in its policing strategy, abandoning the traditional model of policing that relies on random automobile patrols, rapid response, forensic technology in after-the-crime investigations rather than citizen information, and a focus on arrest and incarceration. The new Chicago Alternative Policing Strategy (CAPS) emphasizes the need for community involvement in a proactive effort to prevent crime (Chicago Police Department 1993). The program is relatively new, but the intentions are to actively encourage and support the development of localized citizen and business groups that can cooperate in watching to prevent crime, and to take public police out of their patrol cars and rapid response system in order to put them back on the beat, in large part to establish cooperative relationships with the people in local neighborhoods throughout the community.

Some police are even recognizing the vital role of the private security industry. Following the publication of the Hallcrest Report (Cunningham and Taylor 1985) and a "concomitant national law enforcement summit meeting held between the leadership of law enforcement and counterparts from private security," a number of visible efforts were made to establish liaisons between the two groups (Shanahan 1992: 178). In New York, for example, the Area Police/Private Security Liaison (APPL) program was started in 1986 in order to create a better working relationship between public and private security, to share information, to identify and discuss crime trends, and to facilitate cooperation between the public and the private sector in order to control crime. Over nine hundred private security organizations are now interacting with the New York City Police Department through monthly meetings and through a network of telephone and fax communications, with computer networking on the horizon.[1] Both public police officials, led by the New York Police chief, and private security are finding the arrangement to be increasingly desirable. Numerous other examples of developing public-private cooperation can also be cited (see chapters 2, 7, and 11), even though the process continues to be slow in the face of various laws that limit private alternatives as well as strong political resistance, particularly from police officers and their unions. Shanahan (1992: 178) suggests, for instance, that by 1992 there were "only pockets of effective public- and private-sector operational interface" between police and private security, most notably in Detroit and Washington state.

Public-private interface is actually more widespread than might be suspected, however, because government units are also beginning to return many criminal justice functions to the private sector through contracting out. Halfway houses, drug treatment facilities, and other community-based intermediate sanction programs have been provided by private entities under contract for some time. The provision of secure prisons by private firms, developed and run under contract with federal, state, and local governments, is clearly a growth industry, although the private sector still provides only a small portion of the nation's adult prisons. Governments are also contracting with private security firms to do everything from airport security to guarding government facilities to providing entire police forces, but this government-supported "privatization" process in policing is also modest compared to its potential.

The point is that when questions about crime policy are asked, they should be framed more broadly: "What is the most cost-effective way to reduce crime?" I contend that the answer to this question has to include a significant increase in private-sector input to crime control. As Cunningham and Taylor conclude, "Law enforcement can ill afford to continue its traditional policy of isolating and even ignoring the activities of private security. Indeed, law enforcement and government officials must be willing to experiment with some nontraditional approaches. . . . The creative use of private security personnel and technology may be the one viable option left to control crime in our communities" (1985: 72). The same argument holds for other measures that encourage greater private-sector involvement in criminal justice. Witnesses and victims must be encouraged to report crimes and cooperate in prosecution. Business and residential neighbors must be encouraged to cooperate with one another in either producing or purchasing crime prevention efforts. And so on. In some cases greater privatization requires eliminating artificial legal barriers preventing private citizens and entrepreneurs from performing functions that they would voluntarily carry out if they had not been reserved for public-sector entities. In other cases it will have to involve changes in the institutionalized incentives of public employees and private citizens.

An Overview of What Follows

This book examines each of the categories of private-sector inputs into criminal justice alluded to above. Brief descriptions of the level and scope of various aspects of privatization appear in chapters 2, 5, and 6. Much more detailed descriptions of the actual levels of privatization are available elsewhere (e.g., Cunningham and Taylor 1985; Logan 1990), so a primary focus here will be on the cost and benefits of privatization (see chapters 3, 7, 8, and parts of 4) and the factors that tend to influence the level of private-sector involvement (see chapters 4, 6, 9, 10, 11, and 12).

All of the privately provided criminal justice services obviously involve different costs and benefits. But one potential problem facing those who may wish to use or provide private services in criminal justice appears to be almost universal. Political resistance to private actions in criminal justice is widespread, and no matter what particular service is being provided by a private entrepreneur, many of the same basic criticisms are raised by its opponents. Some of the most pervasive claims made by critics of privatization are economic in nature. For instance, it is often contended that for-profit firms will cut corners and reduce quality (e.g., relative to a public agency producing the same service or relative to that which purchasers expect and pay for), in order to increase profits. In other words, there is supposedly a tradeoff between profits and costs, and private entrepreneurs providing any aspects of criminal justice will opt for lower costs: to the degree that costs are low with private provision of a service, it reflects a reduction in quality. A primary purpose of this presentation is to explore the validity (or invalidity) of such economically based criticisms.

Such criticisms of private actions in the criminal justice arena can be challenged by those inside the relevant industries and organizations, of course, because they are intimately familiar with their own incentives, including the relationships between cost and quality. Their arguments, however, are easily dismissed by critics as "self-serving." Another way to address them is for an "outsider" (someone—such as I—who has never worked for a firm that provides any sort of criminal justice services) to confront them from the perspective of microeconomic theory. A potential disadvantage of such a perspective is that an intimate knowledge of administrative and production processes in these various industries is lacking. But such an intimate knowledge is not necessary for addressing the question of whether the profit-quality tradeoff applies in the universal way that critics contend; the same is true of a number of other economically based criticisms. In fact, intimate knowledge of one of these markets does not provide sufficient arguments to address general criticisms leveled at the large variety of private-sector activities. Thus, the somewhat more abstract but generalizable perspective of an economist may provide a useful set of arguments to counter (or support?) critics.

Microeconomics focuses on explaining or predicting how individuals respond to different incentives and constraints. In the case of crime control, there are a number of different institutional arrangements that can and do apply. For example, private security firms may compete for the business of other private-sector individuals or firms. Or private firms may offer competitive bids for a contract to provide security or policing services, prison management, or some support service to a government entity. Under other circumstances, a private provider may be awarded a contract without having to compete, as when a representative of a government unit negotiates directly with only one firm. Still another possibility is that a public bureaucracy produces the service directly. Various other institutional arrangements are also possible, and each arrangement will create a different set of incentives for the individuals involved. Indeed, in contrast to the almost universal application of many criticisms to every area of privatization in criminal justice, the tremendous variety of institutional arrangements suggests that even if some criticisms are valid under one set of institutions, they need not apply in other institutional settings (it also implies that even if the criticism does not apply in one situation, it may in another). An examination of the potential validity of economically based criticisms of private actions within the criminal justice arena therefore requires consideration of institutional settings.

Efficiency need not be the paramount concern in deciding how to produce criminal justice. It is one of several normative criteria that may be relevant. Indeed, a common and perhaps justifiable complaint against economists is that they tend to emphasize efficiency issues to the virtual exclusion of other norms. And in this regard, some of the objections to private involvement in crime control are not economic in nature. Philosophical or ideological issues (e.g., only the state has the right to punish, so contracting for policing or prison services is wrong) also arise and should be addressed. As an economist, I have no more authority to address such normative philosophical and ideological arguments than anyone else, but I also do not have any less authority than anyone else. Therefore, a broader range of potential normative objectives is considered here than might be expected from an economist. Efficiency, including efficient gains in crime prevention and in rehabilitating criminals through privatization, is still extensively discussed (I am an economist, after all), but justice for victims of crime is actually the primary normative objective underlying my recommendations. Efficiency in crime prevention and rehabilitation of criminals turn out to be complements to justice for victims under the right privatized institutional arrangements, however, rather than substitutes as some policy advocates might expect.

In order to explore the institutional circumstances under which criticisms of privatization may or may not be valid, and to suggest policy changes that can lead to effective and efficient achievement of justice for crime victims, my presentation is divided into three parts, each consisting of several chapters. Part I examines the role of private inputs into the public production of crime control. First, the trends in what many policymakers think of when they use the term privatization in criminal justice—contracting out—are briefly examined in chapter 2. Private firms are contracting with government units to provide a growing array of prison, security, policing, and other criminal justice functions that, for several decades now, have generally been performed by government bureaucracies and their employees. In this context the distinction between public and private is explored, and one of the objections to privatized criminal justice (that only the government should have police powers and the power to punish) is addressed. Chapter 3 focuses on the benefits and pitfalls of such contracting out, allowing these arrangements to provide a benchmark to which both pure market and pure bureaucratic alternatives can be compared. Contracting out can be seen as partial privatization because the supply of criminal justice is privatized. This supply side may be competitive or monopolized, depending on the contractual process. Furthermore, the demand side of the process and the development of the contractual process itself remain in the political arena. Chapter 4 explores the incentives leading to the low level of crucial private-sector involvement in the production of arrest and prosecution, looking at those incentives in the context of an examination of the deterrent incentives that the public-sector criminal justice system produces for criminals. This discussion sets up the rest of the book because the same incentives that lead victims and witnesses to avoid reporting also underlie the widespread private investments in protection and in "private justice." The potential for private-sector production of more effective deterrence is examined in subsequent chapters.

Part II examines fully privatized crime control. Chapter 5 discusses the wide array of private activities that have developed to protect individuals and their property, including everything from participatory neighborhood actions, to individual investments in tools of protection, to the private markets for private police and security equipment. The evidence is somewhat sketchy, but it appears that the private sector actually has a much larger role in crime prevention than the public sector does. Chapter 6 explores both historical and current examples of private justice in America to demonstrate that private justice is a traditional American response to government failure in crime control. The potential benefits and alleged costs of privatization in crime control and justice are examined in chapters 7 and 8, respectively, where it is concluded that the benefits are significant and the alleged costs are exaggerated or nonexistent, at least when those activities are free from manipulation for political reasons. After all, private protection and private justice are situations in which both the demand for and the supply of particular aspects of criminal justice can be largely free of political influence, although, as suggested in subsequent chapters, politically motivated constraints on such private-sector activities can be substantial.

Part III contains policy analysis and recommendations. In particular, chapter 9 asks and answers the question, If privatization is so desirable and public interference in the process so bad, how did we get so much public involvement in criminal justice? The answer requires an examination of the historical evolution of criminal law and its institutions, a process that began in England several hundred years ago and is playing itself out on the streets of America today. The primary conclusion is that when kings took away victims' "property rights" to restitution, the evolutionary path of criminal justice in England was dramatically altered. The development of public courts, prosecution, and policing, with all of their undesirable characteristics, was an inevitable result. The United States inherited a criminal justice system that was already developing many of the problems we see today, including nonreporting of crimes by victims and witnesses, plea bargaining, exclusionary rules, crowded punishment facilities, and police corruption. Chapter 10 focuses on the desirability of returning to a system that strives for victim restitution rather than social engineering goals such as deterrence and rehabilitation. In particular, I contend that restitution should be the primary focus of criminal justice, based on normative goals of promoting liberty, justice, and individual responsibility. The current state of restitution in the law is also discussed, along with changes that would be necessary to refocus criminal justice in order to emphasize restitution. A restitution focus should also have direct impacts on crime reduction, however, by increasing the efficiency of the criminal justice system in terms of several social engineering goals. Therefore, though the arguments for restitution made in chapter 10 reflect a liberty and justice objective, the same conclusions can be supported from an efficiency perspective, as suggested in chapters 11 and 12. Recognizing that the costs that society actually can impose on a criminal depend on the probability that the criminal act will be observed, the probability that it will be reported (given observation), the probability that the offender will be successfully apprehended, the probability that the apprehended offender will be successfully prosecuted and convicted, and the severity of the resulting "punishment" (defined to include restitution), I examine policy alternatives for encouraging greater privatization in each of these areas. Privatization policies and resulting efficiency gains in "watching" to both prevent and observe crime, reporting crimes that are observed, and successfully apprehending criminals are explored in chapter 11. Chapter 12 follows with consideration of private alternatives that will increase the probability of prosecution and conviction and effectively implement just punishment. The efficiency implications of a focus on restitution (both for deterring crime and for developing effective rehabilitation) rather than traditional punishment are important components of the presentation in these two chapters, but an array of other policy options for achieving varying degrees of privatization are also examined—institutional changes that can encourage everything from modest increases in contracting out or private investments in security all the way up to full privatization of the entire criminal justice process.

PART I

Private Inputs for Public Crime Control

2

Partial Privatization

The Level and Scope of Contracting Out in Criminal Justice

The term *privatization* is often used as a synonym for contracting out with a private firm for the production of some good or service that was previously exclusively produced by a public-sector agency or bureaucracy. But contracting out is, at most, only partial or incomplete privatization. The determination of what is going to be demanded from and produced by the firm under contract remains in the political arena, under the influence of interest groups and public officials rather than under the direct control of private citizens acting as individual buyers. Complete privatization in criminal justice involves private-sector control over all of the decisions regarding the use of resources devoted to the protection of persons and property. Conceivably, the resources for the pursuit, prosecution, and punishment of criminals could be included. It is important to recognize that there are likely to be significant differences between contracting out and true or complete privatization. In particular, criticisms of one do not necessary apply to the other, just as the benefits arising under one do not necessarily arise under the other. There can be important benefits arising from contracting out as well as from full privatization, however, and there may also be potentially significant pitfalls under contracting out that are less likely to occur with complete privatization. Therefore, as a benchmark against which to compare full privatization (as well as direct production in a public-sector bureaucracy), partial privatization or contracting out is examined first.

Contracting Out: What Does It Really Mean?

Some people argue that only the government should have police powers and the power to punish, since such powers in private hands will tend to be abused.

In other words, the government must be the monopoly producer of police services, prosecution, and punishment. The fact is, however, that "the government" never actually produces anything. Everything that the government allegedly produces is actually produced by contracting with private entities. Even if a bureaucratic organization such as a police department provides a good or a service, the individuals who work within that bureaucracy are private entities working under contract. They are not owned by the government. They contract to provide their services because they expect to be better off than they would be in an alternative job. The benefits of the bureaucratic job may take many forms, including any pleasure received from helping to produce what a bureaucrat perceives to be in the public interest, a good living to support a family and/or an attractive life style, job security, perhaps pleasure from being in a position of power and authority, and so on. An individual police officer, then, is a private citizen who has been given a tremendous amount of power and discretion (Benson 1981, 1988a, 1988b; Benson and Baden 1985; Rasmussen and Benson 1994; Thornton 1991), and he is in a position to abuse the power that he is given. After all, since he is a part of an organization with virtual monopoly power over the right to coerce, there is relatively little to constrain his tendencies to abuse his position. Not surprisingly, many types of abuse (corruption, physical abuse, falsification of evidence, etc.) occur in great numbers, as explained in chapters 7 and 8.

In light of this discussion, the normative view that government must be the only organization with police and punishment powers, for fear that private entities might abuse such powers, really does not make much sense. The fact that the idea of government production is a fiction actually implies that it makes more sense to have competitive options in order to constrain the ability of individuals to abuse power, an issue explored more fully in chapter 8. In the context of the present discussion, however, this implies that contracting out must occur at some level. The question is whether a single contract with a private entrepreneur, who in turn subcontracts with laborers and other suppliers of input, is superior or inferior to an arrangement in which all workers and managers are under contract as individuals to work within a hierarchical bureaucratic organization. Indeed, when the term contracting out is used by policymakers and policy advocates, it generally can be interpreted to mean that some part of the bureaucratic decision-making hierarchy is replaced by a decision-making hierarchy that operates under a different set of incentives than those within the bureaucracy.

When an agency or a bureau does the production, its manager is under contract to work for a set benefit package (wages, etc.), and the manager in turn contracts with individual citizens for their labor services and other inputs. Similarly, when the function is contracted out, an entrepreneur contracts with the government agency, and in turn he contracts with other individuals for their labor services and other inputs. Contracting out might be seen as simply a replacement of part of the hierarchical decision-making apparatus of an agency or a bureaucracy with an entrepreneur or the decision-making apparatus within a firm, or both. But rather than contracting for a fixed individual benefit package, the entrepreneur contracts for an overall budget from which he must in turn pay for subcontracted suppliers of labor and other inputs. His own return is the residual, what is left over after the service has been produced and all production costs have been paid. This means that entrepreneurs seeking government contracts have incentives and constraints significantly different from those of bureaucratic managers.

Private entrepreneurs offer to produce some good or service in expectation of making a positive residual above costs, which we typically call a profit. However, they also bear the risk of loss, should they fail to produce at the costs they expected to face when they bid for the contract. Civil servants do not generally have to worry about suffering such losses, nor are they allowed to claim positive residuals (at least not legally—corruption in order to capture such residuals is one abuse of power that is quite common, as explained in chapter 8). Thus, when contracting out occurs, part of the decision-making hierarchy involves a risk-bearing residual claimant in the form of a private entrepreneur (or group of entrepreneurial investors) who retains any excess profits *and suffers any losses*. The implications of the resulting differences in incentives are explored in chapter 3.

Contracting for Police and Security Services

Virtually everything that local governments do is being contracted out by some city somewhere, including the provision of fire services, paramedics and ambulance services, road construction and maintenance, water service, parks and recreation services, garbage pickup, tax assessment, court-related services such as "public defenders," police, and jails. State and federal governments also contract for a wide array of services, including prisons and security. Thus, many components of the public sector's criminal justice system are actually being produced by employees of private firms.[1] First, consider contracting for police and security services.

A 1972 survey found no city that contracted directly with a private firm for all police services, and less than 1 percent of the cities surveyed dealt with private firms for subservice functions like crime labs (Fisk, Kiesling, and Muller 1978: 33). This has changed dramatically. Many local governments now contract with private firms for a wide array of traditional police functions, particularly in the area of police support services such as accounting, maintenance, communications and dispatch, data processing, towing illegally parked cars, fingerprinting prisoners, crime laboratory investigations, performing background checks on job applicants, guarding school crossings, directing traffic, transporting prisoners, and guarding prisoners in hospitals (Chaiken and Chaiken 1987: 1–3; Fixler and Poole 1992: 31–32). Security firms also provide personnel to government units for guarding public buildings, sports arenas, schools, public housing projects, convention centers, courts, airports, and other public facilities (Fixler and Poole 1992: 32). Furthermore, some communities are contracting for patrol services. East Hills, Long Island, employs thirty security officers to patrol the town on a twenty-four-hour basis, for instance: the officers are uniformed but unarmed, and they call the local police when they observe a problem (McCrie 1992: 18). Although manufacturing firms and retail businesses rank first and second in contracting with security firms, government agencies rank third, and the expenditures for such services run in the multibillion dollar range (Chaiken and Chaiken 1987: 3). Still, the costs of such contractual services tend to be low relative to the alternative—public production—as explained in the following chapter. As McCrie notes, "the largest employer of security guards in the United States is a federal agency. Those positions could just as easily have been provided by sworn officers, but at higher costs and less flexibility" (1992: 19).

Wackenhut Services, for example, has a long history of contracting with government units. Among its many contracts, the firm supplies complete police services to the Tampa Airport and predeparture security at several other airports. Wackenhut also provides the entire police force for the Energy Research and Development Administration's sixteen-hundred-square-mile Nevada nuclear test site (Poole 1978: 41–42). The firm has a similar arrangement with the Kennedy Space Center in Florida, where it also supplies fire and rescue services. Wackenhut provides security for courthouses in Texas and Florida, armed patrols for the Miami Downtown Development Authority, guards to ride the Miami Metro Rail and the Tri-Rail from West Palm Beach to Dade County, and so on (Reynolds 1994b: 11). Following the murder of a British tourist in a Florida highway rest stop in 1993, the state of Florida contracted with Wackenhut to provide security guards at all state rest stops. Thousands of firms offer similar services.[2]

Private firms have also contracted with the public sector to provide investigative services. For example, in the mid-1960s Florida governor Claude Kirk was not satisfied with the performance of the public criminal justice system in his "war on organized crime" program, so he commissioned Wackenhut to fight the "war" (Fisk, Kiesling, and Muller 1978: 34). The five-hundred-thousand-dollar contract lasted about a year and led to more than eighty criminal indictments—many of those arrested were local politicians and government employees. Another example involves a private firm called Multi-State, which "rented" skilled narcotics agents to small-town police forces in Ohio and West Virginia ("Rent-a-Narc" 1973). The firm was established by a former Columbus, Ohio, police chief and in 1973 employed thirteen former police officers with narcotics experience as undercover agents. In their first few months of operation Multi-State was responsible for more than 150 arrests and the seizure of about two hundred thousand dollars in drugs. More recently, in 1993 the Kentwood, Michigan, police department signed a three-year contract with a private firm to investigate and recover bad checks. The department had been investigating about five hundred check complaints per year (out of the approximately thirty thousand bad checks written in the community), with each investigation taking three to four hours of valuable time away from alternative uses of public police officers' time. The contractor now handles all merchant contacts, telephone calls regarding bad checks, and investigations, in an effort to recover the face value of the check as well as the expenses for both the merchant and the police department.

Chaiken and Chaiken suggest that "only selected functions of police and sheriff departments are being transferred to the private sector, and this practice does not realistically present a threat of total private takeover of entire police agencies" (1987: 1). Although that may be true (counterexamples actually exist and are discussed below), the "selected functions" appear to be expanding in number and scope, as suggested above. In a similar vein, McCrie notes that "no evidence exists that the private sector currently envisions playing a future role as a for-profit policing service in competition with the public police" (1992: 19). This also may be essentially true, given the political and legal barriers discussed in chapter 11 that limit the ability of private citizens to perform some police functions, but a small number of communities have actually contracted for complete police services. Furthermore, this practice could be more widespread if it were not discouraged. It is quite common in Switzerland, where one firm, Securitas, provides police services for more than thirty Swiss villages and townships; Paradise Island in the Bahamas also has a private police force, with much lower incidences of theft, rape, and assault than on the main island of New Providence (Fixler and Poole 1992: 36–38). Thus, though Chaiken and Chaiken suggest that in the United States "no jurisdiction has successfully transferred total police services to the private sector for any extended period of time" (Chaiken and Chaiken 1987: 1), this appears to reflect political forces more than any assessment of cost-effectiveness (Benson 1990: 331–47). For instance, in 1975 Oro Valley, Arizona, contracted for police services with Rural/Metro Fire Department (Gage 1982: 25), but the arrangement was challenged by the Arizona Law Enforcement Officers Advisory Council, which argued that under Arizona law an employee of a private firm could not be a police officer. Rural/Metro could not pay the high legal fees that would have been required to fight the challenge, so in 1977 the arrangement was ended.

Several other contracts like the Oro Valley arrangement have been written elsewhere, however. Perhaps the first local government in modern times to contract out for regular police services was Kalamazoo, Michigan (Wooldridge 1970: 122–23; Fixler and Poole 1992: 33). Kalamazoo contracted for street patrol and traffic control with Charles Services for about three and a half years. The private personnel were sworn in as deputy sheriffs in order to ensure compliance with the law, but the personnel were paid by the hour so that they could be released during slow periods and provided in larger force during peak periods. The arrangement was ended with a court case involving a technicality relating to an arrest. Despite the fact that Charles Services won the case, the arrangement was denounced by a dissenting judge and ultimately undermined. Several other communities have had contracts for police services with private firms that have lasted for at least five years (Fixler and Poole 1992: 34), including Indian Springs, Florida, and Buffalo Creek, West Virginia, for which Guardsmark began providing full police services in 1976 (Poole 1978: 42). Wackenhut had contracts with three separate Florida jurisdictions in 1980 (and had proposals pending with twenty communities in 1985 [Cunningham and Taylor 1985: 47]). Similarly, Reminderville, Ohio, contracted with Corporate Security for police services in 1981 (Gage 1982: 24). Reminderville's contract was challenged by the Ohio Police Chiefs Association, but the association was apparently unable to find anything in Ohio law to prevent it. And after the entire four-officer police force of Sussex, New Jersey, was dismissed in 1993 because of a drug scandal, the community contracted for police services with Executive Security and Investigations Services (Blumenthal 1993). Contracting for all police services is, therefore, a demonstrated possibility.

Contracting for Corrections Services

Perhaps the most visible aspect of privatization in the criminal justice area is contracting for corrections facilities and services. The Federal Bureau of Prisons has contracted out all of its halfway-house operations since 1979 (Poole 1983a: 1). Similarly, in 1985 thirty-two states had nonsecure, community-based facilities (halfway houses, group homes, community treatment centers) under contract (Mullen, Chabotar, and Carrow 1985: 56–68). In that same year, approximately thirty-four thousand juvenile offenders were held in nearly two thousand privately run facilities nationwide. So far, the vast majority of contracting to provide and run entire correctional facilities has been for juvenile facilities and adult services that do not involve substantial security requirements. Several for-profit firms are involved in these markets (although many of these facilities are also operated by private, nonprofit organizations). However, almost all aspects of corrections in publicly run secure and/or adult facilities, including food services, counseling, industrial programs, maintenance, security, education, and vocational training, are under contract with private firms on a piecemeal basis (Logan and Rausch 1985: 307). More significant, though, is the move to privately owned and operated secure institutions for both juveniles and adults.

The first contract for a high-security facility was with RCA, which established a high-security intensive-treatment unit for twenty juveniles at Weaverville, Pennsylvania, in 1975; within eight years there were seventy-three private juvenile facilities in the United States with security systems (guards or security hardware, or both) (Logan and Rausch 1985: 307; Logan 1990). There were no privatized secure adult facilities in 1980, and no jurisdiction other than perhaps the federal government had express legal authority to contract. But by the end of 1994 about one-half of the states had created the legal authority to contract for secure adult facilities, and all three federal agencies that run prisons had the clear authority to do so. Eighty contracts for secure adult facilities with twenty-one different firms were in place in the United States (there were also four each in Great Britain and Australia).

Behavioral Systems Southwest, the first company to operate a major adult detention facility, runs minimum-security facilities for 600 to 700 illegal aliens for the Immigration and Naturalization Service (INS) in San Diego and Pasadena, California, as well as in Arizona (Fixler 1984: 2). The company also had a contract for a facility in Aurora, Colorado, but the contract ended in 1987 when Wackenhut contracted to build a new facility there. Behavioral Systems Southwest also has small contracts with the U.S. Marshals and the Federal Bureau of Prisons. In 1985 the Federal Bureau of Prisons awarded a contract to Palo Duro Private Detention Services for a 575-bed minimum-security prison for illegal aliens. Corrections Corporation of America (CCA), formed in 1983, had two facilities operating by August 1984 (a 35-bed juvenile facility in Memphis and a 350-bed minimum-security jail in Houston for the INS) and thirteen facilities in five states with 3,215 beds by mid-1988.[3] By December 1992 they had facilities in operation or under contractual construction with a rated capacity of 9,045 (*Corrections Today* 1992) and by the end of 1994 they had reached 14,965 ("Privatization Census" 1995: 1). CCA now incarcerates alien criminals for both the INS and the Federal Bureau of Prisons; operates a 250-bed medium-security facility in Hamilton County, Tennessee, and the Bay County jail in Panama City, Florida; and manages the Santa Fe Detention Facility. On July 1, 1988, CCA received a contract from the state of New Mexico to design, finance, construct, and operate a prison to house all of the state's female felons; that was the first private minimum-through-maximum-security state prison in recent history. CCA is the largest private supplier of adult facilities today, followed closely by Wackenhut and Concepts, which had 1992 rated capacities of 6,109 and 4,044, respectively (*Corrections Today* 1992). Several other firms are actively engaged in this market; by June 30, 1993, there were 20,698 adults in sixty-five private corrections facilities operated by twenty-one different firms. The number of firms with contracts actually increased from seventeen to twenty-one between 1992 and 1993, as the number of facilities increased by 14.5 percent (Reynolds 1994b: 32). Still, the "market share" of adult prisons provided by private firms was only 1.5 percent as of June 30, 1993 (Private Corrections Project 1993).

The year 1994 witnessed even faster growth, "No one-year period in the history of privatization comes remotely close in matching the scope and significance of the developments that took place within the private corrections industry during 1994," when the total number of beds in prison facilities under private management reached 49,154 ("Privatization Census" 1995: 1). CCA increased its bed capacity in this one-year period by 65 percent to 14,965, while Wackenhut's capacity rose by 97 percent to 13,636. Those two companies are now multinational corporations with contracts in Great Britain and Australia as well as the United States. CCA was operating fifty-nine facilities in seventeen states, the District of Columbia, Puerto Rico, Australia, and the United Kingdom in August of 1997, at which time an estimated one-hundred private facilities were in operation in the United States (Gunnison 1997).

If the prison building boom that has occurred during the 1990s continues, the industry is likely to continue its rapid growth. Total prison beds increased by 41 percent as 213 state and federal prisons were built between 1990 and 1995, and the prison population rose from about 716,000 to 1.02 million ("Prison Construction" 1997), perhaps suggesting that the pace of construction must slow. However, crowding continues to be a problem with state prisons operating at about 3 percent over capacity and federal prisons at 24 percent over capacity; roughly 25 percent of the fifteen hundred facilities are under court order to limit population or improve conditions. If states continue to attempt to build their way out of the crowded conditions, the future looks good for entrepreneurs in the private prison business, since the fact is that increasing supply will *not* solve the crowding problem. Crowding arises because of both supply and demand conditions, and as explained in chapter 7, the demand side of the prison allocation process is dominated by prosecutors and judges with strong incentives to treat state prisons as common-pool resources, making crowding inevitable unless there are dramatic changes in these incentives (Benson and Wollan 1989; Benson 1990: 143–144; Benson and Rasmussen 1991, 1994b, 1995; Rasmussen and Benson 1994: 17–37). In fact, although most firms wait for a contract before building a facility, CCA is currently building a new two-thousand-bed facility in California at an expected cost of $80 to $100 million with no contract from the state's Department of Corrections. Officials from the Department of Corrections say that they have not even discussed the facility with CCA, but CCA's expectation is "If we build it they will come" (Gunnison 1997). In light of the tremendous level of prison crowding in California, which has almost twice as many prisoners as the state's prison system's designed capacity, CCA is probably correct.

Contracting for Court-Related Services

Few examples of complete contracting out in the area of court services can be found. Instead, even more complete privatization (e.g., arbitration, mediation, private courts, and other less formal ways of imposing private sanctions) is becoming widespread (see chapter 6). Limited contracting does exist, however, in the area of criminal courts. For instance, in 1971 Capital University law professor John Palmer noted that a very large number of criminal misdemeanors were being dismissed every day by the Columbus, Ohio, courts. He also noted that many of these dismissed crimes, particularly involving domestic and neighborhood disputes, often escalated into more serious problems after dismissal. He met with the city prosecutor's office, and together they created the Night Prosecutor's Program. Initially, the program involved assistant prosecutors processing citizens' complaints and scheduling hearings that were heard by law professors from Capital University. During the first year more than one hundred cases were resolved. Then it was determined that law students could also hear cases: students now volunteer in large numbers and are paid for their services. The university has operated the program under contract with the prosecutor's office since that time, and it has evolved from a prosecutor's diversion program to a mediation program. Law students also have become the "intake counselors" who process cases and decide whether they should be referred for prosecution or go into the mediation process. A counseling component was added as social work, psychology, and seminary students were brought in to work with the law students. Columbus's Night Prosecutor's Program has since won numerous awards, and the Department of Justice has promoted its replication elsewhere. It serves as a model for more than fifty similar programs in several other states (Ray 1992: 195).

Contracting for what might be called judicial support services can be found. In February 1980, for example, a Pomona, California, law firm was awarded a contract to provide the municipal court with public defender services (Poole 1980: 1). The contract covered all cases in which the public defender's office could not represent a defendant, primarily because of conflict of interest. There apparently were several hundred such cases per year in the city. Prior to the contract these cases had been handled by individual court-appointed attorneys who were paid by the hour and thus had no incentive to limit the time allocated to their cases. The winner of the competitive bidding process for a 1978 pilot study agreed to payment based on case volume, and in the first eight months of operation, the firm's average cost per case was $205 as compared to the $800 average per case under the previous system; the savings was about 75 percent per case under the 1980 contract. Similar contractual arrangements exist in about 10 percent of the nation's counties (Schulhofer and Friedman 1993: 89). Contracting with private firms for "public defender" services has even become the predominant system in some states, such as North Dakota.

On a less formal basis than the contractual arrangement described above, private defense lawyers perform public defender functions quite regularly. About 60 percent of the nation's counties rely on assigned-counsel programs, wherein a member of the bar can be appointed on a case-by-case basis to defend an accused criminal who cannot pay for his or her own defense (Schulhofer and Friedman 1993: 92). Even when this is not the primary means of obtaining such defense services, a standard practice is for private defense lawyers to represent defendants when a conflict exists between multiple offenders, for example, or when public defenders are not available.

Prosecution by private attorneys also is occasionally practiced in the United States, but such occurrences are rare (Valentine 1992; Reynolds 1994b: 30). Private prosecution was the norm in England well into the nineteenth century (see chapter 9); and as attorneys got involved in prosecution they tended to be under contract with private citizens (Cardenas 1986). There is still private prosecution in England, but only for about 3 percent of criminal cases (police actually took on the prosecution function in England; that contrast with the system that developed in the United States, where politically chosen prosecutors dominate local criminal law).

Conclusions

Contracting out for policing, security, corrections, and court-related services is clearly limited relative to the total numbers of public-sector entities providing the same services. Nonetheless, all such contractual arrangements have grown in numbers and in scope over the last two and a half decades. The data is beginning to come in on the costs and benefits of such partial privatization, so let us turn to an assessment of these contractual arrangements.

3

Potential Benefits and Pitfalls of Contracting Out for Criminal Justice

Why should there be any difference between the quality and costs of services provided by private firms and public bureaus?[1] The Institute for Local Self Government has dismissed contracting out for full police services as infeasible, because "there are no secret methods, known only to the private sector, of running an entire police department" (quoted in Poole 1983b: 10). But the relevant issue is not knowledge or even desire; the fact is that the *incentives* of public bureaucrats are very different from those of private producers (Benson 1995c). As Fitch explains:

> In a market system dominated by private enterprise, the chief guarantor of product quality, the chief incentive to efficient operations, and the chief force operating to hold prices reasonably close to production costs are competition coupled with the profit motive. One of the main objections to the way in which government bureaucracies operate lies in their tendency to disregard and place their own convenience over the needs and wishes of their clientele, which is attributed in turn to absence of any counterpart to the profit motive [*and* competition]. (1974: 509)

The incentives of bureaucrats generally lead bureau managers to strive for expanded discretionary budgets and power, with relatively little concern for efficiency (Niskanen 1975; Benson 1990: 131–47; 1995c; Benson, Kim, and Rasmussen 1994; Benson, Rasmussen, and Sollars 1995c). Civil servants within a bureaucracy are likely to be most concerned with job security or self-preservation, wages and other benefits, avoiding risks and responsibility, and lowering the personal costs of doing the job (e.g., standardizing procedures and routines in order to shift costs onto "customers") (Breton and Wintrobe 1982; Johnson and Libecap 1994; Benson 1995c), all of which tend to stand in the way of efficiency. The frequently noted dysfunctional qualities of civil service systems reflect, at least to a substantial degree, employee pressure that tends to emphasize continuity and seniority over competence as qualifications for higher-level positions, and pressure from employee unions that emphasizes the traditional union goals of more pay, less work, and job security (Johnson and Libecap 1994; Benson 1995c).

Some argue that entrepreneurs have similar incentives to those of bureau managers. They too want to expand and prosper, so they seek economic power. But there is a very important difference between public bureaus supported by taxes and private firms in a competitive market, even if the competition is focused on obtaining contracts paid by tax dollars. Private entrepreneurs' desires for expanding power are limited in competitive markets because they must compete for the attention of consumers with other firms offering similar goods or services. Bureaus also must compete, of course, but they compete with other bureaus, generally with very different functions, for a share of the overall government budget. The difference is significant. Because other firms offer alternative price/quality combinations, customers have choices among a number of similar products; thus, competitive firms must produce something the customers are willing to buy at a price that customers are *willing* to pay. Private firms must *persuade* customers to buy their product rather than the product of the competition by offering a price/quality mix that consumers find to be equal to or better than the price/quality mix offered by someone else. In other words, consumers can do some comparison shopping, thereby gaining information about the actual costs of producing the good and the quality characteristics that are associated with it. There is then a strong incentive for entrepreneurs to look for ways to produce more efficiently, driving down costs and prices, and to develop new and better products in order to increase quality (Kirzner 1997). It is the incentive created by competition that leads entrepreneurs to systematically develop new technologies that reduce costs while increasing both the quantity and quality of output.

A government can coerce taxpayers into buying something they do not want, and because bureaus face relatively little information-generating competition (e.g., other bureaus' outputs are typically very different, so comparison shopping can not provide much information), taxpayers and their elected representatives have relatively little information about alternatives—they do not know whether a bureau's product is being efficiently produced because no competitor is offering to do the job better or at a lower price. Therefore, their incentives to produce at the lowest possible cost and to develop new technologies that lower costs or increase quality are much weaker than those of an entrepreneur in a competitive market. When the lack of competition is added to a bureaucrat's incentives to strive for expanded discretionary budgets and power, and when one considers the rigidities of most civil servant employment systems, which are dominated by people most concerned with job security, increasing wages and other benefits, avoiding risks and responsibility, and lowering their personal costs of doing the job, the inefficiencies of government production are not too surprising. So the question becomes, Can the incentives and competitive pressures of the market system be harnessed through contracting out in order to avoid bureaucratic inefficiencies? Yes, they can be, at least to a degree.

Evidence of Reduced Costs through Contracting

In every area of contracting out with private firms for traditionally government-provided services that has been evaluated (e.g., fire protection, garbage collection, data processing, maintenance, *and* corrections services), contracting out produces savings of from 10 to 50 percent (Poole 1978: 27). Tom Beasley, president of Corrections Corporation of America (CCA), notes that his firm's minimum-security facility for illegal aliens cost $23.84 a day per inmate in 1984, including debt service, profit, and operation; the same kind of facility operated by the federal government cost around $34 per day at that time ("Crime Pays" 1984: 8). More significantly, a number of independent evaluation studies have now been done on private prisons and their costs. They suggest savings of about 20 percent in construction costs and from 5 to 15 percent in private management of prison units (Logan 1990; Logan and McGriff 1989; Bowman, Hakim, and Seidenstat 1993; Brakel 1992: 257–61; Sharp 1991; Archambeault and Deis 1996). For instance, the recently completed and detailed evaluation of Louisiana's two private prisons concludes that over a five-year study period the two facilities were between 11.69 percent and 13.8 percent more cost-effective than the very similar but state-operated prison (Archambeault and Deis 1996: 73). And since private prisons are not state owned, they also generally have to pay state and local property taxes. When this is considered, Sharp (1991: 54) suggests the cost that appeared to represent a slightly less than 10 percent savings in Texas's private facilities actually was 14 percent less than the state's costs.

Unfortunately, no evaluations of contract policing have been done to compare their costs with public police forces, although there is anecdotal evidence of similar savings (Gage 1982; Benson 1990: 186; 1994b; 1996a; 1998b; forthcoming, a). In 1980, for instance, Reminderville, Ohio, and the surrounding Twinsburg Township contracted with a private security firm. The arrangement was made following an attempt by the Summit County Sheriff

Department to charge the community $180,000 per year for an emergency response service with an estimated forty-five-minute response time and an occasional patrol. For $90,000 a year, Corporate Security provided twice as many patrol cars and a six-minute emergency response. The firm agreed to select trained, state-certified candidates for the police positions so the village could choose among the candidates. Corporate Security then paid the seven officers' salaries, provided and maintained two patrol cars, maintained the department's electrical service, communications, and radar equipment, and carried the auto *and liability* insurance for the force (Gage 1982: 23). The community was well satisfied with their private police force, renewing its contract after the initial terms expired. Whether this renewal was put out for a competitive bid or not is not clear, but note that the private firm clearly did face competition—the public-sector sheriff. In this regard, a contracting firm always faces some competition in that there is a public bureaucracy option. If that is the only relevant competition, all the entrepreneur has to do is to offer a better price/quality combination than the bureau, either by increasing quality and holding costs constant or by lowering production costs and price and holding quality constant. More intensive competition with other private firms seeking the same contract increases the incentive to improve quality and lower price.

An arrangement similar to that in Reminderville was established in Oro Valley, Arizona, in 1975, but this one was an even more completely private-sector police force. In Reminderville the village officials hired, fired, disciplined, and organized the police force, but in Oro Valley Rural/Metro Fire Department (which provides fire protection for approximately 20 percent of Arizona's population) took responsibility for full operations management of the police force. Rural/Metro kept all the records required by the state and decided what equipment and how many officers were needed, what salaries to pay, and when to use nonpolice personnel (e.g., to write parking tickets and direct traffic)—all for thirty-five-thousand dollars per year. As a consequence of policies established by Rural/Metro's police chief (e.g., twice-a-day checks of homes whose residents were away), burglary rates in the 3.5-square-mile town dropped from 14 to 0.7 per month and stayed at that level (Gage 1982: 26).

The Oro Valley–Rural/Metro arrangement ended in 1977, as noted in chapter 2, because it was challenged by the Arizona Law Enforcement Officers Advisory Council, and Rural/Metro could not bear the high legal fees required to fight the challenge. It was replaced by a public police department, and in 1982 that department's budget was $241,000, "a typical police operation with typical costs" (Gage 1982: 26).

Incentives to Reduce Costs

Cost savings arise because private profit-seeking entrepreneurs have strong incentives to monitor costs and avoid unnecessarily expensive means of production, perhaps in order to increase profits, but more importantly to attract and keep customers in the face of competitive alternatives. After all, any unnecessary costs cut into current profits and create an opportunity that other entrepreneurs can exploit by offering a better contract when renewal occurs. Thus, for example, a CCA vice president pointed out, "We can . . . get better prices from contractors. Contractors always charge the government more money" (Krajick 1984b: 24). A public employee who negotiates a contract with a private supplier simply has weaker incentives to negotiate hard and to check out the supplier's cost claims than a private entrepreneur does because the private entrepreneur benefits directly and personally from the cost savings, whereas the public employee does not. Given the potential for corruption discussed below, the public employee may be more likely to gain personal benefits by paying high prices to suppliers than by paying low prices (Benson 1981, 1988a, 1988b, 1990: 159–75; Benson and Baden 1985; Rasmussen and Benson 1994: 107–18; Thornton 1991).

Private firms will tend to choose low-cost alternatives when they are available, as long as the cost savings does not reduce the quality of the service provided below the standards demanded by the customer, a customer who is aware of competitive alternatives. Corporate Security's Reminderville police operation purchased a used Kustom HR-12 radar for $350 instead of a new one for $2,600 (Poole 1983b: 11), for instance, a choice that would be very unlikely for a public police department even though the used instrument was perfectly adequate to meet the needs of the community. They also used one-man patrol cars (unlike many public police forces), which studies have shown are significantly more cost-effective than two-man cars (Sherman 1983).

Savings in Labor Costs

Perhaps the major source of savings from contracting out is in labor costs. Even in corrections, with its large outlays for construction of facilities, staffing represents 70 percent of the total costs over the useful life of a prison. CCA reports that because it is not restricted by civil service rules, it pays less in wages than government agencies by hiring nonunion labor. But labor savings go beyond simply avoiding public employee unions. Savings also arise by designing prisons so they need a smaller staff, as Travis Snelling, vice president of CCA, explains:

> The major expense in corrections is personnel, and the area of personnel is a function of good corrections practice and also the design of the building in which you're working. As an example, for a post—and that's corrections vernacular—where you have to have someone doing a function 24 hours a day at a given point in your institution, that's going to take you five-point something people per post. If you can eliminate one post by your architectural design, just one, that'll save you well over $100,000 in a given marketplace, as far as labor cost is concerned. So, if you have a large facility, and you can eliminate one or two or three posts you can start to see those type of savings start to accrue. ("Crime Pays" 1984: 10)

Cost Savings through Flexibility

Another reason for more cost-effective service production by private firms under contract is their flexibility. Fitch argues that dissatisfaction with local government provision of crime control (and many other services) arises at least in part from the fact that government bureaus are not able to quickly respond to changing demands, which is at least partly because of "the political and organizational inflexibility of many local governments" (1974: 502). Therefore, for example, Saint Petersburg, Florida, officials responded to rising vandalism in their parks and recreational facilities by contracting with a private firm rather than adding more city police officers, both because the cost was less and because they realized it would be easier to end a private contract if the need diminished than it would be to reduce the number of public police officers (Fisk, Kiesling, and Muller 1978: 36).

This flexibility has been an especially important consideration in contracting out for corrections. In 1975 the Pennsylvania attorney general informed corrections officials that they could not keep hard-core juvenile delinquents in state prisons. The state's public institutional system was unable to respond quickly to this dilemma, so "they turned for help to RCA, which was then contracting with the state to provide educational programs for delinquents. RCA set up Weaversville [where Pennsylvania's worst delinquents are still kept under RCA's supervision] in a state-owned building in just 10 days and was rewarded with a contract to run it" (Krajick 1984b: 22–23). Similarly, CCA received its contract for the Houston INS facility because it could build in seven months what the government would have spent two or three years and millions of dollars planning. The Federal Bureau of Prisons contracted for its new medium-security facility in 1985 because, as a bureau spokesman notes:

> Rather than build our own institution for something that might be a temporary phenomenon, we decided not to take the risk. Besides it takes two or three years for us to site and build a place. This is an immediate need, which the private sector has offered to fill. If at some point we don't need the place anymore, we can terminate the contract. (Krajick 1984b: 23)

It is much more difficult to "terminate the contract" with a public employees' union and close a publicly owned facility (Wynne 1978: 198–228; Benson 1990: 332–37; 1995c; Johnson and Libecap 1994).

The relative flexibility of private firms is also reflected in the greater likelihood of innovation discussed above. Lou Witzman, president of Arizona's Rural/Metro Fire Department noted, "We have the greatest incentive in the world to innovate, to pioneer, to analyze every little step. Sheer survival" (quoted in Poole 1978: 28). The profit motive, reinforced by the threat of competition for contracts, leads private entrepreneurs to seek cost savings and quality-improving innovations. When firms must compete every year or two to renew their contracts, they must look for ways to keep the cost (and therefore the price) of their services lower than their potential competitors, but they still have to make a profit. Thus, they have a tremendous incentive to look for cost-cutting and quality-enhancing innovations. After all, if a firm can offer better services than potential competitors at similar or lower costs, then that firm will be in a strong position for contract renewal and for obtaining new contracts elsewhere.

Compare this incentive to those of public-sector producers. Police chiefs do not have to see that their departments make profits in order to survive, and they do not generally have to compete with other producers for the attention of consumers (they may have to compete for their appointment, of course, but their organization has a virtual monopoly over production of the service within its jurisdiction). Therefore, they have much weaker incentives to be concerned about production costs. Furthermore, they reap no special reward by successfully producing at the lowest possible cost. This does not imply that police chiefs will be completely ambivalent to costs a department generates; it simply means that they are likely to make a relatively smaller effort to monitor employees to check on wasted time and resources. But the differences go beyond the incentives of public bureau managers. Even a manager who ignored his or her incentives and attempted to act like a profit maximizer (by attempting to minimize the cost of producing the desired level and quality of services) would not be effective, given bureaucratic rigidities (Johnson and Libecap 1994; Benson 1995c). Thus, a study of public production versus contracting out, conducted by New York City's Office of Administration, concludes:

> It is clear that municipal enterprises function under handicaps. Labor productivity is influenced by civil service rules and a union-management situation entirely different from that in private industry. A municipal worker costs more per unit of work. . . .
>
> The point is basically that the rules of the game handicap productivity in municipal enterprise. A good manager will be able to do better than a poor manager, but it will be nearly impossible for him to do as well as he could in private industry, playing under a different set of rules. (quoted in Savas 1974: 492)

The organizational inflexibility inherent in the civil service system prevents management from disciplining inefficient employees unless their behavior is extreme. Lateral movement to adjust manpower needs in the face of changing demands is virtually impossible, as is hiring at any but the lowest grades. In fact, a major labor cost for publicly run prisons under civil service rules or union contracts tends to be overtime. A private firm has more flexibility in hiring and firing and in setting hours and can therefore reduce overtime expenditures considerably.

Economies of Scale

Some may suggest that incentives are not all that matter for contracting out. Potential cost savings through contracting out also appear to arise for production-technological reasons. For instance, economies of scale can differ for different government services. There certainly is no reason to expect that the optimum size for a city in terms of minimizing average production cost is the same for, say, water, sewer, and police services. And there is really no reason to expect that minimum per-unit costs are the same for all police subservices within the same police department. Even if they are, it is doubtful that most police departments are of the efficient size for producing them. As Poole points out: "Whatever the size of the city or county, it's not likely to be the optimum (most efficient) size for producing more than one or two of its public services—if that" (1978: 28).

The implication is that cities can reduce costs by purchasing services from suppliers that can produce at the efficient scale of operation. Some services are likely to require relatively large-scale operations in order to achieve the cost-minimizing level of production. In those cases a single firm may contract with several customers, both private and public. Several cities contract for maintenance of communications equipment, for example, because they do not have enough maintenance work to keep full-time employees busy, and they cannot afford to employ a specialist. Similarly, several small communities in Ohio and West Virginia contracted for professional narcotic agents from Multi-State because their small departments could not afford to staff their own narcotics division with people of comparable skills and experience. Of course, if these static technological factors were the only reason for contracting out, then perhaps efficiency could be achieved through consolidation of jurisdictions or through contracts with other government institutions. Large police or sheriff departments do often provide small communities with policing services in exchange for payments from the local government (Poole 1983b: 11; Freeman 1992: 132). Nevertheless, as suggested above and discussed in more detail below, private entrepreneurs also have stronger incentives to innovate in order to discover the lowest cost means *and scale* of production and to find technologies that efficiently produce a particular service at the scale that the customer wants.

Not all services require large organizations to achieve the efficient size. Some may be more efficiently produced at scales that are substantially smaller than the single public-sector production organization serving a community. One example is the use of private towing services to remove illegally parked cars. These services appear to be done best when performed by a number of small units; besides, it "takes at least a certain amount of police attention away from more important duties, the more so because police forces seem to be incapable of handling towing functions efficiently" (Fitch 1974: 535). Thus, contracting out does not necessarily have to involve big firms with several different jurisdictions or locations as customers; that occurs only when there are substantial economies of scale relative to the size of each jurisdiction. When diseconomies set in quickly, several small firms often can produce more efficiently than a larger bureaucracy.

In sum, there are many reasons to expect lower costs as a result of contracting out, and a substantial amount of evidence indicates that that expectation can be met. Nonetheless, critics have raised concerns about the quality level of government services purchased from the private sector.

Enhanced Quality through Privatization

Mark Cunniff, director of the National Association of Criminal Justice Planners, expects private firms that provide prisons to cut costs by cutting back on services, making the prison situation worse than it already is (Krajick 1984b: 27). Similarly, Sandy Rabinowitz of the American Civil Liberties Union sees the concept of privately provided prisons as "really frightening." The already inadequate food and medical treatment in publicly operated prisons, she believes, only gets worse because of profit incentives. On their face, these arguments may sound reasonable. It is true that when scarce resources are involved, there are always tradeoffs. One way to lower costs obviously is to lower quality, and profit-seeking firms certainly have incentives to cut costs—*if* the cost cutting *does not* result in offsetting reduction in demand and revenue due to buyer dissatisfaction with the quality being provided. However, this is an important "if" that critics generally fail to recognize. Indeed, there are at least three major counterarguments to this concern, given a *competitive* contracting environment (this is an important condition that supporters of contracting also generally fail to recognize, as explained below).

First, as noted above, there may be several ways to cut costs. By more effectively monitoring employees, avoiding unnecessarily expensive means of production, and actively searching for technological advances, private firms can lower costs without lowering quality, and private entrepreneurs have stronger incentives to do these things than public-sector managers have. In fact, effective employee monitoring and the development of new technology can simultaneously lower costs and enhance quality. Thus, in contrast to the assumptions of critics, costs versus quality is not the only potential tradeoff.

Second, a private firm competing to sell services to government units has a reputation to maintain so that it can retain contracts and continue to compete for and attract new customers. A survey of eighty-nine municipal governments regarding contracting out found that the most frequently applied criterion used for awarding large contracts was *documented past performance* (Florestano and Gordon 1980: 32). A firm with a reputation for providing lower quality than expected may not be in business for very long, if competitive alternatives are available.

Third, in a competitive market the quality of the outcome depends more on demand side incentives than supply side incentives. If a government decision maker attempts to get a bargain by limiting payments too much (e.g., relative to the costs of production for the services by a public bureau), a poor-quality service may be provided. Consider the Florida School for Boys at

Okeechobee: The school was taken over from the state in 1982 by the Jack and Ruth Eckerd Foundation, a nonprofit enterprise that had been running "wilderness experience" programs for troubled children for several years. The foundation hoped to do a better job than the state corrections bureau and tried to make improvements in the facility. Neglected buildings were painted and patched, the food was improved, broken toilets and screens were repaired, and dilapidated equipment was replaced. The foundation contributed $280,000 for salaries in 1984 to attract better staff and purchased shoes for inmates and computer terminals for the education program (Krajick 1984b: 27). But even though the facility was clearly improved relative to what it was under bureaucratic control, the American Civil Liberties Union and a coalition of other groups filed suit against the state of Florida because of "cruel and abusive conditions of confinement" at Okeechobee. Allegations included overcrowding, unsanitary conditions, inadequate food and clothing for inmates, poor security resulting in sexual assaults on and beating of inmates, and inadequate medical care and psychological counseling.

Importantly, the Eckerd Foundation was not named in the suit, "nor [did] most of the school's critics blame the Foundation for the alleged conditions there. Critics [said] that Eckerd [had] inherited the fruits of the state's antiquated and harsh policies toward delinquents—policies that [made] it difficult for anyone to run a decent facility" (Krajick 1984b: 25). Florida used Okeechobee as a "dumping ground," sending first-time offenders, hard-core delinquents, and a "large and increasing number" of retarded and severely disturbed offenders there. State Senator Don Childers concludes, "I don't think there's anything Eckerd can do that will have a meaningful effect if they don't control the budget and they don't control who gets sent to them" (Krajick 1984b: 26). Quality services clearly must be paid for, even when profit is not the motivating force for producing the services.

The fact is, however, that private providers who simply must cut costs relative to public production often simultaneously enhance quality because there are ways to cut costs without cutting quality. They choose those means of cost cutting because they want to maintain their reputations in order to compete for other contracts and because governments do not demand so much cost cutting that they are forced to cut quality. Thus, independent observers who monitor private prisons generally praise the quality of their operations (Benson 1990: 190–91; 1994b; 1996a; 1996b; 1998b; forthcoming, a; Logan 1992; Brakel 1992: 261–62; Sharp 1991; Archambeault and Deis 1996). Furthermore, inmates tend to be much better off in private facilities. For instance, a survey of inmates in Texas who were transferred from state to private facilities suggests that the inmates rate the private facilities as "substantially better" in staff treatment, safety, medical care, recreation, education, visitation, and substance abuse programs and that the inmates' mood was substantially better in the private facilities as well (Sharp 1991: 22). The state prison rates better only in the quantity (but not the quality) of food, while the state and private facilities rate the same for other areas of inmate interests. In a comparison of privately and publicly operated corrections facilities in Massachusetts and Kentucky, both staff and inmates rate the services and programs in the private prisons higher than their counterparts in publicly operated institutions. Furthermore, the private facilities have lower escape rates and fewer inmate disturbances (Joel 1993). Similarly, in a study of the CCA-managed Silverdale Detention Center in Chattanooga, Brakel concludes that his findings "resoundingly disprove the trade-off assumption. The gains in efficiency yielded by privatizing the Silverdale facility were in fact found to be accompanied by significant quality improvements" (1992: 261). Brakel examines several dimensions of quality and finds substantial improvements in upkeep and maintenance, safety and security, treatment of inmates, medical services, recreation programs and facilities, religious and other counseling, disciplinary procedures, inmate grievance and request procedures, and legal access. On other quality dimensions that were examined, CCA's performance is roughly equivalent to the previous publicly run arrangement.

The recently completed comparison study of the Louisiana private and public prisons reaches a similar conclusion: "The data analyzed and presented in this study for Fiscal Years 1992–93, 1993–94, 1994–95, and 1995–96 support the general conclusion that the two private prisons—Allen and Winn Correctional Centers—significantly outperformed the public, state-operated prison—Avoyelles Correctional Center—on the vast majority of measures used to compare the three prisons" (Archambeault and Deis 1996: 73). This included the cost savings noted above as well as several measures of quality such as the numbers of "critical incidences"; the safety of the working environment for the facility staff; the safety of the living environment for the inmates; the judicious use of inmate disciplinary actions; the effectiveness and efficiency of security staff employment (the private prisons actually used fewer security personnel but deployed them more effectively than the state facility); the completion rates for inmates taking basic education, literacy, and vocational courses and the proportion of inmates in these programs; and the number of screenings of inmates for placement in community corrections settings. The public facility had no escapes, however, compared to three and five for the private facilities (the opposite result is suggested by the Kentucky-Massachusetts study, and this Louisiana comparison is not statistically significant). The public facility also reports fewer aggravated sex offenses, but the likelihood of reporting such offenses tends to be reduced if they are not dealt with effectively; in this regard "there appeared to be different standards being applied in the private versus the public provisions" (Archambeault and Deis 1996: 39). Finally, the public facility offered inmates more recreation, as well as a broader range of social services, treatment programs, and education programs (but with fewer successful completions, as noted above).

The same conclusion appears to apply for fully contracted or privatized policing (Gage 1982; Benson 1990: 186; 1994b; 1996a; 1996b; 1998b; forthcoming, a), although the evidence is more anecdotal than the evidence regarding prisons, in part because of the small number of privatized police departments (however, the quality of private security services for large private communities discussed in chapters 7 and 8 also supports the expectation that private firms can provide higher quality services at lower costs than their public bureaucracy counterparts). Contracts for specialized support tasks, and even for some traditional police services, also appear to lead to quality enhancement in some cases. For instance, the Kentwood, Michigan, contract for investigation and recovery of bad checks performed quite well during its first year of operation. The national average for recovery of bad checks is about 40 percent, but the Kentwood contractor's monthly recovery rate ranged between 52 and 77 percent over the June 1993 to January 1994 period. As the Kentwood police chief notes:

> The benefit of the program to merchants is obvious. They now have an efficient and effective means to recover their losses from previously uncollected checks. Not only has the paperwork been simplified, but the recovery of losses has improved. In fact, some of the merchants are reporting a reduction in the number of dishonored checks received since the inception of the program. (Mattice 1995)

In other words, not only has the quality of the actual service (collection of bad checks for the benefit of individual merchants) improved, but the service appears to constitute a relatively effective deterrent, thus benefiting merchants in general.

As the various studies of contract prisons discussed above suggest, there may well be several dimensions of quality, and thus although contracting firms may enhance quality on some dimensions relative to a bureaucracy, they may not on other dimensions. In this light it must also be recognized that some critics of contracting out are focusing on a different dimension of (or perhaps even definition of) quality than the actual customers—the public officials who demand and negotiate contract services. For instance, the quality of contract public defender services has been attacked (Wilson 1982). But quality in this case clearly depends on the perspective taken. As Schulhofer and Friedman stress, "[t]he difficulties of privatization in each area are distinct, and potential gains are not always comparable" (1993: 77). For example, public officials who are contracting for public defenders may be much more concerned with reducing court crowding or maximizing criminal sentences in a plea bargaining arena than with the goals of defendants that are stressed by Wilson (1982): acquittal for the innocent or minimization of sentences for the guilty. Thus, there is a conflict of interest inherent in publicly paying for private criminal defense (Schulhofer and Friedman 1993: 74), and a quality product from the payers' perspective may actually entail relatively poor quality from the defendants' perspective (the same is true for public employment of prosecutors who supposedly are representing crime victims, as explained in chapters 10 and 12). In a competitive environment, an attorney who wishes to obtain contracts in the future must develop and maintain a reputation for quality services at the price paid, "but only with those who provide her with business, not with potential defendants themselves" (78). Nonetheless, as Schulhofer and Friedman clearly explain, quality defense from the defendants' perspective is much more likely to be obtained through contracting out, by changing the nature of the contracts, than by expanding the public sector's public defender bureaucracy.

Public defenders generally have very strong incentives to move cases quickly, thus encouraging plea bargaining perhaps even to the degree of not fully or accurately informing the defendant of his options or the probability of success at trial, for instance, so it is not surprising that indigent defendants "commonly mistrust the public defender assigned to them and view him as part of the same court bureaucracy that is 'processing' and convicting them" (Schulhofer and Friedman 1993: 86) (see Schulhofer 1988 and Rasmussen and Benson 1994: 155–64 for examinations of the incentives of such publicly employed public defenders to cooperate with prosecutors and judges rather than with defendants). But contracting out for defense attorney services does not alter those incentives if the contracted fee is based on volume of cases handled, or if the contract requires the provider to handle all cases of a particular type: "Because fees are fixed, either per case or per annum, attorneys have a powerful incentive to avoid *unnecessary* service, but there are few direct incentives for *adequate* service [from the defendants' perspective]. Indeed, global fee and individual fee contracts give the attorney a powerful disincentive to invest time and resources in his indigent fee cases" (Schulhofer and Friedman 1993:

91). Since most private attorneys who contract to provide such services also maintain a private practice, they actually face a tradeoff in the allocation of their time that probably creates even stronger incentives to expedite these publicly funded criminal cases than public defenders have. The problem is greater yet when a private attorney is ordered by the court to provide such services for a fee that is less than what the attorney would voluntarily contract at, but "in many jurisdictions, conscription of unwilling attorneys is a routine feature of the assignment system" (93). However, as Schulhofer and Friedman (1993: 96–122) explain, contracts for defense services do not have to create such incentives.

Schulhofer and Friedman propose various ways to tie the incentives of a contracting lawyer to those of the defendant, and they conclude that the arrangement that is most likely to create incentives to provide quality defense from the defendant's perspective is to develop a voucher system wherein indigent defendants are free to choose their own attorneys and "to provide their attorneys with the same incentives to serve their clients that attorneys have always had when they represent clients other than the poor" (1993: 122). The point is that quality may depend on perspective, and contracts can be adjusted to create whatever level and definition of quality payers want. Thus, the quality of services provided through contracting remains predominantly a function of the demand side of the process. This is the major source of potential problems with contracting out.

Pitfalls of Contracting Out

The primary advantages gained from contracting out are virtually all generated because of the incentives that face private entrepreneurs competing for profits. Thus, if the contract process is not sufficiently competitive, the incentives to provide quality services at a low price may not arise. After all, in a competitive environment, if a contracted supplier does not produce the desired results, the arrangement can be terminated. Furthermore, in a competitive market for contract services, the government unit is not solely responsible for designing a contract; a competitor can offer a different contract form that will instill the appropriate incentives if the government is not satisfied with the services it is getting from a particular supplier under the existing contractual form.

Price and/or quality competition is the automatic safeguard of the market process that forces self-interested individuals to efficiently use the resources they control. In a competitive market, producers must compete for consumers by either (1) offering a product of similar quality for a lower price than competitors offer or (2) offering a better quality product for the price that competitors are charging. Thus, competition tends to produce the quality that consumers want most with the lowest possible price being charged for that quality (or there may be a variety of qualities with varying prices if various consumers demand different price-quality combinations). That is, the firms that win the attention of consumers tend to be the firms that offer a desired level of quality at the lowest possible price. In the market for contract service, the consumer is the government agency letting the contract, so that agency is the most direct determinant of the quality of services. It is also likely to have considerable power to encourage, limit, or redirect competition and to shape the competitive process. When competition is stifled or when it is diverted to other dimensions, the increases in quality and reductions in costs predicted above need no longer arise.

Fisk, Kiesling, and Muller worry that reasonable levels of competition might not exist in the contracting process because "few, if any, private firms exist to provide [certain services] . . . in most places," (1978: 8) but if the market is attractive (profitable) many entrepreneurs will try to enter. These entrants need not be previously existing firms who are already producing the same service. RCA is certainly not known for producing correctional services, nor is Wackenhut, but both are actively pursuing contracts in that area. Control Data Corporation, a conglomerate that deals mainly in computers, has also bid for corrections contracts and has obtained controlling interest in City Venture, which sells vocational training programs to prisons (Krajick 1984b: 24).[2] How do such companies enter the corrections market when they have no previous experience or expertise? It is easy, for as Poole observes, "privatization is nothing more than the application of businesslike ideas to the process of dispensing justice—ideas like specialization, division of labor, and payment for services rendered" (1983a: 3). CCA was founded by Thomas Beasley and backed by the Massey Burch Investment Group, which also started Hospital Corporation of America. Beasley had no prison management experience, so he hired several former corrections officials, including a former commissioner of corrections in Arkansas and Virginia and a retired chairman of the U.S. Parole Commission. CCA is run "with large purchase orders and centralized accounting and management, and by hiring experienced professionals from public agencies to run the day-to-day affairs of the institutions" (Krajick 1984b: 23). The company, which is part of a corporate structure that produced only hospital services fifteen years ago, is one of the most active and aggressive bidders for corrections contracts; through aggressive competition it has become the largest provider of prison beds in the industry, with several facilities in numerous states and in other countries.

There is little doubt that price/quality competition can exist for goods and services sold to governments by contracting firms. As Savas noted, "Under the right conditions, potential contractors will compete vigorously for this [government contract] business" (1974: 489). Competition has in fact intensified as contracting out has developed: "With the increased use of contracting between local governments and the private sector [for public safety services], private firms are responding much more aggressively in pursuing new opportunities" (Freeman 1992: 131). Problems arise if competition is cut off or refocused, however, and unfortunately there are characteristics of government as a buyer of contract services that threaten price/quality competition and therefore the efficiency and quality gains that are available through contracting out.

Bureaucratic Barriers to Effective Contracting

Krajick warns, "Efficient as these profit-making concerns may be, the institutions they run are bound to reflect to some extent the aims, the limitations, and perhaps the abuses of the government systems of which they become a part" (1984b: 23). Government may demand defense attorneys who expedite cases and encourage their clients to plea bargain, for instance, when the clients' best interests might be served by mounting vigorous defenses. More significantly, it may be that governments will do a poor job of contracting, just as they do poorly most of the other tasks they undertake. The bureaucratic attitudes and incentives that influence government production will also affect the contracting process. Consider the belief that "one efficient firm and a knowledgeable government official can reach an agreement to provide services at a cost no higher than it would be if ten suppliers were bidding" (Fisk, Kiesling, and Muller 1978: 5). This attitude could quickly destroy the effectiveness of the contracting process. It is the threat of competition that forces the private firm to produce efficiently. When a single private firm is given a contract with no fear of future competition, it begins acting like a monopolist, not an efficient competitor. Savas contends that the "result . . . that private firms under contract collect refuse more efficiently than government agencies, is probably due more to the differences between competitive and monopoly provision of the service than between private and public delivery" (1982: 146). Public provision is monopolized, but private provision *can be competitive*. Nevertheless, when private firms have exclusive contractually based franchises that do not come up for *competitive* rebidding, the result is more likely to mirror public provision. Fitzgerald cites the case of Pima County, Arizona, where for many years two contractors had exclusive contracts to collect refuse: "When this policy was abandoned in favor of an open, free market, 15 private firms went into competition and prices to consumers were cut in half from what the monopoly holders had charged" (1988: 92).

Civil service rigidities can also stand in the way of savings brought about through contracting. For instance, local governments' ability to lay off workers is often restricted by union contracts or state laws regarding civil service regulations. Thus, employees who lose their jobs to contracting must be transferred to other positions. "This reduces the overall value of the contract because the costs of the contract are reassigned to other departments" (Freeman 1992: 136). One frequent criticism of contracting is that although it may reduce the cost of producing a particular good or service, it does not reduce the cost of government. Rather, costs are shifted into other areas of government.[3] In a study of how chief administrative officers (CAOs—mayors and city managers) gain from decisions to contract, Martin and Stein conclude that "[t]o avoid raising taxes, mayors and city managers appear willing to allow their bureaus to retain all of the savings from service contracting" (1992: 100). Thus, contracting does not necessarily reduce overall government costs relative to what they have been in the past, although it may still tend to reduce demands for tax increases (contracting's costs and benefits should be considered in a dynamic context, after all, since the entrepreneurial discovery process is a vital and ongoing source of gains [Kirzner 1997]). As Martin and Stein explain, CAOs face two distinct political constraints when making contracting decisions:

> The first is a need to promote voter satisfaction by minimizing tax increases. The second is to placate the bureau and agency chiefs and their employees. In this environment, contracting out of services can be a useful stratagem. Contracting can be presented to voter-taxpayers as cost-consciousness evidence by the CAO, and may actually result in a measurable improvement in the quality of services delivered to consumers. . . . In reality, contracting appears to have little [immediate] effect on either aggregate government spending levels or the budgets of government agencies charged with the provision of a particular public good. . . . [An agency] utilizes the contracting gains the CAO allows him to increase the average salary of the remaining employees [and/or to effect the transfer of displaced employees to other areas within the agency]. (1992: 100)

Furthermore, bureaucratic behavior by agencies administering the contract can work to destroy competition in bidding even when the bureau claims to seek competition. This occurs in part because these agencies generally impose a large number and variety of regulations, standards, and other requirements on the contracting process itself and on postcontract production, with the result that

> [t]he high cost of obtaining government contracts, the limitations on salaries and other costs frequently imposed by government regulation, and the problems raised by zealous auditors make government contracting for the typical small firm, and for many large firms a chancy business. The risks impel many firms to limit the amount of government business they seek, and some now go after government contracts only because of ancillary advantages (such as access to information not otherwise available). (Fitch 1974: 518)

The federal government, in contracting out for prisons, for example, specifies standards for all aspects of prison life and stations observers in private institutions (Krajick 1984b: 27).

The excuse for heavy monitoring of private firms under contract is supposedly to prevent dishonest private firms from providing poor services. Of course, a sufficiently competitive contracting process would do precisely that, as potential competitors look for innovations or monitor those providing services, or both, in hopes of spotting inefficiencies or abuses that will allow them to offer a superior contract. But even with all the regulations, many critics remain "afraid that contract prisons will generate the same kinds of scandals as contract nursing homes [and, we might add, contracts for highway construction, production of weapons and other products for the department of defense, and . . .], which despite numerous inspectors and standards have still frequently become substandard facilities" (Krajick 1984b: 27). Such concerns are definitely warranted. After all, as Fitch notes, many of the regulations "have the effect of putting a greater strain on honest firms than on dishonest firms, which can often find some way of beating the regulation, if only by buying cooperation of government contracting officers" (1974: 517). When dishonest firms are allowed to provide inferior services, the reputation of providers in general is tarnished, so honest firms with good reputations who might want to diversify and enter the contract market (e.g., a private provider of medical services who would consider providing nursing home services) are reluctant to do so because of the potential damage it could do to the firm's reputation.

Corruption as a Barrier to Effective Contracting

This brings us to a major potential barrier to price/quality competition in the contracting-out process—corruption. As Poole observes, "instances of corruption have occurred, in cases where the selection process was not an openly competitive situation" (1978: 29). But the threat of corruption goes well beyond that (Benson 1981, 1988a, 1988b; Benson and Baden 1985). Corruption may *prevent* the selection process from being "an openly competitive situation." Political corruption becomes possible when government officials control the allocation of valuable property rights (Benson 1981, 1988a, 1988b, 1990: 159–75; Benson and Baden 1985; Rasmussen and Benson 1994: 107–18; Thornton 1991). Clearly, the right to act as the exclusive supplier of some government service without fear of competition can be extremely valuable, particularly if a public official is willing to look away when a producer cuts quality to increase profits. Thus, "contracts are one of the most common and lucrative sources of corruption in government" (Fitch 1974: 517).

Corruption effectively redirects competition. When entrepreneurs recognize that contracts are going to be awarded on the basis of bribes paid to public officials, they tend to respond to these incentives. The market form of competition that focuses on prices and quality is replaced by a competition to buy contracts with bribe payments. Neither cost savings in order to reduce price nor quality enhancement need play a significant role in the perverted competition that arises when private firms contract with corrupt government officials. In fact, in such cases critics of contracting out for government services may be absolutely right when they argue that private firms reduce costs by cutting quality—but it is not because of market forces. It is because the incorruptible market regulator, price/quality competition, has been terminated and replaced by competition for the attention of and regulation by a corrupt public official. (The same result can occur with public officials who are simply inefficient.) Incentives for private contractors to engage in bribery, kickbacks, and payoffs obviously exist, and corruption is inevitable if public officials in charge of the contracting process are sufficiently self-interested. The level of corruption that has been observed in the criminal justice arena over the past decades (Benson 1981, 1988a, 1988b, 1990: 159–75; Benson and Baden 1985; Rasmussen and Benson 1994: 107–18; Thornton 1991) suggests that this could be a serious problem associated with contracting for various criminal justice functions. That does not imply that private firms should not be considered as providers; if corruption exists in the administration of the system, the bureaucracy is also likely to be corrupt and abusive. Individuals serving as public police officers will simply capture the revenues from corruption rather than private entrepreneurs, and as suggested above, corruption in public police, prosecution, and courts is widespread. The solution to this problem is more likely to be to minimize government involvement in the administration of such a market, rather than to minimize private-sector involvement (see subsequent chapters). After all, even if the contracting process is not dominated by blatantly corrupt public officials and the kinds of private contractors that tend to be attracted to the resulting type of competitive environment, the contracting process can be quite biased.

Political Considerations as a Barrier to Effective Contracting

Entrepreneurs' resorting to bribes in order to purchase contracts is corrupt; but even if they do not bribe, they often can and must pay in other ways for the privilege of getting a contract. As Martin and Stein (1992) explain, the contracting decision is made in a political environment by CAOs concerned with political survival, their own salaries, and job-related perquisites. In this context, competition for the attention of public officials can be quite legal, although it may have little to do with the quality of the product being offered or its price. Even in the area of criminal justice, most government decisions reflect the demands of politically active and powerful interest groups (Chambliss 1964; Chambliss and Seidman 1960, 1971; Eisenstein 1973; Berk, Brackman, and Lesser 1997; Benson 1990: 87–126; Benson, Rasmussen, and Sollars 1995; Benson and Rasmussen 1996b; Rasmussen and Benson 1994: 119–32), and it is not surprising to find that "private contractors doing business with government are . . . one of the principal sources of campaign funds" (Fitch 1974: 516). In fact,

> [i]n the political community, contractors are expected to make political contributions in order to be eligible for contracts. Contributions may take the form of outright bribes and graft but . . . the more popular form is the campaign contribution—outright grants, subscriptions to fund-raising dinners, and so on. Such potlatch may be expected to take its toll by raising the costs of contract services and loosening the assiduousness of inspection, though the more cautious political operators will insist that work be at least passable, and only the more venal will tolerate [extreme reductions in quality]. (Fitch 1974: 513)

This political pressure clearly has an impact on the outcome of contracting decisions. Several respondents to the Florestano-Gordon survey, for example, admitted that "political considerations" had been important "criteria" in awarding large contracts (Florestano and Gordon 1980: 32).

The potential gains in efficiency and quality are themselves at risk because of the nature of the demand side of the contracting equation. Still, if corruption and the bureaucratic tendencies for overregulation do not eventually destroy the potential for cost savings and quality enhancement, then the criminal justice system might be improved through greater contracting. There is yet another potential problem with contracting out, though.

What Do Contractors Produce?

Gains in production efficiency are not desirable if what is being produced is not desirable. When contracting out is considered in the narrow sense of cost reductions or production efficiency, competitive contracting for criminal justice services appears to be desirable (as long as corruption and politics do not undermine the price/quality competition that creates the incentives for cost savings and quality enhancement). But it must be recognized that the lower costs of prisons and policing that can result from contracting out could make criminalization even more attractive as an "easy" solution to a wide variety of political problems. Many of the problems now facing the criminal justice system arise at least in part because of the criminalization of the sale and consumption of various drugs, for instance (Benson 1994b; forthcoming, a; Rasmussen and Benson 1994; Benson and Rasmussen 1994b, 1996a, 1996b), a problem that apparently could be more effectively handled with treatment-based programs than with punishment-based programs (Benson and Rasmussen 1994a, 1994b). This is not an indictment of contracting out per se (treatment-based programs might be and often are contracted out, at least in part). The point simply is that there should also be concerns about the results of enhancing technological efficiency in the production of criminal justice services, given the potential use of the criminal justice system in meeting political objectives.

If Hitler had contracted out the rounding up and extermination of Jews, it might have been accomplished at a lower per unit cost and more Jews could have been exterminated, but the fact that more of these politically defined "criminals" could have been exterminated more "efficiently" in a technological sense does not mean that the contracting out of this process would have been desirable. If through contracting out the costs of operating certain parts of the criminal justice system can be reduced, this may encourage the development of new activities or the continuation of existing criminal justice activities that may be undesirable for various other reasons. Moreover, even for desirable criminal justice functions, the cost savings will be marginal at best because of the remaining problems that exist in criminal justice (Benson 1994b; 1996a; forthcoming, a; Benson and Rasmussen 1994b; Rasmussen and Benson

1994). For instance, a lower-cost policing or corrections sector will not end the problems of crowded courts, prisons, and police files that arise because of the rationing process that characterizes criminal justice (see chapter 8).

Conclusions

Considerable evidence suggests that private firms under contract can simultaneously lower the cost of production and raise the quality of output relative to public producers. That is, the alleged tradeoff between costs and quality does not appear to materialize. Yet, there clearly are examples of contracting out wherein quality is reduced and abuses occur. Although such abuses do not appear to have materialized in the criminal justice area, where contracting is a relatively recent phenomenon, they clearly have in a number of other contracting processes. The fact is that not all contracting out procedures are the same. When contracting is highly competitive, and contracts are awarded on the basis of both price and reputation for quality, quality tends to be enhanced while costs fall. When politics, overregulation, corruption, or general bureaucratic attitudes toward privatization undermine or redirect the competitive nature of contracting, then the result can be very different.

Whether the contracting process is competitive or not is determined not by the contracting firms but by the government. Thus, cost levels and quality are determined, to a large extent, by the demand side of the contracting market rather than the supply side. There is an old cliché that says "You get what you pay for." If public officials will not pay for quality services, they will not get them. And if they allow the contracting process to be influenced by bribes and political contributions, then the private contractors will also get what they pay for: the ability to produce in a noncompetitive environment where they can actually cut quality to enhance profits. As Fitzgerald notes in the case of Pima County refuse collection mentioned above, the way to lower costs and maintain or increase quality involves "getting government out of the business of maintaining the monopoly" (1988: 92) and letting private firms compete for the attention *of private consumers*—that is, privatize the demand side of the refuse collection process.

The best way to avoid the pitfalls of contracting out is to privatize both the demand for and the supply of criminal justice services. More complete voluntarily demanded privatization avoids many of the pitfalls of contracting out and generates more certain benefits, because the potential political and corruption dimensions of competition for contracts are eliminated. That is, privatization of the demand side of the process increases the likelihood of a combination of cost savings and quality enhancement. Can this be done? Yes, but it requires institutional changes. The voucher system proposed by Schulhofer and Friedman (1993) for public defender services is an attempt to place purchasing power in the hands of the actual consumer of such services, for instance, and assuming that quality defense is the true goal of the public defender system, their proposal should enhance quality. Of course, in some areas of criminal justice, demand is already privatized. Citizens are already voluntarily undertaking or purchasing crime control on a large scale in the area of protection of persons and property, or crime prevention, as explained in chapter 5. To see why, first consider the reasons for the low level of vital private inputs to public policing and prosecution, since the same incentives underlie both underinvestment in public (common-access) benefits of law enforcement and increased investment in private benefits.

4

Private Inputs into "Public" Arrest and Prosecution

Vital but Reluctant Victims and Witnesses

According to a recent Bureau of Justice Statistics (BJS) victimization survey (1993), only about 39 percent of all Index I crimes (murder and manslaughter, sexual offenses, aggravated assault, robbery, burglary, larceny, and auto theft) are reported in the United States. About 50 percent of the victims of violent crimes report the crime, compared to 41 percent for household crimes, 92 percent for motor vehicle theft, and 15 percent for the crimes of larceny resulting in losses of less than $50. For consensual crimes such as prostitution, gambling, and illicit drug market activity, the likelihood of reporting is probably even lower, since neither party to the transaction perceives himself or herself to be a victim. In addition, witnesses to such crimes often apparently do not want to "get involved," although the degree of nonreporting in these cases is not known.

Why don't victims and witnesses report more crimes? Victims of and witnesses to crimes respond to incentives, just as everyone else does. They are likely to weight their expected personal costs and benefits of reporting a crime before doing so. The potential benefits of reporting crimes to the public police and cooperating in prosecution presumably are associated with the expectation that the criminal will be punished (e.g., reporting a crime may be motivated by revenge, by the expectation that the criminal will be incapacitated and therefore prevented from harming the victim again, by pleasure from performing a "public duty" that leads to deterrence—survey results that indicate more precisely what expected benefits are important are discussed below). Many of the potential expected personal benefits that victims and witnesses perceive in making their decisions to report can be thought of as the expected publicly imposed costs that the criminals consider when deciding to commit crimes. Other factors influence both decisions, of course. Victims and witnesses also weigh costs associated with reporting (as explained below), as well as the availability of alternatives such as privately imposed sanctions (see chapter 6). And many factors influence criminals' decisions.

The psychological makeup and life experiences of the individual may be of critical importance in influencing the propensity to commit crimes. Substantial evidence also demonstrates that economic opportunities are significant determinants of crime. A person who does not have a job and does not have the skills necessary for obtaining a secure, well-paying job, is much more likely to engage in all kinds of crime than a person with a good job. One reason is that the jobless person's choices are limited, but in addition the consequences of getting caught are less severe. A highly paid individual loses much more income by going to prison than someone with no job, and the impact on a valuable reputation can be even more costly (Lott 1987).[1] In other words, and importantly, most criminal offenders are like other people, including victims, in one important way: they respond to incentives. Considerable evidence suggests that most criminals implicitly weigh the expected benefits of an offense against the expected costs when they are choosing to commit a crime and that one potentially important cost of committing a crime is the severity of the publicly imposed punishment the criminal *expects,* as suggested above. The potential criminal will also consider the expected costs imposed by private sanctions, as discussed in chapter 6 (private sanctions can include ostracism, job loss, violent retaliation, and so on), but the issues explored here are the vital role that private-citizen victims and witnesses play in imposing these public costs and the reasons for their apparent reluctance to do so.

We might think of the expected publicly imposed punishment as the expected price the public sector charges for crimes (it can also be seen as at least part of the expected price that victims receive from reporting crimes and cooperating with public prosecution); the public criminal justice system's effectiveness determines the expected price.[2] This expected publicly imposed price of crime is generally not monetary, of course, although it can be, at least in part (fines are typical for traffic crimes and some other "minor" or misdemeanor crimes). For relatively severe crimes, it generally is the expected time spent under supervision by a public corrections bureaucracy (or under some circumstances, the expectation of capital punishment), subjectively adjusted for the intensity of the supervision (e.g., probation versus various intermediate sanctions, as discussed in Benson and Rasmussen 1994b, versus imprisonment; of course, the punitive aspects of imprisonment itself can vary considerably in severity). Furthermore and significantly, the expected price is also determined by the probabilities of a series of events occurring before sentencing. First, the crime or its consequences must be observed. When a crime has a victim, that is likely to occur, of course, but the quality of observations can also vary, thus influencing the probability of successful prosecution (e.g., is the criminal likely to be observed in the act, producing an eye witness, or will the crime be discovered only after the fact, thus requiring stronger physical evidence for conviction?). With consensual crimes such observation is much less likely, because it requires either that police see the transaction or that some potential reporting witness does. Not surprisingly, those crimes are often much more difficult and costly to enforce.

Second, if the criminal act or its consequences are observed, the observation must then be reported to police, unless the observer is someone in a position to act on the observation (e.g., a police or private security officer). As indicated above, witnesses of crimes often fail to report what they have observed. Witnesses of consensual crimes almost never report them unless they are "snitches" who exchange evidence for money or some other favor, such as freedom from prosecution for crimes they have committed (Cotts 1992). Third, the reported criminal must be arrested. Fourth, the offender must be charged and prosecuted after being arrested. Fifth, the prosecution must be successful before a sanction is imposed. Given a conviction, the criminal can be sanctioned in one of a number of alternative ways, as suggested above. Possible punishments include capital punishment (a highly unlikely outcome except for the most heinous violent offenses), a prison term, supervised release, including probation; immediate release via a sentence that corresponds to time already served in jail, or a fine. As explained in chapters 6 and 12, privately imposed sanctions are real alternatives that should also influence criminal decisions, but here the focus is on the decision to report the crime to the public police and cooperate in public prosecution. Of course, the availability of alternative private sanctions can reduce the incentives to report crimes to the public sector, if the victim or the witness perceives greater net benefits from private pursuit of justice.

Under the assumption that imprisonment is seen as very costly, but probation or other intermediate sanctions are not, the probability of being sentenced to prison is the sixth factor influencing the expected price for the criminal. There is some evidence to suggest that criminals perceive imprisonment to be a more severe sanction than probation; they are much more likely to recidivate if they have been sentenced to probation in the past than if they have served a prison sentence (Kim, et al. 1993). Of course, criminals are likely to see other sanctions as significant as well, so we might conceive of an average expected severity of punishment of some sort, reflecting the probability of each of the different possible sanctions with weights for the perceived severity of each. Such weights are obviously subjectively determined by criminals.

More important, in regard to the issues examined here, is what weights victims and witnesses are likely to assign to these alternatives, since that is what influences their decision whether to report crimes.

Much of the political debate over crime policy focuses on the last step in this expected price calculation: punishment in the form of imprisonment for convicted offenders. This suggests that victims see imprisonment as much more desirable (beneficial) than other kinds of supervision. But from a crime deterrence perspective, the prison sentence may be the wrong focus. The evidence on deterrence suggests that the certainty of punishment is a much more significant deterrent than the severity of punishment. For instance, although imprisonment reduces the probability of recidivating relative to probation, longer prison terms do not appear to further reduce recidivism (Kim et al. 1993).[3] After all, the length of the actual sentence to be served is irrelevant as a deterrent if a criminal does not expect to be punished. Thus, a goal of deterrence implies that the string of probabilities should be receiving first priority in the criminal justice policy debate; the sentencing issue probably should be of concern only if more severe sentences are likely to influence one of these earlier probabilities (e.g., longer sentences could raise expected benefits of reporting for victims).

The first steps in the process almost inevitably must be made by a private citizen. As explained in chapter 5, people are investing a great deal in "watching" (e.g., Crime Watch and patrols, employment of private security, and observation and monitoring equipment such as burglar alarms), and where such actions are taken, crime is clearly deterred (see chapter 7). However, once a crime is committed, relatively few citizens are willing to invest their time and effort in reporting the crime and cooperating with public officials in pursuit and prosecution. Thus, a major impediment to the public-sector criminal justice system's ability to deter criminals occurs at this second type of essential involvement by private citizens. If the public sector is to be successful at raising the expected price that it charges for crimes, an important question must be how to get citizens to provide the vital input of reporting crimes.

One reason citizens report crimes may be apparent from victimization survey results such as those noted above. Motor vehicle thefts are likely to be reported because victims expect to recover their losses through private insurance, and the insurance companies require that the theft be reported (perhaps because they are mandated by statute to do so). In other words, citizens may not expect the public sector to recover their losses, but when they have invested in a private means of protecting their wealth (insurance) they expect to recover anyway and therefore have a strong incentive to report the crime. On the other hand, the costs of filing insurance claims, as well as the costs arising from various deductibles and copayments, mean that recovery of small amounts through insurance is either too costly or not possible; so small larcenies and burglaries are generally not reported. Several other factors affect the personal costs and benefits of reporting, however, and a more complete answer to this question will provide an avenue for policy developments discussed in chapters 11 and 12 that can have dramatic effects on crime.

Why Don't More Victims Report Crimes?

The cost to victims of reporting a crime and then cooperating with prosecution can be staggering. "In contemporary America, the victim's well-being and fair treatment are not the concern of the criminal justice system or any other institution. The victim has to fend for himself every step of the way" (McDonald 1977: 298). In *addition* to the initial loss to the criminal, victims face the costs of cooperating in the prosecution, including (1) out-of-pocket expenses such as transportation, baby-sitting, parking, and so forth; (2) lost wages in order to meet with prosecutors and appear in court, often through several delays; (3) considerable emotional and psychological costs brought on by having to confront an assailant or endure a defense attorney's questions; (4) a great deal of frustration with bureaucratic indifference, delays, the need to tell the same story to several different bureaucrats, and so forth; (5) considerable uncertainty about the outcome of cooperation, because of the likelihood of court dismissals, plea bargaining, light sentences, failure of offenders to appear, and prison crowding that leads to early release; and conceivably (6) retaliation by the offender, in case he or she is either unsuccessfully prosecuted or not confined for very long.

Many of the costs that victims must bear are dependent on the rest of the criminal justice system. For instance, victims can lose wages as they endure seemingly endless delays and continuances caused in part by the huge caseloads that prosecutors and the courts have, and in part by defense counsel tactics. Furthermore, "the criminal justice system's interest in the victim is only as a means to an end not as an end in himself. The victim is a piece of evidence" (McDonald 1977: 299–300). This attitude of indifference is represented in the famous *Miranda v. Arizona* (1966) decision written by Earl Warren, chief justice at that time (or more probably by his law clerks [Fine 1994b: 119]). The case involved Ernesto Miranda, who was arrested for kidnapping and forcible rape and identified in a lineup by the victim and who later gave a detailed oral confession as well as a written one and signed a summary of the confession. Miranda was convicted and sentenced to concurrent twenty- and thirty-year prison terms for kidnapping and rape, but the Supreme Court reversed the conviction because, even though the confession was not forced and the criminal stated that he understood that the confession could be used against him, he had not been informed that he could have a lawyer present during questioning. The Warren decision referred to the rape victim simply as "the complaining witness." This view of victims is regrettably prominent within the public-sector criminal justice system (McDonald 1977; Bidinotto 1994b; Fine 1994b). The police and the prosecutors, harried by bulging caseloads, just want to know the facts and have little time to be concerned about the victim's problems. As an example of some of the related consequences, turnover among assistant prosecutors is very high and a prosecutor's office is usually staffed with young, relatively inexperienced lawyers, which "means that the prosecutors must use an assembly line organization for their work. . . . [D]ifferent prosecutors are stationed along the various stages of the process and handle all the cases that reach the processing stage. . . . This means that the victim, who may have already explained his case to several different police officers now has to retell it to each new prosecutor" (McDonald 1977: 301).

Why would a victim choose to bear such additional costs *beyond* the original loss resulting from the crime? Victimization surveys indicate that the desire for revenge—seeing that the offender is punished—and the possibility of preventing further crimes by the offender are the two most important reasons for those who report violent crimes (Bureau of Justice Statistics 1993: 34). These surveys also suggest that for property crimes, a desire to recover the property (or perhaps more frequently, to collect insurance) replaces the desire for punishment, although prevention of further crimes remains important. Another reason is not evident from the surveys, probably because the questions that would reveal it are not asked. Victims often do not realize how costly cooperating with police and prosecutors will be until after they have reported a crime and experienced the process. As evidence of this, note that victims drop charges or actually refuse to testify for many crimes that they have reported. Once they get involved with the process and are "hit in the face by reality" (as one victim told me in personal conversation), they decide to end their cooperation (this decision can arise for other reasons as well, of course; spouse abuse charges are frequently dropped, for instance). If they expect relatively low costs, an expectation of significant benefits can easily outweigh the costs.

For those who do report, the likelihood of publicly produced benefits may be overestimated, since in reality the expected benefits of cooperation are small for most crimes (unless there is a potential for privately provided benefits through insurance), particularly relative to the costs of cooperating with police and prosecutors: the probability of punishment, of preventing further crimes by the criminal, and of police recovering property are very low even after reporting. Many victims obviously recognize this and choose therefore not to report crimes; but to see why, consider estimates of the actual probabilities generated by the criminal justice system.

Probability of Arrest

The BJS survey on crime victimization (1993: 33) reports that approximately 11 percent of the unreported robberies, 11 percent of the unreported personal larcenies, 12 percent of the unreported household larcenies, and 10 percent of the unreported auto thefts are not reported because the victim believed that the police do "not want to be bothered."[4] Similarly, 13 percent of the unreported rapes are not reported because of a belief that the police are "inefficient, ineffective or biased." These beliefs are apparently justified. A survey of police in New York City indicates that officers respond to only 30.6 percent of the requests for assistance (Donovan and Walsh 1986: 49). Response rates vary considerably across cities and over types of crimes, but whether the police respond or not, the fact is that relatively few arrests are ever made. In 1992, although 64.6 percent of the nation's 23,760 reported murders were cleared by arrest, only 13.4 percent of the 2,979,900 reported burglaries were cleared. Clearance rates for other reported crimes fall between these extremes. Table

TABLE 4.1
Crimes and Clearance Rates, 1992

Crime	Reported Offenses	% Cleared by Arrest*
Murder	23,760	64.6
Aggravated Assault	1,126,970	56.2
Forcible Rape	109,060	51.5
Robbery	672,480	24.0
Larceny	7,915,200	20.2
Motor Vehicle Theft	1,610,800	13.8
Burglary	2,979,900	13.4

*An offense is cleared by arrest if at least one person is arrested, charged, and turned over to the court for prosecution. An offense can also be cleared under a number of exceptional circumstances, such as suicide of the offender or refusal by the victim to cooperate in prosecution.
SOURCE: Bureau of Justice Statistics, *Sourcebook of Criminal Justice Statistics, 1993* (Washington, DC: U.S. Department of Justice, Bureau pf Justice Statistics), tables 3.107 and 4.23.

4.1 provides details for 1992 (1992 data are reported here for comparison because that is the year for which data are available to perform some expected price calculations reported below).

Furthermore, government expenditures for police services rose by 128.5 percent between 1979 and 1990, at which time they reached $31,804,913 (800,459 employees); reported offenses rose by only 7.9 percent, from 12,483,083 in 1980 to 13,468,228 in 1990. Yet, clearance rates rose by only 12.5 percent, from 19.2 percent in 1980 to 21.6 percent in 1990 (and 1990 appears to be the high; clearance rates have dipped back down since then).[5] Thus, large increases in government expenditures on policing do not produce large increases in clearance rates (reasons for this are discussed in chapters 7, 8, and 11).

Probability of Prosecution

If a victim does report the crime, and the criminal happens to be arrested, the costs of cooperation can rise rapidly, as noted above. And to what end? After arrest, a criminal must be charged, successfully prosecuted, and sentenced before any satisfaction is likely to arise, and all of these occurrences are far from certain. For instance, even after arrest, most offenders are not held until trial. They are released, either under bond or on their own recognizance, and ordered to return for trial. But many do not return. Data on the number of people arrested who subsequently are not tried is very difficult to come by, but a study of the New York City criminal justice system's performance in 1971 found that almost one-third of the city's criminal defendants disappeared before their scheduled trial (Landes 1974: 289). Surprisingly, 29 percent of those who disappeared were in the custody of the city's corrections department and were somehow simply "lost" (how this occurred can only be speculated upon, but it is interesting to note that the New York City police department was riddled with corruption at that time [Benson 1981, 1988a, 1988b, 1990: 159–75]). Most of those who are arrested but then disappear before trial are intentionally released, either on bail or on their own recognizance. Some are ultimately recaptured, but many are not.

OFFENDER FLIGHT FOLLOWING PRETRIAL RELEASE

Court backlogs mean that prosecution cannot be immediate. Alleged offenders cannot all be held in jail, both because jail space is limited and because due process requirements in the Bill of Rights require bail. Thus, many arrestees must be released until prosecution can occur. There are two primary mechanisms for initiating release and ensuring appearance for trial: one private and one public.

Historically, defendants for most crimes have been freed from jail when they guarantee their appearance for trial with the posting of a significant monetary bond. Upon appearance, the bond is returned. Because most criminal defendants do not have enough money to post the full bond required for their crimes, a private market has evolved in which a commercial bail bondsman posts the entire bond in exchange for a fee, usually equal to 10 percent of the bond. The bondsman generally also requires a cosigner, such as a family member or a friend, perhaps in order to reduce the risk of nonpayment (although cosigners are probably not in a position to pay the full bond either), but possibly more importantly, to increase the kinds of private-sector pressure that can be brought to bear on the defendant if he or she considers jumping bail. The bail bondsman loses the bond if the defendant fails to appear in court (assuming that the cosigner does not pay). Therefore, in order to avoid the loss (or the costs of trying to collect from reluctant, perhaps judgment-proof cosigners), these private bail bondsmen spend a good deal of time, effort, and money to guarantee appearance. If someone fails to appear, his or her bail bondsman turns to a private market for bail enforcement services. A national network of bounty hunters and other bail-enforcement agents (e.g., private investigators) is notified that the bondsman has authorized the pursuit of the fugitive. These private agents pursue such fugitives in order to either directly apprehend them (the typical outcome) or to locate them and report their presence to local police, who make arrests. Bounty hunters do not get paid unless the defendant is returned to court, so their incentives to find him or her are very strong. One estimate puts the fugitive rate for defendants on private bail at 0.8 percent after three years (Reynolds 1994b). Thus, release under private bond does not reduce the probability of prosecution very much. The same cannot be said for the private market's public-sector counterpart.

The public alternative to the bail system had its origins in the mid-1960s with the goal of helping those accused of nonviolent crimes who could not afford to post a bond themselves. However, "it rapidly evolved into an indiscriminate release mechanism to cap the jail population. It has failed miserably to accomplish any of its aims." The system is administered by tax-funded pretrial release bureaucracies. Its costs are high. For instance, administering the Harris County, Texas, pretrial release program cost an average of $356 per defendant in 1992 (Reynolds 1994b: 18, 19). This agency had one staff employee for every sixteen defendants being supervised, compared to one staff person for every eighty-seven defendants supervised by one of the private bail-bonding companies in Harris County. Alleged offenders are interviewed by pretrial release staff and recommendations are made to judges regarding the release of the defendants. Those released almost never post any kind of monetary bond; rather, they are released under a "personal recognizance bond" (Monks 1986: 8). Essentially, the alleged offender promises the judge that he or she will appear in court when called.[6] Failure to appear presumably means that a specified fine or forfeiture can be collected, but since nothing is paid up front, and the offender probably does not have much that can be seized or the capacity to pay a fine, these "bonds" provide very little in the way of real incentive to appear (Reynolds 1994b: 18), particularly for individuals who expect to be found guilty and punished. Yet this type of "public bail" is very widespread.

Estimates indicate that about 27 percent of the defendants supervised by pretrial release agencies initially do not appear in court (Reynolds 1994b; Carlisle 1992; Bureau of Justice Statistics 1990; Sorin 1986), and such programs have an 8 to 10 percent fugitive rate after three years. However, pretrial release programs tend to release the prisoners who are most likely to appear, leaving the remainder to be dealt with by private bail bondsmen (Carlisle 1992; Bureau of Justice Statistics 1990; Sorin 1986). And significantly, only about 14 percent of those released under a private bonding arrangement initially fail to appear (Bureau of Justice Statistics 1990: 9). Furthermore, as noted above, these private bail bondsmen have a fugitive rate that appears to be less than 1 percent, compared to the 8 to 10 percent for the public alternative (Reed and Stallings 1992: 5).[7] This probably reflects the fact that public police officers are responsible for pursuing fugitives, rather than private bounty hunters, but public police officers rarely do so in any active way. They have neither the incentive nor the resources to pursue such fugitives. The most common way for the public police to capture pretrial release fugitives is in routine traffic stops when they check to see if the driver is wanted (Reynolds 1994b: 19). Thus, many urban counties have more than fifty thousand fugitives from pretrial release programs, and nationally the number probably exceeds a million (Reynolds 1994b: 19).

DISMISSALS

Many people who are arrested are also dismissed without ever being prosecuted, because of insufficient evidence, mistakes in arrests (e.g., arresting the wrong person, violation of due process rules by police, and so forth), or delays in the processing of the case. Another reason for failure to prosecute is that charges may be dropped by the victim because the victim sees how costly the process really is or the victim fears reprisals, or for other reasons (e.g., victims drop charges in many assault cases involving family members). For instance, of the 36,995 cases filed by U.S. attorneys in 1993, 35,809 were terminated that year, and 16.3 percent (5,839) of those terminations were dismissals.[8] In explaining dismissals, prosecutors point to a lack of staff and to police failure to secure items of evidence or lists of witnesses, but many cases also are routinely dismissed because convictions are expected to be difficult to obtain. In this regard, if in the prosecutor's opinion the victim is likely to appear unconvincing or unsympathetic, to have "done something stupid," or to "deserve" what he or she got, or if the victim has a criminal record, the prosecutor will dismiss the case or plea bargain generously.

There is one perverse implication of this tendency. Lower-income individuals are victims of a disproportionate number of crimes, but such victims are also more likely to have criminal records themselves and to make less articulate witnesses. "Thus, it is more likely that these cases are given away by prosecutors than those of higher income victims" (McDonald 1977: 300). This in turn makes lower-income people relatively attractive targets, since the expected price of crimes against them is relatively low. Ironically, one *rhetorical* justification for public policing and prosecution is to ensure that poor victims receive the same justice as rich victims would be able to purchase if private policing and prosecution were relied upon. Instead, the opposite has occurred. As explained in chapter 9, under historic examples of private prosecution, rich and poor victims acted as prosecutors themselves, and before lawyers got involved in criminal trials the victims were generally on a relatively equal footing with defendants (Benson 1990: 66–68; 1992b; Cardenas 1986; Langbein 1979). The implication for the issues addressed here, though, is that victims who are poor also have weaker incentives to report crimes. Since lower-income people are much more likely to be crime victims (see chapter 8), this may have a dramatic impact on the expected price of crime.

How many arrests actually lead to prosecution is generally not known and probably depends on the jurisdiction, but some studies have been done. Over 84 percent of New York felony arrests in 1979 (88,095 out of 104,413) were dismissed (Neely 1982: 16). On the other hand, Benson and Rasmussen (1994a) estimate the probability of prosecution in Florida for robbery and burglary by comparing the number of accused persons to the number arrested in 1992 (data on other crimes were not available). This ratio suggests that 68 percent of the arrested robbers and 82 percent of the burglars were prosecuted. Many of these offenders probably committed several crimes, so these percentages exaggerate the probability of prosecution for any one crime. At any rate, the probability of prosecution appears to vary considerably across jurisdictions and types of crime.

Probability of Conviction

The probability of conviction, given prosecution, appears to be quite high. For instance, Benson and Rasmussen (1994a) estimate that the probability of conviction in Florida ranged from .84 for murder up to .92 for burglary during 1992, suggesting that this is one area of the criminal justice system that may be working well. Offsetting this misleading impression is the fact that prosecutors probably have a good idea of the chances of conviction before they actually file accusations, so if they do not expect to win a conviction, they dismiss the case. Perhaps more significantly, about 91 percent of all convictions in the United States are obtained by plea or charge bargaining (98 percent in Florida) rather than through a trial. Since offenders will agree to a bargain only if they have something to gain, such as a reduction in expected punishment, many of these convictions are for lesser crimes or fewer crimes (or both) than actually led to the arrest (and even fewer relative to the number of crimes the criminal may have committed without being discovered and arrested). How much prosecutors give away in plea and charge bargains is virtually impossible to quantify since "plea bargaining often involves fiddling with the facts" (Fine 1994a: 88) and falsification of the criminal's record (Bidinotto 1994b: 75). Nonetheless, anecdotes can be found regarding criminals' pleading guilty to significantly reduced charges, thus serving short sentences and later committing additional crimes (e.g., see Bidinotto 1994b: 73–75), and some practices are frequent enough to have been documented.

A common practice in Wisconsin, according to Wisconsin Circuit Court Judge Ralph Fine, is that charges of "operating [a] vehicle without [the] owner's consent," a two-year felony, is routinely bargained down to "joyriding," a nine-month misdemeanor (1994a: 87). Joyriding supposedly implies that the car was returned undamaged within twenty-four hours, but this bargain is struck even when the car has been damaged. Such bargains are not unusual. A New York study indicates that a substantial portion of the people arrested as felons are *not* prosecuted and convicted as felons (Neely 1982: 16). In 1979, of the 16,318 felony arrests that led to indictments, 56 percent resulted in guilty pleas to lesser felonies, 16 percent ended with misdemeanor guilty pleas, 12 percent were dismissed after indictment, 3 percent resulted in some other disposition, and 13 percent went to trial. Significantly, the largest number of sentences that did not involve a prison term arose from prosecutors' willingness to permit felons to plead guilty to lesser felony or misdemeanor charges.

A plea or charge bargain is an exchange agreed upon by the negotiating parties, and it might be expected to improve the efficiency of the criminal justice system (after all, voluntary exchange generally makes everyone involved better off, and a more efficient allocation of resources typically results [Coase 1960]). Indeed, the typical justification for the widespread use of plea bargaining is that it relieves some of the pressure on the prosecutorial and judicial systems arising from court crowding and delay. It turns out, however, that this need not be the case. The attorney general of Alaska ordered an end to all plea bargaining in 1975, and subsequent attorneys general have continued the practice. A 1980 National Institute of Justice (NIJ) study of the consequences explains that guilty pleas continued at roughly the same rates because most defendants plead guilty even when the state does not offer reduced charges (Rubinstein, Clarke, and White 1980: 80; Bidinotto 1994b: 76; Fine 1994a: 93–95). Therefore, the NIJ study concludes, "[s]upporters and detractors of plea bargaining have both shared the assumption that, regardless of the merits of the practice, it is probably necessary to the efficient administration of justice. The findings of this study suggest that, at least in Alaska, both sides were wrong" (Rubinstein, Clarke, and White 1980: 102–3). It turns out that cases in Alaska are processed more rapidly now because prosecutors had been spending up to a third of their time bargaining with defense attorneys (46). Disposition times for felonies in Anchorage fell from 192 days to fewer than 90, in Fairbanks they dropped from 164 to 120, and in Juneau the reduction was from 105 to 85 days (Fine 1994a: 94–95).

Similar consequences are observed in New Orleans, in Ventura County, California, and in Oakland County, Michigan, where plea bargaining has been terminated (Bidinotto 1994b: 76; Fine 1994a: 95). In every case prosecutors have been forced to screen cases carefully before charges are brought, and

> ending plea bargaining has put responsibility back into every level of the system: police did better investigating; prosecutors and lawyers began preparing their cases better; lazy judges were compelled to spend more time in court and control their calendars more efficiently. Most importantly, justice was served—and criminals began to realize that they could not continue their arrogant manipulation of a paper-tiger court system. (Bidinotto 1994a: 76)

Sentences for those pleading guilty are more severe, but the courts are not clogged. Bidinotto suggests that the reason is that "it deters crime from occurring in the first place. Since repeat offenders commit most of the crime, careful case screening and 'no-deal' prosecution tend to incapacitate a greater percentage of this group for longer periods—and thus actually reduce case-loads in the long run" (1994a: 76).

If this is true, then why plea bargain? One reason may be the false belief that plea bargaining is necessary for rationing court time, but many rationing mechanisms are actually available (Benson 1990: 136–43). Indeed, the preceding discussion suggests that the alternative that has been adopted when plea bargaining does not occur is more careful case screening. In other words, dismissals probably have risen as fewer of those arrested are actually being charged and convicted. Thus, failure to recognize that scarce court time must be rationed means that the alleged benefits of eliminating plea bargaining may be exaggerated. Plea bargaining reduces the expected punishment for accused criminals, but more careful case screening reduces the expected punishment of arrested criminals (this tendency may be countered to a degree, though, by the incentives police and prosecutors have to prepare cases better, as Bidinotto [1994d] suggests). The point is that public prosecutors retain a good deal of discretion under both plea bargaining and non–plea bargaining regimes, and the result for both criminals and victims is likely to be some reduction in expected punishment (in this light, means of reducing prosecutorial discretion are examined in chapters 10 and 12). Whether this is the case or whether Bidinotto's more optimistic assessment is accurate, the real question should be, Why has plea bargaining evolved as the preferred allocation mechanism?

In contrast to Bidinotto (1994d), many of those involved in the criminal prosecution process contend that plea bargaining is the most efficient means of rationing court time, and the same view has been expressed in the legal literature (e.g., Easterbrook 1983). Efficiency means that net benefits (benefits minus costs) are maximized. The accused criminal who agrees to a plea bargain certainly benefits in the sense that punishment (or perhaps legal expenses) is less than is expected if the case goes to trial. In other words, most accused criminals are probably guilty, so most of them prefer plea bargaining over other alternatives (e.g., more careful screening before charges are filed). Defense attorneys benefit because most criminals (or the government, for public defenders) have very little money to pay the high costs of trial, but the payment they can make is often sufficient to cover the amount of attorney time it takes to negotiate a plea bargain (Fine 1994a: 91; Schulhofer 1988). As one Alaskan attorney told the NIJ researchers, "Criminal law is not a profit-making proposition for the private practitioner unless you have plea-bargaining" (quoted in Fine 1994a: 91). Prosecutors benefit in that their conviction statistics increase and their workload decreases. Both the budget determining process and the political aspirations of prosecutors motivate prosecutors to maximize the number of criminal convictions (Jones 1979: 201; Chambliss and Seidman 1960: 84; Eisenstein 1973; Blumberg 1967; Grosman 1969; Rasmussen and Benson 1994: 158–59). Since there is some probability of loss at trial, whereas a plea produces a guaranteed conviction, plea bargains are very attractive. And as Fine notes, prosecutors want to avoid trial because "trials are hard work and many prosecutors have heavy caseloads" (1994a: 90). Furthermore, although more careful case screening also avoids losses at trial, it means more work for prosecutors *and* reduced numbers of convictions.

Judges may benefit from plea bargaining as well, since their workload is reduced (Schulhofer 1988), an important consideration for most judges if Neely's contention (1982) that judges put a high value on leisure time is correct (and as a judge himself, Neely may know). Certainly, more careful screening of cases by prosecutors should provide similar benefits to judges, since both plea bargaining and screening are means of reducing the flow of cases to trial. Furthermore, plea bargaining deprives judges of the power to determine sentences, so if that power is something that some judges value more than a reduced workload, the use of plea bargains will not make them better off. They supposedly must approve any bargain, but that authority may be largely an illusion. It is clear that prosecutors' preferences tend to dominate over judges' in this system (Downie 1971: 185; Glick and Vines 1973: 73; Rasmussen and Benson 1994: 155–64). Downie cites many examples in support of this contention. For instance, when a Detroit judge began scolding prosecutors and defense attorneys for plea bargaining cases that he felt should have been tried, the lawyers immediately began complaining to the presiding judge, who quickly replaced the malcontent on the bench and made a show of quickly approving all plea bargains (1971: 161–62). And this is not an isolated incident. When Dade County, Florida, Circuit Judge W. Thomas Spencer stopped approving plea deals that he thought were too lenient, public defenders were "outraged" and prosecutors, torn by their desire to appear tougher on crime, still complained of being "swamped with cases" and worried that some cases would be lost because of Florida's speedy trial law . Complaints by both prosecutors and defense attorneys allowed the circuit's chief judge to transfer Spencer to the family court division. The reason: "A judge who can't make deals can't run a courtroom" ("Tough 'No-Plea-Bargain' Judge" 1994). Thus, the benefits to judges are not as obvious or as universal as they are to others involved in the plea bargaining process. Furthermore, there is one party that is probably worse off because of plea bargaining.

Notice that victims have no role in the plea bargain, and not surprisingly, their interests are not likely to be an important consideration. After all, the potential benefits accruing to victims tend to be the satisfaction of knowing that the perpetrator of the crime is being punished and that he or she will be prevented from committing another crime for a significant period of time, but plea bargaining generally leads to shorter sentences than the criminal would expect to result through a trial, reducing both potential benefits for the victim. Victims also avoid the costs that they incur in an actual trial; but since they are not a party to the agreement, their perceptions of such costs and benefits are not considered. The fact is, plea bargaining often makes victims feel violated by the system as well as by the criminals because of plea bargained forgiveness of crimes. Therefore, these exchanges clearly reduce the incentives of some (many?) victims to report crimes. The costs of plea bargaining are apparently greater than the efficiency arguments recognize.

Punishment

Suppose victim cooperation is successful, and a criminal is arrested and convicted. Here, too, the criminal justice system shows little regard for victims, so they may not find the sentence to be satisfactory even when a conviction is achieved. The victim's views on sentencing are still generally not represented to the judge, even though "defense counsel will be allowed to appeal to the judge, to beg for mercy, to try to sway the judge's emotions, and to recount in pathetic details his client's tragic childhood" (McDonald 1977: 301). In fact, most states now allow defendants to tell their story after conviction but before sentencing, and to ask for mercy, although victims generally do not have the right to inform judges about the impact of the crime on them before the sentence is given (Cary 1994: 264). Political demands to have victim representation at sentencing have often been met by the argument that it would be "improper, because the victim would play on the emotions of the judge" (McDonald 1977: 302); some states, though, have begun to change these rules. The rapidly growing victims' rights political movement suggests that victims are not satisfied with sentences, or with most of the other stages of the criminal justice system for that matter.

A number of victim-oriented pressure groups have been formed over the last several years, such as Parents of Murdered Children (POMC) and Mothers against Drunk Drivers (MADD). These groups "are expressing their anger and frustration at judges who hand down lenient sentences, at parole boards who free violent offenders to commit new mayhem, at prosecutors who plea bargain serious offenses down to minor charges, and at laws that allow the guilty to go free on legal quirks or small police errors." Consider the Stephanie Roper Committee, named after a Maryland College student who was raped, beaten, shot, set afire, and partially dismembered by two men who were sentenced to life in prison but who were to be eligible for parole after less than twelve years. This group, with some 11,500 members and 92,000 signatures on petitions, persuaded the Maryland legislature to require a minimum of twenty years in prison before parole can be considered in a capital crime case, to eliminate drugs and alcohol as mitigating circumstances in violent acts, and to mandate that a written victim impact statement be provided to judges before sentencing (Satchell 1985: 15). They have also lobbied for judges to be given the option of imposing life sentences with no parole and for in-person testimony by victims prior to sentencing, as well as for notification of victims and their families before a criminal is paroled.

Political activity by victims' groups has spread throughout the country, and it is clearly having effects on legislatures (see chapter 11 for additional discussion). California's victim assistance programs had been copied by thirty-seven states and the District of Columbia by 1986, for instance (Cardenas 1986: 357). Some states, such as Kentucky, have made it a policy to have prosecutors consult with victims before dismissing a case or completing a plea bargain; Minnesota and others allow victims to speak to the court before a judge ratifies a plea bargain (Evers 1994: 15). Many new statutes passed in response to political pressures from victims' groups (although certainly not all of them) focus on victim input into the punishment or incapacitation decisions or on making punishment more severe. For example, some states now have statutes establishing the right of victims to testify prior to sentencing about the effect of the crime on their lives or to provide a written victim impact statement to the judge before sentencing, and there are now statutes mandating tougher sentencing for various kinds of violent crimes (e.g., crimes against children and sex crimes), as noted above.[9] Other statutes are intended to prevent additional crimes: these provide for notification of victims and their families before a criminal is paroled (perhaps so they can petition the parole board or perhaps so they can guard against revenge), access by organizations to criminal records of anyone seeking a job that brings the person into close contact with children, and numerous other reforms. In addition to lobbying for legislative change, many victims' groups now actively monitor court cases and provide counseling for victims and information for parents.

Despite the victims' movement, most offenders actually prosecuted and sentenced will not go to prison. In Florida the probabilities of imprisonment after conviction for burglary and robbery were estimated to be 26 percent and 46 percent in 1992 (Benson and Rasmussen 1994a). A rough estimate of the cumulative probability of imprisonment, based on 1992 figures, can be determined by calculating the percentage of prison admissions (340,000) relative to total reported crimes nationally (14.43 million). Thus, roughly 2.36 percent of all reported crimes in the nation might lead to an imprisoned criminal. That is not an accurate estimate, because many criminals in prison have committed multiple crimes and because many criminals admitted to prison are non-Index felons who may not have committed any violent or property Index offenses at all. For instance, 61.33 percent of the defendants convicted in U.S. District Courts in 1990 were not convicted for violent or property crimes or weapons charges—they were convicted for drug crimes or "public order offenses"; 45.83 percent of the felony convictions in state courts similarly had primary offenses that were non–Index I property or violent crimes and nonweapons crimes.[10] Furthermore, 43 percent of the 274,613 Index II drug offenders and 37 percent of the 105,484 "other offenses" (offenses other than Index I violent and property crimes, drug crimes, and weapons charges) went to prison, accounting for 41.2 percent of state prison admissions that year. Given a similar figure for 1992, the 2.36 percent estimate derived above would fall at least to 1.39. So it appears that at best, less than 1.5 percent of the felonies reported lead to imprisonment.

Furthermore, even if imprisoned, a felon will probably serve only a small portion of the sentence before being released early or paroled. Average prison sentences vary by crime and by state. In Florida, sentences ranged from an average 21.8 years for murder during 1992 to 4.1 years for theft and fraud, but the average portion of a prison sentence served in Florida was approximately 43 percent in July 1993. And this percentage was much lower in some other states, such as Oklahoma and North Carolina.

Summing Up: What Are the Expected Benefits of Victim Cooperation?

Figure 4.1 summarizes the points made here regarding the expected results of victim cooperation in the form of punishment of the criminal by imprisonment. Other forms of "punishment," such as probation, are more frequently handed down, but the demands of organized victims' groups for more and longer prison sentences suggest that these alternatives are generally viewed as inadequate. This perception is reinforced by the responses to victimization surveys discussed above, which demonstrate that most victims do not perceive sufficient benefits from the public process of policing, prosecuting, and pun-

FIGURE 4.1
Calculating Expected Prison Sentences

Expected Time in Prison =

(1) Probability that Crime Is Observed	X	(2) Probability of Observer Reporting	X	(3) Probability of Arrest	X
(4) Probability of Prosecution	X	(5) Probability of Conviction	X	(6) Probability of Imprisonment	X
	(7) Average Prison Sentence	X	(8) Portion of Sentence Served		

ishing to motivate them to report crimes. Thus, figure 4.1 simply repeats the contention that once a crime has been committed, the expected prison sentence for a criminal is the probability that the crime or its consequences will be observed, times the probability that the observing victim or witness will report the crime (or act on the observation if the observer is a police officer, for instance), times the probability of arrest if the crime is reported, times the probability of being prosecuted given arrest, times the probability of conviction given prosecution, times the probability of a prison sentence given conviction, times the expected prison sentence, which can be approximated by the average sentence handed down by judges, times the average portion of the sentence served before early release.

A rough approximation of the calculation described in figure 4.1, but without the first probability included (there are no data available to measure this probability, but for the types of crimes considered here, the probability that the consequences of the crime will be observed is clearly very close to and implicitly assumed to be 1), can be made for some crimes using 1992 Florida data. Table 4.2 reports approximations of the expected price the criminal justice system is charging for committing robberies and burglaries—and therefore estimates of at least part of the expected benefits a victim might receive from cooperating with the police and the prosecutor. Other violent crimes against persons have relatively higher expected prison penalties than the robbery results reported in table 4.2: a murderer has an expected punishment of 2.99 years, and a sexual offender has an expectation of about 338 days. Property offenses may be common in Florida because there is a very low expected penalty to deter potential offenders. In addition to the burglary figures in the table, those engaged in larceny (theft) face an expected 4.5 days in prison; auto thieves expect about 10 days.

Clearly, the expected prices of most crimes committed in Florida are very low. That is one reason for the high level of crime in Florida. If the primary benefit that a victim anticipates from cooperating with police and prosecutors is that the criminal will be severely punished or incapacitated so that he or she cannot commit more crimes, then nonreporting is very understandable. Why report a burglary and go through all of the hassle, grief, frustration, and monetary costs of cooperating when the average punishment for the burglar is thirteen days in prison because the vast majority are never sentenced to prison and those who are do not serve most of their sentence? (Note that Florida has embarked on a prison building program in order to eliminate early release programs and guarantee that prisoners serve at least 75 percent of their sentence, but this only doubles the expected prison stay to a paltry twenty-six days.)

Furthermore, any hope that cooperating with police and prosecutors will protect the victim or others from the same criminal is a false one. After all, the actual periods of incapacitation, given successful prosecution, are quite short and apparently not sufficient to deter most criminals from further crimes. Roughly 70 percent of the offenders released from prison are rearrested for committing another crime.[11]

Conclusions

The failure of the public-sector-dominated criminal justice system to make arrests after crimes are committed, prosecute criminals who are arrested, and effectively punish those who are prosecuted explains a substantial portion of the criminal activity that threatens Americans today. This same failure also explains, to a large extent, why victims do not report most of the crimes that are committed. As public programs such as pretrial release have been implemented to replace private initiatives such as the market for bail bonds, the

TABLE 4.2
Expected Prison Terms for Robbery and Burglary in Florida, 1992

	(2)	x	(3)	x	(4)	x	(5)	x	(6)	x	(7)	x	(8)	=	Expected Prison Time
Robbery	.70	x	.25	x	.68	x	.85	x	.46	x	8.6 yrs	x	.45	=	65.7 days
Burglary	.60	x	.15	x	.82	x	.92	x	.26	x	5.5 yrs	x	.37	=	12.8 days

problems have become worse rather than better. Thus, wherever possible, the private sector has responded by moving to avoid or reduce the severity of the public sector's failures. The nonreporting stressed above is but one reaction to the high cost of victim involvement with the criminal justice system relative to expected benefits, although it is a reaction that has been common since the inception of criminal law (Benson 1990: 62–63; 1992b, 1994a), as explained in chapter 9. Political action is another, and it will be discussed in more detail in chapter 11.

Yet another response is suggested by the fact that some crimes are likely to be reported even though the victim does not expect the criminal justice system to actually do anything about them. As noted above, crimes are often reported because reporting is required in order to collect insurance. This is particularly true for thefts, including motor vehicle theft, where 9 to 12 percent of the victims cite collection of insurance as a primary motivation for reporting the crime (Bureau of Justice Statistics 1993: 34), and the real impact is probably much higher given the very high reporting rate for auto thefts relative to most other crimes. Thus, victims report the crimes because they have invested in a form of private "protection" of their wealth: insurance. The incentives to substitute private protection alternatives for ineffective criminal justice services are very strong, and substitutes go well beyond insurance to protect wealth after the crime has been committed. Even more direct means of protecting persons and property before a crime is committed are being produced and purchased in ever increasing quantities and varieties. Such activities are attracting considerable entrepreneurial activity as citizens are increasingly looking to the private sector for the protection that they are not getting from public police services. These investments affect criminal behavior by greatly increasing the probability that a crime will be observed. This should deter crimes, and evidence cited in chapter 7 supports this expectation. Of course, not all crimes will be deterred through increased watching efforts, but given an observed crime, the likelihood of punishment rises. A victim can report the crime to the police, but as suggested here, the resulting expected punishment is low. There are many alternatives, however, if victims turn to private justice.

Security managers report that many crimes against business, including pilferage and employee theft, insurance fraud, industrial espionage, commercial bribery, and computer-related crimes, tend to be resolved (solved and sanctioned) within the business organization (Cunningham and Taylor 1985: 11–12). They cite several reasons for internal resolution of crimes, including the expectation that police will give them low priority, the "unsympathetic" view that public officials tend to have regarding business losses, the fact that public police are not likely to have the expertise needed to solve such crimes, the high cost of cooperating with prosecution, and dissatisfaction with the level of sanctions imposed in case prosecution is successful. Therefore, business organizations often impose their own sanctions, such as firing the offender, with considerably greater certainty than the public-sector criminal justice system can be expected to do. Many individual citizens have similar feelings about the responsiveness of the criminal justice system, and in some cases, similar options to impose sanctions. Private justice is therefore an increasingly important response outside the business sector as well. More details on private justice are presented in chapter 6, but first let us examine the kinds of crime prevention activities that the private sector is providing.

PART II

Private Crime Control

5

The Level and Scope of Private
Production of Crime Prevention
and Protection

Lawrence W. Sherman points out that "[f]ew developments are more indicative of public concern about crime—and declining faith in the ability of public institutions to cope with it—than the burgeoning growth in private policing. . . . Rather than approving funds for more police, the voters have turned to volunteer and paid private watchers" (1983: 145–49). But private responses to crime have gone well beyond voluntary participation in watching and hiring guards (Clotfelter 1977: 868) to include the increased use of alarm systems, safes, window bars, and other protection devices. Private-sector involvement in crime control is clearly quite substantial, but much of that involvement goes unnoticed and undocumented. Nonetheless, there have been, over the last three decades, a few valuable surveys and studies that shed some light on the level of privatization. These include studies by Predicast (1970), the Rand Corporation (Kakalik and Wildhorn 1971), the National Advisory Commission on Criminal Justice Standards and Goals (1976), and Research and Forecasts (1983). In addition, Hallcrest Systems conducted a study (Cunningham and Taylor 1985) for the National Institute of Justice (NIJ), and the NIJ followed that up with Strauchs, Cunningham, and Van Meter 1991. There have also been several more narrowly focused academic research projects, studies by research professionals (e.g., NIJ), and a few popular-press publications. Although some of these studies are clearly dated, so that the actual levels of private-sector activity discovered by them may not reflect current levels, an indication of the *types* of private protection that are being demanded and supplied, as well as the *trends* in such activities can be gleaned by examining their findings.[1]

The Demand Side: Prevention, Detection, and Protection Purchased by Individuals, Households, and Businesses

Sherman (1983) classifies crime control into three categories: (1) "watching," (2) "walling," and (3) "wariness." Watching refers to observing people and places that criminals may attack and apprehending criminals in the act. Walling describes actions designed to prevent criminal access to persons or property through the use of locks, bars, fences, and other obstructions. Wariness characterizes adjustments in behavior to avoid the consequences of crime, such as taking self-defense or firearms classes, staying home at night, and leaving lights on when away from home. Private demand for all of these activities is on the rise. Individuals purchase goods like "security" or "protection" by making sacrifices, of course. They often give up money that they could spend on something else in order to buy better locks or alarms, employ guards, and so on, but they may pay in other ways as well. For instance, they may buy more security by spending time watching the street or paying more attention to their surroundings. Like money, time can be spent on other things that give pleasure. And adjustments in behavior, including paying more attention, staying at home after dark, never going out without a companion, dressing in a way that is less likely to attract attention, and so on, all involve costs (sacrifices). In this light, let us consider the kinds of sacrifices individuals and businesses are making in order to buy more security.

Individuals and Households

The Research and Forecasts study of fear of crime asked survey respondents what protective measures they took in their homes and when they went out. "The answers revealed an extremely cautious and security-minded America" (1983: 68). Fifty-six percent of those responding to the survey said that they kept their car doors locked most of the time while driving, and 70 percent did so more often than not. Sixty percent phoned at least sometimes to inform others that they had safely reached their destinations after traveling, and 44 percent indicated that they often planned their travel routes to avoid potentially dangerous places. When going out at night, 25 percent of the sample frequently had a whistle, carried a weapon, or were accompanied by a dog. Fifty-four percent of the women made certain they had a companion for trips at night. Seventy-eight percent of blacks dressed plainly to avoid attracting attention, and 54 percent of the whites surveyed did so (Research and Forecasts 1983: 70, 71, 72, 76).

Almost all respondents to the Research and Forecasts survey (1983: 73) locked their doors when leaving and made people identify themselves before opening doors. Fifty-two percent had added extra locks to their doors, 82 percent had someone watch their homes when they were away for a weekend, and 70 percent had newspaper and mail delivery stopped. In addition, 36 percent of the survey had engraved their valuables in the hope of discouraging theft or aiding in the recovery of stolen items. Approximately one-fourth of the survey sample had automatic timers to switch lights on and off, and many had installed more sophisticated devices to turn the television or stereo on and off as well. Fifteen percent had burglar alarms, and 8 percent barred windows. That was in 1983. Expenditures on security equipment have risen dramatically since then. In 1994 Americans spent an estimated $3.6 billion on alarms and surveillance systems to protect their homes (Lavan 1995).

"Quite often the gun is a household protective device," the report suggests: "Gun ownership clearly has the effect of substantially reducing formless fear" of crime (Research and Forecasts 1983: 91). Fifty-two percent of the respondents to the survey questionnaire indicated that they owned a gun to protect their homes. If this survey was retaken today, the numbers would probably be much higher. Americans are buying more firearms every year (an estimated 4 million handguns, 1.5 million rifles, and 1.3 million shotguns in 1993 [Lavan 1995]). And people are using their guns for protection. Overall, private citizens legally shoot almost as many criminals as public police officers do, and in some jurisdictions citizens legally kill up to two or three times as many violent criminals as do police. There were 126 justifiable homicides by private citizens in California during 1981, compared to 68 justifiable homicides by police (California Department of Justice 1981).

The Research and Forecasts report also examined the effects of rising crime on corporate policy and the lifestyle of *Fortune 1000* business executives. Seventy-five percent of those senior executives reported securing their homes with burglar and fire alarms and said they had guards and guard dogs, had unlisted phone numbers, and/or kept their addresses confidential (Research and Forecasts 1983: 109). Thirty-five percent varied their daily route to work, and 19 percent alternated cars. They also reported substantial investments by their corporations in security for offices and plants, as noted below.

A substantial array of new security devices have been introduced by entrepreneurs since the Research and Forecasts survey. Devices like "the club" to protect cars have been available for only a few years, but they seem to be everywhere, and car alarms are also increasingly common. An even newer device to protect cars, called Lojack, is a radio transmitter that can be hidden inside the vehicle and remotely activated if the car is stolen. Thus, the percentages reported in this survey and others cited here do not appear to hold any longer. Importantly, however, indications are that expenditures on security equipment and the numbers of people using it have continued to grow at a dramatic rate since the surveys were done. Therefore, the substantial levels of private security that they suggest individuals and households employ are all underestimates of what is being done today. The same can be said for businesses.

Businesses

Research and Forecasts' survey results imply that for 46 percent of the surveyed executives nationwide (62 percent of those in large cities), crime in their corporate neighborhoods affected program planning and security policies. Most corporate headquarters had a "vast array" of security procedures and devices: 88 percent of those surveyed had building security checks; 66 percent had burglar alarms; 64 percent had floodlighting; 50 percent had automatic light timers; 48 percent used closed-circuit television; 38 percent had electronic card identification systems; 30 percent had photoelectric timers; and 24 percent employed armed guards (Research and Forecasts 1983: 100). Four hundred of the one thousand companies in the survey used at least six of these kinds of security procedures, and unarmed guards, plainclothes security personnel, and coded door locks were also common. Most of the surveyed corporations also had comprehensive security programs, including education programs for employees (73 percent) and crisis management plans (63 percent), and 62 percent employed a security specialist. The Research and Forecasts report concludes: "It's obvious that the development of a corporate security program is a tremendously time-consuming, cumbersome, and expensive process that places a burden on the employee as well as the employer" (1983: 118).

Office buildings are increasingly being built or reconfigured with security in mind. Many firms are adding guard posts and equipment such as metal detectors, palm readers, and concrete blocks to prevent access. Building managers and operators currently tend to opt for visible guards and various restrictions on entry (e.g., sign-in and -out procedures and confirmation of appointments), but according to Robert McCrie, a professor of security management at CUNY's John Jay College, "there is a clear movement to 100-percent surveillance at building entryways. People entering parking lots and going in and out of buildings will be videotaped. Some buildings are even videotaping elevators" (quoted in Lavan 1995).

Such obvious security devices and personnel tell only part of the story. The fact is that businesses often must take security into account in the initial design and construction of their buildings. Consider Molberg's Designing Jewelers, a long-standing family-owned business in Denver, Colorado, specializing in rare and expensive gemstones for which they design and make settings to sell in their retail establishment. The firm recently had to relocate, and the amount of money spent refurbishing the building for security reasons before they moved would probably shock most of their loyal customers.[2] A Tan TL30 safe designed to take the best thief thirty minutes to crack (cost about $15,000) and the TL15 vault ($20,000) were needed to protect valuable gems. Walls adjacent to the street and parking areas had to be protected by twenty iron-reinforced posts ($2,500) to prevent thieves from crashing a car through the wall and grabbing merchandise, doors and windows had to be replaced with heavy shatterproof glass ($6,850), both burglar and movement alarms ($5,000) with extra phone lines ($6,725) and security cameras were installed, and off-duty police officers were hired as guards during the move and setup. Such security precautions are not unique. Although the value of the merchandise in this store probably exceeds the value in most establishments of similar or even substantially larger size, thus demanding more security precautions than a business with a similar-sized retail facility would generally install, most retailers are forced to invest in some security measures that affect the cost of design and construction of their buildings. Other business locations face similar costs. The design and construction of office buildings is increasingly costly as more and more of them are being built to limit and control access, to make observation more effective, and even to withstand explosions (Lavan 1995).

Total Demand

It is very difficult to determine how much private security is being demanded in the United States. One reason is that much of the expenditure is in terms of time and other sacrifices, rather than in money. Thus, any estimates must be treated with considerable caution. With this in mind, Ayres and Levitt (1996) cite two estimates (one published—Laband and Sophocleus 1992)— that place total private-sector spending to reduce crime at roughly $300 billion annually. If that figure is close to being accurate, and if the estimates of spending on security personnel cited below (about $65 billion in 1994) and on alarms and surveillance systems for homes cited above ($3.6 billion in 1994) are also accurate, then much of the rest of the total is business spending for nonlabor input to security (construction and design, monitoring and surveillance, and so on). Whether those amounts are accurate or not, the total expenditures being made annually by individuals and business firms on security measures must run into the hundreds-of-billions-of-dollars range. Total government spending on criminal justice in 1995 (policing, corrections, and so forth) is estimated to be slightly less than $100 billion (Ayres and Levitt 1996), so even if the estimates of private spending for crime control cited above are double actual expenditures, the private sector's criminal justice role is actually much greater than the public sector's. But the investments in security go even further: people in many residential and business communities are also joining groups and spending time (as well as money, presumably reflected in the estimates cited above) in voluntary crime control activities.

Voluntary Group Actions against Crime

A Gallup poll discussed in Sherman 1983 (145) indicates that organized volunteer crime prevention efforts were in place in the residential neighborhoods of 17 percent of the Americans surveyed. Such activities appear to be on the increase, as explained below. Voluntary groups sponsor and organize youth-oriented activities to keep young people off the streets, cooperate in neighborhood improvement programs, organize property protection activities (e.g., Operation ID), establish escort services, and participate in neighborhood and building patrols. Some groups even buy the streets they live on and fence in the neighborhood.

Group Watching and Patrolling

The best-known and most obvious group activities for protection are group watches and patrols. In 1977 between 800 and 900 resident patrols operated in urban areas with more than 250,000 people, and there were more than 50,000 block watches nationwide (Yin et al. 1977: 13; Pierce 1984). How rapidly this activity is expanding nationally is difficult to determine, but some areas are clearly experiencing rapid growth. Tallahassee, Florida, a community of about 150,000 residents, saw almost a dozen new neighborhood watch groups form between late 1993 and early 1995, and "older, inactive neighborhood-watch groups are once again buzzing with activity" (Cole 1995: 5A).

An estimated 63 percent of the residential patrols examined by Yin and co-workers (1977) are composed of volunteers, 18 percent hire guards, 7 percent pay residents, and the remaining 12 percent use a combination of voluntary and hired watchers. Patrols are active in neighborhoods at all income levels (Yin et al. [1977] estimate that 55 percent of all patrols are in low-income areas, 35 percent in middle-income areas, and 10 percent in high-income neighborhoods). Building patrols frequently operate in low-crime areas for preventive purposes, and neighborhood patrols are often formed in areas experiencing serious crime problems. In 1980 roughly ten thousand of New York's thirty-nine thousand city blocks had functioning block associations to compensate for inadequate city services, and nearly all had some kind of security patrol.

Building patrols, primarily intended to deter crime and keep undesirable strangers out of the building, typically operate in areas that receive little attention from public police. These patrols often place guards at building entrances or gates, and they may also use closed-circuit television and other electronic aids. Neighborhood patrols cover mainly streets and public areas rather than buildings. Unlike building patrols, neighborhood patrols have frequent contact with public police and often may coordinate their efforts with police. If the patrols are responsible for large areas, they are not likely to be able to distinguish strangers from residents, so they have to focus on observing undesirable or suspicious behavior. Neighborhood patrols may operate on foot or in cars, and some observe crime-prone areas from fixed vantage points in buildings. They often employ radios to report observations to a base station or directly to the police.

A typical voluntary patrol might be the East Midwood Patrol in Brooklyn (Podolefsky and Dubow 1981: 84). In 1980 the patrol had 120 volunteer members performing all-night patrols 365 days per year, teaching security techniques to households, and watching for prowlers and muggers. A $10/year donation from the households in the twenty-five-block patrol area covered monetary expenses, and 85 percent of the households contributed in 1980.

Many neighborhood patrols supplement public police services and are organized with the help of the police. Others take a more adversarial role, substituting for a perceived lack of public police presence (Marx and Archer 1971). For instance, the West Park Community Protection Agency was organized by a black resident of Philadelphia because "when Blacks began moving into the area police became lax" (Podolefsky and Dubow 1981: 81). The organizer performed stakeouts and patrols, checked in with businesses, and signed in on police sign-in sheets. The police initially accused him of vigilantism, but they eventually recognized the benefits of cooperating with the West Park patrol group, and after a change in the organization's name, links with police were established. This kind of cooperation does not always develop. The

Black Panthers began as a small ghetto patrol organization to protect the neighborhood from criminals and the police. "Blacks wanted protection from the . . . [police department] that was supposed to protect them," so the Panthers supplied "guards for the guards" by following police cars that patrolled the area and monitoring arrests (Wooldridge 1970: 115). They carried legal weapons to discourage the idle harassment of blacks by police. The Black Panthers subsequently became involved in other controversial projects, and little cooperation between the group and police ever developed.

Patrols and watches are actually only a small part of the overall program of crime prevention that voluntary groups are involved in. Some, such as patrols, are quite time-consuming; others may be less time-consuming but may require more monetary expenditures.

Programs for Youth

"Most of the activities reported as 'doing something about crime,' involve attempts by groups of neighbors to improve the 'quality of life' in their neighborhood" (Podolefsky and Dubow 1981: 44). In particular, voluntary efforts are directed at keeping children from turning to criminal activities. Based on results from a random-digit telephone survey of residents of San Francisco, Chicago, and Philadelphia, Podolefsky and Dubow (1981: 45) suggest that youth-oriented activities account for 19.9 percent of all crime control activities, the largest proportion of all group anticrime efforts. These activities include providing employment or recreation (70 percent of all efforts in this activity group for youths) as well as counseling and dealing with gang problems. It is common for volunteers to see youth programs designed to keep children busy, particularly sports programs, as major contributions to crime control, but many community and neighborhood organizations indicate that "recreation is not enough, there is a need to combine education, economics and recreation" (Podolefsky and Dubow 1981: 48). Thus, community groups also provide activities ranging from job counseling to employment opportunities. One community group responding to this survey even set up a nonprofit business to hire local youths, using funds donated by local businessmen.

Neighborhood Improvement

Voluntary groups pursue programs to (1) improve the physical and social conditions of their neighborhoods or communities, (2) alter conditions seen as particularly conducive to crime, (3) reduce access to the community, (4) make changes that facilitate group watching efforts (e.g., pruning trees and shrubs or installing lighting), and (5) improve the overall economic conditions of the area. Improving or cleaning up the neighborhood is the third most frequently mentioned crime control activity in the Podolefsky and Dubow survey (1981: 53–54), accounting for 8 percent of the responses. Neighborhood groups clean up streets, parks, alleys, business areas, and housing projects and repair or destroy abandoned buildings to make the area more hospitable. They also try to establish or improve neighborhood recreational facilities. One group responding to the survey, for example, claims responsibility for closing six blocks to traffic to allow for children's play.[3]

Property Protection

Community groups promote awareness and home security by holding meetings, arranging lectures, and distributing crime prevention literature (Podolefsky and Dubow 1981: 71). Some groups go beyond simply providing information to organize property engraving (e.g., Operation I.D.) programs. Participants are also urged to display decals that announce to potential burglars that they have marked their property (Skogan and Maxfield 1979). Participation in such programs is estimated to range from 10 to 25 percent in target areas, and 31 percent of those surveyed by Podolefsky and Dubow report marking their property (73).

Personal Protection

Group personal protection activities include escort services and organized responses to signaling devices (e.g., whistles or freon horns), as well as educational programs. Escort services are typically designed for a particular purpose, such as escorting senior citizens when they cash pension, social security, or welfare checks, accompanying children home from day care centers, or escorting women students who must cross a campus after dark.

The Podolefsky and Dubow survey (1981: 76) results suggest that 5 percent of the respondents carried signaling devices. Many people participate in such programs as WhistleSTOP, a community signal system. Participants carry a whistle that they can blow in emergencies or if they encounter trouble in the streets. Other WhistleSTOP members respond to a signal by first calling the police and then blowing their own whistles to signal others that a crime situation or emergency exists.

Private Streets

One of the most complete cooperative privatization schemes in recent history is in place in Saint Louis and University City, Missouri. As Oscar Newman notes,

> the decline of St. Louis, Missouri, has come to epitomize the impotence of federal, state, and local resources in coping with the consequences of large scale population change. Yet buried within those very areas of St. Louis which have been experiencing the most radical turnover of population are a series of streets where residents have adopted a program to stabilize their communities to deter crime, and to guarantee the necessities of a middle-class life-style. These residents have been able to create and maintain for themselves what their city was no longer able to provide: low crime rates, stable property values and a sense of community. . . . The distinguishing characteristic of these *streets* is that they have been deeded back from the city to the residents and are now legally *owned and maintained by the residents themselves.* (1980: 124, emphasis added)

In 1970 Westminster Place in Saint Louis was dying economically. Middle-income residents had seen property values plummet during the 1960s as "urban blight" set in. In addition, an estimated six thousand cars per day used Westminster Place to avoid traffic lights on nearby major boulevards. Prostitutes found the neighborhood to be an attractive business area. But in 1970, "standing up to the urban blight, the crime, and the fear that causes residents to flee, the people of [Westminster Place and several other] neighborhoods . . . found an unconventional solution to a common problem": they petitioned the city to deed the streets to them (Gage 1981: 18). The city complied with this request and many others like it in return for the residents' assumption of responsibility for street, sewer, and streetlight maintenance, garbage pickup, and any security services above normal fire and police protection.

The titles to the streets are now vested in an incorporated street association to which all property owners must belong and pay dues. The street associations, most of which own one or two blocks, have the right to close their streets to through traffic in order to limit cars on the street to those of residents and their visitors. More importantly, "[i]t is *their* street and that ownership gives the neighborhood a high degree of cohesiveness" (Gage 1981: 19).[4] A large study of Saint Louis (and University City) private streets concludes that residents "needed assurance that neighboring homeowners shared both their values and financial capacity to maintain the standards of homeownership. . . . [C]oncern for security of their investment was a critical factor which led urban oriented residents to the selection of a house on a private street" (Newman

1980: 131).[5] As a result of cooperative behavior that produces an increased residential awareness of activities on the streets, along with limited access and in some cases (although limited numbers) security patrols, establishing private streets significantly lowers crime in virtually every category relative to the crime on comparable public streets (Newman 1980: 137, 140): Ames Place's crime rate was 108 percent lower than the adjacent public street, for instance (more details are provided in chapter 7).

The private streets of Saint Louis are definitely not exclusively the domain of the wealthy and the middle class, either. In 1974 Waterman Place, a "lower-class" neighborhood, was experiencing high crime and rapid deterioration. The residents formed an association, obtained permission to privatize the street, limited access by spending forty thousand dollars to erect a gate, and started a block watch. Property values doubled as crime fell and funds were borrowed to improve the street and its housing (Foldvary 1994: 193).

In 1982 the Saint Louis metropolitan area had more than 427 private street–providing organizations (that is, 427 private places reported, but the list was known to be incomplete) (Parks and Oakerson 1988: 9, 84). In two of the Saint Louis area's municipalities, over 50 percent of street mileage is private, and in four others "major" portions of the streets are privately provided (Foldvary 1994: 191).

There are actually many private streets in the United States, as suggested below. What makes the Saint Louis area unique is that, although many streets around the country are private from their inception as proprietary developments, few become private after they have been public. The Saint Louis communities' privatization of previously public streets in response to the demands of a group of neighbors, therefore, involves a more substantial act of privatization than that of residents of new developments supplied by entrepreneurs who build the streets on previously private land.

Cooperation by Business Groups

Growing numbers of businesses are adopting crime control strategies similar to those of the residential groups. For example, "crime on Tennessee Street [a major retailing street in Tallahassee, Florida] had just gotten out of hand," so in 1992 several business owners on the street formed a watch association similar to those in residential areas, and by late 1994, ninety business people were attending monthly meetings, keeping in regular contact by fax regarding criminal activity, and calling police regarding suspected circumstances (Cole 1995: 5A). Of course, such crime prevention efforts by businesses is not new, and many involve much more than cooperative watching by business people. A privately financed police patrol and high-tech security service operates in a twenty-four-block area of downtown Fort Worth, Texas. City Center Security, started by the Bass brothers, who own a number of downtown buildings (Fixler and Poole 1992: 37), assigns fifty guards to patrol the area and has 150 hidden video cameras monitoring buildings and streets, along with a system of computers to link up and analyze information (McCrie 1992: 19).

Other business groups have also formed their own specialized security forces. For example, the railroad police were established by the major railroads in the country at the end of World War I as a complete and autonomous national police force. Railroad police have compiled what must be considered a "remarkable" record of effectiveness, particularly relative to public police forces, as explained in chapter 7, and they continue to operate today. In 1992 major railroads in the United States employed a 2,565-person security force. Businesses (and individuals) do not have to explicitly create these security arrangements, however; entrepreneurs are happy to create and sell such services.

Markets Supplying Specialized Security Services and Equipment

The northern section of San Francisco has sixty-five "private police beats" that are "owned" by private "Patrol Special Police" (Dorffi 1979; Fixler and Poole 1992: 37). San Francisco's Patrol Specials date from 1851 and the gold rush period. They are protected by the city charter and have, with the strong support of the neighborhoods that they patrol, withstood numerous attacks and court challenges led by city police (see chapter 11). All Patrol Specials complete 440 hours or more of police academy training and have full rights to carry firearms and make arrests. Specials are licensed as "peace officers" (they are official members of the San Francisco police department similar to "reservists" and are required to respond to police calls in their area). Once licensed, they can bid on one or more of the sixty-five beats. They are paid by the individual businesses, homeowners, and landlords on their beats. Each patrolman negotiates a contract with each property owner on the beat who wants to purchase his services. Contracts are renewed and renegotiated periodically. The level of attention required by a customer determines the fee. Fees run in the range of twenty-five dollars to thirty dollars per hour, a very competitive price in the San Francisco security market (see chapter 8). On the more lucrative beats, the Patrol Specials employ assistants who complete the same 440 hours of police training, as well as administrative staff and security guards in order to meet their customers' needs. This is but one example of a very large and growing private security market supplying specialized services to meet the demands of individuals and private organizations.

Table 5.1 indicates that large numbers of new firms enter the private security market virtually every year. Between 1964 and 1991, employment by

TABLE 5.1
*Number of Firms and Employees in SIC 7393:
Detective Agency and Protective Services, 1964–1991*

Year	Number of Firms	Number of Employees
1964	1,988	62,170
1965	2,146	71,427
1966	2,418	85,057
1967	2,558	96,614
1968	2,981	118,451
1969	3,145	133,238
1970	3,389	151,637
1971	3,570	163,700
1972	3,822	182,665
1973	4,182	202,561
1974	5,295	249,663
1975	5,533	253,125
1976	5,841	248,050
1977	6,312	268,684
1978	6,204	287,380
1979	6,502	310,333
1980	6,752	337,617
1981	7,126	331,294
1982	8,424	345,874
1983	10,004	361,845
1984	10,059	384,005
1985	10,066	410,625
1986	10,396	430,685
1987	12,201	461,831
1988	11,675	473,308
1989	11,054	482,601
1990	11,681	514,229
1991	12,783	526,435
% change 1964–91	543.0%	746.8%
Average Annual % Change, 1964–91	20.1%	27.7%

NOTE: SIC (Standard Industrial Classification) 7393 was split into 7381 and 7382 in 1988.
SOURCE: Bureau of Census, *County Business Patterns* (Washington, DC: U.S. Department of Commerce, Bureau of Census, 1965–92)

private firms specializing in protective and detective services increased by 746.8 percent, and the number of firms offering such services grew by 543 percent over the same period. The figures in table 5.1 significantly underestimate private security employment, however, because they do not include direct employment of security and investigative personnel by firms, residential developments, and other institutions. For instance, the Sears Loss Prevention Organization employs approximately six thousand security personnel throughout the United States to protect two thousand different properties, a logistics organization, and a private aviation fleet, making it the fourth largest "private police force" in the country (OICJ 1995). A 1970 estimate that did include such sources of security employment put the number of privately employed security personnel at roughly equal to the number of public police, but by 1983 there were over twice as many private security employees as public police in the United States, as citizens hired more and more watchmen, guards, investigators, and highly trained security experts (Reichman 1987: 247). A 1991 NIJ report estimates the ratio to be about 2.5 private security personnel to every public police officer (Cunningham, Strauchs, and Van Meter 1991). An estimated $21.7 billion was paid to an estimated 1.1 million full-time security employees in 1980, 449,000 of them in individual enterprises and the rest involved with contractual services such as those counted in table 5.1 (Cunningham and Taylor 1985: 12). Estimates made in 1991 indicate that expenditures had risen to $52 billion for 1.5 million private security personnel (Cunningham, Strauchs, and Van Meter 1991). Expenditures were estimated at $65 billion in 1994 (Lavan 1995: 3A), and security industry experts expect the growth rate in private security to accelerate even more as private firms take over more responsibility for crime control. Employment of security guards grew by an estimated 11 percent in 1994 alone (Sherman 1995); private security is apparently the second fastest growing industry in the United States today (OICJ 1995). The ratio of private security employment to public police is rapidly approaching three to one (Reynolds 1994b), although expenditures are less than twice as high (e.g., $65 billion compared to about $30 billion in 1994), since income for those employed in the private security market varies more than public police income (from minimum wage up to at least six figures for specialists in security design) but averages less. Even these employment estimates "greatly underestimate the extent of private policing. Surveillance of private places and transactions is being conducted by actors who traditionally have not been counted as among the rank and file of private police" (Reichman 1987: 247), such as insurance adjusters monitoring insurance claims, corporate risk managers, and other "loss consultants."

Private security personnel perform many functions beyond patrolling or guarding residential buildings, neighborhoods, and corporate headquarters. They also provide security for airports, sports arenas, hospitals, colleges, state and municipal government buildings, banks, manufacturing plants, hotels, and retail stores. They provide armored-car services and central-station alarm systems. As McCrie notes, private security may "[m]ake citizens' arrests and may carry weapons; however, both qualities are incidental and supportive to the primary responsibility of deterring crime and providing a variety of support services to the employer or client" (1992: 17). Security personnel include stereotypical minimum-wage night watchmen, of course, but also fully qualified police officers (many public police officers moonlight as private security employees; many others have resigned to enter the lucrative private security market full-time) and highly trained and skilled electronic-security experts. The industry has developed a high level of specialization over the last thirty-five years. In fact, "there is emerging a new security person, highly trained, more highly educated and better able to satisfy the growing intricacies of the security profession" (Ricks, Tillett, and Van Meter 1981: 13).

The market for private security personnel is growing for a number of reasons. Clearly the rising crime rate of the 1960s and 1980s contributed to the industry's growth, but that growth continued during the 1970s, early 1980s, and early 1990s, when crime rates were somewhat more stable or falling. Entrepreneurial introduction of new technologies also plays an important role in the rapid expansion of private security services; new electronic equipment makes detection and deterrence more efficient, but it also requires hiring increasingly more skilled security personnel. It is not just numbers and expenditures that are rising: increasingly sophisticated labor and capital are being combined to produce ever higher levels of security where it is demanded. Training has had to improve dramatically in order to take advantage of the new technology. This in turn makes private alternatives to public police even more attractive sources of security. Thus, the net effect of all private-sector crime control efforts has been to reduce the demand for city police services relative to what it would otherwise be, so there has been a transfer of the policing function from the public to the private sector (Sherman 1983; Poole 1978: 39; Cunningham and Taylor 1985: 2).

Monitoring and Detection Equipment

A 1970 study by Predicast estimates that sales of such equipment grew at an annual rate of 8.8 percent between 1958 and 1963, increasing to 11 percent between 1963 and 1968. Sales of monitoring and detection equipment grew by 7.1 percent per year over the 1958–63 period and 10.4 percent per year from 1963 to 1968. These equipment sales account for considerably less than half the total expenditures on security during this period (41 percent in 1958 and 36 percent in 1968). The largest category of spending is for security personnel (the same is true of public-sector law enforcement services). This relative level of expenditures apparently continued to hold through the mid-1980s (Cunningham and Taylor 1985: 24) as both markets grew. Provision of residential alarm systems (the most frequently used component of security programs for business) was growing rapidly in 1985 (21), for instance, but the growth has probably accelerated. Central stations for alarms are increasingly available from a number of national companies such as ADT, Honeywell, Wells Fargo, Sonitrol, Rollins, Dictograph, and Westinghouse, as well as a large number of small, closely held family businesses that compete successfully with national firms. It is estimated that at least 10 percent of the homes in the United States were connected to central alarm systems in 1990, up from 1 percent in 1970 (Reynolds 1994b: 8).[6] It appears to be safe to say, given the growth in the employment of security personnel and the tremendous technological advances in security equipment, that the growth in the market for such equipment must be at least as rapid as the growth in the market for security personnel and probably much faster. But there is yet another entrepreneurial activity that should be noted.

The Supply of Secure Environments

Given the level of demand for security, it should not be surprising that entrepreneurs are discovering ways to supply a package of services that add up to more secure environments. Thus, residential and business developments are increasingly created with security as one of the design goals and then sold to individuals and businesses that value relative safety.

Private Residential Streets and Communities

Although few examples are documented to the degree that the Saint Louis private streets discussed above have been, many residential developments all over the country actually involve private streets (Foldvary 1994) and some sort of private security arrangements (the same is true for businesses, as explained below). Most of these private neighborhoods and communities are supplied by developers to individual buyers rather than by a local government responding to the demands of a neighborhood group to privatize previously public streets. Many of the private communities (a number of examples are cited in chapters 7 and 8, where their cost-effectiveness is explored) are actually being designed with security in mind. The developers charge for the cost of such designs when they sell the lots or homes, and included in the contracts are various stipulations about regular payments for ongoing costs such as street maintenance, security, and so on. Generally, as residents move in they form ownership associations; at some point these associations join with and ultimately replace the developers in coordinating the purchase of various services, including security.

The development I live in (in Tallahassee, Florida) has private streets owned by the homeowners association. Annual fees for road maintenance are paid, and security factors include only one entrance/exit, rules for traffic flow, and a neighborhood Crime Watch to supplement the county sheriff's provision of general police response. Other new developments in the area have more substantial private security with walls, private security guards, or gates requiring codes for entry. Estimates of the number of people in such "gated" communities range from 4 million in thirty thousand communities (Boaz 1997: 267) up to around 8 million, with .5 million in California alone (John Jay College of Criminal Justice/CUNY 1997b).

Often traced to the publication of a book titled *Defensible Space* (Newman 1972), new private communities (as well as some public communities, including several public housing projects) have been designed and existing communities have been redesigned around ideas of limited access and other principles of "defensible space" (Murray 1995: 350). In many of the private communities, the entire development is walled and security guards are posted at the gates. McCrie also emphasizes that many "[n]ew, planned communities offer the opportunity of providing a private security patrol which operates in effect as a private police department of the community" (1992: 18). He discusses the example of Wynstone, a housing development in North Barrington, Illinois, which provides private security officers who maintain twenty-four-hour access control and traffic control, provides emergency response and loss prevention, and enforces the rules of the development; costs are covered through monthly assessments of home owners established through deed-based contracts with the development. Similar arrangements exist in many developments, including many long-established neighborhoods (Los Angeles neighborhoods such as Bel-Aire and Beverlywood have contracts with Bel-Air Security for twenty-four-hour vehicular patrols [Fixler and Poole 1992: 38]). Furthermore, "[f]ear of crime and demographic changes are causing gated communities, once the domain of only the nation's wealthiest residents, to spring up across the country at prices affordable to middle-class families" (John Jay College of Criminal Justice/CUNY 1997b). New Colony in Howard County Maryland (between Washington, D.C., and Baltimore), which has home prices starting at $94,990 (very modest prices for the area), has a manned guardhouse at the entrance to the subdivision and is attracting single women and single parents as well as young families who want a safe environment for children.

Malls, Office Buildings, and Other Business Equivalents to Private Streets

Enclosed malls and office complexes are attractive to businesses for many reasons. One reason is the attractiveness to customers because of their one-stop shopping convenience. Another factor, though, is that, like many office complexes, they are privately owned and operated. Mall parking lots and corridors are private property like the private residential streets discussed above, although they are often the property of one proprietary entity. Thus, as Mac-Callum explains, security may be part of the contract that businesses purchase from the proprietor or from an independent security firm, but "in a fundamental sense the security of the community is part of the owner's real estate function. . . . [H]e supervises the design of all construction from the standpoint of safety" (1970: 66). The incentive to design facilities with security in mind and to provide adequate levels of security for both businesses and their customers is very strong when a mall or office complex owner must compete with other malls and office buildings to attract businesses. Today, therefore, large malls and office complexes are policed by private security forces, often with the aid of large investments in electronic monitoring and alarm systems. Even larger proprietary operations provide internal security. For instance, Shearing and Stenning (1987b) detail the massive role of private security and the resulting order in Disney World (also see Foldvary [1994]).

Apartment and condominium complexes can operate in a similar fashion. In this case the proprietor is renting or selling space for residential use rather than commercial use, but the incentives to design for security are the same. Such arrangements are apparently quite attractive, and they are available not only for wealthy and middle-income renters. Landlords who own more than fifty low-income and previously crime-infested apartment complexes in several Florida cities are purchasing security services from Critical Intervention Services, a firm discussed below that has specialized in deterring crime in such environments (Boyce 1996). Boaz indicates that an estimated 24 million Americans live in locked condominiums, apartment complexes, and cooperatives, "which are small gated communities" (1997: 267). He explains that these

> [p]rivate communities are a peaceful but comprehensive response to the failure of big government. Like their federal counterpart, local governments today tax us more heavily than ever but offer deteriorating services in return. Not only do police seem unable to combat rising crime, but the schools get worse and worse, garbage and litter don't get picked up, potholes aren't fixed, panhandlers confront us on every corner. Private communities can provide physical safety for their residents, partly by excluding from the community people who are neither residents nor guests. (268)

Clearly, private communities can offer many services that people find desirable, but security is one of the most important ones.

Conclusions

As suggested in chapter 4, dissatisfaction with the performance of the government's criminal justice system means that victims are choosing not to report crimes. Now we see that potential victims are turning to private alternatives for protection in an effort to prevent crime. This avoids the need to call on the public police at all. The privately provided services appear to be preventing a lot of crimes, as explained in chapter 7, but before turning to an examination of the benefits (and potential drawbacks) of private security, let us consider another development. It should not be surprising to find that victims are also turning to private alternatives to resolve crimes and sanction criminals if crimes do occur.

6

Private Justice in America
Historical Precedent and Modern Reality

The high cost of cooperating with police and prosecutors and the diminishing benefits of such cooperation inevitably lead to the development of extrajudicial processes and "self-help" procedures (Nader and Todd 1978: 38), or private justice. Private justice consists of "the localized nonstate systems of administering and sanctioning individuals accused of rule breaking or disputing" (Henry 1987: 45–46), and it has a long and frequently misunderstood history in the United States. Vigilante behavior is a part of our American tradition, for instance, but in contrast to the widespread characterization of vigilantism as "lynch-mob rule," vigilantes almost always were law-abiding citizens enforcing the law and *reestablishing order* in the face of government failure.[1] What really is our heritage of private justice?

Historical Precedent for Private Justice in America

Government law enforcement was not the norm in the original thirteen colonies.[2] Early colonial governments played no active role in apprehending and prosecuting lawbreakers (Cardenas 1986: 366; McDonald 1977), and "[p]olice departments and prosecutors did not exist as they are known today" (Cardenas 1986: 366). Therefore, as McDonald explains, a crime victim had to serve

> as policeman and prosecutor who, if he chose to apprehend an offender and initiate prosecution, did so directly and at his own expense. He did not have to rely on government agencies. On the contrary, he could not rely on them even if he wanted to because they either did not exist or did not perform the function he sought. By the same token, he was obviously not constrained by such agencies to proceed with a prosecution if he chose to withdraw. (1977: 295)

Public courts were available in most colonial capitals, but distance and poor roads made use of them for many colonists very expensive. Thus, government trials could be and frequently were simply bypassed in favor of direct bargaining or third-party arbitration or mediation, with restitution to the victim from the offender being the dominant sanction. Again, as Cardenas explains, early Americans held

> a restitutive theory of justice whereby forced reparations by the criminal to the victim were ordered, but punitive measures taken against the criminal to the benefit of the victim were also demanded. For example, a convicted thief would not only be ordered to return stolen property, but would also be forced to pay treble damages to the victim.
>
> When the offender was indigent, which was often the case, the crime victim generally was authorized to keep the offender as a servant or the victim could sell the offender's services. The duration of servitude was fixed. (1986: 367)

Despite the lack of public police services and the focus on restitution for victims, however, the victim did not have sole responsibility for enforcement. Reciprocities were strong. Neighbors or villagers aided a victim in pursuit, in part because they might require similar aid in the future and/or had in the past (these communities tended to be very close-knit, depending on each other for many things besides protection against and pursuit of criminals). Therefore, "while criminal prosecutions were brought in the name of the state, they were in effect private prosecutions in which the state usually did not play an active role and did not have a vested interest" (McDonald 1977: 295).

All of this changed fairly quickly in the original thirteen colonies, however. Government judicial officials advocated public prosecution very early in North America. "The heavy emphasis on private initiative for law enforcement had resulted in low status and pay for the public officials within the judicial system; additionally, expected revenue for government coffers from court-ordered fines never materialized because most crime victims who successfully apprehended their offenders privately settled their dispute" (Cardenas 1986: 369). An effort to increase judicial revenues was a major spur for the development of public prosecution in several colonies (although the excuse often cited was to aid the crime victims who were poor, an issue addressed in some detail in chapter 9). The attorney general of Virginia had authority to prosecute cases of special importance to the crown in 1643, for instance, but by 1711 the office had appointed in each county deputies who fully exploited this right as well as prosecuting most routine cases (Cardenas 1986: 370). In 1751 all crime victims in Virginia were ordered to confer with the deputy attorney general before they filed a criminal prosecution (to fully appreciate this order, it should be considered in the context of English criminal law of the time, as discussed in chapter 9), and by 1789 those deputies had virtually complete control of prosecution within their counties.

In some colonies, particularly those with a large Dutch population, public prosecution took root even faster. The Dutch government had criminal cases prosecuted by a public official called a *schout,* and the Dutch colonies in North America adopted the same system. After the English gained control of these colonies, they revoked all Dutch law and government except for the *schout.* This officer, who eventually became a sheriff, retained the power to prosecute. In addition, both Scottish and French law involved public prosecution, and these systems may also have influenced some of the colonial governments. At any rate, Connecticut established a system of public prosecution in 1704 and other colonies followed suit. Public prosecution was firmly in place within the thirteen colonies when they declared their independence.

Public prosecutorial bureaucracies grew up quickly, and fines found their way into state treasuries rather than victims' pockets. The rise of public prosecutors does not imply, however, that these public services were immediately widely used. Many victims and their reciprocal support groups, even during the post-Revolution period, pursued and then settled with an offender directly if he or she was willing to pay restitution. This private justice was used in part because access to courts remained difficult and costly: poor roads made distances significant. But perhaps private justice was also preferred because the offender's payment went to the victim rather than to the state. Thus, many private citizens continued to essentially treat crimes as torts and avoided the public prosecutors and courts.

Some may deny this conclusion (the lack of detailed records does not prove such a denial, of course), but even if it is not true in general for the original thirteen states, there can be no question regarding the lack of public courts, public prosecutors, and even enforcement of government-established statutes or precedents among most inhabitants of the new American society. In particular, many communities bound together by strong reciprocal ties based on religion or ethnic background (e.g., Quakers, Mormons) chose to establish and enforce their own laws even when public law and enforcement mechanisms were available (Auerbach 1983; Benson 1991b). Similarly, groups joined together to establish law and order as a consequence of reciprocal economic interests; this occurred both within merchant communities in the original states and within frontier associations that moved west at a rate that far outpaced the geographic expansion of government institutions. For these voluntary communities, law existed and order prevailed without the formal institutions of local, state, territorial, or federal governments. The law and order that existed for virtually the entire westward expansion was based to a large extent on private-sector production of law and law enforcement (Valentine 1956: 10; Anderson and Hill 1979; Benson 1991b). In most cases there was no alternative, but the fact is that a private-sector enterprise of law was chosen mainly because it worked.

Did it really work? What about the widely held perception that the eighteenth-century American West was a lawless society dominated by violence, where the strongest and most ruthless ruled by force? It is true that miners, farmers, ranchers, and many other individuals moved westward much more rapidly than government entities could expand the state's law enforcement system, particularly from 1830 to 1900. But this does not mean that the frontier was lawless. As economic historians Terry Anderson and P. J. Hill conclude after considering several of the nongovernmental systems of law enforcement that existed, "the western frontier was not as wild as legend would have us believe. The market did provide protection and arbitration agencies that functioned very effectively, either as a complete replacement for formal government or as a supplement to that government" (1979: 27). Similarly, UCLA historian Roger D. McGrath concludes that "some long-cherished notions about violence, lawlessness, and justice in the Old West . . . are nothing more than myth" (1984: 259). These quotes may not be very convincing, given the widespread beliefs regarding violence in the frontier West, so let us briefly examine the historical "evidence" of such violence.

Violence in the West: Myth or Reality?

That the West was a wild, violent, and lawless place is not just something that is popularly believed but rejected by researchers. Many historians have held the same opinions.[3] According to Elliot, the American frontier was a place "where a man could exist without tribute to tax collectors, or law makers, and if he moved fast enough he did not need to defer even to his neighbor's opinion" (1944: 189). This lack of effective government, Elliot suggests, encouraged a sense of individualism that *supposedly* produced frequent violent confrontations, particularly in the mining and cattle frontier. Similarly, Mondy (1943) notes that men found no stable social order waiting for them as they moved westward. This lack of social order *presumably* forced frontiersmen to act independently and to establish social relationships without the framework of an existing order. The resulting lack of law and order, Mondy concludes, led to frequent violent confrontations and deaths. Mondy also cites the physical and cultural isolation of the frontier communities as contributing factors to the problem of violence.

Interestingly, Elliot and Mondy provide *no proof* of widespread violence on the frontier. They simply *assume* (or *assert*) that violence was prevalent and then proceed to explain why that should be the case. In the same vein, Geis writes, "We can report with some assurance that, compared to frontier days, there has been a significant decrease in [crimes of violence]" (1967: 357). But Geis also cites no evidence. Frantz (1969) even suggests that American violence today reflects our frontier heritage, without demonstrating that the frontier was violent.

Is there any real evidence of relatively violent behavior in the West? Some historical accounts focus on a particularly notorious event or individual, and such events and individuals certainly existed. But there appears to be a serious selection bias problem when the entire West is characterized on the basis of the conclusions of such studies. Interestingly, however, even those studies discover a good deal of social order. Holden (1940) examines the Texas frontier from 1875–90, for instance, and finds that many kinds of criminal offenses common today were nonexistent. Burglaries and robberies of homes and businesses (except for banks) simply did not occur. Doors were not locked, and hospitality was widespread, indicating that citizens had relatively little fear of invasive violent or property offenses. Shootings did occur, but they typically involved what the citizenry considered to be "fair fights." Stage and train robberies occurred, but these incidents were isolated from most citizens and caused them little or no concern (Holden 1940: 196).

Drago (1970) also examines specific cases of violence that broke out over the use of range lands, but like Holden, he points out that such confrontations were not very common. A number of authors have written about gunfighters in the West (Burns 1926; Lake 1931; Connelley 1933), and it is true that some gunfighters participated in a number of killings. The vast majority of people, however, were not involved in or even touched by such violence. Furthermore, many western historians, particularly those during the 1920s and 1930s such as Burns (1926), Lake (1931), and Connelley (1933) "tended to exaggerate the exploits of the gunfighters and even to romanticize and ennoble them" (McGrath 1984: 264). More recent writers (e.g., Waters [1960], Steckmesser [1965], and Rosa [1968]) depict gunfighters as considerably less noble, and "the number of men killed by the gunfighters is also, for the most part, considerably reduced by the revisionist historians of the 1960s" (McGrath 1984: 264).

The reasons for the violent behavior exhibited in specific events or by specific notorious individuals, according to those historians who extrapolate these events or individuals to conclude that violence was a widespread phenomenon, are the nonexistence of government institutions of law and order, the isolation of communities, and the need for individuals to defend themselves and pursue attackers themselves or in conjunction with vigilante committees, who generally contributed more to violence than to order. Beyond these problems with law enforcement, there were supposedly many sources of confrontations, such as scarce land, large numbers of saloons, and gambling and prostitution establishments.[4]

The conclusion that the western frontier was a lawless, violent place comes from one of two sources: (1) it is simply *assumed* that since the West had no effective government law enforcement apparatus, it *must* have been lawless and violent; or (2) specific examples of violent individuals or events are *assumed* to represent the general character of the western frontier. After a careful review of the literature, McGrath concludes that

> the frontier-was-violent authors are not, for the most part, attempting to prove that the frontier was violent. Rather, they assume that it was violent and then proffer explanations for that alleged violence. These explanations are based on conditions that the authors think were peculiar to or exaggerated on the frontier and to the personality traits of the frontiersman himself. The authors reason that it must have been the unique frontier conditions and the frontiersman's personality that caused the violence.
>
> Their conclusions are not based on a thorough investigation of *all* forms of violence and lawlessness in the West or even in a particular town or region. . . . These authors provide a less than complete—in some cases a highly selective and perhaps unrepresentative—picture of frontier violence and lawlessness. (1984: 270–71)

Significantly, there is a growing literature that concludes that the West was not very violent. Hollon finds that the western frontier "was a far more civilized, more peaceful and safer place than American society today" (1974: x). According to him, violence became a problem in the West only *after* urban development (and urban development was often accompanied by public legal institutions). Similarly, Prassel concludes: "[I]t would appear that, in the American West, crime may have been more closely related to the developing urban environment than the former existence of a frontier" and that in general the westerner "probably enjoyed greater security in both person and property than did his contemporary in the urban centers of the east" (1972: 22). Both Hollon and Prassel also provide reasonable explanations for the widespread but mistaken impression that the frontier West was a violent place. Prassel points out that, in part because of the general *absence of disorder,* the notorious actions of a few individuals received undue attention. He also emphasizes that western fiction, movies, and television all create very inaccurate perceptions of the West. Hollon makes similar arguments, suggesting that the western frontier has a poetic image, in which its extremes, both good and bad, have been exaggerated. Even so, however, Hollon and Prassel are surprised to find that the West was really quite orderly. Prassel writes, "[C]onsidering the factors present it is surprising that even more murders, assaults, and robberies did not occur [in the western frontier]" (1972: 23). Similarly, Hollon concludes that "it is miraculous that the last and largest frontier region in the United States was settled in as orderly a fashion as it was" (1974: 125).

Hollon and Prassel are not the only scholars to recognize that the frontier West was not the lawless society of popular fiction or of academic assumption. Perrigo (1941) is surprised at how orderly the mining camps were. Similarly, Dykstra (1968) finds that Kansas cattle towns were not especially violent or lawless. Furthermore, he finds little evidence of conflict between Texas cattle drives and farmers along their routes. Conflicts that arose were generally resolved without violence through the efforts and programs of cow town businessmen. These historians do not offer explanations for their surprising findings, and their inability to explain the social order that was actually the norm in the West is typical of much of the historical literature. McGrath concludes that

> the frontier-was-not-especially-violent authors, while contending that there was relatively little violence on the frontier, nevertheless indicate that the unique frontier conditions which the frontier-was-violent authors enumerate were present, and they believe that those conditions *should* have caused violence. That those conditions did not do so suggests that they might have actually promoted peacefulness—though none of the frontier-was-not-so-violent authors proposes such a connection. (1984: 270–71)

But this is not quite accurate. As economic historians Anderson and Hill explain:

> The West during this time often is perceived as a place of great chaos, with little respect for property or life. Our research indicates that this was not the case; property rights were protected and civil order prevailed. Private agencies provided the necessary basis for an orderly society in which property was protected and conflicts were resolved. These agencies often did not qualify as governments because they did not have a legal monopoly on "keeping order." They soon discovered that "warfare" was a costly way of resolving disputes and lower cost

methods of settlement (arbitration, courts, etc.) resulted. In summary, . . . a characterization of the American West as chaotic would appear to be incorrect. (1979: 9)

In other words, the American West of the nineteenth century was not lawless; it was just "stateless." Much of the real violence in the West arose with the arrival of the state: the violence perpetrated on American Indians by the U.S. army, some of which spilled over onto civilians (Anderson and McChesney 1994). Anderson and Hill (1979), Umbeck (1981a, 1981b), Reid (1980), Benson (1991b), Morriss (1997), and others illustrate the role of private arrangements in making and enforcing law in the American West by examining the historical literature on and the records of the legal systems established by organizations such as land claim clubs, cattlemen's associations, wagon trains, and mining camps. Let us briefly consider a sampling of these private agency legal systems in the American West.

Land Clubs

Private citizens began moving into the western lands that were supposedly owned by the United States government long before this "public domain" was surveyed or available for sale. These squatters had no claim to the land under federal law. Thus, disputes over the possession and use of the land or its products could not be settled under state law even if courts had been available. "The result was the formation of 'extra-legal' organizations for protection and justice. These land clubs or claim associations . . . were found throughout the Middle West" (Anderson and Hill 1979: 15).

The land clubs and claim associations each adopted their own written contract setting out the laws that provided the means for defining and protecting property rights in land. They established procedures for registration of land claims, as well as for protection of those claims against outsiders, and for adjudication of internal disputes that arose. The reciprocal arrangements for protection would be maintained only if a member complied with the association's rules and its court's rulings. Anyone who refused would be ostracized. Boycott by a land club meant that an individual had no protection from aggression other than what he could provide himself.

Wagon Trains

After gold was discovered in California in 1848, large numbers of people began moving across the continent in wagon trains. Members of these trains "created their own law making and law-enforcing machinery before they started" (Billington 1956: 99). In many cases the members of a wagon train agreed to adopt a formal contract laying out a basic set of rules that would govern them during the journey. These laws varied from train to train, but there were several general tendencies. Most trains waited until they were out of the jurisdiction of state law, for example, and then selected officers with responsibility for enforcing their own rules. The previously agreed to contracts generally included voting eligibility and decision rules. They also typically provided for means of amending the contract and for the banishment of law breakers from the train. More specific rules often included the procedure for organizing jury trials; laws regarding gambling, intoxication, and Sabbath-breaking; and penalties for failure to perform certain tasks such as guard duty. But most important, the negotiated contracts "included a very well accepted set of private rights especially with regard to property" (Anderson and Hill 1979: 22). Respect for rules of private property was paramount, as Reid (1980) demonstrates in considerable detail.

If one train's contract did not suit a traveler, he or she was free to join another, and often many trains were available to choose from at embarkation points. Furthermore, if a group on a train found after departing that the majority's interpretation of the contract was different than they had expected, then train members could opt out of a contract and form a new arrangement with others who were similarly dissatisfied. This possibility was recognized in most contracts by formal procedures for the dissolution of jointly held property in the event of a breakup (Anderson and Hill 1979: 19).

There were few instances of violence on the wagon trains even when food became extremely scarce and starvation threatened. When crimes against persons or their property were committed, the judicial system as detailed in a train's contract would take effect. The actual adjudication processes varied, but most wagon trains specified some type of arbitration proceeding. The offender did not necessarily have to be threatened with violence from the members of the train itself because ostracism in the form of banishment from the group would often be sufficient.

Mining Camps

Hundreds of thousands of people seeking gold arrived in California within a very short period of time. Umbeck (1981a: 67) explains that "[a]t the territorial and federal level there were no legal institutions restraining the behavior of miners. . . . [E]ven if there had been such institutions, they could not have been enforced. By the end of 1848, or the beginning of 1849, the miners began forming contracts with one another to restrain their own behavior."[5] California did have some representation of federal authority in the form of military posts, but their primary function was apparently to take care of Indian troubles; they did not exercise any authority over the mining camps. Furthermore, if they had, they clearly would have been enforcing a very different set of laws from those that governed the mining camps. In fact, it is questionable whether any state or federal government law existed that could have applied to the camps, since, as Umbeck explains, "from 1848 to 1850 California was without any mining law, Mexican or American. From 1850 to 1866 the only federal law made all miners trespassers on California's public mineral lands" (1981a: 70).

California state law defining rights to mineral lands could not be applied after 1850 because all the land in question belonged to the federal government. The state did pass a law in 1851 regarding mining disputes (sec. 621 of the Civil Practices Act, quoted by Umbeck), but it declared that evidence in a mining case before the state courts would include "the customs, usages, or regulations established or in force at the bar or diggings embracing such claims, and such customs, usages and regulations, when not in conflict with the Constitution and laws of this state, shall govern the decision of the action" (1981a: 71). Thus, the state approved and agreed to enforce the miners' voluntary agreements. It may appear that this statute put the state government's power behind the private laws of the mining camps, but the fact is that the camps also enforced their own laws. Prior to 1852 the state government did not even attempt to enforce laws against murder and robbery, let alone private laws regarding illegal—from the perspective of federal law—mining claims.

The earliest contractual arrangements that developed (primarily before 1850) involved small groups of miners. The only contractually controlled activities related to gold mining, and the agreement typically involved equal shares of all gold found. Generally, agreements among larger groups were not needed since gold deposits were very widespread and relatively few miners were in the area. This was not to last. The Harbor Master's Office in San Francisco reported the arrival of almost 40,000 people from throughout the world in 1849; the population of California was estimated at 107,000 by the end of 1849 and reached 264,000 by the end of 1852 (Umbeck 1981a: 89).

As the size of the mining population grew and the mineral lands became relatively more scarce, contractual arrangements began to change. One of the most striking features of miners' law was its flexibility in adapting to new situations (Morris 1997: 28–33). Rather than sharing the gold from a joint production effort, for instance, each individual was given the exclusive rights to a specific piece of land, and "[o]wnership of the gold went with the land" (Umbeck 1981a: 90). Those property rights were assigned and enforced by the miners themselves. The first step in the process of contractual law and order was a "miners' meeting" for the purpose of setting up a "mining district." Such meetings were apparently organized when the need arose—that is, when minable land became scarce enough to create the potential for disputes and violent confrontations. The laws set by miners' meetings were always chosen by majority rule, but individuals who did not agree with the majority were not forced to accept its rules. They were free to move to a new location or to otherwise opt out of the contract for reciprocal protection of rights (Morriss 1997: 29). If a minority disagreed with a majority, they could set up their own separate mining district. Thus, those governed by a particular set of laws actually *unanimously* consented to be so governed (Anderson and Hill 1979: 19).

One result of these initial meetings was specification of the geographic boundary of the mining district (the area over which the laws of the group would apply) and the size of the piece of land each miner could claim within that area. Claims were allocated on a first-come-first-served basis. In order to retain rights to a claim, a miner was required to work it a specified number of days out of each week. Then, as long as a miner complied with these rules, the entire community of miners were obliged to defend his rights under the privately contracted set of laws of the district. "If the miner failed to comply with the terms of the contract, his claim was considered by others to be nonexclusive and open to any jumpers" (Umbeck 1981a: 93). Thus, the reciprocal arrangements for protection were backed by ostracism.

Umbeck (1981a: 114) points out that some mining camps hired an enforcement specialist, although most enforced their laws through group action. Some camps also appointed or elected an *alcalde,* or justice of the peace, to act as an arbitrator in mining disputes. In such cases, if decisions were acceptable to the majority of miners, the arbitrator was backed by the community at large. When the majority disagreed, a new *alcalde* was appointed. Most districts did not elect any arbitrator, however. More typically, when a dispute arose, each party appointed a representative and these two picked a third. Then the three would arbitrate the dispute. Again, the decision was backed by ostracism if it was acceptable to the other miners in the district. Yet another alternative for dispute resolution was a "miners' court." By this method, a subset of the miners in the district would be summoned when a dispute arose. A presiding officer or judge was then elected and a jury was selected. The rulings of the arbitrators or the miners' court were rarely disputed, but if one was, a mass meeting of the camp could be called to allow a dissatisfied party to plead his case and possibly get the decision reversed (Anderson and Hill 1979: 20).

Rights to mineral lands were not the only laws in the mining camps. Canlis, in his examination of the evolution of law enforcement in California, finds that miners possessed a strong desire for organization and law (1961: 2). Consequently, they established and enforced a full range of private property law. As Morriss explains, in light of the rapidly evolving technology in mining and the entry of new miners, as well as the nature of the California environment, "the miners needed a legal system which could deter theft and murder, establish and protect property rights in mining claims, and adapt to rapidly changing conditions" (1997: 28). Reid notes, "Apparently one need only state the proposition that America's mining frontier was lawless to prove the fact. . . . [but] Contemporaries who experienced that 'rampant' lawlessness in California would have been amazed by the descriptions written during the twentieth century about their society. They thought it was more law abiding than lawless" (1980: 3–4). The fact is that there were very few robberies, thefts, or murders (Reid 1980: 5; Canlis 1961; Morriss 1997: 34–35) despite the absence of locks and guards and the widespread practice of property owners' leaving their valuables (including gold) unattended for long periods. Property rights apparently were very secure (Canlis 1961).[6] Violent crimes occasionally occurred; but if sufficient illegal activity arose, miners would arm themselves (the fact that miners were generally armed provided a powerful deterrent [Umbeck 1981a: 110; Morriss 1997: 34]) for protection and/or for vigilante groups to reestablish order. Even so, the resulting violence was minimal. Criminal law in the miner's camps was quite effective; murders and thefts were actually very rare. The contractual system of law effectively generated cooperation rather than conflict, and on those occasions when conflict arose it was, by and large, effectively quelled through nonviolent means.

Miners' law was displaced by the government's legal apparatus everywhere that it existed. In some areas it lasted for many years, though, and the fact that it did not last even longer everywhere does not imply that it failed to meet the needs of the miners. As Morriss (1997: 51–54) explains, the reasons for the imposition of law by federal, state, and/or local government reflected very different incentives. For one thing, the tremendous wealth being produced in the mining territories was seen by both federal and state authorities as a significant opportunity to increase revenues, and revenue collection requires a source of coercive law enforcement for success. In addition, many individuals recognized that they could extract advantages, including wealth from such revenues, through the political process if they could establish local governments. In essence, a class of political "entrepreneurs saw opportunity in prospecting in government" (52). Morriss also points out that many who saw the potential for opportunistic behavior in the mining areas, whether by prospecting through government or through other dishonest swindles, robbery, and so on, recognized that they "required a corruptible judicial forum" to protect them, and they recognized that miners' courts were difficult to corrupt. These various interests combined to stimulate the development of government institutions as replacements for miners' law, particularly where mining evolved from the highly mobile placer process into the more and more capital-intensive process of underground mining. Not surprisingly, the resulting governments were often not very effective sources of law and order, at least in the eyes of most citizens. In many cases miners' courts continued to function even when state or local courts were in place in the community (55). Perhaps more significantly, in several instances the resulting law enforcement was so ineffective or so corrupt that private citizens had to reestablish law and order through vigilante organizations.

Vigilante Justice in Response to the Failure of the Public Sector's Law Enforcement

The two cases of vigilante action that are perhaps the best known both occurred in San Francisco.[7] By the late 1840s in San Francisco, anyone accused of a crime who could be caught was supposedly arrested by the publicly employed sheriff and tried in the next Court of Sessions, which met every two months at the county seat. But with the swelling of San Francisco's population during the early period of the gold rush, this public law enforcement apparatus simply could not handle the rising tide of crime. Even those criminals who were caught frequently escaped or were released before a trial could be arranged. The city's press was urging drastic action by early 1849, but the citizens of San Francisco held back until February of 1851.

On February 19, 1851, the owner of a San Francisco clothing store was robbed and beaten. The sheriff arrested two men and charged them. A large number of people gathered the next day before the city offices, demanding quick action against the accused. A committee of fourteen prominent citizens was chosen to take charge of the case. The government authorities were invited to participate but declined, although they raised no resistance and handed over the prisoners. The gathering adjourned as the committee impaneled a jury and appointed three judges and a clerk. Two "highly regarded" lawyers were appointed to represent the prisoners. After the jury heard the case, nine voted guilty and three voted for acquittal. Some in the crowd that had gathered to hear the decision demanded that the accused be hung anyway, but the committee refused. The prisoners were turned back over to the authorities. But the impetus for a vigilante organization was now in place.

Some three thousand citizens gathered in early June during the trial of a suspected arsonist, and over the next few days separate small groups of businessmen spontaneously began meeting and discussing the possibility of forming a "committee of vigilance." These groups did not merge for several days, however. Finally, a "selected group of responsible citizens" was called together and a committee was formed, on June 10, 1851. The June 13 *San Francisco Alta* printed a statement from the committee:

> Whereas, It has become apparent to the citizens of San Francisco that there is no security to life and property, either under the regulations of society as it at present exists, or under the laws as now administered, therefore, the citizens whose names are hereunto attached, do unite themselves into an association, for the maintenance of the peace and good order of society and the preservation of the lives and property of the citizens of San Francisco, and do bind themselves each unto the others, to do and perform every lawful act for the maintenance of law and order, and to sustain the laws when faithfully and properly administered. But we are determined that no thief, burglar, incendiary or assassin shall escape punishment either by the quibbles of the law, the insecurity of prisons, or laxity of those who PRETEND to administer justice. (Quoted in Valentine 1956: 28)

This statement was followed by the committee's regulations and a list of its members.

The committee took its first action even before the statement in the newspaper appeared. On the night after they organized, John Jenkins was caught stealing a safe from an office. Two of the vigilantes assisted in the capture and took the prisoner to their headquarters rather than the sheriff's office. A trial was immediately organized, and since Jenkins had been caught in the act, he was easily convicted. The verdict was to hang Jenkins immediately (the statutory penalty under California law for grand larceny at that time was death, so the committee's punishment was consistent with the state's law).

One of the biggest sources of criminals moving into California was the British penal colonies in Australia. The vigilantes began boarding every ship entering the port from Australia to examine the papers of all who wished to disembark. If someone did not have a permit to land issued by the U.S. Counsel in Sydney, he was not allowed to enter San Francisco. The committee paid the cost of having several people sent back to Australia; others were allowed to go on to other ports. The committee also invoked an old Mexican "ostracism" law that forbade admission to the territory of anyone previously convicted of a crime in some other country. Thus, many residents of San Francisco were examined by the committee (each could offer evidence on his own behalf) and expelled from the city. Many others simply left to avoid the process.

The committee offered a five-thousand-dollar reward for the capture of anyone found guilty of arson, and committee members patrolled the streets at night to watch for fires. After these actions were taken, fires in San Francisco diminished noticeably.

"There was no question that the Vigilantes had become the most powerful force in the city and had the support of most of the citizens" (Valentine 1956: 74). The only opposition was apparently from those who saw their political power in the city slipping away. California's governor, yielding to pressure from local politicians, issued a proclamation on August 20, calling on all citizens "to unite to sustain public order and tranquillity, to aid the public officers in the discharge of their duty, and by all lawful means to discountenance any and every attempt to substitute the despotic control of any self-constituted association, unknown and acting in defiance of the laws, in the place of the regularly organized government of the country" (quoted in Valentine 1956: 75). Then on August 21, as the vigilance committee was preparing to hang two previously tried and convicted criminals, the sheriff and a small group of police arrived at committee headquarters with a warrant of habeas corpus procured at the request of the governor. There was a sufficient number of vigilantes to resist, but the prisoners were turned over to the sheriff's authority. No action was taken against the criminals by the public authorities, however, so two days later an organized group of thirty-six vigilantes went to the jail and removed the two prisoners. The two men were hanged seventeen minutes later. The governor was not heard from on the vigilante issue again.

This double hanging was the last major act of the committee. The committee officially made ninety-one arrests during its hundred days of action. In addition to the four who were hanged, one was whipped (a punishment not at all uncommon at that time), fourteen were deported to Australia, and fourteen were informally ordered to leave California. Fifteen were handed over to public authorities, and *forty-one were discharged* (two others for whom no decision is recorded were apparently discharged). "The record is eloquent in itself. It speaks of moderation and of the attempt to render justice" (Stewart 1964: 319). But this moderation was evidently more effective than the public law enforcement system had been. Crime declined so rapidly that for a short period, San Francisco was a city of considerable order and safety (Valentine 1956: 78).

The committee announced that it was suspending action as of September 16, 1851. An executive committee was appointed to act as a "watchdog of public order," but it took only two actions, both in support of city officials. Although the vigilante movement subsided almost as fast as it had begun, the precedent had been set. One remnant of that period remains to this day, suggesting that the citizens of San Francisco were not willing to put full reliance in the public sector: privately provided security from the Patrol Specials discussed in chapters 5 and 7 was started in 1851.

The deterrent impact of the 1851 actions by the vigilantes was very short-lived, so in this sense one might contend that the movement failed, although its immediate impact on crime and social order was clearly quite dramatic. Of the spring of 1855, Valentine writes, "[T]he criminals were making out better than the honest men in the political atmosphere of San Francisco. A machine modeled on Tammany Hall controlled the city government and was also at war with another machine . . . for control of state officers and federal patronage" (1956: 87). On April 22, 1855, the *San Francisco Herald* called for "a return of the good and vigorous days of the vigilance committee" (quoted in Gard 1949: 161).

Between November 1855 and May 1856, more than one hundred murders were committed in San Francisco (Gard 1949: 165). One occurred on November 17, 1855, when a machine politician, Charles Cora, shot and killed William Richardson, the U.S. Marshall. Richardson was unarmed. Cora was arrested, but he was not very concerned. The sheriff was one of his "cronies," and several of the best lawyers in the city were retained to defend him. The trial was held on January 3, 1856, but "[t]he jury was fixed, the witnesses were rehearsed in perjury, and the proceedings were a farce. On the seventeenth the jury reported disagreement, as planned by Cora, and was discharged" (162).

On May 14, 1856, James King of William, publisher of the *Bulletin*, noted that James Casey, a city supervisor, had been a convict in Sing Sing. That evening as King was walking home, Casey shot him, and that night the committee on vigilance was revived as some ten thousand citizens gathered in the streets demanding action. Within two days, fifty-five hundred members were officially enrolled in the committee, and many more contributed funds (Gard 1949: 163). Casey had been arrested and was being held by the sheriff in the city jail. On May 18 some five hundred vigilantes approached the jail and threatened to destroy it with cannon fire if both Casey and Cora were not turned over to the committee.

Cora went on trial for the murder of Richardson on May 20 before the vigilante court. James King of William died that afternoon, and Casey also went on trial. On May 22 both politicians were found guilty of murder and sentenced to hang. But "[t]his was no judicial farce or lynching mob" (Valentine 1956: 131). The defendants chose their own counsel, and the jury, after hearing evidence from both sides, reached a unanimous verdict. The two men were hung within a few hours of King's funeral.

The committee remained active for another three months, as its membership grew to eight thousand (in those three months there were two murders in San Francisco as compared to the more than one hundred that took place during the previous six months). During June and July the committee put many of the city's undesirables on outbound ships. On July 29 two more murderers were hanged. But the 1856 vigilance committee faced a much more difficult task than simply crime control: political corruption was rampant and "[t]he committee had to deal with men like Sheriff Scannell, a former Hound; Ned McCowan, a judge; Billy Mulligan, a sheriff's deputy; Rube Maloney, a governor's handyman; and D. S. Terry, a Supreme Court Justice" (Valentine 1956: 171). The committee, after dealing extensively in the political arena, relinquished the power they had wrestled from the corrupt politicians. On August 18, 1856, the committee on vigilance disbanded.

Similar stories, generally on a smaller scale, can be told about numerous other communities in the American West. For example, Henry Plummer was the sheriff of Bannock, Montana, in 1863. He was also the organizer of "an intricate network of bandits, agents, and hideouts in southwestern Montana" (Gard 1949: 171). He led about one hundred "road agents"; his deputies were horse thieves, stagecoach robbers, and murderers. Plummer himself participated in numerous robberies and was responsible for several deaths. Records suggest that the sheriff's road agents killed at least 102 men (Morriss 1997: 81). When the citizens finally organized their vigilante justice, they hanged Plummer and twenty one of his gang in six weeks, banished several others from the area, and frightened most of the rest off. The Montana vigilante courts were like their San Francisco counterparts in that "[t]hey had good leadership and seldom acted except in extreme cases. Usually they gave the defendant an opportunity to clear himself if he could. . . . [T]he [Montana] vigilance committees were called into existence by frontier necessity. When the need for them passed, they quietly and quickly faded away" (Gard 1949: 188).[8]

Generally vigilante movements involved efforts to enforce law and *reestablish order* by law-abiding citizens who intended to live and interact in the community for many more years. Nevertheless, many historians cite vigilantism as an example of lawlessness in the West. McGrath discusses vigilantism in his section "The Frontier Was Violent" (1984: 265–66), despite the fact that after his extensive examination of the vigilante activities in the mining camps of Aurora and Bodie, California, he concludes that "[i]n each case they were supported by a great majority of the townspeople, including the leading citizens; they were well regulated; they dealt quickly and effectively with criminal problems; they left the town in more stable and orderly conditions; and when opposition developed they disbanded. . . . The vigilance committees were organized, not because there were no established institutions of law enforcement and justice, but because those institutions had failed, in the eyes of the vigilantes, to provide justice" (255–56). Similarly, Canlis, though agreeing that the San Francisco committees were well organized and orderly and that they got rid of "some disreputable and despicable characters," concludes that "there can never be any justification for their [the vigilantes'] overall acts in a society as well organized as San Francisco was at this time." He finds it "strange indeed that the constitutional government of the time did not put down by force . . . this group which had taken the law into its own hands" (1961: 13). But who was really outside the law in this case? The government's officials either failed to enforce the law as perceived by the general citizenry, as in 1851; or as in 1856, those officials were themselves in violation of the law. The vigilante organizations formed to reestablish law and order, not to defy it.

The view that a vigilante movement under any and all circumstances is an example of lawlessness reflects one of the most serious flaws in belief that law is only what public courts, legislatures, or others backed by state authority say it is. Under such a view of law, "there is no recognition that . . . a single source of legal power . . . may be so ineptly or corruptly exercised that an effective legal system is not achieved" (Fuller 1964: 157). But the power of a legal authority is not absolute, even when it is in the hands of the state. As Hayek observes, "the allegiance on which this sovereignty rests depends on the sovereign's satisfying certain expectations concerning the general character of those rules, and will vanish when this expectation is disappointed" (1973: 92). This fact, that government law is not paramount, but rather that there is some implicit constraint on power or authority (an overriding social contract), is probably not widely perceived today. Yet it is a firmly established force in American history. Revolutionaries chose to break from England and its law to establish their own legal system, and similar "vigilantism" on a smaller scale has been a common and frequent occurrence since. Importantly, however, this generally does not result in lawlessness. Law still prevails as private law enforcement arrangements arise to supplant inept, inefficient, or corrupt public institutions.

Conclusions Regarding the History of Private Justice
in the United States

This discussion really tells only a small part of the story of the role that private justice has played in the settlement of the American West. Its primary purpose is simply to illustrate that the private sector has had a *very* significant historical role in the production of law and order in America. When state-backed law was unavailable or undesirable to a particular group, private options filled the void.

I do not intend to suggest that all so-called vigilante movements and other private-sector uses of force were desirable. There may well have been some that gained something close to monopoly control over a community and essentially used their power to establish a new and even less just "government." If a private organization uses coercion and violence to gain virtual control over an area, as the Mafia has in Sicily, for instance, the institutional arrangements of such organizations take on the same characteristics that government legal institutions exhibit (Benson 1994c). Some movements that might be called vigilantes probably also directed their actions against people who were not criminals (e.g., attacks on former slaves in the South), just as governments all over the world have done, although obviously on a much smaller scale than that of governments. Governments have been and continue to be the most effective and active organizations for mass murder that have ever been created.

During this century alone fifteen government murderers are responsible for killing an estimated 151 million people *aside from those they have killed during warfare* (Rummel 1994), and many others clearly have killed or arranged the killing of many more innocent victims than any private organization that ever existed, including organized crime. Of course, not all governments are so murderous, as Rummel (1994) explains. Democracies, and particularly democracies that are constrained by constitutions or institutions that are intended to protect individual liberty, are much less likely to murder innocent victims than totalitarian regimes. The obvious implication is that not all governments are equal, as many people who support government initiatives readily point out. But the same is true of private institutions. The fact that the Mafia acts as an "enforcer" or a "protection racket" and can produce tremendous injustice does not mean that all nonstate institutions that enforce rules or protect people and property are going to produce injustice. The outcome depends on the incentives and constraints facing those who are involved. Blanket condemnation of private justice based on selected and limited observation, are clearly no more warranted than blanket condemnation of governments based on observations of what has happened this century in places like the Soviet Union under Stalin, China under Mao, Germany under Hitler, and the other twelve megamurdering states. On the other hand, neither is a blanket claim that government is the appropriate holder of a monopoly over police powers and the right to punish warranted by examining a selected sample of late-twentieth-century democracies. Public institutions of law enforcement were not always well received in these democracies either, and for good reason, as suggested in chapter 9. Furthermore, a realistic assessment of the performance of these so-called democratic legal institutions suggests that they leave a lot to be desired, even today. That appears to be the assessment made by many Americans, at any rate, because the historical examples of private justice discussed above are actually historical analogies for what is happening today.

The fact is that even after public institutions for law enforcement are in place, and even if the government is supposedly democratic, a sufficient breakdown in the public provision of law and order "must—if we are to judge the matter with any rationality at all—release men from those duties that had as their only reason for being, maintaining a pattern of social interaction that has now been destroyed" (Fuller 1964: 22). Such a breakdown in the government's legal system did occur in San Francisco and most other places where vigilante action was taken in the American West (Gard 1949; Valentine 1956; Stewart 1964; McGrath 1984; Benson 1990: 315–21; 1991b; Morriss 1997), and significantly, such a breakdown is increasingly apparent today as well, both in civil and in criminal law. The response is also similar: private alternatives are arising to establish justice and social order. To illustrate how the private sector is responding to government failure in the legal system, first consider the shift of dispute resolution into private forums.

Modern Private Courts for Civil Justice, and Some Implications for Criminal Justice

It is estimated that during the 1950s at least 75 percent of all disputes between businesses in the United States that could not be resolved through negotiation or mediation were settled through private arbitration rather than public-court litigation (Auerbach 1983: 113). The use of commercial arbitration has continued to expand at a rapid pace since then (Benson 1995a, 1997a, 1998a). Indeed, private arbitration in America has a history that is at least as long as that of vigilantism. Merchants established their own arbitration arrangements in the American colonies, and those arrangements grew in importance as the economy evolved. Government courts of the period simply did not apply commercial law in what the merchant community considered to be a just and expeditious fashion: "Not only did courts, according to one New York merchant, dispense 'expensive endless law'; they were slow to develop legal doctrine that facilitated commercial development" (Auerbach 1983: 33). The use of commercial arbitration continued to expand throughout the eighteenth and nineteenth centuries as virtually every new trade association and commercial organization formalized its own arbitration arrangements (Jones 1956; Benson 1995a). In this century commercial arbitration has made "the courts secondary recourse in many areas and completely superfluous in others" (Wooldridge 1970: 101).[9]

Arbitration is also increasingly important for disputes between businessmen and employees and between businessmen and customers. The American Arbitration Association (AAA), which may handle about a fourth of the business arbitration in the country (trade associations handle the vast majority of such disputes), had a list of approximately three thousand labor arbitrators in 1981 and administered some seventeen thousand labor cases a year (Denenberg and Denenberg 1981: 10). Similarly, the Federal Mediation and Conciliation Service had a roster of about fourteen hundred arbitrators for labor disputes and reported that around fourteen thousand arbitration appointments were made. Labor arbitration has a long and well-documented history, but consumer arbitration may be less well-known despite a considerable history of its own. For instance, the New York Stock Exchange formally provided for arbitration in its 1817 constitution, and it "has been working successfully ever since," primarily to rectify disputes between New York Stock Exchange members and their customers (Lazarus et al. 1965: 27). Today arbitration between businesses and consumers is increasingly widespread. The Council of Better Business Bureaus (BBB) operates arbitration programs for consumers in many parts of the country, and they encourage businesses to precommit to arbitration of customer complaints (Denenberg and Denenberg 1981: 6). Several automobile manufacturers have contracts with the BBB to arbitrate car owners' complaints. In addition, the AAA arbitrates over 15,000 auto insurance cases per year (8). Insurance companies were reportedly arbitrating over 50,000 claims per year by 1970 (Wooldridge 1970: 101). The National Association of Home Builders has a home owners warranty program that offers arbitration of buyers' complaints against the association's builders. The warranty had been applied to roughly 950,000 homes by 1981, and the AAA resolved 1,800 cases in 1980 (Denenberg and Denenberg 1981: 5). Medical malpractice arbitration, begun in 1929, is on the rise as malpractice litigation has become more costly and widespread. For example, subscribers to the Kaiser Foundation of health plans of California, the nation's largest prepaid medical care system, agree to arbitrate any claims when they sign up. The hospital and medical associations in California sponsor a two-hundred-hospital arbitration system, and the AAA also offers medical malpractice arbitration (10).

Rent-a-Judge Justice

In 1976 two California lawyers discovered an 1872 statute that says individuals in a dispute have the right to a full court hearing before any referee they choose (Poole 1980: 2; Granelli 1981: 1; Pruitt 1982). At that time California had a seventy-thousand-case public court backlog, with a median pretrial delay of fifty and one-half months (Poole 1980: 2). The two lawyers, who wanted a complex case settled quickly, found a retired judge with expertise in the area of the dispute, paid him at attorney's fee rates, and saved their clients a tremendous amount of time and expense (Granelli 1981: 1–2). There is no count of the number of rent-a-judge cases tried since 1976, but the civil court coordinator of the Los Angeles County Superior Court estimates that several hundred disputes in the county were settled through this process during the next five years. Most of the cases involve complex business disputes that litigants "feel the public courts cannot quickly and adequately" try (Pruitt 1982: 51).

Entrepreneurs quickly recognized an opportunity, and they began developing for-profit private-court firms in the late 1970s and early 1980s. These firms now seek out business rather than waiting for lawyers to approach them; they advertise in business magazines and other outlets that they offer quick, low-cost, and just dispute resolution services in virtually every state. Judicial Arbitration and Mediation Services Company (JAMS), started in 1979 by a California state trial judge (Phalon 1992: 127), is one of those aggressive businesses. It has grown to be the largest firm in the industry. Civicourt in Phoenix and Judicate in Philadelphia have offered quick and inexpensive dispute resolution since 1983 (Koenig 1984; Meyer 1987; Hannon 1986). Judicate went public in 1985 with sales of stocks. As of March 1987, Judicate employed 308 judges in forty-five states and has been called the "national private court," although it is actually only the third largest of the private court firms (Phalon 1992: 127).[10] The Washington Arbitration Services, established in 1981, has four franchised offices around the state. Judicial Mediation of Santa Ana, California, and Resolution of Connecticut are more recent entrants into the private court market. One of the earliest for-profit dispute resolution firms was

EnDispute, which opened in Washington, D.C., and Los Angeles in 1982 and offers minitrials. The firm has become the second largest in the industry, adding offices in Chicago; Cambridge, Massachusetts; and Santa Ana, California; and it is continuing to expand into other large markets. Minitrials are now considered an attractive option for companies involved in what are expected to be large, time-consuming, expensive litigations.

The two largest firms in this market, JAMS and EnDispute, recently attracted large investments by venture capitalists ($17 million was paid for a 60 percent share of JAMS and $3 million was invested in EnDispute), not as start-up money, but as "late-stage expansion investments that have enabled JAMS and EnDispute to push their hearing rooms into big-city markets (New York, for one) that should add significantly to revenues." The two companies enjoyed gross revenue growth of 130 percent (EnDispute) and 826 percent (JAMS) between 1988 and 1992 in reflection of the "demand for relief from the jammed dockets and killer jury awards of the courts" (Phalon 1992: 126). This has occurred in the face of rapid entry into the industry and increasing competition. It was estimated that there were more than fifty private for-profit dispute resolution firms operating in the United States in 1992 (Ray 1992: 191). These private courts have moved from business disputes into personal injury disputes, divorces, construction warranty disputes, disputes over loan defaults, and so on. They offer a number of options, including binding arbitration, mediation, minitrials, and various "hybrid mediation arbitrations" that can be held in a courtroom atmosphere or not, depending on what the disputants want: "Flexibility is the operative word" (Phalon 1992: 126; also see Ray 1992).

Alternative Dispute Resolution and Criminal Justice

Why discuss this use of private courts for civil disputes in the context of an exploration of privatization in criminal law? In part because they are a response to government failure in the provision of legal services and add further evidence that the private sector can offer viable alternatives. More important in this context, however, is that, as Denenberg and Denenberg point out, private "[d]ispute resolution is a method whose potential applications are limited only by the ingenuity of the potential users. It satisfies a widely felt need for flexible, accessible justice" (1981: 26). For instance, since the 1960s arbitration or mediation has been used in a growing number of programs to resolve "conflicts that courts may find too trivial or too elusive: domestic quarrels, squabbles between neighbors and similar animosities among ethnic groups" (15). Beginning with the largest cities (Los Angeles; Philadelphia; Kansas City; Atlanta; San Francisco; Miami; Boston; Garden City, New York; and Cleveland), such "community mediation centers" or "community dispute resolution programs" are spreading all over the country. They seek compromise solutions to disputes by using neighborhood volunteers to serve as mediators. These programs have gone beyond domestic and neighborhood disputes, however, to consider criminal incidents. In one example, a Los Angeles grocer filed a complaint against a black youth who robbed his store. The store owner did not want to involve the police because he wanted to avoid alienating his black customers (18).

One of the earliest community dispute resolution projects was run by the AAA in Philadelphia; it began hearing minor criminal cases in 1969. The success of this private alternative provided much of the impetus for the movement of minor criminal cases into neighborhood justice centers. During the 1970s and early 1980s, the AAA became increasingly involved in minor criminal and civil disputes, such as neighborhood fights and juvenile offenses (Poole 1978: 55) through its Community Disputes Division. Similar arrangements with local courts also exist, such as the Columbus, Ohio, arrangement with Capital University discussed in chapter 2. Some of these alternative courts might more accurately be described as contracting-out arrangements than fully privatized courts.[11]

An even newer but related institution is specifically focused on resolution of crimes. Victim-offender mediation (VOM) is spreading rapidly throughout the United States, Canada, and Europe, with about 150 programs in the United States in 1995 (Umbreit and Stacey 1996: 30). These programs offer mediation between victims and the criminal offenders, generally seeking restitution for the victims and reconciliation. Victims are able to express the full impact of the crime on their lives, to find out why the offenders targeted them, and to directly participate in determining how to hold the offender accountable. Offenders can also tell their story and explain how the crime has affected them. Most (over 90 percent in one large survey [Umbreit 1995: 272]) result in an agreement regarding compensation to the victim from the offender, and most of these agreements (over 80 percent in the same survey) are fulfilled by the offender. The VOM option is typically limited to juvenile crimes and/or nonviolent property crimes, taking referrals from courts or prosecutors. Their development might be traced to the community dispute resolution movement mentioned above, but more direct predecessors are the Victim-Offender Reconciliation Program (VORP), first introduced in the United States in 1978 through a joint effort of the Mennonite Central Committee and the PACT (Prisoner and Community Together) organization in the Elkhart, Indiana, area (Umbreit 1995: 264), and the restitution centers that have been developed by criminal justice agencies (generally probation departments).

The Elkhart VORP was modeled after the initial Canadian VORP developed in 1974, and similar programs have been developed by private organizations such as church-related groups (Mennonites appear to have the leadership role in advocating such arrangements, but other churches are also starting and supporting them) and community groups in a number of other places. Most of the church-related programs receive no funding from the government, but the disputes they resolve are generally referrals from criminal justice authorities. Community-based programs are developed for the most part by private nonprofit organizations but tend to work more directly within the criminal justice system, in part because they have more difficulty raising funds than the church-related groups. Thus, they may fit the contracting-out model more than the private justice model. The number of government-run victim-offender mediation programs is also increasing; they are being developed by probation agencies, courts, and even sheriff departments. These are obviously not private justice alternatives, but they do illustrate that alternative dispute resolution is a real possibility for at least some crimes. Umbreit contends that "victim-offender mediation is no longer simply an experiment but is now established as an important and growing subfield of alternative dispute resolution" (1995: 263).

An even more recent program of direct negotiation and mediation has been imported from Australia: Family Group Conferencing (e.g., see Umbreit and Stacey 1996; Pranis 1996). As with victim-offender mediation, a mediator facilitates direct negotiation between the victim and the offender, but in this case several more people are involved. Other people in the community that were affected by the crime (the victim's family, neighbors who feel threatened, the offender's family, the arresting officer, and perhaps others) join the victim, the offender, and the mediator and speak their piece, offering their reactions to the crime, restitution suggestions, ideas about how to implement the agreement, and perhaps their own services as a resource for the victim, the offender, or both (Umbreit and Stacey 1996: 33). The result can be an even more powerful experience for the offender and the victim than VOM is, and it can create stronger bonds within the community in an effort to reintegrate the offender and the victim into the community after the offender has admitted and felt remorse for the crime and has taken responsibility for making amends.

At this time these formally recognized private alternatives to public courts are not widely employed for crimes (see chapter 10 in this regard), and they are not options that victims can typically choose without the consent and referral of criminal justice officials. Perhaps as a result, less formal institutions actually tend to dominate private criminal justice.

Informal Justice

When the criminal justice system fails to punish criminals to the degree that victims and potential victims feel is appropriate, or if the cost of achieving publicly imposed punishment is high, individuals are motivated to employ self-help solutions to exact punishment. A victim may personally take revenge, or groups of neighbors may act together. Even when neighborhood dispute resolution arrangements are not formally developed by third parties (e.g., the AAA) and recognized by the government, they often exist. Informal private justice may be substantially less costly than formal alternatives, after all, and the benefits may be much more certain.

Private Justice in Neighborhoods

A close-knit group of neighbors may enforce criminal law, even when doing so violates another law as defined by the state. Within such groups recognized procedures often exist, as Ellickson suggests. In the groups of neighbors he observed, the offender is informed of the "informal debt" so that it can be resolved voluntarily by making a "side-payment." If this restitution debt is not paid, "truthful negative gossip" is spread about the unpaid debt, and once the members of the group have been informed of the offense and the refusal to pay the debt, some appropriate amount of the offender's assets are either seized or destroyed (1991: 213–14). In fact, gossip itself can destroy an important asset: the offender's reputation. Thus, such a group may simply ostracize an offender, refusing to interact with him in any way. As Ellickson notes, "the basic logic of the system is transparent: the remedial devices most likely to be costly in and of themselves are not made available until less costly approaches have been tried without success" (214). Of course, if the sequence and severity of remedial steps are sufficiently well established that they are well-known within a group, they should deter offenses by group members while also creating strong incentives for members to pay "informal debts" when they arise.

If the government does not recognize such "restitutive punishment" and attempts to prevent it; or if the offense is too severe to expect that an appropriate restitution can be paid; or if the offender is not a member of the group, making the reputation threat of gossip not viable; the victim will not be satisfied until the final step in the sequence outlined by Ellickson is carried out. The demand for retribution remains, and self-help may be the only option. The result need not be violent or destructive, however: it can involve the seizure of an asset, although this may not be a possibility because such a seizure might be treated as a theft by the government. Thus, self-help may take the form of destruction of an asset (vandalism) belonging to an offender, which is likely to be easier to cover up than a seizure (Ellickson 1991: 217), or even physical punishment (assault). Under such circumstances, a considerable amount of "crime" may be "undertaken to exercise social control" (213).

Self-help is not the only mechanism for retribution. Informal or formal associations may also aid the victim in the "criminal" extraction of revenge. That is, vigilante actions may result. Recognition of the fact that a group will take such actions is also a deterrent, of course. Therefore, under some circumstances at least, members of a group may want to develop a reputation of being willing to "take the law into their own hands." For example, neighborhood groups can "sanction wrongdoers" (e.g., drug addicts, pushers, drunks, prostitutes, gangs, and troublesome families) in an attempt to expel them from the community. After the murder of a seventeen-year-old youth, a community group in South Philadelphia organized a demonstration to pressure drug dealers (who apparently were not connected with the murder) to leave the neighborhood. Between five hundred and nine hundred residents marched to the residence of two dealers and shouted at them for forty-five minutes to get them to leave. The dealers did not return (Podolefsky and Dubow 1981: 64). Such activity is increasingly common (Carlson 1995b).

Because private citizens do not own public streets, they cannot evict individuals who use those streets for activities that can have significant negative impacts on private property values in the neighborhood.[12] The most obvious examples of such activities are street drug and prostitution markets. Although consumption of drugs and prostitution services need have no spillover effect on members of a community if they are carried out in privacy, when they involve street markets, spillovers do occur. Robberies increase, because both buyers and sellers of drugs and prostitution services are attractive targets (they are often carrying cash and/or drugs, and they are unlikely to report the theft), but since robbers may have imperfect information about who actually is involved in such markets, others can also be robbed. As thieves become familiar with the neighborhood, they also may pick out attractive targets for burglary. Traffic flow increases as buyers cruise the neighborhood looking for sellers, and congestion rises. Violence can increase when sellers compete for turf, and innocent bystanders can be and frequently are injured or killed. As a result of such activities, property values decline and citizens of the neighborhood face rising risks.

Organizations of private citizens can bring a great deal of pressure to bear on such activities. Consider the Fairlawn Coalition, formed in what was a disintegrating working-class neighborhood of the Anacostia section of Washington, D.C. This group was founded by Edward Johnson after he helped a neighbor repair a shattered front door following the second burglary of the house in a month. Johnson recognized that the people of the neighborhood were letting the criminals who were perpetrating such crimes "stand on the corner and no one called the police until something happened. We were just as responsible as the police for letting these kids hang around the corner" (quoted in Carlson 1995b: 64). The Fairlawn Coalition, consisting mostly of middle-aged or older church-going citizens, many of whom are women, retired, and/or grandparents, focused its initial efforts at the intersection of Seventeenth and R Streets, Southwest, where a thriving drug market existed. They could not intimidate the drug dealers and thieves who gathered on the streets by threatening force, so they adopted a much more passive approach. They wore "safety orange baseball hats" in order to distinguish themselves from the drug dealers and other criminals, marched to the intersection, and simply spent the evening standing on the corner making those who regularly used the area for drug dealing and/or spotting targets for thefts uncomfortable. The dealers made intimidating gestures and threats but soon left. The next night the Orange Hats (as they have now been dubbed) returned, and they did the same until those engaged in the street activities moved on. With this initial success, the Orange Hats began to invest in equipment to help make undesirables more uncomfortable. They bought two-way radios to communicate with one another and obtained a video camera. They started setting up the video camera across the street from any open-air drug market: "The effect was immediate. Drug dealers evaporated. Buyers avoided the corner" (Carlson 1995b: 64). One former crack dealer recalls that the video camera made him so nervous that he left the area because he did not want to be anywhere near the Orange Hats, and users have made similar statements. The group added to its repertoire, recording license plate numbers of suspicious cars and carrying regular cameras, snapping pictures of individuals suspected of wrongdoing. By and large, these are pure scare tactics. The cameras often do not even have any film, although they do have flash bulbs, and the same is true of video cameras.

Carlson suggests that the Orange Hats wield another weapon as well—shame:

The fact that the Orange Hats are middle-aged and church-going works to their advantage. To teen-age crack dealers, watching the group march up to the corner on Saturday night with bright hats and walkie-talkies is like having parents show up at a beer party in junior-high school; it spoils the mood. And in this case, the profits. The Orange Hats realize what the police often do not: Even drug dealers—especially drug dealers—have appearances to keep up. (1995b: 64)

The Orange Hats have changed the behavior of drug dealers and users in their neighborhoods. The dealers are probably still selling drugs, and the users are probably still buying drugs, but the drug market has been forced to relocate or move underground where it does less harm to those who are not part of the market. The Orange Hats maintain that if an individual wants to use drugs in his or her own home, he or she is free to do so, but they do not want the drug market in their neighborhood where it lowers property values and spills over into property crimes and violence. Residents and businesspeople in Fairlawn overwhelmingly agree that the Orange Hats have made their community safer "with moral force alone."

In many neighborhoods, driving drug markets off the streets is not enough. When markets move indoors within the neighborhood, they can still have negative consequences for other residents. Buyers and thieves may still be attracted, creating excessive traffic flow and violence. Buildings used for drug trading often are allowed to deteriorate (the "crack house" phenomenon), lowering the value of other property in the area. But tactics similar to those employed by the Orange Hats can also be directed at these indoor markets. One of the best-known examples of such activity is from the Mantua section of Philadelphia, where Herman Wrice, a former operator of a drug rehabilitation program for addicts, founded "Mantua Against Drugs. The organization had one aim—to rid Mantua of crack houses" (Carlson 1995b: 58). Wrice maintains that the way to solve the crack problem is to get neighbors involved. His organization goes only into areas where they have been invited by a group of five or six neighbors who are willing to work both with his group and with each other. Such a group must come to him first; then they are invited to a meeting of Mantua against Drugs (meetings are held once a week in the Grace Lutheran Church) where volunteers recount past successes and explain the way the group works.

The process involves a Thursday night march to a targeted crack house by members of the group wearing white hard hats for identification. They also carry bullhorns. At first, the dealers respond with jeers and threats, but soon they retreat inside their houses. The marchers do not leave, however. They wait for the buyers to arrive. When a buyer approaches, the marchers begin singing "Drugs are no good, drugs are no good," and the buyers turn away. They keep it up for several hours, singing out to the dealers that "If you keep selling crack we will be back." Then the group returns on Friday and Saturday during the day to clean up the area, mow the lawns, and pick up trash. Each night they assemble again with their hard hats and bullhorns and chants. Wrice has developed a good relationship with police, who often stop by to lend their support, despite being unable to legally act against the dealers without sufficient "probable cause."

Drug dealers find their business cut off. In addition, the process is "embarrassing"; as noted above, drug dealers want to maintain their images. Often this is enough to close the crack house, although occasionally dealers turn violent. The marchers then respond in kind. Wrice notes, "We've been in pushing matches, brick throwing. We throw bricks back if you throw at us. We're not going to stand there and take it. We didn't come here to be nice. . . . We're not brave people. We worry about it, too. But we worry more about having a crack house in our neighborhood" (quoted in Carlson 1995b: 60). When the constant pressure from the marchers proves to be insufficient, Wrice's group turns to additional sanctions. They attempt to find out if the residents have paid their electric, water, and gas bills, and if they have not, which is often the case, they pressure the utility company to cut off service, and they escort the representative who must go to the house to do so. Often, cutting off electricity and water can be enough to close a crack house; but if it is not, they report to the city's code enforcers that there is a sanitation problem with the house, and bureaucratic harassment from city inspectors starts. The inspectors ask for rent receipts; if none are produced, the dealers are assumed to be living there illegally, and an eviction notice is issued. Police get involved at that point, not because of the illegal drug activity, for which they may have insufficient evidence to act, but because of the eviction notice.

If this tactic does not work (e.g., because the dealers pay their utilities), Wrice turns to yet another. The organization attempts to track down the owner of the house. When the owner is found, Wrice tells him or her that the city can confiscate the house unless the dealers leave; this threat often induces owners to work with Wrice (often they are happy to do so anyway, because they have not been able to collect rents).[13]

Wrice's group has expanded its efforts beyond crack houses.[14] For instance, street dealers often use pay phones to receive orders, and buyers use the phones to call dealers on their pagers. Wrice has persuaded the phone company to replace touch-tone pay phones with rotary-dial phones, which are incompatible with pagers, reducing the incentive for drug dealers to hang around on the streets. He has also taken his confrontational tactics into the courts in an effort to "scare judges" into treating dealers from their neighborhood seriously. Carlson notes, "In a city where judges are elected, a few members of Mantua Against Drugs assembled in the court room can add thousands of dollars to the price of bail" (1995b: 61). And when a defense lawyer claims that the accused is really a first-time minor player, Wrice and his group dispute the statement with firsthand observations.

Wrice admits that his solutions "aren't always above board, but drug dealing isn't either," and the Department of Justice must agree. They have been sending Wrice around the country to explain his tactics to citizens and police in other communities where crack houses prove to be a problem. Similar groups have sprung up following his lectures, some with considerable success (Carlson 1995b: 61–63). Carlson concludes, quoting a lawyer from Baltimore, "who has seen some communities successfully expel drug dealers and others sink deeper into chaos, . . . it is easy to tell which neighborhood will recover. 'If there are five people who will stick together . . . it's just a matter of time before that block is clean'" (1995b: 65).

Private Justice within Business Organizations

Neighborhoods are not the only private organizations developing informal mechanisms to achieve private justice. Business firms face significant losses because of crime and a relatively unresponsive public-sector criminal justice system, so many of them have also developed their own methods of sanctioning wrongdoers.

The U.S. Department of Commerce defines "ordinary crime" against business as burglary, robbery, vandalism, shoplifting, employee theft, bad checks, arson, and credit card fraud. The costs of these crimes for businesses can be "staggering" (e.g., in 1981 U.S. supermarkets alone were estimated to have lost a billion dollars to shoplifting), and among them, "employee theft may be the most pervasive and costly." It is estimated that about one-third of the employees in any organization steal, and Fireman's Fund Insurance Company estimates that one-third of all business failures are caused by employee theft (Cunningham and Taylor 1985: 8). These are thefts that are presumably prosecutable; but in reality, police tend to give them little time or attention, and the public-sector criminal justice system in general tends to be "unsympathetic to business losses due to crime" (11–12).[15] Thus, the most frequently investigated crime by security personnel working within business organizations is employee theft, and the majority of security managers for business firms report that employee theft (and most other "ordinary crimes" against business) are resolved either through their own investigations followed by direct contact with a public prosecutor, thus bypassing public police, *or* "more often, within the organization," avoiding public prosecutors and courts as well—close to half of all employee thefts are resolved internally with private procedures and privately imposed sanctions (11). The procedures may be formal, including adjudication by internal disciplinary bodies, boards, or panels (Henry 1987: 46), or informal with confrontations and negotiation between security personnel or managers and accused offenders. The private sanctions include dismissal, suspension without pay, transfer, job reassignment or redesign to eliminate some duties, denial of subsequent advancement, and restitution agreements.

Such private justice clearly reduces the demands on the public sector's criminal justice institutions. Some observers suggest that within business organizations, "private justice may exert far greater control on citizens than the criminal justice system itself" (Cunningham and Taylor 1985: 12). The same is probably true for many neighborhoods in America's cities.

Conclusions

Civil liberty concerns about private judges mandating punishment will probably prevent the development of a large system of formal private-sector criminal courts such as that which is evolving for civil disputes. Of course, as suggested in chapter 2, even judges employed by the government are private citizens under contract to provide the service. Nonetheless, the political costs associated with any attempt to obtain a legislated sanctioning of private courts so offenders and victims can choose them over the government's courts appear to be very high at this time. Formal private courts would move into criminal justice very quickly if they were allowed to, but this is unlikely without significant changes in criminal law (see chapters 10 and 12 in this regard). In their absence, informal mechanisms for imposing private sanctions are developing, because of dissatisfaction with the public sector's criminal justice system.

Informal sanctioning actions, particularly when they involve violence or destruction, are not necessarily to be commended, but they must be noted in order to stress that private individuals, when faced with a choice between breaking a legislated law and enduring harmful personal effects of the actions by other persons, may choose to break the law. Vigilante-like self-help by individuals and groups is a natural reaction to threats that arise because the criminal justice system has been unable to provide adequate protection and/or punishment, and it has a long history in the United States. What we are seeing is a repeat of that history but in the face of a relatively strong public sector that can prevent some of the more open and formal vigilantism that characterized earlier episodes of private justice. Still, it appears that, as Shearing and Stenning argue, there is "compelling evidence . . . [that] what we are witnessing . . . is not merely a reshuffling of responsibility for policing public order but the emergence of privately defined orders, policed by privately employed agents, that are in some cases inconsistent with, or even in conflict with, the public order proclaimed by the state" (1987a: 13–14). Private justice may not be as widely practiced as the private protection activities outlined in chapter 5, but it clearly is another private initiative that is likely to have a significant impact on decisions to commit crime wherever it is effectively and persistently applied.

7

The Benefits of Privatization
Theory and Evidence

The rapid growth of private-sector efforts to prevent crimes and to resolve them once they are committed suggests that these private alternatives must be generating considerable benefits relative to the alternative of investing more in the public criminal justice system.[1] Of course, there may also be undesirable consequences of privatization, as suggested by the discussion of some of the characteristics of private justice (although they arise, in part at least, because such vigilante actions are treated as illegal, forcing those taking them to attempt to avoid detection). And markets are certainly not perfect, as advocates of public production always stress (although the alleged imperfections tend to be exaggerated—see chapter 8). But government is also far from perfect. Thus, "we are choosing between two techniques that will produce less than if we lived in a perfect world" (Tullock 1970: 127–28). In light of the fact that neither option is likely to be ideal, an important question is, How can the scarce resources used for crime control be allocated most effectively?

Answering this question requires comparing the alternatives. We should not simply look for market failures and, upon finding some, advocate the government alternative. Any observed market failure should be weighed against government failure. In doing so we shall find that there is a growing amount of empirical evidence suggesting that specialized uses of private resources in crime control are relatively efficient and in many cases considerably more effective than publicly allocated resources. Furthermore, there are strong theoretical reasons for expecting significantly superior performance by the private sector in crime control. This chapter will focus on these potential relative benefits by examining some of the reasons for and consequences of government failure in allocating scarce resources and by comparing the relatively more efficient market alternative. Chapter 8 reverses the focus by considering several of the most frequent market failure arguments against privatization in criminal justice and then asking if the public alternative actually provides an improvement over the market.

An understanding of the relative advantage of markets requires an understanding of some basic economic principles. I apologize to those readers who are already familiar with such principles; for those who are not, I only hope that the following presentation provides enough discussion to allow you to appreciate its relevance to the question at hand. The basic underlying principle of economics is scarcity. There are not enough resources (labor, land and other natural resources, capital, knowledge) to produce everything that people want. Therefore, choices must be made. Every good or service that is produced requires resources that could be used for something else. So the true (economic) cost of producing one good is the most valuable alternative that must be sacrificed. Essentially, there are always tradeoffs, and since people want scarce resources to be used to satisfy their desires rather than someone else's desires, they will compete to influence the allocation of the resources. Scarcity inevitably leads to competition, but the nature of that competition is determined by "the rules of the game." Scarce resources must be rationed among potential alternative uses, but there are many different rationing mechanisms that might be established, and the rationing process that is established (the rules of the game) determines the nature of the competition that arises. The following discussion focuses on the rationing procedures and the competitive process that arise in the public sector and in the market, and on the incentives that those rationing techniques create.

Rationing Scarce Resources through Government

Governments have the power to tax, and they can use that power of *coercion* to produce "services" whether they are actually valued relative to the costs or not. In a democracy taxpayers supposedly can "throw the rascals out" if they are forced to buy something they do not want or to pay more for something than they are willing to pay. Unfortunately, this simplistic view of democracy is far from reality. The fact is that the typical voter/taxpayer does not really know what is being purchased with tax revenues, let alone how cost-effective the production of some particular service happens to be.

Information and Monitoring of Performance

The lack of knowledge about government is not surprising. In fact, it is perfectly rational, because citizens have very weak incentives to obtain the information required to effectively evaluate government performance, even in a democracy. After all, there is no guarantee that the individual's evaluations, after taking the trouble to seek information, will matter at all. As Friedman suggests,

> Imagine buying cars the way we buy governments. Ten thousand people would get together and agree to vote, each for the car he preferred. Whichever car won each of the ten thousand would have to buy it. It would not pay any of us to make any serious effort to find out which car was best; whatever I decide, my car is being picked for me by the other members of the group. Under such institutions the quality of cars would quickly decline.
>
> That is how I must buy products on the political marketplace. I not only cannot compare alternative products, it would not be worth my while to do so even if I could. This may have something to do with the quality of the goods sold on that market. *Caveat emptor.* (1973: 180–81)

It certainly does have something to do with the quality of government output, because it affects the incentives of those who cast votes, pay taxes, and/or consume the outputs produced through government, and this in turn affects the incentives of those who produce the outputs. Furthermore, the problem goes well beyond what Friedman's example suggests.

Voters do not choose individual products like cars. They generally vote for a political candidate offering to advocate a bundle of goods and services, some of which may be desirable for a particular voter while others are not. To make a good decision (i.e., obtain enough information to actually vote for the candidate who will advocate the policy bundle closest to the voter's preferred bundle), the voter would have to determine what each candidate is actually offering (not always an easy task, given the obfuscation that politicians often practice in an effort to keep voters from finding out about the costs they are likely to bear if the candidate is elected), weigh the attractive parts of each candidate's offered bundle against the unsatisfactory parts, and then compare these weighted bundles of costs and benefits. If the voter makes the considerable investment in time and effort that this would take, there still is no guarantee that the preferred candidate will win or that if he wins he will be able to achieve the goals he promises to advocate, or that he will even advocate the promised policies.

The costs to a voter of making a bad decision (e.g., voting for a candidate who actually will not advocate the voter's preferred bundle of policies, given the candidate field available) are also very low. The chances that a particular vote will be decisive are very remote. The candidate may not win at all; and if he does win, the chance that he will be able to get the undesirable set of policies implemented is also low. Even if the candidate who wins is inept, a liar, or totally corrupt, the individual voter who supported the candidate because of an uninformed decision will bear only a small part of the costs. The costs are shared by widely dispersed taxpayers, some of whom voted for the same candidate and many of whom did not.

Given the high personal costs of gathering information about alternative candidates, the substantial uncertainty about obtaining any personal benefits from investing in information gathering, and the low personal costs that occur if information is not obtained, individuals who have the right to vote and individuals who are forced to be taxpayers have relatively weak incentives to inform themselves. Indeed, most potential voters do not even bother to vote, and virtually everyone who does is far from fully informed. It is widely argued that low voter turnout (and even the lack of knowledge that voters have about alternatives) reflects voter apathy, but this clearly is not the case. Many people are very concerned about what the government is doing for (or to) them, but they rationally choose not to invest in information about candidates or to vote because they recognize that the costs of doing so exceed the benefits.

Most citizens also have weak incentives to gather information regarding the general workings of the bureaucracies that actually carry out most of the policies for their government, although they may know a lot about some policies that have large impacts on their well-being (e.g., farmers probably know about various agricultural subsidies and other farm programs that can increase their incomes by thousands of dollars, utility company executives know a lot about the utility rate hearing process because it can increase or decrease their company's income by millions of dollars, potential criminals probably know about prison crowding and its implications for the portion of a sentence that might be served because of the impact on their expected costs). In general, however, the cost for most people of gathering information about individual government activities exceeds the likely benefits of doing so (therefore, people who buy bread do not pay attention to the wheat program because it only costs them a few dollars a year, residential consumers of electricity do not know about rate hearings because their expenditures probably only change by a few dollars a year as a consequence of the process, people who have not been and do not expect to be victimized do not pay much attention to the causes of prison crowding, etc.). This generates an environment conducive to interest group influence on government decisions, since members of focused interests invest time or money to organize and to purchase specialists (lobbyists) in order to influence and then monitor performance in government production related to the issues that have large impacts on them (additional discussion of such political competition appears below).

therefore, even imperfect private alternatives may be superior to government production. A couple of examples of factors influencing public-sector rationing of criminal justice resources should make this point even clearer.

EXAMPLE 1: PUBLIC RATIONING OF PRISON SPACE

Many punishments other than imprisonment are available to judges, and some are frequently employed, but the incentives to consider them are relatively weak because sentencing decisions are made in a political environment in which local judges and prosecutors have "free access" to state prison space (federal judges and prosecutors have similar free access to the federal prison system). Inasmuch as prosecutors and judges have incentives to demonstrate to their local constituencies that they are "tough on crime," imprisonment is a relatively attractive punishment. Even if they recognize that their actions add to the prison crowding problem, the political support they get from their "tough" image should exceed their personal costs (possibly the anxiety associated with the recognition that they are crowding prisons and raising costs to society at large). Perhaps more important, however, prosecutors and judges generally are locally elected officials with a mandate to alleviate local crime problems. Their job is not to avoid crowding state prisons, but to protect local citizens and punish criminals who attack them.

Local citizens elect judges and prosecutors who they think will be tough on crime, so prosecutors who have a "tough" image because they get a large number of prison sentences are probably doing the job their constituents elected them to do. Local citizens reasonably expect to be more effectively protected if known criminals are sent off to the state prison than if criminals are placed on locally supervised probation or in a localized intermediate-sanction program. No matter how intensive the supervision is in such localized programs, the criminals in them clearly pose a greater threat to the prosecutor's constituents than they do from a state prison. Thus, all local prosecutors and judges have incentives to choose imprisonment relatively frequently. If there is no quota system in place that forces a judge and prosecutor to limit the flow of criminals into the state prison (e.g., sentencing guidelines determined by the availability of prison capacity rather than by legislators' political goals to appear tough without paying for it [Benson and Rasmussen 1994b]), then crowding is inevitable because there is no effective coordination of the sentencing decisions of the dispersed local judges.

The local officials may well be aware that their decisions in aggregate are crowding the state system, but there is no way of comparing the threat posed by a felon from one district to the threat posed by another district's felon who might be released early (e.g., there is no price to signal the relative merits of imprisoning the two offenders). Even if there was, of course, the threat posed by a felon within a district *to the citizens of that district* is clearly greater than the threat posed by a felon released to another district. Thus, the local prosecutor and the local judge, whose primary concern is local public safety, will naturally put more weight on putting the local felon in prison than having the felon from another district in prison. The effect is that prosecutors and judges as a group crowd the common-access prisons. Inevitably, virtually every prisoner sent to the state system forces the release of someone already there who has not yet served his full sentence; almost no prisoner serves a full sentence (even those politicians advocating more severe punishment generally advocate that prisoners serve 75 or 85 percent of their sentences).

Prosecutors and judges are not the only officials whose uncoordinated decisions lead to prison crowding. Legislators can also crowd the criminal justice commons since, like judges and prosecutors, they have weak incentives to conserve scarce prison resources. When passing laws that increase the penalties, such as mandatory minimum sentences, the legislature's actions mandate more crowding of prisons. Of course, the legislature also has the power to offset the resulting overcrowding: it can increase the budgetary allocation for prisons in order to expand the number of prison beds, or it can pass sentencing guidelines that severely constrain judicial discretion. Minnesota actually established capacity-based sentencing guidelines, but the temptation to create the appearance of being tough on crime without actually paying for it ultimately prevailed, and crowding reemerged (Lawrence 1991). This is not surprising, since individual legislators also have a local constituency demanding that they do something about local crime conditions *without* raising their taxes. Thus, legislators can reap political benefits by passing longer sentences for crimes, appearing to be tough on criminals, while downplaying the fact that their actions can undermine other aspects of the criminal justice system. Since expanding criminal justice resources involves the politically unpopular task of either cutting other government functions or raising taxes, the politically astute course of action is to crowd the common-access prisons.

Even if sentencing guidelines could be created that might serve to coordinate sentencing decisions across judicial districts and influence the inflow decisions of judges and prosecutors, at least to a degree, those sentencing decisions are not coordinated with prison release decisions (parole or other early-release programs). Therefore, it may well be that the prisoner who is released poses a much more significant threat to society than the entrant who forced him out. For example, on November 28, 1988, only ten days after being released from a Florida prison, Charlie H. Street murdered two Metro-Dade police officers. Street had a rap sheet over twenty pages long and had been sentenced to a fifteen-year term for attempted murder. He served only half that sentence before he was released. Frank Stephenson explains:

> One week before Street walked out of Indiantown's Martin Correctional Institution, 14 worthless-check writers were issued their prison blues in Florida. The "paper-hangers"—cops parlance for habitual bad check writers—were finally getting what they deserved—an overdue stretch in the Big House.
> Problem was, the Big House wasn't big enough to hold the paper-hangers and Charlie, too. (1994: 9)

Regrettably, this story is far from unique. Frank Potts was released from the Florida prison system in 1988 as well, after serving six years of a fifteen-year sentence for molesting an eleven-year-old girl. He was set free despite a parole examiner's warning that Potts was not a good candidate for parole "now or in the future" and accompanying prediction that Potts would recidivate. After several years Potts was arrested in Alabama and charged with molesting another eleven-year-old girl, but in addition, an intensive investigation was instigated to determine whether Potts is guilty of at least thirteen murders in six states. A representative of the Florida Department of Corrections, recently asked why Frank Potts was released in 1988, explained that "the agency is bound by mandates from the courts and the legislature. In the mid-1980s, the prison system was inundated with inmates carrying minimum-mandatory sentences during the country's initial skirmishes in the war on drugs" (Pudlow 1993: 1).

Florida was building prisons during the 1980s and sentencing guidelines were in place, but drug criminals were flowing in faster than space was being added. During fiscal year 1983–84 there were 1,620 admissions to Florida's prisons for drug offenses, accounting for 12.9 percent of all admissions. By 1989–90 this figure had risen by 875 percent to 15,802 admissions, or 36.4 percent of the now much larger total. At the same time, the legislature passed an array of longer minimum mandatory sentences for drug criminals. Because prison resources are scarce, getting tough on drug offenders resulted in leniency for other criminals.

Florida had to implement an "administrative gain time program" in February of 1987. The consequences were dramatic. Before 1984 prisoners in Florida typically served more than 50 percent of their sentences, but by the end of 1989 the average prisoner served only 33 percent of his or her sentence; in fact, about 37 percent of the prisoners released in December 1989 had served less than 25 percent of their sentences, and some had served less than 15 percent. Those released early included violent offenders like Street and Potts who were recognized by corrections personnel as serious threats to the community.

The crowding of prisons forces corrections officials to decide what portion of each prisoner's sentence will be served and who will be released early as judges send them more prisoners. The decision may be constrained by legislative mandates regarding minimum mandatory sentences, gain time programs, good behavior, and so on, but decisions must be made. In some cases a hearing is held and individuals serve as judges of the likelihood that the criminal will commit another crime (e.g., as with a parole board); in other cases a bureaucratically determined formula reflecting time served, prisoner behavior, and other factors determines who will be released next (e.g., Florida's experiences with early release in the late 1980s occurred when the state was phasing out parole). There is no mechanism to compare the benefits of keeping the prisoner to be released with the benefits of incarcerating the new prisoner. With no coordinating system in place, bad-check writers and drug users can go into prisons and force violent offenders out the back door.

EXAMPLE 2: RATIONING OF PUBLIC POLICE RESOURCES

Prison crowding is only one of the consequences of the way the public sector allocates resources. Property crime rates in Florida were falling in the early 1980s, from 7,465.2 reported crimes per 100,000 population in 1981 to 6,892.4 in 1983. Nonetheless, in 1984 Florida law enforcement joined the war on drugs declared by the Reagan administration, allegedly because it was a way to solve Florida's crime problem: drug use was widely believed to be a primary cause of property crime because it is assumed that users must steal to support their habits. In reality, even though many property and violent criminals do consume drugs, the majority were nondrug criminals before they began consuming drugs, and most drug users are not active nondrug criminals (evidence developed in Rasmussen and Benson 1994 suggests that probably only about 25 to 35 percent of drug users are active property criminals), so drug use is not a very good indicator of nondrug forms of criminality. Property criminals who also use drugs may focus on different criminal activities than nondrug users (robbery may be more attractive than burglary, for instance, because users may want cash rather than stereos, jewelry, etc.), but the propensity to commit crimes in general does not appear to change. Nonetheless, drug arrests rose dramatically over the next five years, from a 1983 level of 358.6 per 100,000 population to 668.3 in 1989 (Rasmussen and Benson

1994: 36). What were the results of this new offensive in the war on drugs? One was the prison crowding problem discussed above, but there were others, too.

The diversion of scarce police resources to focus on drug markets is a primary factor in explaining the 16.3 percent increase in Florida's property crime rates from their modern low in 1983 to their historic maximum of 8,019.1 per 100,000 population in 1989 (Benson and Rasmussen 1991; Benson et al. 1992; Benson, Kim, and Rasmussen 1998; Rasmussen and Benson 1994: 94–101). In 1983 Florida police made 3 times as many property arrests as drug arrests, but by 1989 this figure had fallen to 1.8. As police efforts increased against drugs, efforts against property crime diminished, and property crime rates rose. Benson, and co-workers (1992) estimate that a 1 percent increase in drug enforcement in Florida relative to enforcement directed at reported crimes leads to a decrease in the probability of arrest for property crime of between 0.20 percent and 0.34 percent. Drug enforcement relative to property crime enforcement actually increased by about 40 percent in Florida between 1983 and 1989, so the reduction in the probability of arrest for property crimes, and therefore in the expected punishment for such crimes, was dramatic (see chapter 4 for a discussion about the importance of expected punishment as a deterrent). Many factors explain property crime, but after controlling for these other factors, Benson and Rasmussen (1991) estimate that the reallocation of police resources to focus on drug crime directly explains an estimated 40 to 50 percent of the increase in property crime rates in Florida over the 1984–89 period, and the increased prison crowding just discussed, with its shorter sentences served by property criminals, probably explains another significant part.[2]

The criminal justice system's focus on drug enforcement clearly imposes substantial unintended social costs, in part by diverting scarce police and prison resources from other public safety concerns. But what about the benefits in terms of reduced drug use? A recent Rand corporation study suggests that another dollar spent on drug treatment is seven times more effective at reducing cocaine use than another dollar spent on criminal justice drug control activities (Rydell and Everingham, 1994). These researchers suggest that reducing criminal justice expenditures on drug control by 25 percent and doubling treatment offered to users would reduce cocaine use and save $2 billion. Thus, even if controlling drug use is the goal, the current level of criminal justice investment in drug control is clearly excessive. Furthermore, moving many drug offenders out of prisons and into alternative treatment programs would increase the portion of sentences served by nondrug criminals even without spending the $2 billion in savings on prisons (Benson and Rasmussen 1994b). Another reason for the ineffectiveness of criminal justice drug control activities (Miron and Zweibel 1995), except for some potential short-term impacts, is that drug-market entrepreneurs inevitably introduce innovative new products, product procedures, and marketing institutions (e.g., new smuggling techniques and routes, new production locations, bribery of law enforcement personnel) that undermine law enforcement gains (Rasmussen and Benson 1994: 67–92). Cocaine prices actually fell through most of the 1980s, for instance, suggesting that supply was increasing faster than demand, despite the large-scale interdiction efforts by law enforcement. So what motivated the massive reallocation of policing and prison resources that occurred during the 1980s?

The most recent battle cry in the war on drugs in the United States was sounded by President Reagan and was clearly part of his agenda by 1982 (Wisotsky 1991). But such an offensive has to be waged, in large part, by state and local "troops," and the fact is that state and local law enforcement agencies generally did not significantly increase their efforts against drugs in a dramatic fashion until 1984, when a substantial reallocation of state and local criminal justice resources toward drug enforcement began (Benson, Rasmussen, and Sollars 1995; Rasmussen and Benson 1994).[3] There are a number of possible explanations for the upsurge in local drug enforcement: Perhaps local elected officials, representing median voter preferences across the nation, coincidentally demanded that their police departments escalate the War on Drugs. There are strong indications that this explanation does not hold, however (Rasmussen and Benson 1994: 122–27). In 1985 "public opinion" surveys suggested that drug use was not considered to be an especially significant problem. It appears that illicit drug policy in the 1980s was a case of policy changes leading public opinion (see Stutmann and Esposito 1992 for confessions of a senior Drug Enforcement Agency official regarding "selective distortion" techniques used to manipulate the press and public opinion).

Another explanation for the trends in the reallocation of local police resources over the 1984–89 period is that powerful interest groups demanded the war. It would be surprising if this were not the case, since as Chambliss and Seidman conclude, "every detailed study of the emergence of legal norms has consistently shown the immense importance of interest-group activity, not the public interest, as the critical variable" (1971: 73). Similarly, Rhodes points out that "as far as crime policy and legislation are concerned, public opinion and attitudes are generally irrelevant. The same is not true, however, of specifically interested criminal justice publics." (1977: 13). More recent research im-

plies similar conclusions but also makes it clear that one of the most important "specifically interested criminal justice publics" consists of law enforcement bureaucrats (see, e.g., Berk, Brackman, and Lesser 1977; Benson 1990:
105–26; Rasmussen and Benson 1994: 119–73; Benson, Rasmussen, and Sollars 1995; Benson and Rasmussen 1996b). The significant political role that
entrepreneurial bureaucrats have played in the development and evolution of
drug policy is widely recognized (see Thornton 1991; Benson, Rasmussen, and
Sollars 1995; Benson and Rasmussen 1996b; and Rasmussen and Benson
1994: 127–32). The same is true for the 1984 changes. In particular, the most
compelling explanation for this upsurge in drug enforcement effort is that
state and local police officials faced an exogenous change in bureaucratic incentives created by federal legislation (and by the Department of Justice's subsequent expansion of the incentive-creating implications of that legislation)
that was demanded by federal, state, and local police officials (Rasmussen and
Benson 1994: 119–73; Benson and Rasmussen 1996b; Benson, Rasmussen,
and Sollars 1995).

One section of the Comprehensive Crime Act of 1984 established a system
whereby any local police bureau that cooperated with federal drug enforcement authorities in a drug investigation would share in the money and/or
property confiscated as part of that investigation. As a result, police departments could increase their budgets without going through the typical budget
approval process, even in states whose own laws or constitutions limited confiscation possibilities or mandated that seizures go someplace other than to law
enforcement. The Department of Justice went even further, however, by agreeing to "adopt" seizures that did not occur in the context of an investigation involving a cooperating federal agency. Local police then began to circumvent
state laws by having federal authorities adopt their seizures.[4] Thus, under the
1984 federal statute, a substantial percentage of these seized properties were returned to the agency that seized them, even if the state's laws mandated that
confiscations go someplace else. This asset seizure law not only established a
way to "tax" involvement in drug markets, but it required that the resulting
revenue go to the tax collection agency (the police), thus creating relatively
strong incentives to collect the tax.[5]

Perhaps police bureaucracies advocated such legislation and joined in the
drug war because they perceived it to be in the public interest. There is considerable evidence suggesting that the opportunity costs of resources allocated
to the War on Drugs have been very high, however, as noted above, and a good
deal of evidence also indicates that many law enforcement bureaucracies engaged in substantial misinformation campaigns in order to exaggerate the se-

riousness of the problems associated with drugs and the potential benefits of a drug war (see, e.g., Lindesmith 1965; Kaplan 1970, 1983; Richards 1982; Barnett 1984; Michaels 1987; Bennett and DiLorenzo 1992; Stuttman and Esposito 1992; and Rasmussen and Benson 1994: 129–31, 141–46). Randy E. Barnett (1984: 53), a former criminal prosecutor, reports that it was chiefly as a result of information promulgated by police that the widespread belief developed that drugs are the cause of much of what is wrong with society (e.g., see Office of National Drug Control Strategy 1990: 2). Thus, the federal statute appears to explain a substantial portion of the changes in the allocation of local police resources after 1984.

The point is that allocation decisions in the public sector's criminal justice system are made on the basis of numerous factors. Allocation is, in part, by first-come-first-served, but because public officials generally have a great deal of discretion, political motives as well as the self-interest motives of police bureaucrats are also very important. There also clearly is a "market-like" allocation for some aspects of the criminal justice process: those with the greatest ability and willingness to pay politicians and other public officials with campaign contributions or other kinds of support (including bribes) often get the most out of the system. All of these rationing mechanisms create an environment in which uses of scarce resources that may be relatively valuable can be and often are crowded out by other less valuable uses. Because of the political and bureaucratic nature of the allocation process, Richard Neely, Chief Justice of the West Virginia Supreme Court, concludes, "[I]t is not that community enforcement [e.g., voluntary patrols, private security, etc.] is the *best* alternative for controlling crime; rather, it is that community enforcement is the *only* alternative for controlling crime" (1992: 188)

Rationing of Scarce Resources through Market Prices

When a consumer "casts a vote" (spends a dollar) in the market place, the consumer knows that the vote is decisive, in contrast to the votes cast in the political arena. No one else shares in the decision or in its consequences (certainly a partner or spouse may have some say before the vote is cast, but once the vote is cast the result is a "done deal"). The consumer owns the product (or service contract) that is purchased and therefore is in a position to decide how it will be used (as long as the use is legal and consistent with the contract). That means that the consumer can get as much benefit from consumption of the product as is legally and subjectively possible. Furthermore, though the consumer does obtain a large bundle of goods and services, the expenditure for each component of the bundle is recognized because the components are purchased individually. In the political arena taxpayer/voters are forced to buy a large bundle of products (or more accurately, uncertain promises) with a single decision.[6]

These circumstances imply that consumers buying in markets have very strong incentives to gather information, compared to the motivation of taxpayer/voters in the political arena, because the individual consumer receives the benefits from a good decision (the purchase of a product that truly provides more satisfaction than any alternative purchase, given the consumer's money income, or number of votes, and the money prices of alternatives). The consumer also bears the costs of a bad decision (the purchase of a product that gives less satisfaction than some alternative would have provided, given money income and prices). Therefore, consumers *benefit directly* from any time, effort, and expenses invested in information gathering and evaluation that increase the likelihood of a good decision. Furthermore, they have access to much better information than voters do.

Prices and Reputations as Sources of Information

Consumers making purchases in a market buy individual units of products and pay prices per unit, so they can compare the per-unit prices of competitive substitutes in order to help determine value. They can also compare the characteristics of the individual products and/or the reputation of their producers (past performance records) in order to determine relative quality. Consumer information is clearly not perfect, and information is costly to gather, so mistakes can be made; but alternatives actually *exist* that can be compared on the bases of price and quality rather than on the basis of politicians' promises about future policy efforts (reputations can also be important indicators of the credibility of political promises, of course, but the fact that most people do not effectively monitor the performance of their elected officials means that reputations can also be manipulated by selective distortion).

RELATIVE PRICES

The prices of products inform consumers about the value of the resources being used to produce the specific goods and services they are considering. High market prices imply that some of the resources are quite scarce (e.g., they have alternative valuable uses, and because they are available only in limited amounts, people who want those alternatives are bidding up the prices of the resources) and therefore quite valuable. This creates incentives to look for lower-priced substitutes and conserve the relatively scarce resources. Low prices imply relative abundance, so the search for substitute goods leads to the substitution of abundant resources for relatively scarce resources. Consumers do not have to actually know what resources are being used or how rare and valuable they may be, because the prices paid embody the relevant information. Without such product-specific prices as measures of value, those who consume government-produced goods really cannot compare value. They are therefore much less likely to recognize lower-cost substitutes and shift demands in order to conserve the most scarce and valuable resources.

Producers also have better information about what consumers want in markets than they do in the political arena. The prices of different goods and services in the marketplace inform producers of relative consumer evaluations and serve to coordinate society's resource allocation decisions by influencing relative profits. If consumers are willing to pay high prices relative to the current cost of the resources being used, the resulting profits attract investments and entrepreneurial entry, whereas low prices relative to costs of production result in losses, followed by disinvestment and exit. Thus, prices also transmit information to producers that allows them to shift resources and specialize in order to more accurately (and more profitably) meet the specific desires of individual consumers. Legislators and public bureaus such as police departments cannot take advantage of price signals in deciding how to allocate scarce resources that they control, but private producers in a competitive market *are forced* to pay attention to price signals.

Because so much information is embodied in prices, they serve to *coordinate* the decisions of diverse independent decision makers, both consumers and producers. When consumers want more of some good or service, they bid the price up, and producers who see the higher price relative to costs move resources into that market in order to earn profits. The resulting increase in competitive supply pushes the price back down, although generally not to its original level—if consumers want more of something, they generally should pay more for it, because the scarce resources used to produce it have alternative uses that must be sacrificed. If consumers do not like what a producer is providing or the price being charged, they turn to alternatives. Entrepreneurs must respond with new products and/or lower prices, or they go out of business. Furthermore, because consumers are free to immediately shift their allegiance in a market if someone offers them a better product and/or a lower price, entrepreneurs are motivated to invest in research and development in order to attract consumers and their dollars away from other potential purchases. Since public bureaucrats cannot capture the profits that might result from an innovation, their incentive to discover new and better ways to serve their customers is much weaker.

THE PROFIT MOTIVE AND REPUTATION AS A SIGNAL OF QUALITY

Private entrepreneurs are residual claimants. That is, they are able to retain any profit (revenue from the sale of a product that exceeds the expenditure for the resources used to produce it) while also bearing any loss if production costs exceed revenue. The resulting profit motive provides a strong incentive to produce at low costs, but since consumers are free to choose how they will spend their money, the only way that a private entrepreneur can legally obtain customers and profits is by *persuading* people that a quality service is being offered at a reasonable price, relative to the options available. Private producers cannot simply cut costs by cutting quality and continue to count on an undiminished flow of revenue, because consumers will turn to substitutes that are of higher quality for the same price or of the same quality with a lower price. Thus, competition forces private firms to offer relatively high-quality services at relatively low prices. Moreover, entrepreneurs who want to be in business for a long time have the incentive to invest in building a good reputation by providing a good value for the money and standing behind the product (e.g., via guarantees and cost-effective maintenance services). A producer can thereby attract repeat business; as consumer loyalty increases, others see the customers' satisfaction and try the product. The resulting reputation becomes increasingly valuable, and loss of such a reputation can be very costly. If a reputable firm suddenly started reducing quality relative to price, consumer complaints would mount, word would spread, and the firm would quickly begin losing customers and revenues. Therefore, once a firm has a reputation for quality, the incentive to maintain it is very strong.

Firms' investments in building and maintaining reputations mean that consumers do not have to directly determine the precise quality of the good before making a purchase; they can use the seller's reputation as a credible signal of quality. Furthermore, other entrepreneurs trying to compete with the reputable firm will have to compete against both the firm's price and its quality. As Gustave de Molinari recognized almost a century and a half ago in his analysis of private security, the "option the consumer retains of being able to buy security wherever he pleases brings about a constant emulation among all producers, each producer striving to maintain or augment his clientele with the attraction of cheapness or of faster, more complete and better [services]" (1849: 13). And significantly, the relevant definition of quality is the consumer's definition, not the seller's. Successful firms (firms that survive in a competitive environment) must be responsive to consumer desires.

Price/Quality Competition and Efficiency

The importance of multidimensional competition for clientele, and of survival in a competitive market, should not be overlooked in a discussion of efficiency in resource allocation. Entrepreneurs in the private sector must compete for consumer dollars, and consumers choose among the options available. Thus, competition is in terms of both price and quality, and firms that fail to compete effectively by offering a quality product at a low price do not survive.

Consider the San Francisco Patrol Specials discussed in chapter 5. Entry into the market is clearly limited to a degree, because Patrol Specials must undertake 440 hours of training and obtain licenses and because the number and size of private beats are apparently predetermined. Even so, competition is significant because the number of licensed Patrol Specials exceeds the number of beats available; individual license holders can also bid for more than one beat. Furthermore, private security is available from other sources, including other private security firms in San Francisco that do not have a licensed beat, as well as internal employment of security personnel, at least for many of the businesses purchasing services from the Specials. Self-protection efforts such as installation of various security devices and equipment are also an option. And the city police department administers a program that provides off-duty police officers to serve as location-specific security. Therefore, customers choosing to purchase services from the Patrol Specials could actually buy additional security from many competitive sources, including public police officers. Given the level of competition in the provision of security, and the fact that the Patrol Specials have been in existence for over 145 years, it appears that the Specials are producing for very satisfied customers: that is, the quality of their services is high, relative to the prices that are paid for the services.

The satisfaction of Patrol Specials' customers is illustrated by the fact that nine times in recent decades, the public police have advocated imposing restrictions on what the Patrol Specials can do, but in each case the Specials have received strong political backing from the people in the neighborhoods they protect, and they have beat back each of the police department's proposals. The price of Patrol Specials' services is in the $25–$30-per-hour range, compared to a $58-per-hour price tag for the services of an off-duty police officer (OICJ 1995).[7] Therefore, the Specials appear to be quite competitive in terms of price, at least compared to the publicly administered option. Furthermore, the flexibility they offer, including a willingness to provide the level of security each customer wants, and the fact that they are geographically focused so that they become intimately familiar with the neighborhood and its residents, make their services very attractive to a wide array of clients.

In competitive markets the prices that consumers are willing to pay for goods or services reflect the benefits they expect to obtain relative to the benefits arising from spending their money on competitive alternatives. Under these circumstances, if a consumer contracts with Patrol Specials or any other private security provider for protection, or if the consumer buys a gun, installs an alarm, joins Crime Watch, or uses any number of other voluntary options, then the decision implies a rational, efficient allocation of protection resources in view of the level of uncertainty that exists. Such a decision reflects the fact that there are several competitive alternatives in specialized goods and services for protection that can be compared on the basis of price and quality and that provide benefits the public police cannot or will not provide. As San Francisco attorney Ephraim Margolin notes in explaining the popularity of the Patrol Specials, "The police are now in central stations. The police don't know neighborhoods. They should but they don't. The specials are filling a void" (OICJ 1995). The Patrol Specials have filled the void since 1851, clearly meeting the market test of survival and implying that they efficiently provide a quality service, relative to the alternatives available (including the alternative of relying on public policing and/or buying extra security from public police officers). Many other private security arrangements have similar satisfied customers, as suggested below.

One advantage of more complete privatization is that allocation by price replaces dramatically less efficient rationing techniques.[8] In contrast to the first-come-first-served, political, and/or bureaucratic discretion methods that dominate the allocation of public criminal justice resources, a market system allocates scarce resources on the basis of willingness to pay, so goods and services tend to be allocated to their most highly valued uses. Furthermore, the price-rationing process itself does not consume massive amounts of resources directly, as many of the alternatives do. Competition to influence the allocation of resources still occurs, but when a scarce good or service is rationed by price, people who value it *and* are able to pay the price get to determine its use, and those who are unwilling or unable to pay the price do not influence its use. In order to be in a position to pay the prices necessary to influence the allocation of goods and services, people need money. The allocation process itself consumes far fewer resources, then, because the competition is directed toward obtaining money. In a market economy the primary way to get money is either to sell the use of resources to entrepreneurs who combine resources in order to produce things consumers value, or to become an entrepreneur who employs other resources (labor, land, capital). Therefore, the competition to obtain goods and services through markets tends to actually require the production of more goods and services. The net effect is that the availability of goods and services tends to expand rather than contract the way they do when resources are used up in nonproductive competition (e.g., by standing in line, by employing people as lobbyists who could actually produce something new, by spending a of lot of time and effort producing proposals that are not successful) as people compete for control of scarce resources.

In reality, of course, there are other margins of potential competition for money. Theft is one, and so is competition in the political arena for transfers through taxation and redistribution payments (e.g., welfare, farm subsidies, small-business loans, high wages for bureaucrats relative to what they could earn in the private sector [see Johnson and Libecap 1994 for evidence of such high wages]). Theft clearly is a possibility under other rationing mechanisms, too, since no matter how a person obtains a good, someone else can try to steal it. Furthermore, political competition either totally dominates or serves as an option for all of the other rationing mechanisms too. For instance, rationing by waiting can lead to demands for quotas, and political influence can determine the allocation of those quotas; rationing by merit can lead to political competition to determine the merit criteria (so income levels, racial and ethnic background, political affiliation, and so on, can all become meritorious or unmeritorious through political decisions). In a relative sense at least, then, allocation through prices is an efficient rationing mechanism because fewer resources tend to be used up in the rationing process itself, and the competition for money often leads to even greater availability of goods and services.

When individuals turn to the market in order to obtain something that is supposedly available from some nonmarket source, it is often because they are unable or unwilling to incur the costs associated with trying to influence the nonmarket rationing outcome. They expect to be better off by purchasing a substitute from the market. Their purchases from the market reflect rational decisions, given the alternatives, and tend to be efficiency enhancing. In the case of crime control services, market options can be attractive because the costs of trying to influence the allocation of public crime control resources is very high, or because public bureaucrats cannot (or will not, given bureaucratic discretion and pursuit of their own well-being) effectively provide the desired quality of services at reasonable costs, or because the public sector has misallocated resources to relatively little-valued uses as a result of the poor information-transferring mechanisms that are at work. After all, preferences and desires vary considerably across individuals, so the product variety and mix that one person wants need not be the variety and mix that another prefers.

Bureaucrats are not likely to produce the variety of services that each individual wants, in part because they have no readily available information on consumers' relative evaluations of the options. They are much more likely to provide a relatively homogeneous, one-size-fits-all service than a market is. It is easier to do that than to try to gather all the information needed to meet the diverse demands of individuals. Alternatively, some variety and a mix of services may be produced, but they are likely to be the variety and mix *that the bureaucrats themselves think should be highly valued* (perhaps because they gain more personal satisfaction thereby, including serving their own subjective view of the public interest). There may also be some outside influence from powerful political interest groups (and from individuals and organizations willing to pay bribes for special privileges or services). Those who do not find the resulting services attractive and who do not want to play political games (or pay bribes) opt for private security alternatives.

Here is an example: The American Banking Association and the American Hotel-Motel Association retain the William J. Burns International Detective Agency to investigate crimes committed against their members. A bank security director pointed out why. "[I]t was necessary to employ private investigators because the public police and investigative forces were too busy to devote the amount of effort required by [banks]" (Kakalik and Wildhorn 1971: 112–13). Cunningham and Taylor (1985) find that this view is prevalent in private business organizations. Private investigators therefore are frequently employed to do things that public police will not do, such as preemployment background checks or undercover work to detect employee dishonesty or customer shoplifting.

Private security guards and patrolmen, and voluntary watch and patrol organizations, also do things that the public police cannot or will not do, such as making routine checks on buildings for residents or businesses and "watching to prevent" crime. And, as McCrie notes, "The existence of such a formidable corps of security personnel is only possible because the private sector in this century wants more security than government can or will supply" (1992: 17).

Specialization and Increased Efficiency

The private sector tends to do well what the government criminal justice system does badly, in part because consumers generally have narrowly focused concerns. When they pay a private firm to alleviate those concerns, they can hire someone with focused expertise. Both the evidence and economic theory tell us that when resources *specialize* in their area of comparative advantage, economic efficiency is enhanced. More is produced with the same resources, or fewer resources are needed to produce the same level of output. Beginning in 1982, for instance, Amarillo, Texas, authorized Allstate Security to respond to subscriber alarms (Fixler and Poole 1992: 30). The police department was relieved of responding to an average of eight alarms per day and saved an estimated 3,420 person-hours per year (a time saving with the same impact as adding 1.75 employees per year to the police department). Since private security personnel are less expensive than public police officers, the result was a reduction in the monetary costs of alarm response. Significantly, the cost is also shifted from general taxpayers to the individuals who actually use and benefit directly from alarm services. Responding to false alarms is expensive for police departments, but those who generate the false alarms have little reason to be concerned about them when taxpayers in general bear the costs (Benson 1990: 98–99). Shifting the response function to a private security provider who can then charge for the service creates a much stronger incentive to avoid accidentally or carelessly setting off an alarm.

Public police specialize too, having homicide, vice, robbery, burglary, and traffic divisions, and others, but the range of private security options is much greater (and the allocation of public police resources among these special focuses is not necessarily responsive to citizens' demands or designed to maximize effective crime control either, as suggested above in the discussion of asset seizures and drug enforcement). Security personnel range from minimum-wage guards who work on a temporary basis, to full-time guards with relatively few investigative skills, to security personnel who also provide a bundle of various complementary services, to trained professional investigators, to highly trained individuals who specialize in electronic monitoring, to experts in security system design. Security equipment ranges from the simplest locks to the most complex alarm and monitoring equipment.

Consider an example of a specialized private security effort that is specifically focused on certain types of criminal activity: the railroad police. Recall that at the end of World War I, railroad police were established as a complete and autonomous police force. They quickly compiled what must be considered a remarkable record of effectiveness, particularly compared to that of public police forces. Between the end of World War I and 1929, freight claim payments for robberies fell by 92.7 percent, from $12,726,947 to $704,262. Furthermore, arrests by railroad police produce a substantially higher percentage of convictions than is achieved by public police: a five-year sample from the Pennsylvania Railroad, for instance, indicates that 83.4 percent of those arrested are convicted; a thirteen-year sample from another line shows a 97.47 percent conviction rate (Wooldridge 1970: 116). A study of railroad police over the first three-plus decades of their existence suggests that the overall conviction rate from their arrests was close to 98 percent, with an average of 60,000 arrests per year (Dewhurst 1955: 4). Wooldridge observes that the primary reason for this success is that the railroad police specialize in one area of enforcement, developing "an expertise not realistically within the grasp of public forces" (1970: 117). Although the railroad police do not get any attention from public officials as they debate public policy, they remain a powerful crime control force. In 1992 major railroads in the United States still employed a 2,565-person security force of fully commissioned law enforcement officers whose clearance rate, adjusted for underreporting, is 286 percent of the similarly adjusted rate, for public police (Reynolds 1994b: 11–12): 1992 data suggest that railroad police clear about 30.9 percent of the crimes reported to them, whereas public police clear about 21.4 percent; but because of their relative effectiveness, it is estimated that 75 percent of all crimes against railroads are reported to their police force, compared to roughly 39 percent for public police. Therefore, adjusted for reporting, clearance rates are 8.1 for public police and 23.2 for railroad police. This kind of specialization and the consequent gain in proficiency (and efficiency) often characterize private-sector security and investigative firms.

The major intended benefit of specialization by the private security firm is a localized deterrent effect in the geographical area (neighborhood, private community, shopping mall, business establishment, home) or the functional area (e.g., railroads) protected by the specialized security arrangements. Such focused specialization is intended to make it less likely that a criminal will succeed in his or her attempt at theft or violence within the protected area. Thus, the potential cost of attacking the protected target is relatively high because of a higher probability of the criminal's being observed and captured, or, in the case of some investments like armed guards or firearms, a higher probability that the criminal will suffer personal injury or death. One consequence is that criminals may simply choose other less well-protected targets, of course. Therefore, a short-run impact of specialized private security may be greater criminal activity elsewhere (the same is true if one public policing jurisdiction increases its crime control effort relative to another [Rasmussen, Benson, and Sollars 1993]). Entrepreneurs will recognize the new opportunity, however, and happily offer more security personnel and/or equipment for these new targets as well, spreading private security to other geographic and/or functional areas. This suggests that there is a second potential effect. As the potential cost of committing crimes rises in more and more places, potential criminals are less likely to become actual criminals, so the overall propensity to commit crimes falls: there is a potential general deterrent effect. This is particularly true if it is difficult for the criminal to determine whether private security personnel or equipment is in place or not. The recognition that there is a relatively high probability of private protection creates more uncertainty and tends to reduce the overall level of crime.

This process of generating general deterrence is quite different from the public criminal justice process. The public sector seems to focus on catching and punishing criminals after a crime is committed (see chapters 11 and 12 in this regard), on the assumption that spending resources on punishment provides an effective general deterrent. Private security focuses on preventing crimes against specific targets, but as such protection spreads, an unintended benefit can arise: criminals find fewer and fewer attractive targets and perceive a rising price of crime because of the increased chances of being observed, so they are less likely to commit crimes. This is the way markets work, of course. As Adam Smith (1976) pointed out over two centuries ago, markets harness the self-interests of individuals trying to maximize their own well-being; the result is maximization of the "wealth of nations." Hayek (1937) further explains that prices coordinate the dispersed information possessed by the many buyers and sellers in the market and that no central planner or bureaucracy has sufficient information to design a system that can come remotely close to the undesigned spontaneous order of the market in maximizing the well-being of the population. The question here is, Does this same argument apply with regard to the protection of persons and their property? Let us consider the evidence.

Evaluating Private Security

Since the goal of private security is localized deterrence, the first question to be considered is, How effectively is this goal achieved? There are a number of possible examples of focused efforts to protect individuals' property that might be discussed. For instance, a National Institute of Law Enforcement and Criminal Justice study of four cities concluded that households that engrave identification numbers on their property appear to reduce their chances of being burglarized, and surveys of people involved in similar projects in seventy-eight other communities indicated similar results ("Operation Indent" 1975). The most relevant examples for our purpose, though, involve the kinds of security activities that the public sector presumably can produce, so that the consequences of private protection can be compared with the consequences of potential public alternatives.

Localized Deterrence

Donovan and Walsh (1986) provide what may be the closest thing to a full-scale evaluation of a large private security system with their examination of the effectiveness of private security for Starrett City, a 153-acre apartment complex in a high-crime area of the East New York section of Brooklyn, with fifty-six residential buildings containing 5,881 apartment units and about twenty thousand racially and ethnically diverse but largely middle-income residents (at the time of the study almost two-thirds of the residents were white, over 20 percent were black, 8 percent were Hispanic, 5 percent were Asian, and about 2 percent were of other racial/ethnic backgrounds; median income in the complex was twenty-four thousand dollars in 1984, although some poorer families also lived there as some apartment rents were subsidized under Title 8 funding; most residents were office or blue-collar workers or city employees). Starrett City also has eight parking garages and one outdoor parking lot, a shopping center with twenty-five businesses, an elementary school, an intermediate school, two nursery schools, a recreation complex (facilities for swimming, basketball, tennis, meetings, etc.), and various open spaces and parks. At the time of the evaluation, Starrett City's fifty-four-person private security force included thirty-four officers with general patrol duties, a six-officer K-9 unit, and a five-officer "anticrime" unit, which patrolled in civilian clothes. The director of security is a vice president in the corporation, but most day-to-day activities are supervised by a site manager (a captain) and seven sergeants who oversee patrolling and the anticrime units.

The Donovan-Walsh study (Donovan and Walsh 1986; also see Walsh, Donovan, and McNicholas 1992) employs a number of research methods and sources of information, including the records of both the Starrett City Security Unit and the New York Police Department, self-administered questionnaires for Starrett City security personnel and residents, direct interviews of the Starrett City business community and security unit as well as New York Police Department personnel, and field observations of residents and security personnel during their daily activities. They note that outwardly, Starrett City appears to be a relatively safe and stable community. The appearance of stability is confirmed by the survey of residents. Some 62.7 percent had lived in the community for between six and twelve years in 1986 (the complex was twelve years old at the time of the survey). The most important factors explaining why residents moved into Starrett City are its affordable rent (37.4 percent) and the desire to live in a "safe neighborhood" (21.3 percent; this is a more important concern among blacks [35.5 percent] and Hispanics [48.5 percent], perhaps because they perceive that their alternatives generally are significantly less safe) (Donovan and Walsh 1986: 54). Other important factors include potential crime-related issues such as its desirability as a good place to raise children (7 percent, again relatively more important for blacks and Hispanics with 12.2 percent and 15.7 percent, respectively, reporting this as their prime motivation for moving) and the deterioration of the person's former neighborhood (9.9 percent). And the vast majority of survey respondents, 88.8 percent, feel safe within the community (Donovan and Walsh 1986: 56), whereas only 40.8 percent feel safe outside the confines of Starrett City.

This perception of relative safety is apparently warranted: the report concludes that "statistically, Starrett City must be considered one of the safest communities in the United States" (Donovan and Walsh 1986: 36) (there are many other private developments all over the country that probably have comparable safety; they simply have not been studied). Table 7.1 lists the 1984 and 1985 reported crimes per thousand persons within Starrett City; within the Seventy-Fifth Police Precinct, in which the community is located (Starrett City accounts for 16 percent of the precinct's population [Carlson 1995a: 71]); within New York State; and for the United States as a whole. Starrett City had far fewer reported felonies than any of the other reporting categories. This difference does not appear to reflect a tendency for nonreporting by residents, either: they were apparently much more likely to report crimes than other residents of the Seventy-Fifth Precinct, as evidenced by the fact that they reported many more incidents of criminal mischief, trespass, petit larceny, reckless behavior, and disorderly conduct than were reported to public police. This probably reflects recognition that the public police and courts will do very little if anything in response to such reports, whereas private security will respond (an issue discussed below). Thus, 77.5 percent of the residents in the survey said they would report an assault to their private security force; only 12.6 percent would call the New York City Police Department.

TABLE 7.1
Reported Crimes per 1,000 Residents, 1984 and 1985

Crime	United States		New York State		75th Precinct		Starrett City	
	1984	1985	1984	1985	1984	1985	1984	1985
Murder/ non-negligent manslaughter	0.08	0.08	0.10	0.10	0.30	0.22	0.00	0.05
Rape	0.36	0.39	0.32	0.32	0.90	0.83	0.05	0.10
Robbery	2.05	2.14	5.07	4.56	16.00	15.51	3.60	2.57
Aggravated assault	2.90	3.20	3.66	3.86	6.10	6.88	1.90	1.05
Burglary	12.64	13.41	12.57	12.55	15.40	15.26	2.10	0.40
Grand larceny	27.91	30.49	27.55	28.41	12.10	11.64	2.90	1.30
Vehicle theft	4.37	7.27	6.51	5.90	10.10	9.51	1.80	1.10

SOURCE: Donovan and Walsh 1986: 31.

Similarly, 97.1 percent of the thirty-five retail businesses within Starrett City would call the private security force if they had a problem, and only 2.9 percent (the manager of thirty stores in a chain, only one of which is in Starrett City) would call the New York police (Donovan and Walsh 1986: 75). The "concern shown by security personnel for care of property and prevention of disorder as well as the safety of residents and visitors" is what explains the high level of reporting in Starrett City (Donovan and Walsh 1986: 36). A large majority of residents (89.1 percent) clearly recognize that the reason for the relative safety of their community is its security force; in fact, a majority suggest that they would move out if the security force was not there (Donovan and Walsh 1986: 61).

The benefits of safety are not only for residents. In part because of their feelings of safety, 82.3 percent of the residents do a majority of their shopping in the Starrett City shopping center, where security is provided from 8:00 a.m. until 12:00 midnight. Shopping centers in general are relatively safe, of course, because they generally have a full-time private security presence. The only areas outside Starrett City where a majority of the surveyed residents (55.9 percent) feel safe are in other shopping centers, but 84.6 of the respondents feel safe shopping at their local stores, perhaps because this shopping center is inside the Starrett City complex and therefore has an added umbrella of private security not present at other shopping malls (familiarity also means that they can estimate the risks more accurately, so there is less uncertainty).

Now let us consider the alternative: Why do the public police provide less effective localized deterrence? Obviously they do, given the numbers in table 7.1. During 1985 Starrett City security officers responded to 13,248 requests for services (only 8.35 percent were for crime reports; 4.36 percent were for disputes, and 87.28 were "service calls"). If the New York Police Department had been responsible for these calls, the Seventy-Fifth Precinct would have faced an 18 percent increase in calls, assuming that all of them would have been made (Donovan and Walsh 1986: 68–72). Donovan and Walsh estimate that the added cost for public police in the absence of the Starrett City security force would have been a minimum of about $750,000 per year because of the additional officers who would have been needed. The fact is, however, that economically it would be "practically impossible to replace the Starrett City security department on a person-for-person basis" (Donovan and Walsh 1986: 81). The police in the Seventy-Fifth Precinct actually responded to only 30.6 percent of their calls for service, compared to the 94.44 response rate for Starrett City's security force (Donovan and Walsh 1986: 49); Donovan and Walsh recognize that fewer officers would have been employed to serve these residents. The $750,000 estimate essentially assumes that four additional police officers would have been assigned to the area in order to replace the fifty-four-person security force, resulting in a lower level of protection and much higher crime rates. The greater propensity to report crimes in Starrett City, noted above, suggests that only a portion of the calls would have been made to the public police in the absence of private security; but the reduced security presence and the reduced probability of reporting mean that crime would have been much higher in the area without the private security presence, so crime-related calls could actually increase. Clearly the public police are unable or unwilling to duplicate the level of localized deterrence that people want and are willing to buy from private security.

ADDITIONAL EVIDENCE

Carlson notes, in discussing the "Grand Central Partnership," an organization of more than six thousand businesses employing a private security force to patrol an eighty-block area around New York's Grand Central Station, that "over the years, police have adopted a laissez-faire view of minor lawbreakers" (1995a: 70). The Grand Central security force has not, however, and not surprisingly, crime rates in the area they began patrolling in 1988 fell by 20 percent within two years, by 36 percent after three yeas, and by 53 percent after five (68). Even the city's assistant chief of police sees the result as "phenomenal" (68).

Rossmoor, a private development covering about seven square miles in Walnut Creek, California, started with about eighty-three hundred exclusively adult residents in 1979 (children are not allowed except for short-term visits, and residents must be forty-five or older) and is protected by private security (Dart 1992: 118–20). The twenty-two-officer security force maintains a guard post at the only entrance to the complex and responds to approximately nine hundred calls per month made to its own dispatchers (two full-time and two part-time dispatchers are employed for this purpose, in addition to the security force). The unarmed security force is approximately the same size as a city police force handling that number of calls, although the mix of calls appears to differ significantly, just as in Starrett City. The vast majority of calls are not to report crimes; instead, they involve medical emergencies and crime prevention actions such as vacation checks and escorting visitors. The security force has not been granted police powers by the government, so its personnel's authority to arrest is the same as any private citizen's, and they must call the public police when a criminal incident actually occurs, but deterrence is so effective that Walnut Creek public police respond to only about twenty-five such calls a year from Rossmoor. Nonetheless, it is estimated that in 1980 if Rossmoor had terminated its private security arrangement, Walnut Creek would have created two additional twenty-four-hour patrol beats at a cost to city taxpayers of about $1.5 million per year (Dart 1992: 119). In comparison, the twenty-two-person private force and related security arrangements cost Rossmoor residents $555,000 in 1979. The amount reached $900,000 in 1989, still far below the estimated cost of a much smaller public policing presence that would have replaced it a decade earlier. Thus, for Rossmoor (and for Walnut Creek taxpayers), Rossmoor's private security force appears to be very cost-effective. These conclusions probably apply to most other private developments with limited access and a private security force.

VOLUNTARY COMMUNITY EFFORTS

Patrols and neighborhood watches are also effective crime prevention alternatives (Yin et al. 1977: 30). Little in the way of statistical or experimental analysis has been done to verify this, but there is considerable anecdotal evidence. For instance, the 1993–94 period saw a 21 percent drop in reported crimes in Tallahassee, Florida, from 9,603 to 7,583. Although a number of anticrime steps had been taken under the new police chief, Tom Coe, he attributes the decrease to the fact that the people of the community got involved. Specifically, almost a dozen new crime watch organizations were started in residential neighborhoods between late 1993 and early 1995, along with a business district organization with a similar purpose, and several older inactive Crime Watch programs were revitalized. Police Chief Coe contends that "the police have very little to do with crime when it comes down to it," but what can reduce crime, he believes, is empowering "the people to protect themselves" (Cole 1995: 5A).

Similar results appear to arise from more aggressive community efforts such as those discussed in chapter 6, on private justice. In 1989 District 16 in Philadelphia, the section of the city in which Herman Wrice later started Mantua against Drugs (see chapter 6), had the highest crime rate in the city. Mantua itself had 1,644 serious felonies (murder, rape, robbery, burglary, and aggravated assault) reported that year, one for every fifteen of the community's twenty-five thousand residents. By 1993 the number of major crimes reported was down by 40 percent to 990, and it apparently was not due to increased numbers of arrests (Carlson 1995b: 61): drug arrests fell from 326 to 241, for instance, as Mantua against Drugs forced many drug market participants to move out of the area. Since crime rates fell throughout the city over this period, the overall reduction in crime may not be attributed entirely to Wrice's efforts to bring neighbors together to take back their neighborhood and to the citizens' responses to those efforts. Nonetheless, serious crime in Mantua decreased at more than twice the rate occurring in Philadelphia as a whole, suggesting that "[c]riminals in Mantua didn't just stop committing as many crimes. Something, or somebody, made them stop" (62). Similar success stories can be told for communities ranging from Taylor, Texas, to Marion, Indiana, to Fairlawn in Washington, D.C. (Carlson 1995b).

PRIVATE STREETS

Because private security efforts focus on protecting private property, one way to encourage more private security clearly is to privatize more property. One particular privatization option—private streets—deserves mention here, since there is some evidence of its relative effectiveness. Newman's study of private streets in Saint Louis concludes that such cooperative behavior has substantially reduced crime. A comparison of crime rates on private streets with those on adjacent public streets shows significantly lower crime in virtually every category (Newman 1980: 137, 140). Ames Place, a private street, had a crime rate that was 108 percent lower than the adjacent public street, for instance.

Some observers argue that the lower crime rates on the private streets of Saint Louis are the result of limiting access, not privatization. Certainly an argument that limited access reduces crime might appear to make sense, at least on the surface, but the fact is that closure of public streets to through traffic has been tried elsewhere with little success. Indeed, within two years of the publication of Newman's earlier book, *Defensible Space* (1972), which advocated street closures and other neighborhood redesigns to change residents' behavior toward crime, "major demonstration projects" were under way, including a Department of Justice experiment in Hartford, Connecticut, that closed streets and assigned police teams to the neighborhood. In addition, a number of new public housing projects were designed around ideas of limited access and other principles of "defensible space" (Murray 1995: 350). In Hartford, "to the disappointment of the project directors, police statistics did not show any dramatic drop in crime" (Gage 1981: 20). Results were similarly disappointing elsewhere. As Murray explains: "The most provocative hypothesis of defensible space has been that residents would change their behavior, defending their space against criminals given the right environmental design. This has not been demonstrated. . . . [A] better physical environment has not been proven to produce new anticrime behaviors" (1995: 350). Yet, Saint Louis's private streets clearly have lower crime rates compared to nearby public streets and compared to the preprivatization period for the private streets themselves. Why? Because people must have the capacity and incentive to defend even defensible spaces.

The fact is that private streets have things going for them that public street closures and even redesigning of a neighborhood environment alone do not. For one thing, ownership gives the neighborhood a high degree of cohesiveness. Privatization creates a bond through joint ownership that encourages reciprocal cooperation in crime prevention. For another, all residents sign a contract agreeing to property use and maintenance. They have legal obligations to cooperate and reasons for communicating on a wide variety of issues, one of which is clearly likely to be crime control. Furthermore, and perhaps more important, ownership gives residents powers that they do not have when the streets are publicly owned—they can do something about undesirable people or behavior, because as owners they have the right to ask someone to leave; if the request is refused, they can call their neighbors, their security personnel, or even the public police to remove uninvited trespassers. If a stranger enters the area, he is likely to be noticed and observed until he demonstrates that he belongs, perhaps by visiting a resident who obviously knows him. If this does not happen, he will attract more attention and, recognizing this, will probably move on. Residents on public streets cannot legally act until after a crime has been committed, and then they must call upon public police. The incentives to watch and to cooperate to prevent crime are apparently much stronger when streets are privatized.

Privatization of streets appears to have the greatest effect in deterring particular types of crimes: specifically, crimes against persons and crimes of opportunity, such as assault, purse snatching, and auto-related theft are reduced significantly through privatization of streets (Newman 1980: 142). Criminals apparently realize that private street residents are more likely to notice them, so they look elsewhere for victims.

BUSINESSES AND BUSINESS GROUPS

The Starrett City, Rossmoor, Saint Louis, and other examples discussed above are geographically limited (but fairly large) residential communities; similar results also appear to arise, however, with functional specialization. For instance, Timothy Hannan finds that private guards in banks, by their presence, "significantly reduce the risk of robbery. Accepting point estimates, the magnitude of this reduction is approximately one robbery attempt a year for those offices which would have otherwise suffered a positive number of robbery attempts" (1982: 91). Similarly, but on a broader scale, Charles Clotfelter considers the impact of private and public security services on the sectors of (1) manufacturing and wholesaling and (2) finance, insurance, and real estate; his empirical results "indicate that private protective firms are more effective than public police at protecting firms in these industries" (1977: 874) (the same is true for railroads, as noted above). He also concludes that private protection is more effective and more readily responsive in areas experiencing rapid population growth.

Experimental studies reinforce the specific deterrence implied by such statistical studies. The Western Behavioral Science Institute examined various security measures using Southland Corporation's 7–Eleven stores. They employed former armed robbers to rate a large number of stores according to their attractiveness as robbery targets ("Holding Down Holdups" 1976). Then, using a sample of 120 stores of similar attractiveness, 60 were left unchanged as a control group and experimental changes were tested on the other 60. The changes were quite inexpensive (about one hundred dollars per store), including actions like stripping store windows of ad banners after dark and posting signs reading "Clerk cannot open this safe." The result was a 30 percent lower robbery rate in the test stores than in the control stores during the first eight months of the study. Prior to the study, Southland was experiencing an average of one robbery per store per year, so a 30 percent reduction is far from trivial.

Other private protection and detection devices appear to have similar impacts. For instance, FBI officials in the Washington, D.C./Maryland area have recently reported that the changing behavior of bank robbers also indicates the deterrent impact of private security equipment (John Jay College of Criminal Justice/CUNY 1997c). The increased security measures taken by banks in the urban and suburban areas of Washington, D.C., and Maryland have induced bank robbers to search for other, less secure targets. The result is a drop in bank robberies in these urban/suburban areas and a dramatic increase in robberies in small-town branches in rural Maryland. One particular security measure apparently is particularly significant in this shifting pattern of bank robbery. Bulletproof glass was installed to protect tellers in banks throughout Prince George's County, and bank robberies are substantially lower there than in a similar adjacent county. Effective location-specific deterrence (whether through private security or public actions) apparently does lead to a shift in criminal activity to a new location, as suggested above, rather than to an immediate overall reduction in crime (Rasmussen, Benson, and Sollars 1993). But as more rural banks perceive the increased risks, they will also invest in more security, and because the level of these private security measures tends to spread quite quickly, making bank robberies more and more costly for the criminal, they ultimately should reduce such crimes.

It should not be surprising to find that specific deterrence is effectively produced by private security efforts. People are voluntarily participating in or purchasing a tremendous amount of these services, and the purchases have been increasing at a rapid rate. It is hard to imagine that this would occur if the benefits were not significant. But what about the argument that as private security spreads, general deterrence results?

General Deterrence

Most studies of general crime deterrence examine the effects of public-sector efforts and ignore the potential effects of private-sector deterrence. In this regard, many statistical studies using aggregate measures of police resources in statistical equations intended to explain crime rates do not find a significant relationship between police budgets or levels of staffing and crime rates (e.g., Swimmer 1974; Allison 1972; Thaler 1977; Hakim 1980; Buck et al. 1985; see Cameron 1988 for other references). Similarly, though crime rates are generally negatively and significantly related to the probability of arrest for the crime being studied, the probability of arrest often does not appear to be significantly related to measures of aggregate police resources using simultaneous equation estimators (e.g., Ehrlich 1972, 1973; Mathur 1978; Carr-Hill and Stern 1973; Furlong and Mehay 1981; Wahlroos 1981; Cameron 1988). Because measures of police resources have failed to consistently show a negative influence on the crime rate, either directly, on the one hand, or indirectly through the probability of arrest, on the other, critics such as Cameron (1988: 308) question the validity of the general deterrence hypothesis. Their views are not warranted. Benson, Kim, and Rasmussen (1994) explain that the reason public police resources often do not appear, in empirical studies, to have a deterrent impact is that police have discretionary power to allocate those resources. Essentially, given the lack of substantial variation in aggregate police resource measures, increased deterrence for one crime is generally achieved through a reallocation of police resources, and when resource allocation is controlled for, support for the deterrence hypothesis clearly surfaces (Levitt 1997; Benson et al. 1992; Benson, Kim, and Rasmussen 1998). The implications of this underlie the consequences discussed above of the widespread reallocation of policing resources during the 1980s. In other words, although public police can deter crimes, they often do not appear to do it effectively.[9]

A recent comprehensive study by Zedlewski (1992) uses 1977 data from 124 Standard Metropolitan Statistical Areas in an effort to analyze the effect of both public police and private security on the overall safety environment of communities and on offender decision making. Despite the poor data on private security efforts other than estimates of security employment, his results are intriguing. As with much of the literature on general deterrence just discussed, he finds no deterrence impact of increased public police resources on the level of reported crimes. It appears, then, that the arguments of Benson, Kim, and Rasmussen (1994) actually explain the lack of apparent deterrence: although deterrence may be possible, additional public police resources are generally not being effectively allocated to deter crimes.[10] Zedlewski also supports the deterrence hypothesis; he finds an impact of private security employment on crime and concludes "that greater levels of security personnel are associated with reduced levels of community crime. It suggests that investment in private security produces spillover benefits to the community at large. Crime is not only displaced; it is somewhat discouraged" (1992: 51). In light of these findings and the general lack of empirical findings of deterrent effects from additional public police resources, Zedlewski predicts that "[a]n inability to produce predictable increases in arrest rates, coupled with demonstrably effective private security systems, indicates that safety investment in private security will grow more rapidly than investment in police" (1992: 51), a prediction that is easy to make since that is already occurring (Sherman 1983; see chapter 5).

SELF-PROTECTION

Individual self-protection efforts may be effective for specific deterrence and may also produce general deterrence. Because of the controversy surrounding firearms and violence, firearm ownership has attracted more study than other specialized forms of protection. Kleck (1991: chap. 4) estimates, from survey data, that civilians use guns for self-defense between eight hundred thousand and 2.5 million times per year. Roughly 8 percent of these uses are to prevent sexual assaults, about 29 percent involve defense against nonsexual assaults, 22 percent are induced by attempted robberies, 33 percent are against burglars, and 16 percent involve trespass (these percentages add up to more than 100 because some criminals simultaneously attempt more than one type of crime, e.g., assault and robbery). Kleck's estimates imply that more people defend themselves with a gun than the police arrest for violent crimes and burglary (Evers 1994: 7). Knowledge of the potential dangers posed by armed victims generates considerable incentive to avoid victims who are known to be armed. Surveys of prisoners "uniformly find felons stating that, whenever possible, they avoid victims who are thought to be armed, and that they know of planned crimes that were abandoned when it was discovered that the prospective victim was armed" (Silver and Kates 1977: 151). The evidence regarding the specific deterrent effects of bank guards discussed above (Hannan 1982) supports this survey result, and it is not surprising in light of the risk criminals face when confronting an armed victim.

A growing body of evidence suggests that fear of confronting armed victims has a dramatic general deterrent effect for crimes (e.g., Silver and Kates 1977; Cook 1979; Kleck and Bordua 1983; Benson 1984a, 1986a, 1990: 239–42; Lott and Mustard 1997). Cook (1979) uses cross-section data to examine the relationship between armed robbery rates and the strength of gun control laws. He finds that areas with strong gun controls have higher levels of armed robbery than areas with weaker controls. This may imply that when individuals' ability to defend themselves with guns is limited, they are perceived by criminals to be more vulnerable to crime and therefore are more likely to become crime victims. That is, criminals expect low probabilities of gun ownership and therefore are attracted to the area. Of course, there is a danger in such an interpretation because correlation does not necessarily imply causation. In this case the correlation may arise because the strictest gun controls are in high-crime areas as a result of the mistaken but widely held belief that guns cause crime (Benson 1984a, 1986a). There is, however, more persuasive evidence of a deterrent effect arising from gun ownership.

Some of the best evidence of the general deterrent effect of gun ownership for protection comes from the impact of publicized programs to provide training in firearm use for potential victims. One such effort was sponsored by the Orlando police department between October 1966 and March 1967. The program was designed to train women in the safe use of firearms because of the sharp increase in rapes in the city during 1966, and it was widely publicized in Orlando newspapers. Kleck and Bordua (1983), in their examination of the consequences of this program, report that the rape rate in Orlando fell from a 1966 level of 35.91 per one hundred thousand inhabitants to 4.18 in 1967. This was clearly not a part of any general downward trend, since the national rate was increasing and rates in surrounding metropolitan areas, as well as in Florida as a whole (excluding Orlando), were either constant or increasing over the same period. Furthermore, the decrease did not reflect a continual downward trend for Orlando, since the trend had been erratic but upward for the previous several years. It seems obvious that the knowledge that potential rape victims might be carrying a gun and might know how to use it is a significant deterrent; additional evidence arises from a comparison of the change in the rape rate, which was the crime category targeted by the program, to other Orlando crime rates. Rates for virtually all crimes were rising or constant in Orlando, the surrounding metropolitan area, and Florida over the 1966–67 period. There was one exception besides rape, however. The Orlando burglary rate also declined, but this actually tends to strengthen the argument that gun ownership for protection has a deterrent effect, since burglary would seem to be the most likely crime category other than rape in which a criminal might confront an armed female victim.

The Orlando example is not unique. Publicized training programs in the use of firearms have led to reductions in armed robberies in Highland Park, Michigan; drug store robberies in New Orleans; and grocery store robberies in Detroit (Kleck and Bordua 1983). When potential criminals become aware that potential victims might be willing and able to protect themselves with a gun, the increased perceived risk of committing a crime leads to the abandonment of at least some potential criminal acts. Cook (1979: 755) provides an idea of the potential magnitude of this risk with his calculations based on Atlanta data. He concludes that a robber in the city doubles his chances of dying by committing only seven robberies, because of the risk of being counterattacked by a victim. Of course, such location specific risks may also lead to the choice of a victim in another area where guns for protection are less likely: location specific gun control could easily lead to higher crime rates in another area, as the Cook (1979) results cited earlier imply. To the degree that gun control laws are constraining, private citizens' potential options for responding to this shift in crime are limited by the government, not by a market imperfection.

Reviewing the evidence of gun ownership and deterrence from several sources led Kleck and Bordua to conclude: "[I]t is a perfectly plausible hypothesis that private gun ownership currently exerts as much or more deterrent effect on criminals as do the activities of the criminal justice system. . . . [T]here is the distinct possibility that although gun ownership among the crime-prone may tend to increase crime, gun ownership among the noncriminal majority may tend to depress crime rates below the levels they otherwise would achieve" (1983: 271). A recent study by Lott and Mustard (1997) provides even more powerful evidence of a deterrent effect of fear that a victim may be armed. Their detailed statistical analysis, using several different data sets and statistical techniques, concludes that a statute that simply recognizes a citizen's right to carry a concealed weapon significantly deters violent crimes without increasing accidental deaths. They estimate that if the states that did not have right-to-carry laws in 1992 had adopted such laws, approximately 1,570 murders, 4,177 rapes, and more than 60,000 aggravated assaults would have been prevented. The obvious implication is that when potential criminals recognize that there is a high probability that a potential victim will be armed, they are much less likely to confront the victim. These results clearly support Cook's (1979) findings that gun controls tend to increase crime, since laws allowing noncriminals to carry concealed weapons are essentially the opposite of gun controls.

SECURITY TECHNOLOGY AND EQUIPMENT

Ayres and Levitt (1996) provide a very thorough empirical analysis of the impacts of Lojack, a hidden radio transmitter installed in cars that can be remotely activated if the car is stolen. These devices greatly reduce the expected loss for car owners who use them: 95 percent of the cars equipped with Lojack are recovered, compared to 60 percent for non-Lojack-equipped cars. Therefore, the estimated mean loss per auto theft for cars equipped with Lojack is about 25 percent of the expected mean loss for cars without the device. However, this direct benefit for the individual using the device is only part of the total benefit arising from its availability and use.

Lojack is similar to a concealed weapon in that there really is no visible indication that a vehicle is equipped with the device. A potential car thief does not know whether a potential target vehicle is protected by Lojack or not, just as a potential assailant or robber does not know whether a potential victim in a right-to-carry state has a gun or not. Its consequences are also similar. Ayres and Levitt (1996) find that Lojack has a significant crime-reducing effect: a one-percentage-point increase in installations of the device in a market is associated with a 20 percent decline in auto thefts within large cities and a 5 percent reduction in the rest of the state. Since other crime rates are not correlated with such a drop in auto theft and installation of Lojack, the obvious implication is that many potential auto thieves are aware of the increased probability that they will be arrested, and they are deterred as a consequence. After all, the probability of a successful arrest for stealing a Lojack-equipped car is over twice the probability of a successful arrest for a car that is not so equipped. Ayres and Levitt conclude, "Lojack appears to be one of the most cost-effective crime reduction approaches documented in the literature, providing a greater return than increased police, prisons, job programs, or early education interventions" (1996: 30). They estimate that the marginal social benefits of installing another Lojack, including the increased likelihood of recovery of the car itself if stolen and the overall increase in general deterrence, are fifteen times the marginal costs.

Acres and Levitt (1996) describe the result in terms used in classic market failure analysis, implying that the market is undersupplying the product because it cannot charge for the external benefit in the form of general deterrence. An alternative interpretation is offered in chapter 8, where it is contended that such underinvestment in general deterrence can be seen as a result of the property rights that the government has dictated, and therefore as a government failure. Beyond that, it is easy to show that part of the under supply clearly reflects government constraints. Introduction of the product into a market requires approval by state attorneys general and local police, and the time delay for approvals after application has ranged from fourteen weeks up to *seven and a half years*. Therefore, though Lojack was introduced in Massachusetts in 1986, it was serving only twelve approved markets in December of 1994 (some are statewide, but some are local; the product was available in only thirteen of the fifty-seven U.S. cities with more than one hundred thousand residents). Such delays can have a significant effect since installation is almost always in new cars, and new car sales in a given year account for less than 10 percent of sales of registered cars. Furthermore, only a small proportion of the new cars get the device (which costs about $600 at installation plus annual service charges), particularly when it is first introduced in a market. Over time, installation rates increase as consumers become aware of the product and its benefits, particularly in markets where auto theft rates are high.

Even if individuals might tend to underinvest in Lojack because they do not receive all of the benefits, it does not follow that there will be a "market failure," because there is a potentially effective market mechanism for internalizing the benefits of devices like Lojack. As Acres and Levitt (1996) note, auto insurance rates are already being adjusted to reflect the installation of Lojack. Currently, they suggest, these insurance adjustments are far below the "socially optimal level," but that could easily reflect the fact that the technology is new and only available in a few markets; the insurance companies have not had sufficient information to determine the potential gains to them in the form of overall reductions in auto theft claims. As this information, including studies like Acres and Levitt 1996, becomes available, competitive insurance companies are likely to change rates in order to encourage more installations, *if* they are free to do so. It must also be recognized, however, that insurance markets are heavily regulated in many states. For instance, Massachusetts mandates a 20 percent discount on the comprehensive portion of auto insurance if Lojack is installed, and insurance discounts in other states are also typically capped at 20 percent. Some of the Lojack discounts are not set by regulation, perhaps suggesting that the insurance companies are choosing them, but the fact is that as a consequence of interest group influences on insurance regulations, the upward rate adjustments companies are allowed to make in the face of various high-risk indicators are often severely limited (those who would have to pay the highest rates because of their risk-taking behavior have relatively strong incentives to organize and demand lower rates, claiming discrimination, and the political process responds to such demands [Stigler 1971; Benson 1984b, 1990: 105–15; 1995c; Berk, Brachman, and Lesser 1977; Johnson and Libecap 1994; Neely 1992; Rasmussen and Benson 1994: 127–32]). This forces insurance companies to cross-subsidize risky behavior by charging customers who take actions to make themselves relatively less risky (e.g., those who install Lojack) more than the companies would if they were free to set appropriate risk-adjusted prices. The result is an inefficient allocation of resources, relative to what might be "socially optimal," but it reflects government failure, not market failure.

Conclusions

Many recent studies of private security see the trends in increasing privatization as a process of substitution of relatively effective private security for relatively ineffective public police as citizens resist increased taxes to fund more policing while simultaneously increasing their purchases of private alternatives (Sherman 1983; Cunningham and Taylor 1985; Clotfelter 1977; Benson 1990: 261–62; 1996b; Zedlewski 1992: 52). The benefits of privatization of criminal justice are apparently perceived to be considerable by actual consumers, even if many policy advocates and police bureaucrats deny that they exist. The empirical evidence cited above suggests that consumers are in fact correct and that their substitution efforts are rational. Furthermore, the theoretical analysis explains why the benefits should actually arise. Private markets have the advantages of freedom of choice and competition, better information, and the cost-minimizing/quality-enhancing/innovating/specialization incentives of profit-seeking entrepreneurs, and they avoid the inefficiencies that arise with non–price rationing. Some contend, despite the evidence and theory, that these advantages do not actually arise, claiming that the simplistic theory does not account for serious flaws in markets (and if pressed, that the evidence is insufficient or invalid or produced by biased researchers). Others claim that rationing through private markets tends to cause problems that outweigh any efficiency advantages (e.g., distributional or equity problems, and abuses of power). Therefore, let us turn to a comparative institution analysis of some of the more prominent of these alleged market failings and shortcomings.

8

Alleged Market Failures in a Privatized System of Criminal Justice

Are They Valid?

A number of arguments against privatization of law enforcement are in fact arguments commonly raised against market processes in general. They are arguments made by lobbyists and other policy advocates, including bureaucrats and public-sector union representatives, who oppose privatization of an existing government activity or who want to develop some new government program. Such individuals either do not understand the way competitive markets work; or they refuse to believe that they work the way they do; or they know perfectly well that their arguments are not valid, but they make them anyway because they are effective in the political arena, where information is poor and costly to obtain, making "selective distortion" a very viable tactic (see chapter 7). Such criticisms include assertions (1) that the profit motive leads to poor-quality service because profiteers cut costs, an argument already addressed to a degree in chapter 3, and (2) that the market process results in an inequitably large dispersion of wealth, or in the case of private security, that the rich will be more than adequately protected while the poor, who are "powerless" in the marketplace, will not be sufficiently protected. A third argument commonly made against privatization in criminal justice is, in a sense, a combination of these two. It is contended (3) that if private citizens are given police powers, that is authority to act as police, or even if they are permitted to take on some of the functions of public police, they will abuse their power. This abuse is expected to arise because, as a result of profit-seekers' cost-cutting incentives, the people employed in private security tend to be of "poor quality." In addition many citizens (it is claimed) are powerless to protect themselves against private security abuses since such abusive behavior is not effectively constrained by the various constitutional due-process requirements imposed on public police. These arguments will be examined below, where both theoretical counterarguments and evidence will show all three to be invalid, relative to the public sector. That is, the incentives and constraints that arise in competitive markets create an environment in which such problems are highly unlikely, whereas the incentives and constraints that exist in the public sector create an environment in which they are quite likely to occur.

A different argument is made by many "economic theorists." Law in general and policing in particular are said to be *public goods.* Most people probably think that this term simply means "a good produced by the public," but this is not the case, at least as the term is used by theorists. Perhaps the most widely accepted definition in the academic literature involves two elements: nonexcludability and indivisibility or nonrivalrous consumption (Cowen 1988: 3). Nonrivalrous consumption means that even though one person consumes the benefits of the good, another person (and generally many other persons) can consume the same benefits. Thus, for instance, if police produce effective general deterrence in a community, the fact that one person benefits from that deterrence does not prevent all of the other citizens from consuming the same undiminished benefits. Nonexcludability means that not only can many people consume the benefits, but also that they cannot be prevented from consuming them even if they do not pay their share of the costs. This creates *free-rider* incentives. Individuals recognize that they can consume the benefits without paying, so they will not voluntarily pay. This in turn allegedly means that private producers will not produce the good because they cannot collect revenues to cover costs, or at least, that they will not produce enough of the good because, although everyone may not free-ride, some will.[1] Given such free-riding, the market will fail to produce enough of the good; this provides a justification for coercive taxation to collect from free riders. It does not follow that a public bureau must produce the good, however, so the public-good argument is not a justification for public provision. Instead, it implies that the government must serve as a collection agent; that could be done by taxing in order to pay private providers under contract. Actual public provision requires consideration of other factors (e.g., relative efficiency and quality, potentials for abuse, and so on).

At any rate, it is frequently claimed that law and order is one of the "important examples of production of public goods," and because of free-rider incentives "private provision of these public goods will not occur" (Samuelson and Nordhaus 1985: 48–49). The level of security and justice provided through voluntary associations and markets clearly demonstrates that the strong claim by Samuelson and Nordhaus is wrong. Nonetheless, there may be some free-riding that results in consumption of some benefits for which producers cannot charge. For instance, Tullock makes the following claim:

Let us say that hiring a police force having a reasonable degree of efficiency would cost each individual ten dollars a year. If I refuse to contribute my yearly allotment, I will receive almost as much protection as if I did make the contribution . . . and I would, on the whole, be wiser not to pay. On the other hand, if everybody made this calculation, we would have no police force and thus would all be worse off than if each paid the ten dollars. Therefore, we join together and form a police force that has as one of its duties coercing people into paying the ten dollars. (1970: 83–84)

If this contention is valid, it may be that the private sector will provide inadequate levels of at least some types of policing and therefore that the government must be involved in the process, at least to some degree. The public-good argument is addressed in the concluding section of this chapter (and also in chapters 9 through 12, although not often explicitly). But first let us consider the arguments over privatization that are more common in the press and in political debates.[2]

The Profit Motive, Cost Cutting, and Poor-Quality Services

Private security firms allegedly will cut corners in order to cut costs and increase profits. As evidence of such quality cutting, many cite the widely held belief that security personnel are "undertrained" relative to public police, "old," and "high-school dropouts" ("Private Police Forces" 1983). Carlson (1995a: 68) agrees with this characterization, but then explains the great lengths to which one particular private security system (the Grand Central Station area example mentioned in chapter 7) went in order to avoid employing people like this. His findings are not surprising, however, since the underlying premise is false. These quality-cutting incentives hold only when sellers have short-term profit goals or when the market is not competitive. There are con men and hucksters in some markets who move into an area for a short period, defraud a number of consumers, and move on; but no matter how uninformed consumers might be, it is unlikely that many of them would buy security services from such fly-by-night operations. A sense of permanence and a reputation for quality services would clearly be much more important criteria for consumers choosing the provider of such services than the quality-cutting argument assumes. That is why firms invest in building a reputation by providing quality—such investments pay off in higher long-run profits (see chapter 7). As for competition, the number of private protection and detective agencies in the United States probably exceeds thirteen thousand today, and competition is fierce. When competitive firms have long-range profit goals, their incentive is to beat the competition by offering the same quality of service at lower prices (and therefore lower cost) or a superior quality at a comparable price (i.e., to raise quality without increasing costs). After all, profits are *total revenues minus total costs,* so when reducing costs by reducing quality means losing customers and revenue, profits fall.

But what about the evidence? It also is not valid. There are some relatively old security guards, of course (there are old policemen, too), and there are security personnel with little or no training, but that is not the norm. Cunningham and Taylor's extensive survey (1985: 89) found that private security forces had an average age of between thirty-one and thirty-five and that over half (59 percent) had at least some college education. Similarly, the average age of the Starrett City security force was thirty-nine in 1986, 83.3 percent of the officers had at least a high school education, 70.4 percent of them had prior security experience before taking the Starrett City job (over 25 percent had been employed as either public or military police officers), and all of these security officers had prior security training, either from another security agency or from the New York City Police Academy (Donovan and Walsh 1986: 37–42). Their annual salaries averaged thirty-one thousand dollars in 1995 (Carlson 1995a: 70).

As for those minimum-wage night watchmen and guards who have little training or expertise, the fact is that it would be foolish to employ a person with the training of an urban police officer as a night watchman (e.g., to check IDs and set off an alarm in the event of trouble) or to pay the twenty thousand to forty thousand dollars it would cost to hire that person. On the other hand, it would be foolish to hire someone to design and initiate a corporate security system who has only the training and skills of an urban police officer. In general, public police in a community are similar in background and training after all. A public police department often requires fairly similar training for all of its officers, even sending them through its own training facility. Public police officers are therefore a one-size-fits-all product that may well be appropriately trained to provide quality services for some security functions. But they are clearly overtrained to supply other services, which means that using them is not cost-effective (the price paid for the service is too high). Furthermore, they are undertrained compared to the skills needed to effectively perform still other security functions (i.e., the quality they can provide is poor). In other words, given the wide variety of security needs in society, the public police are not likely to be in a position to provide cost-effective quality services for many people seeking security.

In this regard, it also must be remembered that quality can mean different things to different people. A low-wage watchman may provide a high-quality service relative to the price paid, for a business owner who simply wants someone to watch for strangers in order to deter criminals who might otherwise see the business as an easy target. If a crime occurs despite the watchman's presence, then the investigating public policeman who wants to make an arrest may think that the watchman is a poor-quality law enforcement agent because he cannot provide a detailed description of the perpetrator of the crime or because he is not particularly articulate and may therefore be a poor witness. But after the fact, the watchman is simply a private citizen who is a witness to a crime, and there really does not seem to be any reason to expect the watchman to be a better witness than any other private citizen. The police (or the taxpayers) do not pay the watchman's salary; the businessman does, and the businessman wants a low-cost proactive source of deterrence, not a trained observer who can facilitate reactive arrests. Thus, criticisms by police regarding the lack of quality among watchmen they interact with may be totally irrelevant for the person paying the watchman's salary.

Such criticisms should also be considered in light of the underlying self-interest motives of police. For instance, a substantial portion of the public police officers in the country moonlight by selling their services in the private security market when they are off duty. Thus, at least some public police officers have every incentive to propagate the belief that private security personnel should have the training and skills of a public police officer, in hopes of undermining their competition by reducing the demand for low-priced substitutes for the services they would like to provide. Furthermore, many police officers also recognize that the growing private security market is creating substitutes for the public police, reducing the demand for and therefore the budgets of public police services relative to what they would experience in the absence of such competition. Therefore, they have incentives to use "selective distortion" tactics as discussed in chapter 7, in an effort to limit the demand for such competitive substitutes (see chapter 11 for additional discussion in this regard).

In contrast to public police departments, market entrepreneurs are willing to offer a wide variety of services, depending upon the variety of demands that consumers have. The market does provide minimum-wage watchmen to those consumers who demand them, and the quality of services received is clearly sufficient to satisfy the demand *at the price paid,* or the service would not be purchased. If customers want private security with other qualifications, they can buy the level of training and expertise that is required to provide the quality of services desired. In ethnically diverse Starrett City, for instance, the security force was also ethnically diverse (50 percent white, 35.2 percent black, and 14.8 percent Hispanic, compared to the Starrett City population, which was 64 percent white), and importantly, 26.1 percent of the officers spoke at least one language in addition to English, a feature that "greatly enhances the security unit's ability to break down barriers that are often experienced by non-English-speaking citizens in their dealings with government agencies" (Donovan and Walsh 1986: 40). Furthermore, "virtually ignored [by the critics of private security] are the many thousands of well-qualified proprietary loss control personnel" (Bottom and Kostanoski 1983: 31). In fact, increasing technological sophistication in electronic detection equipment plays an important role in the increased proficiency of and demand for private security, but that equipment calls for skilled personnel. Thus, "there is emerging a new security person, highly trained, more highly educated and better able to satisfy the growing intricacies of the security profession" (Ricks, Tillett, and Van Meter 1981: 13). The current trend in private security clearly is away from the stereotypical old, untrained night watchmen toward more training and an upgrading of personnel, practices, and procedure, as should be expected given the increased demand for private protection against property and violent crimes, the increasingly sophisticated technology available for security, *and* the level of competition that has developed. Entrepreneurs must continually offer better services as technology advances in order to be competitive, and such services also tend to involve lower prices.

Abuses of Power

A closely related criticism of private security is that these organizations or their employees will abuse their powers (Carlson 1995a: 69). In what may be the most well-developed criticism of privatization in law and order (but see Friedman 1984 for explicitly developed counterproofs), Landes and Posner argue that

> the private enforcer is paid per offender convicted, regardless of the actual guilt or innocence of the accused. There are several ways in which the enforcer can increase his "catch" and hence his income, by augmenting the supply of "offenders." (1) He can fabricate an offense. (2) He can prosecute an innocent person for an offense that in fact occurred. (3) He can encourage an individual to commit an offense that he would not have committed without encouragement, and then prosecute him for the offense; this is the practice known as "entrap-

valid is not known, but it would be foolish to suggest that private security firms never employ people who are likely to be abusive. Mistakes happen. Nonetheless, the complaint levels appear to be quite low, and that is not surprising.

Private firms must satisfy customers in order to stay in business. Furthermore, they can be held liable for harm that their employees inflict. Security firms buy liability insurance to cover this contingency, and if it was a serious and frequent problem, such insurance would be extremely costly. Therefore, a security officer who abuses shopping mall patrons will not be a security officer for long. And security firms have strong incentives to screen employees if they can (see chapter 11 regarding government barriers that limit their ability to screen). For these reasons, firms in private competitive markets are not nearly as likely to offer poor-quality services and abuse their powers as is frequently claimed. Government bureaus often provide poor services, however, and bureaucrats can be very abusive. For instance, Judge Richard Neely explains that in order to understand why judges act the way they do, we must consider the interaction of judges with the structure of the courts, for it is the institutional setting that generates much of the behavior we observe:

> Certain personal vices are not remarkable in people employed outside the judiciary (immediately arrogance and indolence spring to mind). And if the people appointed to the bench exhibited various qualities to excess before their appointments, they would not have been selected. It is the nature of the judiciary, with its life tenure, or long elected terms, that it can encourage arrogance and indolence as the occupation of salesperson tends to mask them. (1982: 35)

This is a very important point. The fact is that many individuals, whether publicly or privately employed, might abuse their positions by cutting costs, doing poor quality work, and bullying—*if they can.* The institutional arrangements within which people perform their tasks determine whether or not such abuses can be carried out, and competitive markets supply one of the best (if not *the* best) institutional arrangements for discouraging abusive, inefficient behavior.

It also must be recognized that an individual who is not fully liable for the consequences of his or her actions is likely to be *relatively* unconcerned about those consequences. A civil suit brought against an abusive private security firm can be very costly, perhaps even destroying the business. In a suit against a public law enforcement agency, however, taxpayers pick up the tab, so the cost to the manager of that bureau is relatively small. Furthermore, unlike private employers, governments are often not liable for the actions of their employees, as a recent Supreme Court decision reveals. In 1991 a woman was severely injured by an Oklahoma sheriff's deputy who had been hired in spite of his criminal record. Writing for the majority in overturning a lower court award of $818,000 in damages, Justice Sandra Day O'Connor stated that Congress did not intend to hold local government liable for harms to citizens that arise from isolated bad hiring decisions (Epstein 1997). Even if someone who is carelessly hired or trained to be a police officer uses excessive force and violates a person's constitutional rights, a local government is not likely to be liable for damages.

Public officials are immune from liability under many circumstances. A policeman cannot even be sued for false arrest, for instance, unless the plaintiff can prove his or her innocence *and* that the police officer had no reason to suspect that individual. In addition, no legal claim against the government or its officials can be made by an innocent person who is wrongly imprisoned. It might be recognized that the government has made an error, but government officials have the *right* to make such errors and are not liable for them even when the mistake has devastating impacts on private citizens.

Consider the case of *Warren v. District of Columbia*, 444 A.2d. 1 (D.C. Ct. of Ap. 1981), for example. In this case three rape victims sued the Washington, D.C., government because of negligence on the part of the police. The case brought out the following facts (Evers 1994: 7): Two of three female roommates were upstairs in their apartment when they heard men break in and attack the third. They made repeated calls to the police for help. After about thirty minutes, their roommate's screams had stopped and they assumed that the police must have arrived. They went downstairs where, for the next fourteen hours, they were held captive, raped, robbed, beaten, and forced to commit sexual acts upon one another and to submit to the sexual demands of the criminals. It seems that the police had lost track of the repeated calls for assistance. Yet, the District of Columbia's highest court absolved the police and the city of any liability, stating that the police do not have a legal responsibility to provide personal protection to individuals. This ruling is completely consistent with a number of court rulings and statute law from several states (31). But imagine what a jury would award to a plaintiff in a civil case for negligence on the part of a private security firm that resulted in harms such as this!

A private security firm cannot afford to be careless in the way it serves its customers. Public police can. Thus, public employees who provide law enforcement actually have the type of incentives that some critics have attributed to private security, but they are not regulated by the threat of competition at anything close to the level that exists in private markets, and they do not face the same liability rules that private firms face. Consequently, public producers are far more likely to react to those incentives than are private producers.

It is difficult to determine how much police abuse actually occurs, because most complaints are investigated internally, and police officials naturally do not want to provide information about such complaints or their outcomes because they do not want to tarnish the image of the department (Benson 1988a, 1988b). In fact, police departments generally refuse to release such information. A series of lawsuits brought by reporters seeking "freedom of information" access to files on citizen complaints against police officers have been working their way through the courts in the last few years, however, some of which promise some potential access in the future (John Jay College of Criminal Justice/CUNY 1997d). In Wisconsin a case filed by three Madison newspapers seeking access to files on citizen complaints was successful about two years ago, although police compliance has been less than perfect. Following the court order, the Madison Police Department released sixteen citizen complaints but refused to provide information about the people making the complaints or about how the complaints were disposed of. The newspapers went back to court, and the judge ordered release of that information. But then the newspapers discovered that the department had actually withheld information about complaints made by fellow officers and by other government employees, so they went back to court again, and that case is pending. The first district court of appeals in Milwaukee also ruled (following police refusal of a request by a newspaper in that city) that Milwaukee police do not have a blanket right to keep personnel records secret. In contrast, however, there is a 1996 Rhode Island Supreme Court case indicating that the open-records laws exempt the disclosure of some records, including those pertaining to law enforcement officers, and police organizations are working hard to prevent disclosure, employing "experts" to file depositions on behalf of the police departments, and lobbying legislatures.

Nonetheless, there is anecdotal evidence of considerable police abuse. Courts have considered cases wherein public police accidentally (e.g., the *Warren* case just discussed) or intentionally (the Rodney King case) abuse innocent citizens and criminals alike, and other stories of abuse are quite common. Consider the "drug squad" activities in Volusia County, Florida. This specialized squad seized over $8 million (an average of five thousand dollars per day) from motorists on Interstate 95 during a forty-one-month period between 1989 and 1992. The tactic was to selectively stop people driving south on the freeway for minor traffic violations (following too close, improper lane change, etc.). Allegations now suggest that a "drug profile" was being used and most of those stopped clearly were Hispanic or black. After the stop, the officer would ask permission to search the car (perhaps intimating that refusal was probable cause so a warrant could be issued). Then, any fairly large amount of cash was seized because it was alleged to be proceeds from drug sales. How many of the victims of this seizure operation were drug traffickers? There is no way to know, since no drug charges were levied and no trials occurred. Indeed, no traffic citations were even issued in the large majority of the instances that resulted in seizures. It is clear that many were innocent victims, however (and even if they were not, the Constitution presumably mandates that they be considered innocent until proof beyond a reasonable doubt of guilt is produced). Three-fourths of the 199 seizures were contested, but money was not returned when such challenges were made, even if no proof of wrongdoing and no criminal record existed, and even if the victim presented proof that the money was legitimately earned. Instead, the sheriff's forfeiture attorney handled settlement negotiations.

Only four people ultimately got their money back; one went to trial in civil court but lost and has appealed. In the face of the high litigation costs of a trial, the rest have settled for 50 to 90 percent of their money after promising not to sue the sheriff's department. Of course, they also had to pay their attorneys a third or more of the money actually returned. And unfortunately, this is not an isolated incident. A repeat of the Volusia County episode is now playing out in Louisiana, where out-of-state drivers are the favorite targets because they are much less likely to contest a seizure than in-state drivers. A seizure-motivated drug raid in California led to the death of a home owner who made the mistake of grabbing a gun to defend himself when his door was broken in, apparently by unknown assailants. The raid was apparently "justified" because an uncorroborated paid informant reported that a member of the household had some marijuana, but during the resulting investigation it was discovered that the police raiders had obtained an assessment of the value of the property because they intended to seize it.

The differences between public institutions and competitive private institutions go well beyond the difficulty of holding public officials accountable when they do poor jobs. The fact is that private producers are rewarded for providing what consumers want—effective protection that prevents crime. Public bureaucrats obtain their rewards through the political process, where rewards are frequently tied to some measurable representation of the *size* of the bureaucracies' operations, such as numbers of arrests and numbers of convictions (Sherman 1983; Benson 1990: 130–32; 1995b; Rasmussen and Benson 1994: 131–32; Benson, Kim, and Rasmussen 1994; also see chapter 11). This can lead to considerable abuse of innocent parties. In April of 1991, for instance, a Belize Air International flight from Miami to Belize and back had a routine stopover in Honduras. Honduran authorities boarded and asked for permission to search the plane. The unsuspecting crew gave their consent, and one crew member even assisted in the search. They were astounded when forty-eight kilos of cocaine was discovered. It turns out that the drugs had been planted by American law enforcement personnel as part of a sting intended to expose smuggling into Miami, but they had not informed the crew, the passengers, or the Honduran authorities. Three crew members and three passengers were taken to the local jail, where they were held for eleven days and repeatedly tortured with electric shocks and rubber hoses, all the while protesting their innocence. This appears to be an extreme case, but similar incidents of carelessness on the part of American drug agents, arising in conjunction with their efforts to make arrests and convictions, are not uncommon, and some have been even more catastrophic. An elderly clergyman died of a heart attack after agents broke into the wrong apartment and roughly restrained him as they carried out their search; similar mistakes, but with less dire consequences, have also been reported.

Not surprisingly, police are also frequently accused—with considerable justification—of entrapment and of generating false evidence in order to achieve an arrest or a conviction (e.g., see Cotts 1992; Herbert 1997). And such actions can also have terrible consequences. Consider the April 1997 execution of David Wayne Spence in Texas. Spence was accused and convicted of the brutal murder of three teenagers in 1982, but "Spence was almost certainly innocent" (Herbert 1997). Apparently, the case developed against Spence was put together by a former narcotics officer working for the county sheriff who "conducted an obsessive, unprofessional and widely criticized campaign to nail Spence . . . [and] cobbled his case together from the fabricated and often preposterous testimony of inmates who were granted all manner of favors in return" (Herbert 1997). The police department homicide detective actually charged with investigating the case and the retired lieutenant in charge of the division responsible for investigation of murders both believe Spence was innocent of the murders, and none of the physical evidence from the case can be tied to Spence. Yet, the jury was not made aware of the situation surrounding the investigation, and Spence was convicted. Whether Spence actually was innocent or not, such results are disturbingly common. After one informant confessed to perjury in twelve 1988 cases in exchange for payments or other inducements, the Los Angeles district attorney was forced to review more than ten years of convictions based on informant information. Cotts concludes that the use of informants to generate convictions has been "over-zealous and unscrupulous" (1992: 41). But the problems go well beyond the use of criminals as informants. Scandals regarding police forensic experts deliberately falsifying evidence in large numbers of cases in order to gain convictions have surfaced in at least two states in recent years, and even the FBI's crime lab has come under serious suspicion for sloppy work if not deliberate falsification. The list of abuses could go on, but the point is that public police are much more likely to perpetrate the kinds of abuses that Landes and Posner (and others) attribute to private protection in the quotation above, than private protectors are.

Markets Favor the Rich

Yet another argument against privatization is that only the wealthy can afford private security. In reality, however, historical evidence suggests that private arrangements have been made to ensure that attacks against poor victims are brought to justice. In his analysis of private law and order in medieval Iceland, for instance, Friedman (1979: 406) explains that victims were given a *transferable* property right, the right to restitution, which meant that "a man who did not have sufficient resources to prosecute a case or enforce a verdict could sell it to another who did and who expected to make a profit in both money and reputation by winning the case and collecting the fine. This meant that an attack on even the poorest victim could lead to eventual punishment" (1997: 406).[4] In addition, the wealthy in Iceland were not immune from prosecution. *Anyone* refusing to pay restitution was outlawed, and an outlaw who defended himself by force was liable to pay for every injury inflicted on those trying to bring him to justice. Thus, the private sector can produce and has produced arrangements to prevent favoring one group over another in the justice process.

Rich and poor certainly do not necessarily have access to precisely the same private security resources in a modern market economy, of course. A wealthy person may be able to buy services from others, whereas a poorer person may have to directly contribute to production of the service (e.g., by actively participating in a neighborhood watch). As Lott (1987) stresses, however, one who earns a high wage should be able to employ security services because that person's own time has relatively valuable alternative uses. Thus, an array of private personal, participatory, and hired security is available; individuals can choose according to their willingness and ability to pay, either with money or with time. It may appear that poor people living in high-crime areas are left to fend for themselves, staying indoors, avoiding the appearance of having money, or paying protection money (or joining the criminal element in order to avoid being its victim), and certainly many make such choices. Another choice, though, is to organize for protection. Examples of organized private justice, such as the Orange Hats and Mantua against Drugs discussed in chapter 6, are frequently located in working-class or poor neighborhoods because the public police are unwilling or unable to provide those areas with adequate crime prevention and protection.

Furthermore, to the degree that poor people would be willing to pay something for private security even though they may not be able to individually engage it, there is a potential profit available that may attract an entrepreneur. If some way can be discovered to pool the limited monetary resources of a group of poor people, all of whom are willing to pay something more for security, then the service will be provided. This is not just an idle suggestion. It is motivated by recent developments in Florida. Critical Intervention Services (CIS) is a relatively small firm in Tampa, Florida, that has specialized in providing private security to landlords who own apartment complexes priced to attract low-income tenants. When such a complex is the focus of a lot of criminal activity, the rents tenants are willing to pay are likely lower than they would be in a safe environment. Furthermore, even if they cannot pay much more for housing in a safer environment, the crime problems lead to more rapid turnover among tenants and to higher vacancy rates. The crime also can lead directly to property damage. Therefore, landlords have incentives to purchase security in order to increase the value of their rental properties, whether by raising rents, lowering vacancy rates, or reducing costly property damage.

CIS offers to supply security services of a type specialized to deter crime in such environments. Their guards are all state certified, meaning that they have taken sixty-eight hours of training, but CIS requires at least eighty additional hours of training annually. Their salaries start at about two dollars an hour above the average for security guards, and they also get overtime pay, medical and dental benefits, life insurance, and a 401(k) retirement plan. Clearly, CIS is trying to provide quality services and is rewarding employees relatively well for working in a relatively dangerous environment (only 10 percent of their applicants are hired, and 70 percent of those do not make it through the six-month probationary period, but those who remain after the screening tend to stay—turnover among CIS employees is much lower than for the industry as a whole). The guards "dress to intimidate the bad guys" (Boyce 1996): their uniforms are black, they wear polished combat boots and bulletproof vests, and they carry .357 magnum pistols, mace, and two-way radios.

Regulations of private security in Florida allow the CIS personnel only limited powers to arrest, so their main tactics are intimidation of criminals, observation and information gathering in order to inform landlords about trouble-making tenants who should be evicted, and building good relations with law-abiding residents. Therefore, CIS employees play ball with kids and help them with homework (CIS is also considering developing awards for good school performance), distribute Christmas presents to needy youngsters, hand out replicas of their badges to kids, respond to residents' concerns, and so on. As the firm's founder explains, "once you get to know the kids and their parents, crime goes down" (quoted in Boyce 1996). Since CIS began offering its services in Tampa in 1991 (with a two-thousand-dollar loan from the founder's father), it has received requests for much more service than it can actually supply (probably in part because the firm is so selective in employment); nonetheless, CIS has expanded into Miami, Jacksonville, and Orlando as its revenues have grown from $35,000 to roughly $2 million in 1996. The firm was providing security for fifty apartment complexes that year, and crime has dropped by an average of 50 percent for those complexes. Local police acknowledge that crime also tends to drop in the areas in which CIS is present, and both tenants (except those who want to prey on their neighbors) and landlords are very pleased with the result. After all, as a sheriff's department major from Tampa, commenting on CIS personnel, states, "they're committed to the community. I have never encountered that before" in these neighborhoods (quoted in Boyce 1996). He also notes that the department has never received any complaints about CIS officers. The CIS example is a recent development, but its success is certain to be noticed, and similar services could develop in many other places.

Where private security options are limited or prevented by government actions, however, the poor certainly may have relatively limited choices. The current politicized system of justice attempts to keep individuals from considering some options because other individuals or groups have the power to make decisions for them. Since the poor generally have less political power, it should not be surprising that some of the options that are eliminated have a relatively large impact on them. For instance, purchase of a gun for protection is a relatively low-cost option. Gun controls prevent this option, or at least raise its costs. The effect on someone with considerable wealth is minimal because that person can employ licensed security personnel who can be armed if it is desirable, live in a private development with limited access and guards, buy alarms and alarm services, and so on. If poor individuals' options are much more limited so that a gun is an attractive self-protection option, government-imposed limits on gun ownership can substantially reduce their safety, given the evidence cited in chapter 7. The government limits on private security discussed in chapter 11 may also limit low-income individuals' options. Furthermore, private purchases are restricted because taxes are collected to force the purchase of public police services, meaning that taxpayers are forced to pay for those services and their mistakes whether they want to or not. As a consequence, the poor are actually much worse off under the current system than they would be under privatized law enforcement.

Some might retort that the poor often do not pay taxes and that whatever public law enforcement they get is more than they would get in a private arrangement. But their rent includes the capitalized taxes of landlords, and the prices they pay for other goods and services cover sales taxes and corporate taxes paid by producers, so such an argument is not really valid. More fundamentally, the nonmonetary cost of the public-sector criminal justice system is disproportionately borne by the poor.

Active outdoor drug markets and their accompanying spillovers are tolerated in poor neighborhoods but not in wealthy ones. In general, wealthy and middle-income neighborhoods are much safer than poor neighborhoods, so if "equal protection" by public police is really the goal (rather than discriminatory protection of those with political influence), there should be a huge public police presence in poor neighborhoods relative to other areas. There is not, and as a result virtually every type of crime is more likely to be perpetrated against a poor person than against a wealthy one. The probability that a woman from a family making under three thousand dollars a year will be raped is almost four times that for a woman from a family that makes twenty-five thousand dollars or more; similar statistics apply to other violent crimes (Neely 1982: 140). Furthermore, since such victims are also more likely to be less-than-articulate witnesses (or to have criminal records themselves), "it is more likely that these cases are given away by prosecutors than those of higher income victims" (McDonald 1977: 300). And perhaps most significant, as Neely explains, "[I]n terms of tax revenues, the release of dangerous felons is very cheap. The cost of the sanction is then shifted . . . [to the poor] because that is the class that disproportionately bears the brunt of crime" (1982: 140). In other words, many of the negative consequences of the common problems arising in the allocation of public-sector crime control resources fall disproportionately on the poor. Thus, for the poor, privatization actually means the potential for reducing contact with a system to which they currently contribute but from which they feel alienated and moving to a system wherein they get the protection and justice they pay for.

Conclusion: Public Goods versus Common Pools

Market imperfections in crime prevention and protection are not nearly so severe as many political critics of private law enforcement suggest, particularly relative to government failure when the public sector attempts to provide the same services. The evidence regarding government failures in criminal justice becomes overwhelmingly clear whenever it is carefully examined.[5] But if these arguments are true, how in the world did we get in such a mess, with huge public expenditures on the inefficient criminal justice system and substantial legal barriers to more efficient private alternatives? (Those barriers are discussed in chapter 11). Maybe there is yet another type of market failure that explains this. As suggested above, theoretical economists' predominant justification for public policing and other law enforcement functions is that these functions are public goods characterized by nonexcludability and indivisibility or nonrivalrous consumption, which leads to free-riding and underproduction by the private sector. The theory of public goods is certainly not universally accepted, however, and its application to policing and law enforcement has been challenged.

An important theoretical point was made by Demsetz (1970). He distinguishes between public goods and collective goods, with a public good involving nonrivalrous consumption and a collective good involving nonexcludability as well (i.e., Demsetz's collective good is the traditionally defined public good). He contends that when exclusion is possible, indivisibility and nonrivalrous consumption will not stand in the way of private production of public goods as he defines them, and following the publication of Demsetz's (1970) article, "many economists concluded that non-excludability is generally the only serious problem in the provision of public goods" (Cowen 1988: 9). Goldin (1977) goes one step further, explaining that there are actually no goods that are *inherently* public goods because there are always institutional choices available that can be used to exclude, that is, to create a situation of selective access. Even if Goldin is wrong, Hardin (1982: 178–79) points out that if the supplier also produces a good that is highly complementary to the public good, and nonpayers for the complement can be excluded, then the "auxiliary" good can be used to undermine free-rider incentives. Such tying arrangements characterize the private provision of lighthouses in Coase's famous counterexample (1974) to the public-goods argument and the private provision of policing and roads in Benson 1994a.

Tullock (quoted near the beginning of this chapter) conditions his public-good/free-rider explanation of public policing by writing "*If* I refuse to contribute my yearly allotment, I will receive almost as much protection as if I did make the contribution . . . and . . . *if* everybody made this calculation, we would have no police force" (1970: 83–84, emphasis added). But what if the "if" statements do not hold? An alternatively and perfectly valid theoretical argument is that *if* property rights are perfectly defined and assigned to private individuals, efficiency alone determines the allocation of resources, so no external benefits that can be consumed by nonpayers (or external costs borne by those who cannot influence the decision or consume the benefits) arise (Coase 1960).

In reality, none of the "if" statements made above hold completely. Commodities generally have many attributes, and the bundle of rights associated with them can include some rights that assign attributes and related benefits to particular individuals, while still other attributes are held in common so that everyone has access to their benefits. Law and order, and even more specifically police services, clearly can be so characterized. Many of the benefits of policing can be internalized by individuals. Assets and persons can be protected through watching, walling, and wariness, and these policing functions can be and are in fact produced by the private sector. Similarly, organizations such as private residential developments, shopping malls, and business complexes can internalize the deterrent effects of policing that are specific to their property boundaries, and they do so effectively. Despite the ability to capture private benefits of many aspects of security, however, it appears that some benefits of some attributes of policing services may be captured by nonpayers who have common access to them. Patrol of a public street may deter crime and benefit everyone along the street whether everyone pays or not, for instance, and since under the law all citizens have common access to public streets, they cannot be excluded from consuming the benefits of such deterrence. Similarly, successful arrest, prosecution, and punishment of a criminal after a crime has been committed may have a general deterrent effect (or perhaps the criminal can be rehabilitated by the so-called corrections system so that he or she commits no more crimes against anyone in society, reducing everyone's chances of being victimized; even if not, incapacitation of criminals prevents them from attacking other victims). Private citizens do not have incentives to pay for such general deterrence benefits that others can capture, so presumably they must be coerced into paying for publicly employed resources such as police, prosecutors, and prisons intended to produce general deterrence. This sounds like the result of free-riding in the production of general deterrence as in Tullock's argument, but there is another way to look at it.

Free-riding arises because a consumer of benefits does not have to pay. In crime control, people who already bear costs are reluctant to pay more for services that others will able to benefit from. This is a subtle difference but an important one. Effective public policing and successful public prosecution both require privately provided resources as well as public resources, as explained in chapter 4. The fact that people may not cooperate in pursuit and prosecution may appear to provide evidence of free-riding, but describing victims as free-riders seems inappropriate since they have already borne considerable costs. Nonreporting is rational, given that the benefits created through the arrest-prosecution-punishment of criminals after the fact are primarily common-access benefits of general deterrence. There is an underinvestment by individuals in privately provided resources required to produce such common-access benefits, as suggested by the evidence discussed in chapter 4. This does not have to be the case, however, because private property rights can be assigned to important benefits of pursuit, prosecution, and punishment, creating much stronger incentives for private investment in these activities. Recall the discussion of restitution-based justice in colonial America, for instance (and see chapters 9 through 12 for additional discussion of this issue). When victims have property rights to restitution, a very important private benefit arises from successfully apprehending and prosecuting law violators (Benson 1992b, 1994a, 1996c).[6] Effective collection of restitution requires cooperation (e.g., of witnesses, of neighbors who could aid in pursuit and testify for prosecution, etc.), but it can be carried out by voluntary associations or private firms, and free-riding does not have to be a problem (Friedman 1979; Benson 1992b, 1994a, 1996c; see chapters 9 through 12).

The point is that different institutions (property rights) lead to different incentives, as Goldin (1977) emphasizes. Friedman (1984: 380) even contends that any inefficiencies that may exist in private enforcement of law "can be eliminated by minor changes in institutions." Whether such changes are minor in the current political environment or not may be questionable, but it is clear that many of them are fairly obvious when the possibility of privatization is seriously considered rather than being rejected out of hand. In this light, however, the benefits of law enforcement activities associated with the public sector (pursuit after the crime, prosecution, punishment, perhaps patrol of public common-access streets) must be recognized for what they really are: common-access benefits rather than public goods.[7] After all, the two characteristics of common pools clearly apply. There is an underinvestment by individuals using the common-pool resources (e.g., victims and witnesses), and crowding is a serious problem that reduces the quality of the outputs being produced. For instance, millions of reported crimes are backlogged in police files getting little or no attention, plea bargaining is used for over 90 percent of all convictions in order to relieve court crowding, and because of crowded prisons most criminals are sentenced to probation and those sent to prison are released early. All of these crowded commons imply that deterrence is less effective than it would be in the absence of crowding. Privatizing at least some of the benefits of pursuit, prosecution, and punishment can yield a very different outcome.

It might be argued that the subtle distinction made above is not really a distinction at all. In other words, nonexcludable public goods and common-access resources are simply two terms for the same concept. The public-goods terminology seems to imply, however, that nonexcludability is an intrinsic problem that cannot be resolved without coercing free-riders into paying for the service. The common-pool terminology emphasizes that incentives arise because of the existing definition of property rights and therefore that another property rights assignment can alter such incentives. Thus, the public-good/free-rider argument does not explain why we have gotten into this mess either. In fact, it is really an ex post rationalization of public provision of policing rather than an ex ante explanation for its historical development (Benson 1992b, 1994a).

The actual explanation for the large and inefficient publicly provided criminal justice system is implicit in this discussion of the common-pool nature of public-sector crime control. The fact is that a wide variety of private contractual arrangements already exist when sufficient private benefits to crime control exist (e.g., prevention and protection), and with changes in property rights to other benefits of crime control (e.g., creating a true right to restitution if a crime is committed), many of the remaining underinvestment incentives associated with policing (and prosecution) services can be eliminated. Perhaps the best way to see how we might get out of the mess we are in is to see how we got into it. Therefore, before turning to specific suggestions for legal and institutional changes, let us travel back in history to Anglo-Saxon England in order to see that the development of public fines and property confiscations as royal sources of revenue also involved the elimination of private rights to restitution and that powerful incentives to cooperate in pursuit and private prosecution were thereby eliminated. It was the removal of these incentives that in turn led to the development of criminal law, including the public bureaucracies for policing, prosecution, and punishment.

9

Why Is the Public Sector So Involved with Criminal Law Today?

A Theoretical and Historical Analysis

In order to understand why the modern criminal justice system relies so heavily on the public sector for policing, prosecution, and punishment, we must look back in history.[1] We must begin centuries ago in England, since the basic institutional arrangements of the American legal system were inherited from the British system. The chain of reactions to actions taken by English kings as they began to concentrate and centralize power will be traced to their modern consequences. In particular, development of monarchical government led to the creation of criminal law as a source of royal revenues, and this criminalization took away the private right to restitution and significantly reduced the incentives to voluntarily cooperate in law enforcement. A very different set of institutions evolved as a consequence. Before examining the relevant legal institutions and their evolution, however, we turn briefly to the incentive structure underlying a hypothetical restitution-based legal system with private-sector policing in order to facilitate the description of the largely stateless legal system that existed in Anglo-Saxon England.

Restitution and Incentives to Cooperate in Law Enforcement

The current institutional system of criminal law, wherein individuals have common access to police services and criminals are adjudicated and punished by the state, is not the only institutional system that is possible for the production of law enforcement. To see this, assume that the offenses now considered as crimes against persons or property are treated as torts. That is, if an accused offender is determined to be guilty of violating some victim's rights, the punishment is restitution in the form of a fine or indemnity to be paid to the victim. Furthermore, as is generally the case with tort law, assume that the aggrieved party must pursue prosecution. Pursuit and prosecution are much more effective, however, if several people cooperate in their production. Cooperation of nonvictim witnesses can be essential for prosecution, for example. Furthermore, pursuit by the victim alone is less likely to succeed than pursuit by a large group or by trained specialists hired by a group. The offender is more likely to elude a single pursuer or a nonspecialist, and the offender is also more likely to violently resist an untrained individual than a large group or a specialist.

Individuals never know whether they will be the victim of an offense in the future, but they assign some positive probability to being victimized. An individual also does not know whether an offender will be physically, politically, or economically strong enough to resist the individual's efforts to apprehend and prosecute. Cooperation is desirable, but if each opportunity for pursuit of an offender is treated as a one-time event (e.g., a one-shot game) by victims, witnesses, and others in a position to aid in pursuit and prosecution, then cooperation is unlikely because only the victim gains from the cooperative exchange. As Buchanan and Tullock point out, however, such a "collective choice is a continuous process, with each unique decision representing only one link in a long-time chain of social action" (1962: 37). That is, most individuals in a group are involved in various long-term relationships (for theoretical purists, they are in a repeated game setting with finite but uncertain horizons), and when each individual has some probability of becoming a victim at some point, cooperation becomes possible (Axelrod 1984; Ellickson 1991; Benson 1994c, 1997b). Under these circumstances, individuals may have incentives to voluntarily exchange obligations to support one another in pursuit and prosecution. Of course, if individuals can express a willingness to cooperate and obtain benefits from the cooperative arrangements but then not actually reciprocate when called upon, such an arrangement will either fail to develop or break down if established. In a close-knit community with ongoing mutually beneficial interactions (repeated games), however, a commitment can be made credible if there is a credible potential response by the other party or parties (that is, if the tit-for-tat response may be sufficient punishment for the cheater [Axelrod 1984]). If an individual recognizes that refusal to cooperate with a victim at one point in time will mean that others will not cooperate with that individual in the future, then the incentives to cooperate can be quite strong.

Saxon Law

primitive Germanic tribes from which the Anglo-Saxons descended,
was the basis for reciprocal recognition and enforcement of law (Lyon
83). Germanic tribes were divided into *pagi,* which were in turn com-
f kinship groups called *vici.* A *pagus* apparently consisted of one hun-
en or households (59). The kindred was reciprocally responsible for
ion, and for pursuit and prosecution when an offense occurred (rele-
ffenses are discussed below). Successful pursuit and prosecution resulted
ment of restitution defined by a system of *wergeld* or man-price *(wer).*[3]
the property rights to restitution were clearly defined and widely

er explains that public meetings were held to

ourage the parties to settle their differences or at least submit them to ar-
ration. The parties can air their grievances before their fellows, and with
mmunal advice perhaps reach a compromise. If the parties cannot agree,
community does not act as a judge or jury, but may agree on the test
ich the parties, or one of them, should perform to establish the truth of
e matter. Procedures of this sort do not evolve through coercion, but par-
s who do not cooperate may be put outside the protection of the com-
unity. (1971: 10)

vici were more than just reciprocal policing arrangements, however; the
red also had a "duty to make amends" for the offenses of one of its mem-
against someone from another *vici* (Lyon 1980: 83).[4]

he Anglo-Saxons carried their customary legal system to Britain begin-
g in about 450 A.D. By the tenth century, there was a clearly recognized
glo-Saxon legal institution called the *hundred.* The primary purposes of the
dreds were rounding up stray cattle and dispensing justice (Blair 1956:
), although they were also the locus of a number of other important social
ivities and the providers of a number of jointly produced services, such as
d maintenance (Benson 1994a). When a theft occurred, the men of the sev-
l tithings that made up a hundred were informed and they had a reciprocal
ty to pursue the thief. A tithing apparently consisted of a group of neigh-
rs, many of whom probably were kin. These voluntary groups provided "the
lice system of the country" (Stephen 1883: 66), but their role went well bend policing; they also "made everyone accountable for all his neighbors."
deed, social relations were generally maintained only with people who
ared surety protection through association with a tithing and a hundred
iggio 1977: 274).

Even the bilateral repeated-interaction situ
weaker incentives to cooperate than those that e
dividual enters into several different ongoing re
different individuals. These various relationshij
tion, trade, religion, or any number of other da
(Benson 1994a, 1994c); they do not need to hav
ing. To the extent that reputation travels from or
refusal to cooperate within one interaction can
enter into others, the potential for a credible res
forms of social pressure or ostracism can be broug
ation in law enforcement. Individuals who do not I
others in pursuit and prosecution can even be excl
cial interaction with other members of the group (
tivities). In other words, because each individual ha
position in the community and building a reputatic
investments can be "held hostage" by the communit
to insure that the commitment to cooperate is credi
stances, the dominant strategy almost always is to bel
teractions whether they are part of an ongoing relatic
North, and Weingast 1990; Schmidtz 1991: 102; I
1994c). There clearly is a simultaneous development o
forcement and other forms of interaction, since most in
degree of certainty about legal obligations (Benson 198

This discussion of an alternative institutional arrang
ment is not merely hypothetical. It describes a number
pological, and modern legal systems. The makeup of su
the institutional arrangement that produces the reput
peated-dealing interactions, may reflect family and/or r
1991b, geographic proximity as described by Klein (199
and Benson (1992b, 1994a), functional similarity as
(1989a, 1995a, 1997a, 1998e) and by Milgrom, North, ar
or contractual arrangements as discussed by Friedmar
(1992, 1993), and Umbeck (1981a). And not all of the e:
cal (e.g., see Ellickson 1991). Criminal law in modern Japar
mon with these examples (Evers 1994), as explained in ch;
ticularly important example is Anglo-Saxon England (Ben
1992b, 1994a; Berman 1983), because American criminal I
tions were, in large part, transplanted from England.[2]

The tithing and hundred organizations also performed the local judicial function. Four members of each tithing in a hundred served as *suitors* of the hundred court. "The court consisted of the suitors collectively, but a representative body of twelve seem to have been instituted as a judicial committee of the court" (Stephen 1883: 68). This committee arbitrated disputes between members of the tithings in the hundred. When the committee could not determine guilt or innocence in a particular case, it was appealed to what Anglo-Saxons believed was a higher authority: their God. In such cases, trial was by ordeal, and the survivor of the ordeal was assumed to have been saved by God because he was innocent. Thus, Anglo-Saxons essentially saw trial by ordeal as trial before God, God serving as an arbitrator. Many observers have disparaged such "primitive barbarism," but trial by ordeal must be considered in historical context. The lack of modern methods of gathering evidence meant that disputes might be unresolvable through peaceful means, and a violent confrontation between the parties and their support groups could easily develop. Such violence could be very costly for the entire community. Ordeal certainly may have indicated guilt for some who were innocent and vice versa, but if everyone shared a strong belief in God, the guilty party would expect to be revealed. Thus, strong incentives would exist to confess and pay restitution in order to avoid the ordeal. Furthermore, fear of the ordeal might well have been a powerful deterrent. Thus, although it may be true that the determination of actual disputes resolved through ordeal could easily be unjust (presumably the overall odds were something close to fifty-fifty, roughly the same—according to Gordon Tullock–for modern jury trials), the threat was such that relatively few trials actually occurred because of deterrence and admissions of guilt.

Disputes between individuals who were not in the same hundred were handled by a shire court. All the suitors in the hundred courts within a shire were also suitors in the shire court, but again a twelve-man committee provided the arbitration function, supplemented by the threat of trial by ordeal. There was apparently a third court for disputes between individuals who did not reside within one shire (Stephen 1883: 67).

A primary reason for recognizing reciprocal duty in the Anglo-Saxon system was that offenses thought of as crimes today were treated as torts, with economic restitution as the major form of punishment.[5] A well-established set of rules arose some centuries before there were written records, defining as illegal a large proportion of the offenses that appear in a modern criminal code and specifying the restitutions that must be paid for the various offenses (Stephen 1883: 53).[6] In particular, Anglo-Saxon rules of conduct were very concerned with protection of individuals and their property. Offenses against individuals were minutely provided for, and theft was extensively treated. With regard to property law, "it is possession that has to be defended or recovered, and to possess without dispute, or by judicial award after a dispute real or feigned is the only sure foundation of title and end of strife. A right to possess, distinct from actual possession, must be admitted if there is any rule of judicial redress at all" (Pollock and Maitland 1959: vol. 1, 57).

Disputes were subject to arbitration (including the possibility of arbitration by God) ending in a prescribed payment to the winner (Stephen 1883: 62). Restitution could be made for any offense if it was the first offense committed by the aggressor (Pollock and Maitland 1959: vol. 2, 50; Stephen 1883; 58). Even a "deed of homicide can be paid for by money . . . the offender could buy back the peace he had broken" (Pollock and Maitland 1959: vol. 2, 451). Refusal to submit to a trial would result in a legal right for the accuser (and his support group: kin or tithing) to take the life of the accused (Stephen 1883: 62). Likewise, refusing to accept the restitution payment put the accuser outside the law (Pollock and Maitland 1959: vol. 1, 47–48). Refusal by either party to yield to the hundred court's decision thus led to outlawry and the potential of a *blood-feud.* An outlaw was ostracized by the society in general, and physical retribution became the responsibility of the entire community. Outlaws were also outside the protection of the law, so their property could be taken by victims and/or tithings.

Numerous institutions were developed that clearly had as one of their functions the reduction of the potential for a violent confrontation. For instance, though some scholars view outlawry and blood-feud as the primary legal sanction prior to efforts by kings to force acceptance of economic restitution (e.g., Lyon 1980: 84; Hume 1983–85), in all likelihood, given the incentives and institutions arising in such legal systems, the blood-feud was a valid recourse only after an attempt had been made to go to trial, long before kings became active in law. Support for this view comes from the numerous anthropological studies of law in primitive societies (Benson 1989b, 1991a; Pospisil 1971) and from studies of other medieval legal systems, such as Iceland's (Friedman 1979; Solvason 1992, 1993) and Ireland's (Peden 1977). The earliest written codes were articulations of existing customs, so the *wergeld* system probably preceded their appearance in such codes. As with primitive customary law in general, the threat of violence was used to create incentives for a peaceful settlement (see Umbeck 1981a, 1981b and Benson 1994c in this regard). Other institutions intended to limit violence include the surety function of tithings, the development of arbitration tribunals and trial by ordeal, and the development of restitution as a mandatory substitute for retribution. Furthermore, for certain offenses involving especially large restitution payments, an offender was given up to a year to pay (Pollock and Maitland 1959: vol. 2, 451), and "slavery [more accurately, indentured servitude] was a recognized penalty when the thief was unable to make restitution. This . . . might be regarded as handing over the debtor's person by way of compensation rather than as punishment in the modern sense" (Pollock and Maitland 1959: vol. 2, 449).

By the time laws began to be recorded, ealdormen (later called earls) had become a king's appointed representative in a shire and, by the ninth century, part of the evolving aristocracy. This appointed position probably evolved from a tribal or kinship arrangement involving a well-respected individual (elder) whose opinion carried particular weight in the community. Early codes make it clear that "the ealdorman, and the king at need, may be called in if the plaintiff is not strong enough himself" (Pollock and Maitland 1959: vol. 2, 48). Thus, the threat of ostracism was backed by the most respected and powerful members of the Anglo-Saxon community. A strong offender might resist if he had little to fear from tithings or hundreds made up of free peasants, but when his entire community backed the ostracism, it was probably a very significant threat. In fact, if a victim had to call upon an ealdorman or king, the potential cost to the offender increased considerably. He would have to pay both restitution *(wer)* to the victim or his kin and another fee *(wite)* to the king or ealdorman who used his power to bring about a settlement. Kings and ealdormen had no sovereign powers to coerce compliance, however. An ealdorman or king's "business is not to see justice done in his name in an ordinary course, but to exercise a special reserved power which a man must not invoke unless he has failed to get his cause heard in the jurisdiction of his own hundred" (Pollock and Maitland 1959: vol. 2, 40–41). This institutionalization of a king's role in the justice process, and in particular a *payment (wite)* to the king for performing his role, was one of the first steps in what would soon become a rapid extension of the king's legal activities. The institution of kingship did not develop for the purpose of establishing internal law and order, however.

Around 450 A.D. Saxon or Jutish war chieftains led the first of the Germanic raiding parties into Britain; others quickly followed. Those chieftains were war leaders whom freemen *chose* to follow (Blair 1956: 196), and their tenure was temporary unless warfare was continuous and they could continue to persuade their followers that they could gain from such activities. For those Anglo-Saxons who moved into Britain, warfare apparently became virtually permanent, because efforts were continually being made to expand landholdings. Military ability won for a small group of war chiefs prestige *and* land, and their accumulated wealth allowed some to set themselves apart as kings. The primary reason for voluntarily following a war leader was the anticipation of gains, partly in the form of land. Thus, early kingship required reciprocal recognition of duty, reflecting the solid contractual foundation of leadership during this period. War chiefs provided followers with battle equipment, food, and war booty (including land) in exchange for their support in war. In fact, the word *king* derives from the Old English word *cyning*, and the earliest records use the phrase *ceosan to cyninge*, which means "choose as king" (Blair 1956: 198). Kingship was contractual rather than hereditary, and appointment of a successor was not automatic; nor was a kingship considered a position for life. Kings tried to establish a system of life tenure and hereditary succession early in the Anglo-Saxon period, but these efforts were never completely successful (Lyon 1980: 39, 59; Blair 1956: 197), as indicated below. If a king's successor was endowed with military ability, followers would often choose to follow him, however, so the "kingdom" would last; and if the king could establish a blood descendant with similar ability as his successor, precedent for a hereditary dynasty would be established.

Competition for land and kingship was intense. Between the years 450 and 600, the number of kingdoms declined until reasonably well-established dynasties existed in seven fairly well-defined regions of Britain. Throughout this period the primary function of kings was to carry out warfare. They apparently did not presume to be lawmakers, and law enforcement remained in the hands of local reciprocally established groups. The next 250 years saw further consolidation, with three kingdoms (Northumbria, Mercia, and Wessex) moving to positions of dominance. During most of this period, warfare was between the various Anglo-Saxon kingdoms. In the late eighth century, however, Vikings began to raid the English coast. The English seaboard was too long to defend without a greater concentration of military force than any of the kingdoms controlled, and the Scandinavian invaders ultimately destroyed all the kingdoms except Wessex. Alfred, king of Wessex, fortified southern England and begin a gradual unification process. His son continued the reconquest of Danish holdings. By 937 "the older political system had perished through the disintegration or destruction of several once independent kingdoms upon which that system had rested and its place had been taken by the single kingdom of England" (Blair 1956: 87). It is clear, then, that the reason for the development of the institution of kingship and the formation of the English kingdom was not a need for establishment of law or maintenance of *internal* order.

By the early eleventh century, many of the relatively localized functions of ealdormen (e.g., within a shire) had also been taken over by royal appointees (sheriffs). The earls that remained, now clearly designated as royal appointees, were lords over much larger areas (several shires). Thus, the aristocracy that survived the long period of warfare was quite strong and relatively concentrated. At the same time the well-being of nonnoble freemen in England declined considerably, producing "semi-servile communities in many parts of the country" (Blair 1956: 262).[7] These institutions of government evolved, in large part, because of external conflict (warfare), in order to take land from other groups or to protect existing holdings. Each earl and each sheriff retained a substantial military force, so kings gave privileges and support to the sheriffs and earls in exchange for their military support in warfare. The earls and the sheriffs also served as administrators for various localized functions of the king. For instance, because the king's land was widely dispersed, sheriffs administered the local land holdings, accumulating the produce for the kings to consume. In addition, they were responsible for collecting local tolls and other revenues for the kings (other functions are considered below). As payment for these administrative activities, the earls and kings could retain part of the revenues and produce. Throughout the centuries of warfare, however, kingship and its local administrative arms also acquired important legal ramifications. In particular, Anglo-Saxon kings began to see the legal process as a mechanism for obtaining revenue and for granting favors to powerful followers in recognition of their support.

Kings and Law in England

As Anglo-Saxon England gradually yielded to consolidation and centralization of power, the king's role as a lawgiver was also gradually established. Well before the Norman Conquest, for instance, outlawry began to involve "forfeiture of goods to the king" rather than the potential for confiscation by victims and tithings. Kings also gradually added offenses against others to those that required payment of *wite*. More significant, violations of certain laws began to be referred to as violations of the "king's peace," with fines paid to the king rather than to the actual victim (Pollock and Maitland 1959: vol. 1, 49).

The concept of the "king's peace" traces directly to Anglo-Saxon law: every freeman's house had a "peace"; if it was broken, the violator had to pay. Initially, the king's peace simply referred to the peace of the king's house, but as royal power expanded, the king declared that his peace extended to places where he traveled, then to churches, monasteries, highways, and bridges. Eventually, it would be "possible for royal officers such as sheriffs to proclaim the king's peace wherever suitable" (Lyon 1980: 42). The expansion in places and times protected by the king's peace meant greater potential for royal revenue through legal actions. These imposed changes were not appreciated by the peasant freemen, because the true victim of an offense claimed as a violation of the king's peace received little or no restitution.[8] Thus, "there is a constant tendency to conflict between the old customs of the family and the newer laws of the State" (Pollock and Maitland 1959: vol. 1, 31–32).

The "profits" from enforcing the king's peace accrued only to the king or those to whom he had granted an "unusual favour" (Pollock and Maitland 1959: vol. 2, 453). Royal profits from justice probably were only a small component of total income for Anglo-Saxon kings. They were becoming an increasingly important component, however, for at least two reasons. First, such income was relatively liquid. The potential for taxation was modest. By far the largest component of royal income came from the king's landholdings, but this income was largely in the form of agricultural produce, which could not easily be transported or sold. Therefore, kings and their households traveled from estate to estate throughout the year, consuming each estate's output before moving to the next. Fines collected through the king's evolving legal functions, in contrast, could be stored and "spent" in a much greater variety of ways. Second, marginal changes in royal revenue could be made relatively easily by mandating changes in the law (e.g., extending the king's peace to other offenses, increasing the *wite*); it was more difficult to increase most other sources of revenue. The same advantages accrued to the aristocrats to whom the king granted jurisdictions.

Law enforcement and its profits became something the king could exchange for support in the political arena. As Pollock and Maitland stress, one of the

> bad features of pecuniary mulcts was the introduction of a fiscal element into the administration of criminal law. Criminal jurisdiction became a source of revenue; "pleas and forfeitures" were among profitable rights which the king could grant to prelates and thegns. A double process was at work; on the one hand the king was becoming supreme judge in all causes; on the other hand he was granting out jurisdiction as though it were so much land. (1959: vol. 2, 453–54)

Ealdormen were granted special status as royal representatives within shires; they received "one third of the fines from the profits of justice" and one-third of the revenues from tolls and other duties levied by the king (Lyon 1980: 62–63), in exchange for mustering and leading men into combat, representing the king in shire courts, and executing royal commands, as suggested above. Furthermore, "by the reign of Edward the Confessor judicial profits had come to be lumped in with the farm of the royal manors and all these had to be collected by the sheriff" (65) in exchange for part of the profit.

During the early Anglo-Saxon period, the king's council probably consisted of local elders, and early royal law always included recognition of consent of the group of "wise men of the nation." Later, the king's household, the earls, and the church would be represented in the council, and some authoritarian laws began to reflect the interests of these groups. More important, their interests were closely intertwined with the king's interests because of royal grants and privileges. Thus, codes began to reflect the desires of the king. Little substantive change from customary law was made in the definition of offenses, however. The most significant changes were probably in the specifications of *wite* for kings and lords and the designation of increasing numbers of offenses as violating the king's peace.

Early Norman Rule

The successful Norman invasion of 1066 brought significant changes in the English legal system. Although the Normans were in no position to simply overturn most rules of conduct provided by Anglo-Saxon law, some important institutional changes occurred immediately. Saxon kings had gradually been concentrating and consolidating power through reciprocal arrangements with earls, sheriffs, and the church, but the Normans quickly established "an exceedingly strong kingship" (Pollock and Maitland 1959: vol. 1, 94). William seized virtually all the lands of England and established a system of feudalism. He granted fiefs to Norman barons and the church in exchange for various payments and services (e.g., military support and local administration of the king's properties and revenues). The Norman kings also expanded the use of law and law enforcement to generate revenues needed to finance their military operations, to enhance their own wealth, and to buy the support of powerful groups (Lyon 1980: 163). In this regard, one of the earliest and most significant changes the Normans made in English law was replacing the old restitution-based system *(wer)* with a system of fines and confiscations along with corporal and capital punishment (Pollock and Maitland 1959: vol. 1, 53). The withdrawal of the right to restitution had significant implications for the institutions of law enforcement, because it substantially reduced citizens' incentives to maintain their reciprocal arrangements for protection, pursuit, prosecution, and insurance, and to participate in the local court system (operating at the levels of hundreds and counties at this time).

Apparently many of the hundreds ceased functioning altogether under William. Other private benefits arising from local cooperation also began to disappear, largely as a result of Norman takings, so it should not be inferred that the withdrawal of the right to restitution was the only relevant factor in undermining the tithing and the hundred. For instance, after the Norman seizure of much of the land in England, the Normans granted large tracts to barons and the church in exchange for support, and as noted in Darby 1973: 85, enclosure of some land soon followed. In particular, the land held directly by the lords, called the demesne, could be enclosed. Other types of land were controlled by freeholders, who paid rent to the lord, and by the villeins, who provided labor to the lords. Estimates from the Hundred Rolls of 1279 indicate that the demesne involved about 32 percent of the arable land at that time (86). The Statute of Merton (1236) also permitted the lords to enclose large portions of the "waste," the high woodlands and unimproved pastures that lay in clumps around the arable lands, and grazing was significantly restricted in the vast royal forests and parks "in the interest of the chase" (Darby 1973: 98–99). With increasing enclosure, the potential for straying cattle was diminishing, so the value of the corresponding cooperative function of the tithing was also declining. Then in the 1400s, as wool prices rose relative to grain prices, the lords evicted large numbers of tenants and enclosed large tracts of land, converting to sheep pastures much land that had been used for crops and stubble fields upon which cattle grazed. Hundreds of local villages were abandoned (Darby 1973: 210–11). Many of the remaining kinship groups and tithings were broken apart as people were driven from their traditional homes. Thus, for a number of interrelated reasons, the reciprocity-based tithings and hundreds dissolved or became ineffective, and Norman kings were forced to attempt to establish new incentives and institutions for law enforcement in order to collect their profits from justice.

As the business of justice increasingly became the accumulation of royal revenues rather than restitution, the Normans instituted a local arrangement called the frankpledge. With similar functions to an Anglo-Saxon tithing, the members of a frankpledge were commanded to pursue and capture thieves and perform court duties. Based on requirements of feudal obligation rather than reciprocities, the frankpledge was also ordered to ensure the appearance of members in court. If a frankpledge failed in its mandated legal functions, the group could be fined. Thus, the positive incentives under the restitution system were replaced with negative incentives (threats of punishment). These incentives were apparently much less effective, however; there is substantial evidence of large numbers of incidents in which entire communities were fined (Lyon 1980: 196).[9]

Power was also centralized by the Normans, who established close surveillance by the central administration of local organs of government (Lyon 1980: 148). The Anglo-Saxon shire became the Norman county, and barons appointed as sheriffs by the king quickly became the most important local officials in the Norman system. Sheriffs' legal functions were numerous. For instance, they were the king's permanent judicial representatives, presiding over the county court, and they were responsible for ensuring the attendance of members of these courts and those summoned to appear. That is, they attempted to revitalize the functions of the participatory Anglo-Saxon court system. In addition, they impaneled inquisitional juries for the king, enforced the centralized royal courts' decisions, led the pursuit of law offenders, made arrests, and carried out the orders of royal writs. In exchange for their services, sheriffs were given control of tracts of land, but they "derived their largest income from what they extorted from the people. . . . This was a perquisite of the office and was taken for granted; it was why so many men were willing to pay dearly for the office" (170). Sheriffs gained considerable power and wealth, so at times they were actually in a position to challenge the kings. When the sheriffs revolted, or just became too greedy and siphoned off too much revenue, the king began taking away some of their powers. For instance, sheriffs lost the privilege of considering the king's pleas as kings established residential justices, who were, in turn, soon replaced by itinerant justices sent out from the court to travel from county to county.

The first permanent tribunal representing the king, beyond the king's own council or *curis regis,* consisted of Henry I's financial administrators.

> Twice a year this group, taking the name of "the exchequer," . . . received the royal revenue, audited the sheriffs' accounts and did incidental justice. From time to time some of its members would be sent through the counties to hear the pleas of the crown, and litigants who were great men began to find it worth their while to bring their cases before this powerful tribunal. (Pollock and Maitland 1959: vol. 1, 109–10)

By 1135 the exchequer court had developed its own legal tradition; it imposed swift justice on royal debtors and assessed substantial fines on people who did not meet their financial obligations to the king.

Early Norman Law

Beginning with Henry I, royal legislation become increasingly important (Pollock and Maitland 1959: vol. 1, 111). During Henry's reign an attempt was made to translate the codes of the Saxon king Edward. Three new law books were added to the translations, however. "These law books have . . . one main theme. . . . An offense, probably some violent offense, has been committed. Who then is to get money, and how much money, out of the offender" (106). Revenues from law enforcement and their allocation were obviously the most important consideration in royal law. Most offenses under the early Normans were still defined by Anglo-Saxon custom, but the number of offenses that were considered to be violations of the king's peace rather than torts was significantly increased. An important factor in the growth of this list of offenses was the king's "need of money; to increase his income the king only needed to use his prerogative and throw his jurisdiction over another offense" (Lyon 1980: 189). In addition, in order to expand the profits to be made from justice, Norman kings and their justices began to permit appeal to a royal court. The appellor could accuse the wrongdoer of violating the king's peace along with the actual offense, and the accused could not deny breaking the king's peace. Creation of this fiction meant that practically any offense could be interpreted as a violation of the king's peace (190).

The Norman kings also brought the concept of felony to England by making it a feudal crime for a vassal to betray or commit treachery against a feudal lord. Feudal felonies were punishable by death, and all the felon's land and property were forfeited to the lord. Soon felony began to develop a broader meaning: "Again royal greed seems to be the best explanation for the expansion of the concept of felony. Any crime called a felony meant that if the appellee was found guilty his possessions escheated to the king. The more crimes called felonies, the greater the income, and so the list of felonies continued to grow throughout the twelfth century" (Lyon 1980: 190).

As the discretion of the kings and their courts increased, so did the arbitrariness of punishment: "The outlaw forfeits all, life and limb, lands and goods. . . . The king may take life and choose the kind of death, or he may be content with a limb. . . . Under the new Norman kings, who are not very straightly bound by tradition . . . the kings could favour now one and now another punishment" (Pollock and Maitland 1959: vol 2, 461–62). When justice becomes discretionary, it becomes arbitrary.

Institutions of Law Enforcement

Many foundations of the modern English system of law were laid during the reign of Henry II, a man who was "hungry for political power, both abroad and at home" (Berman 1983: 439). When Henry II came to power, he consolidated and expanded his revenue-collecting system (Pollock and Maitland 1959: vol. 1, 153). The king's courts quickly took on many of the functions that had historically fallen to county and hundred courts. The judicial functions of the exchequer also evolved rapidly, and the barons of the exchequer began considering cases that had nothing to do with the traditional disputes regarding royal finances, except that they generated royal revenues. The upper exchequer became "the first of the great common law courts to split off from the royal court" (Lyon 1980: 282), and by 1165 the ministers of the exchequer were referred to as justices.

By 1168 circuit tax collectors, who were also the itinerant justices, had become another great subdivision of the royal court. The itinerant justices conducted royal inquests regarding financial issues and issues of justice, and they transmitted royal commands to counties and hundreds. The justices also amerced frankpledge groups that failed to or refused to fulfill their policing duties, fined communities that did not form all men into frankpledge groups, and amerced both communities and hundreds that failed to pursue criminals or to report all crimes through inquest juries. Such amercements were increasingly important.

The growing scope of royal justice created a backlog of cases for the king and his council, so in 1178 Henry established a permanent *curia regis* court to hear all suits except those that required his personal attention. This court met throughout the year and almost always at Westminster, becoming the first centralized king's court. The treasurer always sat on the ten- or twelve-man court, indicating the vital role of justice in revenue collection.

Henry II also used inquisitional juries extensively. The juries' primary functions were to inform the king's justices on various matters and make accusations. Sheriffs made the appropriate arrests and established jails to contain those accused by the juries. Trial was not by jury, however: it was still by ordeal. The development of the inquisitional juries and the growth of the king's court were not independent events. The lack of incentives to voluntarily participate in the local hundreds and the desire to centralize judicial power forced the use of itinerant judges and led to the development of local juries of inquisition.

Criminal Law

Henry and his judges defined an ever growing number of actions as violating the king's peace (Pollock and Maitland 1959: vol. 1, 141). These offenses came to be known as crimes, and the contrast between criminal and civil causes developed: *criminal causes referred to offenses that generated revenues for the king or the sheriffs rather than payment to a victim.* Strong incentives for a freeman to have an offense considered as civil meant that "the dilemma 'criminal or civil' is offered to every plea" (Pollock and Maitland 1959: vol. 1, 455; also see Laster 1970: 75). Furthermore, "the king got his judicial profit whether the accused was found guilty or innocent" (Lyon 1980: 295), because an innocent verdict meant that the plaintiff was heavily amerced for false accusation. Of course, this further reduced the incentives of crime victims and frankpledge groups to report crimes.

Jury Trials

Most civil cases were jury trials by the time of the reign of Edward I.[10] These juries, which consisted of men of the community who presumably had witnessed the offense or otherwise had knowledge of the facts, were impaneled by the sheriff to hear the pleading and render a verdict. Trial by ordeal effectively ended for criminal cases in 1215, and no one seemed to know what to do with those accused of crimes and overflowing the crowded jails (Lyon 1980: 450). Writs had developed for obtaining jury trials in a few criminal cases, but not for most criminal trials. For instance, an accused could obtain a writ to have a jury determine whether the accuser had made charges because of malice. These juries were called petty juries to distinguish them from the grand or inquisitional juries. The stage was thus set for criminal jury trials.

The petty jury comprised the same men who sat as an inquisitional jury. As a result, the prevailing opinion of the day was that trial by jury virtually guaranteed a guilty verdict, and there was considerable resistance by the accused to acceptance of a jury trial. Justices therefore began to search for ways to force defendants to accept a jury trial. Some defendants were locked in prison for a year and a day with little food and water, but still many refused to accept a jury trial. In 1275 the first statute of Westminster declared that those accused of a felony who refused to accept a jury inquest would be "put in strong and hard imprisonment." Accused felons were loaded with heavy chains and stones, placed in the worst part of the prison, and given a little water one day and a little bread the next until they either agreed to trial by jury or died. Many chose to die. After all, if found guilty in a trial, the accused would be executed and forfeit all property to the crown, but death under "hard and severe pressure" with no conviction meant his property went to his family.

The composition of the petty jury gradually began to change toward the end of the thirteenth century. The grand jury was augmented by men randomly chosen from neighboring communities. Occasionally, such juries would even reach not-guilty verdicts. The witness-bearing character still dominated, however, and throughout the thirteenth century petty juries were groups sworn to tell what they knew about a case. The presentment jury and the petty jury would not be completely separated until the mid–fourteenth century, and it would be another five hundred years before juries could be characterized as impartial (Lyon 1980: 452).

Consequences of the Elimination of Restitution

By the end of the reign of Edward I, the basic institutions of criminal law had been established, and in many instances older custom had been altered or replaced by king-made rules to facilitate the transfer of wealth to the king and other relatively powerful groups. Victims' resistance to the development of criminal law, along with the resulting loss of restitution and its accompanying incentives, meant that English citizens had to be "forced into compliance by a slowly evolving carrot and stick policy" (Laster 1970: 76). Efforts to force formation of frankpledge groups was noted above, but in addition, royal law declared that the victim was a criminal if he obtained restitution prior to bringing the offender before a king's justice where the king could get his profits.[11] This was not a strong enough inducement, so royal law created the crime of theftbote, making it a misdemeanor for a victim to accept the return of stolen property or to make other arrangements with a felon in exchange for an agreement not to prosecute. The earliest development of misdemeanor offenses involved only "crimes" of this type, and Pollock and Maitland suggest that

> [a] very large part of the justices' work will indeed consist of putting in mercy men and communities guilty of neglect of police duties. This, if we have regard to actual results, is the main business of the eyre. . . . [T]he justices collect in all a very large sum from hundreds, boroughs, townships and tithings which have misconducted themselves by not presenting, or not arresting criminals. . . . [P]robably no single "community" in the county will escape without amercement. (1959: vol. 2, 521–52)

More laws were added. For instance, civil remedies to a criminal offense could not be achieved until after criminal prosecution was complete; the owner of stolen goods could not get his goods back until after he had given evidence in a criminal prosecution; and a fine was imposed on advertisers or printers who advertised a reward for the return of stolen property, no questions asked. Coercive efforts to induce victims and communities to pursue and prosecute criminals were not successful, however, and state institutions gradually took over production of these services.

Justices of the Peace

An early development in the evolution of public policing and prosecution was the explicit creation of justices of the peace in 1326. At that time JPs were simply "assigned to keep the peace," but in 1360 they were empowered "to take and arrest all those they may find by indictment or suspicion and put them in prison" (Stephen 1883: 190). More than thirty statutes were issued from the late fourteenth to the middle of the sixteenth century, establishing various functions for JPs in the criminal process (Langbein 1974: 66). For example, although victims or their support group continued to be required to pursue criminals and prosecute cases, after a 1555 statute, JPs were obliged to take active investigative roles in felony cases; to organize cases for prosecution, including examination documents; to assist the assize judge in coordinating the prosecution at trial; to bind over for appearance all relevant witnesses, including the accusers and the accused; and to act as a backup prosecutor when a private citizen was not available (Langbein 1973: 334). While JPs were not paid for performing their required duties, a public element had clearly been introduced into the prosecution.

That was inevitable. Not only was restitution gone as a positive incentive, but victim participation in criminal justice was becoming expensive. When a victim filed a complaint before a JP, he might have to pay for subpoenas and warrants if his witnesses and the suspect were not present. Other fees were incurred for the recognizances in which he and witnesses were bound over for trial, for the clerk of the peace or of the assize for drawing up the indictment, for the officer of the court who swore the witnesses, for the doorkeeper of the courtroom, for the crier, and for the bailiff who took the prosecutor from the court to the grand jury room (Beattie 1986: 41). Beyond those fees, the level of the cost of attending court was uncertain, because the length of the wait for an appearance before a grand jury and the timing of the trial were not known. A victim often had to incur costs of food and lodging for both himself and his witnesses. With the ever declining incentives for victim participation in crime control, crime was naturally on the rise. Public policing and prosecution had to be developed.

This was especially true of urban areas, where growing gang crime was soon to become particularly troublesome. International military involvement served as a major impetus for the development of public prosecution and police during the eighteenth and nineteenth centuries (as well as prisons and other public institutions of criminal justice). The economy could not quickly absorb the large influx of veterans following a war (Beattie 1986: 228). Instead, "the conclusions of wars in the eighteenth century brought 'a great harvest of crime.' . . . The peace brought back to England large numbers of disreputable men who had spent several years being further brutalized by service in the armed forces, without any provision being made for their reentry into the work force" (226). Returning veterans had considerable training in *organized violence,* however, so "[i]t is hardly to be wondered at that some might employ these same skills at home if it seemed necessary. It was the power of such men in gangs . . . that frightened so many commentators" (227). Large-scale gang crime proved to be difficult for the existing criminal justice system to handle, given the weak incentives to participate in pursuit and prosecution.

As early as 1729, the central government began to support local law enforcement in Middlesex, where the seat of government and the residences of most government officials and parliamentarians were located. Thus, government officials transferred the cost of law enforcement in the area where they lived and worked onto general taxpayers, while the rest of the citizenry was forced (under statute) to provide their own policing and prosecutorial services. In 1729 the government chose to financially support one Middlesex JP to provide criminal investigative and prosecutorial services; he became known as the "court JP." Similar arrangements developed in London soon thereafter (Langbein 1983: 76). Little record of the first court JP remains, but dramatic developments occurred under the second and third, Henry and John Fielding (63). Forces set in motion by the original development of the justice of the peace accelerated during the Fieldings' tenures, and several interrelated institutional developments followed, feeding on and aiding one another.

The Beginnings of Rules of Evidence

As victim participation in law enforcement declined, JP duties *and* discretion increased. For instance, the "crown witness" program arose as a result of the JP's growing discretion regarding the decision to prosecute after his pretrial investigation. One gang member was admitted as a crown witness and excused from prosecution in exchange for testimony against his fellow gang members. This became the primary strategy for combating gang crime. Criminal court judges recognized a problem with crown witnesses almost immediately: "[T]he danger is that when a man is fixed, and knows that his own guilt is detected, he purchases impunity by falsely accusing others" (*Regina v. Farler*, 8C and pp. 106, 108, 173 Eng. Rev. 418, 419 [Worcester Assizes 1837]). As a result, "the crown witness system led to one of the earliest manifestations of what came to be the laws of criminal evidence, the corroboration rule" (Langbein 1983: 96). By 1751 a mandatory corroboration rule was in place as a directed verdict standard, and judges dismissed cases if the prosecution was solely founded on uncorroborated crown witness testimony (98). In *Rex v. Atwood & Robbins* (1788), crown witness evidence was declared admissible "under such directions and observations from the Court as the circumstances of the case may require, to say whether they think it sufficiently credible to guide their decision in the case" (1 Leach at 465–66, 168 Eng. Rep. at 334–35 [1788]). This is the beginning of what has developed into the often detailed instructions to the jury by common-law judges regarding the rules of evidence. It traces directly to increases in JP discretion resulting from victims' lack of incentives to participate in law enforcement and prosecution.

A standard practice under the crown witness program was to set up a competition between suspected criminal gang members. The one offering the most evidence against the largest number of potential criminals received exemption from prosecution; the losers generally had to admit guilt in an effort to compete, however, and the courts became concerned over the use of such confessions. A 1783 ruling gave "no credit" to a confession "forced from the mind by the flattery of hope, or by the torture of fear" (*Rex v. Warickshall* 1 Leach 263, 168 Eng. Rep. at 235 [1783]), providing precedent for the confession rule, which "presaged the future of the Anglo-American law of evidence. It was an "exclusionary rule" . . . excluding from the trial jury concededly probative information for fear that the jury lacked the ability to evaluate the reliability of the information properly. . . . [T]his way of handling criminal adjudication . . . was a recent invention . . . and one whose origins have yet to be explained" (Langbein 1983: 104). But the explanation lies in forces set in motion hundreds of years earlier in the transformation from a system of privately enforced customary tort law to publicly produced criminal law. Each change created problems that required additional change.

Criminal Lawyers

Prior to the mid-1700s, the accused spoke in his own defense in a criminal trial, because there were no defense lawyers. This did not put the accused at a great disadvantage, however, because prosecution was also performed by non-lawyer victims. Indeed, there was a substantial level of acquittals in the seventeenth century (Langbein 1978: 267; Beattie 1986: 418). But as a result of weakening victim incentives to prosecute, public-sector involvement in criminal prosecution had increased with the increasing role of JPs. Then lawyers were employed by the government as prosecutors in a long series of "State Trials" involving political crimes such as treason, as well as in some important criminal cases.[12] This set a precedent for private citizens, and by the mid-1730s, some wealthy victims employed prosecution attorneys in order to avoid the time costs of direct participation.

Prosecution counsel were not used in great numbers, and they did not significantly change the character of criminal trials, but there was a significant consequence of their participation (Beattie 1986: 354): judges began to allow defense counsel if prosecution counsel was employed, and defense counsel had a tremendous impact on the criminal trial. First, access to the accused was sharply limited. Second, the counsel had to know what the case for the prosecution was in order to defend his client. Consequently, "[i]n place of the rambling altercation that had persisted into the practice of the early eighteenth century, the criminal trial underwent that articulation into prosecution and defense 'cases' that so characterizes adversary procedure." Third, the demarcation of prosecution and defense cases meant that the burden of "proof could be recognized and defense motions for directed verdict at the conclusion of the prosecution case could come into play" (Langbein 1983: 131). Fourth, the possibility of remaining silent to avoid self-incrimination became an option and ultimately a privilege. The idea that a defense was not necessary unless the prosecution had fully demonstrated guilt was forming (Beattie 1986: 375). Finally, excluding evidence became a significant issue: allowing defense counsel meant that objections to the admissibility of evidence were much more frequently taken, and the attention of the judges was increasingly directed to the subject of evidence (Langbein 1983: 131).

The two institutional changes of rules of evidence and defense counsel quickly began to feed on one another. Defense counsel called on the existing rules of evidence and questioned the admissibility of evidence not covered in the first rules. Rules of evidence began to evolve, becoming increasingly complex. "These adaptations were meant as patches, applied for the purpose of repairing the inherited system. . . . No one could have foreseen that adversary procedure harbored an inner dynamic toward complexity so relentless that it would ultimately render criminal jury trial unworkable as a routine dispositive procedure" (Langbein 1983: 134). Alternatives became necessary.

Plea Bargaining

A gradual increase in guilty pleas appears in the assize records as early as 1586. Many of those pleas involved altered indictments to allow for less severe punishment than would have been required under the original charges (Cockburn 1985: 65). Cockburn proposes two reasons for what may have been the beginning of informal plea bargain arrangements. First, the government was trying to avoid loss of forfeitures as a consequence of acquittals, so judges preferred to obtain a conviction on lesser charges. Second, "the assize system, with its fixed schedule and inability to guarantee the attendance of trial jurors and local magistrates, was peculiarly incapable of absorbing increases in judicial business. When such increases occurred suddenly, as they apparently did on at least three occasions in Elizabeth's reign, traditional trial procedures came under intolerable pressure" (69). Apparently, the same cyclical forces, arising from involvements in wars, that put pressure on all the other aspects of the criminal justice process led to some plea bargaining. Nonetheless, it appears that the summary character of criminal trials without lawyers meant that plea bargaining generally was not necessary. For example, in London before the end of the eighteenth century, "so rapid was trial procedure that the court was under no pressure to induce jury waivers. We cannot find a trace of plea bargaining in the Old Bailey in these years" (Langbein 1978: 278). Plea bargaining became increasingly important as the pace of trials slowed with the advent of lawyers and rules of evidence, however. Other allocative mechanisms conceivably could have evolved, as explained in chapter 12, so the question becomes, Why has *widespread* use of plea bargaining developed rather than some other solution to the problem of crowded court dockets?

One reason is that it evolved easily from what came before. As JPs began to do pretrial preparation of prosecution, they obtained discretionary power to decide whether to prosecute or not. It was a relatively small step to exempt a criminal from prosecution for some crime in exchange for a guilty plea to another crime (Langbein 1979: 267). Another factor leading to plea bargaining was the insistence on trial by jury rather than by judge. Recall that juries initially were resisted as they were used to expand the power of the kings, but distrust of judges also was substantial. In addition, as Langbein explains: "[t]he seventeenth-century political trials [the so-called State Trials] that were the source of so much of the esteem in which the jury was held were responsible for a good deal of continuing distrust for the English judiciary. The behavior of Justices Scroggs and Jeffreys was not easily forgotten even after the independence of the judiciary was established" (1979: 269). In other words, two legal institutions developed by kings became the alternatives as sources of determination of guilt. Both had been despised and resisted for centuries, but mistrust for the one that had the most involvement by private citizens, *in the context of the criminal law as it developed to assist the kings,* that is, juries, was clearly not as great as mistrust for the other, the royal judges. Thus, juries became widely viewed as the only potential safeguard against the further manipulation of the law enforcement apparatus for the political or financial benefit of the kings and other powerful political entities.

Another factor helps explain the ease with which plea bargaining was adopted. "As the emphasis shifted from restitution to the victim . . . to punishment for alleged crimes committed 'against the state,' the punishment exacted by the state became more and more severe" (Rothbard 1977: 262). Facts in capital cases that had involved restitution in pre-Norman times, such as unplanned homicide and nonviolent thefts, were frequently manipulated by inquisitional juries to prevent capital punishment, thus blunting royal criminal law (Green 1985). Jury mitigation continued to reduce the severity of punishment in certain cases, relative to the level of punishment mandated by royal law, and it became particularly important during the seventeenth-century political trials (xviii). Plea bargaining was another way to mitigate legislated punishment that juries, JPs, and/or judges viewed to be too harsh to fit the crime.[13]

Punishment by Imprisonment

The Anglo-Saxons did not consider prison to be an appropriate punishment. It would force the offender to be idle, making it difficult for him to pay his restitution, and it would be costly to the community. However, prisons, or *gaols,* were used on a small scale as early as the tenth century to detain individuals accused of an offense but awaiting trial. By Henry II's time, detention prisons were becoming quite common as trials increasingly had to wait for the arrival of an itinerant judge. Henry III also used prisons to prepare an offender to pay a fine, and imprisonment as a form of *punishment* arose chiefly in conjunction with the refusal to pay an amercement. Prisons were also used to force those accused of crimes to plead in order to proceed to trial, as noted above, as individuals were put in prison and piled with chains and stones until they either agreed to plead or died. Imprisonment was not a significant form of punishment, however, nor did it involve a significant public expenditure, as it does today. In fact, jails were not publicly financed. Sheriffs or others who obtained the right to run a jail, frequently by paying a fee to the crown, earned their income by levying charges on prisoners and selling them special accommodations (Beattie 1986: 290; Stephen 1883: 484). The evolution of publicly financed imprisonment as an important form of punishment is closely intertwined with the issues discussed above, though. In particular, jury nullification in capital crimes left no significant alternative punishment.

The only real option to a death sentence was release (perhaps with branding), and jury (and judge) mitigation meant that criminals were often released.[14] A 1597 act created an alternative. Pardons could now be granted for capital offenses, subject to acceptance of transportation out of the country, and merchants willingly transported healthy criminals to sell them into indentured servitude. Removal of some criminals to various British colonies in Africa and later in America soon followed.

A postwar crisis in crime arose in 1713, 1714, and 1715, at the same time that a change in the character of government occurred. The new government was anxious to gain support of powerful political elements, many of which were concerned about crime, and it was "strong enough, both politically and financially, to ensure that any new powers they were granted could be put into effect. One result was the Transportation Act of 1718" (Beattie 1986: 503). England had undergone a significant "financial revolution" during the previous twenty years, which had substantially expanded the state's revenue sources and its ability to tap them. Thus, the new government was willing to commit funds to crime control in order to meet the demands of powerful political interests. In fact, the eighteenth century witnessed a gradual increase in government financing of many aspects of criminal law, as it declined in importance as a revenue source relative to other forms of revenue and as crime was increasingly seen as a problem by powerful political groups (recall the development of court JPs during this period, for instance, and see the discussion of policing below).

The transportation of criminals reached its peak in the 1750s and 1760s, and faith in its deterrent effect began to wane in the face of a series of crime crises following wars. Houses of correction had been used to "reform" vagrants and some criminals by subjecting them to hard labor, and influential voices advocated that such arrangements be used more extensively for criminals.[15] On top of the growing political pressure, the American Revolution suddenly completely closed the American colonies to transportation. Parliament approved confinement at hard labor in 1776, as a temporary substitute for transportation. The London merchant community was a major supporter of the bill; thus, convicts were to be used to dredge sand and gravel from the Thames to improve navigation on the river. The prisoners were to be housed on ships in the river, called hulks. Many of the practices established to punish and manage the convicts on board the ships anticipated fundamental aspects of the penitentiaries that would follow (Beattie 1986: 567). Prisoners wore uniforms, for example, whipping was allowed for misbehavior, and good behavior could earn early release.

Hulks were soon seen as institutions that did more to corrupt men than to reform them, and demands were made for prison reform. The Penitentiary Act of 1779 was passed, supposedly because conditions in hulks had become "hideous" and the mortality rate was quite high. Perhaps a more important factor, though, was the security problem; several battles between prisoners and their keepers had erupted, and several men had escaped (Beattie 1986: 573). The legislation dictated that prisons be constructed wherein prisoners could be held in solitary confinement, thus reducing the interaction between prisoners and reducing the chance of organized riots, but funding was not allocated and the prisons were not built. Therefore, the 1779 act did not eliminate the hulks or change conditions on them, and they remained the only significant alternative to transportation. The hulks and houses of correction were expensive to operate, costs were rising, and the hulks could not absorb the "skyrocketing" convictions of the period (Beattie 1986: 593). Finally, in 1786, political pressure forced the government to act. Despite heavy costs, the cabinet chose to transport prisoners to Botany Bay in New South Wales, Australia (Beattie 1986: 599), presumably because it was less costly than building prisons, and transportation again became the primary punishment alternative.

Government had demonstrated a willingness to bear large costs to "punish" criminals by developing the hulks and then covering the costs of transporting criminals to Australia. The houses of correction and the hulks also established that prisons could be used as politically acceptable means of punishment. All that was required now was "larger economic resources and more concentrated and activist political power and . . . [even] greater participation of the state in the administration of justice" (Beattie 1986: 617). By the early 1800s, imprisonment was the major form of punishment for felons in England, and parliamentary actions in 1823, 1865, and 1877 effectively transformed England's system of punishment into a public prison system financed by tax revenues.

Public Police

Pursuit of criminals and protection from them remained a mandated duty of all private citizens, perhaps with the assistance (or the coercive urging) of semiofficial sheriffs and JPs, at least until the nineteenth century. Incentives to participate were weak, however. In order to strengthen the incentives for private citizens to pursue criminals, Parliament enacted the first important public reward statute in 1692; it offered rewards of forty pounds for apprehension and *prosecution* of highwaymen. This was a large amount of money, and over the next fifty years a number of other statutes were passed setting various rewards for aiding in the conviction of burglars, horse thieves, cattle thieves, sheep thieves, shoplifters, coiners, and people who returned from felony transportation early. All of these were felony crimes, for which no victim could anticipate collecting restitution; the need for the reward system is but one more reflection of the indisputable fact that criminalization and the demise of the restitution system had undermined the incentives for private citizen involvement in the public criminal justice system. The public reward system strengthened incentives for growth of a professional "thief-taker" or bounty hunter industry to replace the private policing and prosecutorial system.

This was an easy development because private thief-takers had actually existed for some time, pursuing and capturing offenders and recovering property in order to obtain rewards offered by individuals and private organizations. The increased use of these specialists reflects the fact that as trade, commerce, and eventually industry developed, income rose and individuals' opportunity costs of actual participation in criminal justice rose: "Busy middle-class folks increasingly searched for substitutes for their active participation in the criminal justice process" (Morn 1982: 2). Of course, as these same people gained in wealth and political power, they also demanded that the state do more to protect them from criminals, and the public reward system was one of the early responses to such demands. Significantly, *public* rewards also created incentives to falsely accuse people of felonies, since rewards were not paid unless a felony conviction was achieved. The private reward system had not suffered from this problem because those rewards were paid upon return of property, not upon conviction.

The first historical record that hints of a problem with the public reward system is the 1732 conviction in London of a man who attempted to prosecute an innocent person as a highwayman in order to collect the reward; there is evidence that this same man had successfully prosecuted and received rewards in other counties (Langbein 1983: 108). Furthermore, the practice of extortion based on the threat of falsely turning someone in for a reward was apparently not uncommon, but the problems did not really come to public attention until August 1754, when "there broke one of the greatest scandals ever to taint the administration of criminal justice in England, the Macdaniel affair. It came to light that a gang had been prosecuting innocent men to their deaths in order to collect reward money." This was one more indication of the problems with the evolving government participation in the prosecutorial process:

> The Macdaniel scandal put the [public] reward system under a cloud of doubt from which it never recovered. Nevertheless, it continued to function into the nineteenth century before the paid professional police force finally displaced it. Here again, as with the crown witness system, the people operating this ramshackle prosecutional system felt compelled to rely upon an evidence-gathering technique of manifest untrustworthiness. That left it to the law courts to try to repair at the trial stage failures of institutional design in the pretrial process. The consequences would long outlive the institutions whose shortcomings were at fault. Professional police and prosecutors we would ultimately get but we would never recover the criminal trial we were about to lose. (Langbein 1983: 114)

Rules of evidence continued to grow; but in addition, events such as the Macdaniel scandal added some impetus to the demand for public police.

The reliance on private policing had already changed modestly in 1737 when George II began paying some London and particularly Middlesex watchmen with tax moneys (privately employed watchmen had existed from about 1500 on, paid by private individuals or private organizations [Ricks, Tillett, and Van Meter 1981: 2–3]). In addition, Henry Fielding's system required people who could seek out and apprehend suspects, assist in the retaking of goods, patrol, and infiltrate gangs. In the early 1750s, he began organizing a force of quasi-professional constables (Langbein 1983: 67). Because Fielding was a magistrate of the court, this group had some "public" status, but their income came from rewards for criminal apprehensions. By 1792 seven other magistrate offices in the London area had organized similar operations. The Macdaniel affair distressed John Fielding because he was afraid that it might taint the reputation of his band of constables, called the Bow Street Runners, who depended on rewards as a primary source of income. Thus, this scandal added fuel to the argument that a publicly salaried police force was needed so that such incentives could be eliminated. Fielding even suggested that certain supplementing rewards occasionally offered by the crown be stopped. The patchwork system intended to supplement the failing victim and frankpledge policing and prosecutorial system was clearly flawed, and "Fielding continuously agitated for governmental financial assistance so his platoon could be regularly salaried . . . [but] Englishmen opposed on principle the idea of public police during Fielding's lifetime. They feared the relation between police and what is known now as the police state" (Wooldridge 1970: 119–20).

In 1822 Robert Peel was appointed home secretary. Peel believed that "you cannot have good policing when responsibility is divided" (Post and Kingsbury 1970: 13) and that the only way to consolidate responsibility was through a government monopoly. But it took Peel some time to actually set up a public police department. Even after Parliament gave Peel the authority and financing to form a London metropolitan police department in 1829, there was substantial opposition from the populace. Englishmen knew that the French public police, established in 1667, had always provided the king with detailed information about citizens and that even after the revolution police had opened mail, controlled the press, and made arrests and imprisonments without trial. Citizen concerns were apparently justified. Between 1829 and 1831, three thousand of the eight thousand public police officers (referred to as "Peel's bloody gang" or "blue devils") who had been hired were fired for "unfitness, incompetence, or drunkenness" (Ricks, Tillett, and Van Meter 1981: 6). Substantial opposition prevented the full-scale development of public police for some time, but support gradually increased in the face of war-induced cyclical upsurges in crime. And once powerful individuals and groups began to see that they could shift the cost of their own protection to taxpayers, support for public police grew more quickly (Beattie 1986: 67). For instance, the London merchants had been financing a private police force to patrol the Thames docks, and the new publicly funded police force absorbed this private force, taking over the merchants' costs and providing them with the same benefits.

Public Prosecution

Englishmen also resisted public prosecution for a long time because "a private prosecutorial system was necessary to check the power of the Crown. If not so limited, the power of criminal prosecution could be used for politically oppressive purposes" (Cardenas 1986: 361). Considerable power in prosecutorial management had accrued to JPs, however, particularly in the London/Middlesex area during and after the Fielding era. But JPs apparently preferred not to personally perform the trial prosecution function. That role remained largely in victims' hands, and JPs tended to delegate their evolving trial prosecutorial or testimonial duties to constables. Of course, private victims received no restitution, and they had to bear substantial costs in fees, time, and trouble, so it was not surprising when many citizens became willing to yield the prosecution role to someone else. Fear of public prosecution was primarily directed at the central government, so a localized bureaucracy was the natural government organization to take on such duties.[16] Thus, "police departments instituted the policies of receiving the complaints of crime victims, investigating the charges, and if prosecution was believed appropriate, of bringing the charges against the offender and managing the prosecution within their own office" (363). Police officers were soon conducting prosecutions. To this day "English common law maintains that . . . when a police officer initiates a criminal proceeding he is legally acting . . . as a private citizen interested in the maintenance of law and order" (365). Thus, theoretically at least, private prosecution remains. By 1900, though, police were prosecuting around 97 percent of all crimes, and there is now a growing trend in England for police departments to retain permanent prosecuting solicitors.

Conclusions

The evolution of England's criminal law system was altered by a long history of direct commands intended to serve the self-interested goals of kings, their bureaucrats, and politically powerful individuals and groups. These changes substantially weakened private citizens' incentives to participate in voluntary law enforcement arrangements and ultimately forced the government to provide bureaucratic alternatives. The fact that the state has taken such a prominent role in criminal law is not a reflection of the superior efficiency of state institutions, but a result of the state's undermining the incentives for private participation in criminal law. It was concluded in chapter 8 that public-good justifications for a government-dominated criminal justice system and institutions *must* be viewed as *ex post* rationalization rather than as *ex ante* explanations of their development, but this conclusion appears to apply more broadly to any and all "public interest" justifications.

Criminal Law in America

Many of the basic rules that characterize modern criminal justice in the United States were simply imported from England. Thus, our concepts of crimes versus torts, felonies, misdemeanors, plea bargaining, and exclusionary rules reflect the developments described above. Furthermore, the same kinds of institutional adjustments have followed as lawyers have become involved in criminal trials, which in turn have grown ever longer and more costly, and as public police, public prosecution, and public prisons have evolved. These institutions developed in the United States shortly after they did in England, in large part because the foundations of American criminal law were laid in England. Some of the developments, such as the inception of public courts and prosecution, were briefly discussed in chapter 6. In addition, watchmen paid by private individuals or organizations, and later by government, were established in the colonies in reflection of the English system, and private thief-takers were widely used. New York City began paying watchmen out of public funds in 1783, and other large cities soon followed, with the exception of Boston, which was still relying on private guard services as late as 1821 (Morn 1982: 12). "But the establishment of the London Metropolitan Police system in 1829—with its uniformed patrolmen, centralized leadership, and disciplined regimen—found few admirers in America" (Post and Kingsbury 1970: 14); public policing took even longer to develop.

After the first true public police force was established in New York in 1844, other cities followed suit shortly. From the outset, however, these police departments were used primarily for political purposes. Crime control was, at best, a secondary concern. First of all, local elected officials used their police departments as a way to reward political supporters, much as early Norman kings granted some of the profits of justice to their powerful baronial supporters. A newly elected mayor typically fired virtually the entire police department and replaced it with his own supporters. Bribery was often necessary to obtain a position on the police force; that practice was financially reasonable, given the potential payoff from police corruption (Benson 1981, 1988a, 1988b, 1990: 159–75; Benson and Baden 1985; Rasmussen and Benson 1994: 107–18; Thornton 1991). At any rate, mayors and their political machines then used their police departments to control the city for their own benefit. Thus,

> [t]he last half of the nineteenth century and the first decade of the twentieth century saw the police become puppets in the politicians' hands. Their primary function was to maintain the status quo. . . . [A] police system was allowed to develop which was corrupt and completely inadequate. The American police were, to a degree, a part of the criminal element, rather than being a force which controlled criminality. (Ricks, Tillet, and Van Meter 1981: 8)

The corruption in San Francisco's public police that led to the 1856 vigilante action discussed in chapter 6 was not an unusual case. In fact, it was very much the norm for cities all over the country. It is not surprising that public distrust of the urban police departments, and especially the detective bureaus, was widespread throughout the period (Morn 1982: 12). Police detectives were generally (and often justifiably) believed to be closely linked to the criminal element and to be working as spies for politicians.

On top of police departments' being corrupt tools of corrupt politicians, the political process virtually guaranteed that the public police would be inefficient and ineffective at actually controlling crime. Police were appointed because of their political connections, or because they bribed someone with political connections, rather than because they had abilities or expertise that would make them good crime control or investigative officials. As a rule, they served for relatively short periods, so such expertise was unlikely to develop, and objectivity was sacrificed in favor of political consideration and/or corruption. Politics also determined the geographic allocation of police resources, so inefficient communications and coordination typified nineteenth-century police departments. It is clear that the growth and development of public police through the nineteenth century was generally a direct result of their usefulness as political tools, not because they provided superior criminal justice. They may have had some impact on crime, but that does not appear to explain their growth (in many instances the police impact on crime was to facilitate its organization by accepting bribes in exchange for providing support for powerful criminals' activities, and the powerful criminals were often powerful politicians).

The poor performance of public police is evidenced by the fact that this same period saw the birth and rapid development of the modern private security industry (Ricks, Tillett, and Van Meter 1981: 9). "Public attitudes were predictable. . . . [And] [c]onsequently, several retired constables established private police agencies to protect property, restore stolen goods for a commission, and, whenever possible, circumvent the official criminal justice system" (Morn 1982: 14). Many of the largest and most well-known private detective and protection agencies that exist today were formed during this era of highly corrupt and ineffective public police, including the Pinkerton Detective Agency, Wells Fargo, Brinks, the railroad police, and the Burns Detective Agency (near the end of the era in 1909). They protected private property and transported valuables, investigated crimes, arrested criminals, and provided all the types of crime control services that public police are expected to provide today, but they did it when public police were much more obviously inadequate for the task. Indeed, the nineteenth- and early-twentieth-century public police compare poorly to their private-sector counterparts, who developed a reputation for integrity and efficiency during the same period that has survived and prospered to the present day.

Some of the most egregious problems with public policing, prosecution, and punishment in the nineteenth century may appear to be irrelevant today. In fact, however, crime statistics suggest that other problems may be much worse, and many things have not changed at all. Police still cannot solve crimes by organized criminal groups without practicing modern versions of the crown witness program, buying off criminals in order to testify against their fellow gang members (Cotts 1992; Rasmussen and Benson 1994: 165–66). Prison crowding persists, just as it did when the hulks floated on the Thames (Benson and Wollan 1989; Benson and Rasmussen 1994a, 1994b; Rasmussen and Benson 1994: 18–37). Large numbers of police are still part of the "criminal element" as recurrent corruption scandals plague most city police departments (Benson 1981, 1988a, 1988b, 1990: 159–75; Benson and Baden 1985; Rasmussen and Benson 1994: 107–18; Thornton 1991). Victims still do not report most crimes, as explained in chapter 4, because the costs of doing so outweigh the benefits. Plea bargaining now accounts for 91 percent of all criminal convictions nationwide and up to 98 percent in some states. And so on. What can be done? Perhaps the answer is not to "build more prisons and employ more public police," as today's politicians seem to believe. Perhaps it is not to develop a "bigger and better" version of some government program, as has been done throughout most of this century. Perhaps the answer is to turn back the clock in an effort to reestablish the incentives for greater private-sector involvement in criminal justice that disappeared centuries ago in the face of efforts by kings to expand their revenues and power.

10

Restitution in a Rights-Based Approach to Crime Policy
Individual Responsibility and Justice for Victims

Gary W. Bornman, a bank robber serving a seven-year sentence in the Federal Correctional Institute in Marianna, Florida, writes in a very powerful letter to the *Tallahassee Democrat:*

> I'm sure when a rape victim is being raped she doesn't care if her attacker was an abused child. By allowing this blame-laying, we're telling the rest of society that it's OK to rob and murder as long as you have a good excuse. What happened to taking responsibility for one's own actions?
>
> As someone who has spent the better part of his life behind bars, I've never run into a guilty criminal. To hear them tell it, everyone but themselves is to blame for making them commit the crime: their mother, the victim, society itself. Isn't it about time that we stop all this nonsense and start holding criminals accountable for their actions? (Bornman 1995)

I agree.[1] There should be no excuse for committing a crime against a victim, and when such a crime occurs, the criminal must be held responsible.

Before we discuss how to do that, it should be recognized that making policy recommendations such as those that follow is a normative exercise. The questions asked are What *should* be done about crime and (given the answer) How *should* we go about achieving the objective? The answers depend on the normative objectives of the person proposing them. Therefore, the normative perspective behind the proposals should be stated up front. Most economists focus on efficiency as the normative goal of their policy proposals, but the dominant goal of the proposals made here is to ensure liberty and justice. In reality, however, liberty, justice, and efficiency are generally complementary goals, and it appears that they are complementary in the area of crime policy as well. Thus, the incentives created by an emphasis on liberty and justice should lead to more efficient institutions for doing justice. This chapter focuses on the liberty and justice goals; the issue of efficiency is treated somewhat in chapters 3, 7, 8, and 9, and it is also the focus of chapters 11 and 12.

Liberty, as used here, means neither freedom from responsibility, nor freedom from "worry" (perhaps because the government has promised to take care of everyone), nor freedom to do as one pleases regardless of the impact on others. Liberty means being unhindered in the pursuit of one's own interests, as long as that pursuit does not impinge on someone else's liberty. That is, liberty is "an absence of imposed costs" (Lester 1996) by others upon an individual and by that individual on others. An individual's freedom to act in his or her "domain," then, is coupled with a responsibility to respect other people's freedom to do the same thing. Without a wedding of freedom and responsibility, liberty has no real meaning, because the fruits of one person's alleged freedom can be destroyed by another person. That is why the rights to "life, liberty, and the pursuit of happiness" as envisioned by the founders of this country included a recognition of the sanctity of private property rights.

Property rights as conceived here include both economic rights and civil rights. All people should have property rights to the full privileges of citizenship, just as they should have property rights to their person, including the fruits of their labor, as well as to their land, their capital equipment, and their other economic resources. Private property rights involve an individual's right to use the things (economic resources, privileges of citizenship, etc.) that are owned by that individual for whatever purpose the person wants (presumably in the pursuit of personal happiness) as long as that use does not infringe on someone else's property rights. For economic resources, that includes the rights to consume the resources, to earn income from their use, to exclude others from consuming or using them, and/or to alienate (e.g., sell or voluntarily give away) those resources. But for property rights to have any real meaning, they must be accompanied by obligations. Everyone must have an obligation to respect other people's private property rights, or those rights have little value. It is the existence of such obligations that actually creates property rights in the first place. Without obligations to respect other people's property rights, the pursuit of happiness is transformed into a competition for the fruits of or sources of one another's wealth (taking income and resources from others) rather than the production of new wealth (Benson 1984b, 1994c, 1997b).

From the normative perspective of liberty, all individuals should be treated as free and responsible beings as long as they live up to their responsibilities to others (i.e., respect other people's property rights). Someone who, in the exercise of free will, intentionally violates another person's property rights through theft or violence essentially forfeits his own property rights (economic and civil) until justice is done. As Lester (1996) explains, "knowingly to take or damage another's goods [property rights] is to cede the claim that he take or damage your goods up to the same value. Knowingly to damage, violate, or use another's person is also to cede the claim that your victim have some physical damage, violation, or use done to you up to the pain, inconvenience, and indignity you imposed." That is, the victim has the right to retaliate against *any* intentional imposition of costs (Lester 1996; Rothbard 1973, 1977, 1982). In Bidinotto's words, justice should be seen as "a moral principle recognizing causality and attribution of individual responsibility in social relationships. The principle of justice holds that because individuals are thinking causal agents, they are morally responsible for the social consequences of their actions, and must be treated accordingly" (1994c: 191). When individuals fail to live up to their obligations to respect others' rights, thus taking someone else's property, they must be held responsible: justice demands that action be taken to "reflect those negative consequences of harm and injury back onto the criminal," as Bidinotto (1994c: 194) contends. Furthermore, from the normative position of liberty and justice taken here, those individuals must be responsible to their victims rather than to "society" or the state, *because* they have violated their victims' property rights.

Criminals should lose many of their own property rights unless and until they have restored the property they have taken, diminished in value, or destroyed. The restoration can be either in fact (e.g., return of stolen property and any other costs to the victim that arise because of the theft) or in kind (e.g., sufficient compensation so that the victim is in a position to once again pursue happiness in a fashion comparable to that which existed before the offense). In Anglo-Saxon England an offender could "buy back the peace" by paying the victim of his actions, but refusal to pay put the offender "outside the law," meaning that he had no property rights (no one had an obligation to respect his claims). As in Anglo-Saxon England, making criminals responsible for their actions should mean making them responsible to their victims, and refusal to accept that responsibility should result in loss of all civil and economic rights. Justice for the victim of crime should be the primary goal of crime policy, so that when a crime is committed, the right of the victim to be restored should be paramount (but in addition any costs borne by others who assist the victim, many of which are currently borne by taxpayers but could be privatized, should be paid by the offender).

Individual Responsibility: Making Criminals Pay

There should be no excuse for intentionally violating someone else's rights (Bidinotto 1994a, 1994b, 1994c, 1994d; Barger 1994). The fact that the offender is unemployed or poor, is addicted to drugs or alcohol, was abused as a child, has no father in residence, is a member of a minority group being mistreated now or suffering from past mistreatment, and/or is young, does not excuse crimes against innocent victims. (Past mistreatment of the offender is a violation of rights, or course, but it does not give him or her the right to violate the rights of anyone except the person[s] responsible for the mistreating. And if policymakers decide that there is a lower bound on the age of the responsibility, then those who are responsible for the behavior of juveniles—parents or guardians—should be held accountable for the crimes that juveniles commit.) As Bidinotto (1994a: 14) notes, "influences" are not "causes"—the way a person responds to his or her environment is determined by the choices the individual makes. Most people who are poor, young, members of abused groups, and so forth, do not commit crimes. The fact that some do reflects the choices they make in the face of the same circumstances that others suffer under and choose not to commit crimes; those who do harm other people and/or their property therefore should be held responsible for any negative consequences of those choices. The arguments made here echo many that are raised by "conservatives," of course, but for different reasons and with different implications.

In the current criminal justice environment, precisely the opposite seems to be the case, at least to many victims of crime and many who fear being victimized. Criminals are seen by many who "study" them and make policy recommendations about them as products of their environment with no control over their actions. Because they came from a bad home or neighborhood, they presumably cannot help but be criminals. These "excuse makers" may not be able to convince victims and their families of the validity of their arguments, but they certainly have been able to convince many potential criminals, as the quotation from Gary Bornman introducing this chapter suggests. Almost every criminal now claims to be a victim, free of blame for his or her actions. Criminals have been taught that they do not have an obligation to respect other people's lives and property. Thus, the "excuse-making industry," to use Bidinotto's (1994a) term, has had the effect of undermining individual responsibility and creating an environment that fosters and even excuses crime.

Today we are clearly seeing a conservative political backlash against the predominantly "liberal" excuse makers. Demands for longer prison sentences, more prisons, and expanded use of capital punishment to hold criminals accountable for their actions seem to be dominating the political debate. These demands do not reflect the normative position taken here. Although the normative approach (or approaches) to crime underlying conservative policy prescriptions also implies that individuals must be held accountable for their actions, the nature of that accountability differs significantly from the accountability arising from the liberty-and-justice reasons that underlie the arguments made here. Accountability in the form of punishment may be used for the utilitarian or social engineering purposes of conservatives, such as deterrence, incapacitation, retribution, and even the rehabilitation that apparently is implied by modern liberal norms (Logan 1995; Bidinotto 1994c; and see chapter 12). These are not the primary goals that are being advocated here: as Logan suggests, punishment should not be seen as "a tool of social engineering; [but rather, as] an expression of our sense of justice" (1995: 84). Accountability is required because justice *for victims* mandates it. But in reality, as Bidinotto explains, "[t]oday, they [victims of crimes] are too often forgotten people in our legal system; and their cries for justice must be heard and answered" (1994a: 6).

In contrast with conservative crime policy prescriptions so prominent in the political environment today, justice for victims does not necessarily imply longer prison sentences, more prisons, and expanded use of capital punishment. Justice for victims does not even demand imprisonment, unless imprisonment to supervise the criminal as he works off his debt to the victim is the only way to assure payment. When a criminal violates another individual's rights, justice demands that action be taken to "reflect those negative consequences of harm and injury back onto the criminal," as noted above, but doing so through imprisonment also reflects negative consequences onto taxpayers and, more significantly, *fails to deflect the negative consequences from the victim.* The criminal may indeed "pay for his crime" if the punishment is severe enough, but others are forced to pay for it, too. Taxpayers bear the cost of building and staffing prisons, consumers of other government services (e.g., education) see those services cut in order to pay for prisons, and the victims generally still suffer the costs of the crime itself along with additional costs discussed in chapter 4 that arise from cooperation with police and prosecutors in order to convict and punish the offender. Thus, the negative consequences of the crime are not removed from the victim, since the victim receives nothing that restores the value that has been taken or destroyed. The victim's capacity to pursue happiness has not been and cannot be fully restored. Perhaps the victim gets some satisfaction in the form of revenge from having the criminal punished, but such revenge is not likely to be a good substitute for being restored. Justice for victims requires more than punishment as negative consequences are reflected onto the criminal. Justice requires that the negative consequences also be deflected away from others. The criminal alone should pay.

This is where the emphasis on liberty and justice departs from most current conservative policy prescriptions. For example, although Bidinotto may be closer to a libertarian stance than to a conservative one on a number of issues, he has become a very visible, powerful, and articulate spokesman against the liberal-dominated excuse-making approach to crime policy that tends to prescribe treatment of the underlying "causes" (i.e., excuses) for crime. He makes the conservative case as well or better than almost any of the politically prominent conservative spokesmen, so let us focus on his arguments. First, note that Bidinotto sees restoring the victim simply as one of the utilitarian (or social engineering) strategies of crime control, lumping it with liberal goals of prevention, treatment, and rehabilitation, as well as conservative objectives like deterrence, incapacitation, and what he sees as traditional views of retribution. He does admit that "[o]f all utilitarian strategies, making the criminal 'restore' his victim by paying back the costs of the harm done is closest to the principle of justice [that he advocates]" (Bidinotto 1994c: 183), but rather than victim restoration, he advocates "moral retribution . . . to reflect those negative consequences of harm and injury back onto the criminal" (194). He suggests that restitution or fines might be sufficient for some minor crimes, but that for "more serious offenses, prisons are an unavoidable punitive measure" (196). The reasons for lumping restitution with "utilitarian" objectives are not particularly clear, given Bidinotto's cry for justice for victims. He distinguishes between "moral retribution" and revenge (194–96), for instance, but the fact is that about the only satisfaction the victim might get when a criminal is imprisoned is some "pleasure" of revenge (and perhaps some reduction in anxiety because the criminal is incapacitated). And importantly, it is likely to be the personal costs and benefits that motivate victims to cooperate with police and prosecutors, as indicated in chapter 4, *not* some abstract concept of moral retribution.

Bidinotto also dismisses restitution as a policy goal because "in practice, it has proven to be hard to enforce. Thanks to their irresponsible lifestyles, criminals often remain poor and infrequently employed. Outside of a prison work environment, it is difficult to compel them to pay back their victims. In addition, it is hard to translate damages for some kinds of crimes into dollar terms" (1994c: 183–84). All of this may be true, *in the current institutional environment,* but none of it needs to be true, given appropriate institutional changes.

Numerous historical examples exist of different institutional environments that encouraged the effective use of restitution (Peden 1977; Pospisil 1971; Goldsmidt 1951; Hoebel 1967; Friedman 1979; Solvason 1992, 1993; Benson 1986b, 1989b, 1990: 11–30; 1991a, 1992b, 1994a; and see chapters 6 and 9), and modern Japan also focuses on restitution (Evers 1994), as explained below. Therefore, with sufficient institutional changes of the type proposed below and in chapters 11 and 12, restitution could be a very viable practice.

Bidinotto's own policy prescriptions are also difficult, if not impossible, to achieve in the current institutional and political environment dominated by excuse makers, conservative and liberal advocates of various social engineering goals, and criminal justice bureaucrats whose livelihood depends on pursuit of those goals. He would do away with all of the social engineering objectives that dominate the current criminal justice environment; and in order to achieve "moral retribution," he would redefine the concept of crime to involve only an "intentional, non-consensual act entailing the initiation of force, fraud, or coercion against another person or persons" (1994c: 192). Recognize that this definition eliminates all so-called "victimless" or "consensual" crimes such as prostitution, drug consumption, gambling (that is not fraudulently rigged), and so on that are so popular among many conservative policy advocates. Bidinotto generally does not explicitly recognize this, although he does suggest legalizing drugs, in part to alleviate prison crowding so that moral retribution can be achieved when crimes, as he defines the term, are committed (1994d: 291–92). This clearly separates Bidinotto from the majority of conservative policy advocates, but it really is a logical implication of most normative positions underlying conservative views (the obvious exception being those conservatives who want to use government to legislate morality as they perceive it, including the so-called religious right), and a number of prominent conservatives do advocate drug legalization. The point is that achieving Bidinotto's policy prescriptions also requires some very dramatic changes in the criminal justice system, changes that are not necessarily any more dramatic than those required to create an effective restitution-based system. And furthermore, as suggested below and in chapters 11 and 12, a focus on restitution in a privatized criminal justice system would result in the pursuit and prosecution of offenses involving the "intentional, non-consensual act entailing the initiation of force, fraud, or coercion against another person or persons" in order to "reflect those negative consequences of harm and injury back onto the criminal" *and* away from victims. Thus, the redefinition of crime and the objective Bidinotto presumably wants to be imposed through legislation and government spending (of taxpayer's dollars) would naturally evolve. Under these circumstances, so-called victimless or consensual crimes would also get little or no attention, depending on how far in the direction of a fully privatized system we move, regardless of whether statute law is changed or not.

Clearly, many of the issues that characterize the most well-developed conservative views about retribution (at least from a logical perspective) are also relevant to the liberty-and-justice perspective, but the principal policy conclusion is not. The difference is that a goal of full restitution also generally produces moral retribution (the shifting of costs back onto the criminal), as suggested below, whereas a goal of retribution through physical punishment generally does not produce full restitution. It is doubtful that the family of a murder victim is fully satisfied if the murderer is executed, for instance. Critics of restitution can point out that no monetary restitution will probably be sufficient to restore them, either, but receiving as much financial restitution as possible, perhaps with the balance as physical retribution (Lester 1996), is likely to come closer to full restoration than capital punishment, let alone imprisonment for life or something substantially less. Furthermore, under the right institutional environment (e.g., the markets for prison labor discussed in chapter 12) financial retribution and physical retribution in the form of incapacitation might be achieved simultaneously.

Restitution and/or Retribution

In tort law, when a person is injured, the negligent party is liable for damages, that is, for restitution. Furthermore, if something more than simple negligence is evident, if the harm arises out of some intentional act (e.g., providing misleading or false information that culminates in the accident, or hiding information about potential harms that arise when using a particular product), then punitive damages can be awarded; that is, the victim can be compensated for more than the actual *measurable* damages done. Some observers support punitive damages for social engineering purposes: punitive damages may serve as a deterrent to such intentional harms, for instance. Although this may well be the case, there is another more important reason for *legitimate* punitive damages:[2] justice demands that they be paid. As Lester (1996) observes, for instance, payment of measurable damages alone is essentially "buying crime" by paying for it afterward. But as Rothbard (1973, 1977, 1982) explains, restitution should be the price paid by the offender *to persuade* the victim not to exact some other sort of punishment. Clearly, then, the payment must be enough to satisfy the victim's desire for retribution. From the perspective of liberty and individual responsibility emphasized here, these so-called punitive or retributive damages are actually restitutive.

Consider an intentional tort in the form of withholding knowledge about known dangers involved in using a product. An individual should have the right to be informed about the potential harms that can arise in using a product purchased from someone else, given that the seller is exclusively aware of that potential. Information about a product's potential dangers is an attribute of the product that should be transferred when the product is sold. In essence, one of the attributes of the product that the buyer pays for is any relevant knowledge of its potential harmful characteristics that the seller may possess. Therefore, intentional misinformation or even intentional failure to inform is an intentional taking of the buyer's valuable property rights. Such information is obviously valuable, as exemplified by the fact that the buyer is likely to pay less for the product when the information is provided; that is, the seller captures more wealth by withholding such information (e.g., by not transferring the property rights to all of the attributes of the product). Thus, the real damage to the victim of an intentional tort goes beyond the measurable costs to the victim (medical costs, property damage restoration, lost wages or profits, etc.); so-called punitive damages are in order. But these damages are punitive only in the sense that they are above the damages for measurable harms. They are restorative in the sense that they compensate for the tortfeasor's taking of the plaintiff's property, the attribute of the product associated with the withheld knowledge, which resulted in the buyer's paying more for the product than he would have, given such knowledge.

Like tortfeasors, criminals should be held accountable for the measurable damages they do, but since crimes with victims are intentional harms, criminals' restitution payments should cover both measurable damages for the restoration of property or health (or if restoration is impossible, as with severe physical harm or murder, for the present value of the stream of lost income) and so-called punitive damages to compensate for the invasion of another person's property rights. Some writers (e.g., Evers [1994] and Lester [1996]) refer to this as punitive restitution, or perhaps retributive restitution; but as explained here, it can be seen as full restitution since not all harms are measurable on a case-by-case basis (an estimated valuation of these costs can be discovered, however, as explained below, so they are not necessarily arbitrary). The criminal invasion of another's property rights is itself a harm, even if no measurable damages are done. A burglar who breaks into a house by picking a lock (so no measurable property damage is done) and is caught before taking anything still owes the intended victim for violating the sanctity of his or her property rights. A person who attempts murder and fails has still invaded the intended victim's property rights and should pay damages. Thus, payments characterized by many (e.g., Evers 1994; Lester 1996) to be punitive or retributive are perceived here to be restorative, because they are restitution for the invasion of another person's property rights. Indeed, if a victim is not satisfied with a restitution payment based on measurable damages, and he or she demands additional "punitive damages" or "retribution," that suggests that the victim has not been restored. Full restoration arises when the victim is satisfied, not when his out-of-pocket or measurable costs have been paid.

This view of restitution is not without its potential problems. In particular, payment of damages for unmeasurable harms creates incentives for victims to claim more damages than what was actually done. There is a potential "holdout" problem if the victim has the right to be restored *and* has the power to determine the level of unmeasurable damages that will be sufficient to achieve restoration. Such a victim is in a position to behave opportunistically and impose a larger fine on the offender than what actually is sufficient for restoration. If determination of damages is achieved through direct negotiation between a victim and a criminal, perhaps aided by a mediator, and if a victim refuses to settle for what should be a reasonable payment, the offender is being victimized by the former victim. This is in part why, in restitution-based systems such as the one discussed in chapter 9, a third-party dispute resolution system has virtually always evolved to mediate or arbitrate the victim's claim. An arbitrator has the power to determine what a fair payment is after listening to the claims and counterclaims and considering evidence about the level of unmeasurable damages by looking at "tradition and practice" or "community standards of reasonableness" (that is, customary law), perhaps demonstrated by past negotiated settlements as well as past judgments for similar offenses (Pospisil 1971; Goldsmidt 1951; Peden 1977; Friedman 1979: Benson 1989b, 1990: 11–30; 1991a, 1992b, 1994a). A mediator can rely only on his ability to persuade, although considerable social pressure is often also applied to accept a "fair" restitution, that is, one consistent with customary standards (Barton 1967). That fact also explains why customary standards have evolved into explicit rules (e.g., custom is recognized in a judgment, that judgment becomes precedent for similar cases, etc.) regarding appropriate or fair damages for specified offenses in virtually all such arrangements, and why the victim is obliged to accept what the arbitrator and/or the commonly perceived rules determine to be fair payments for particular offenses (Goldsmidt 1951; Barton 1967; Peden 1977; Friedman 1979: Benson 1989b, 1990: 11–30; 1991a,

1992b, 1994a). As Hayek (1937, 1967, 1973) explains, one reason for the evolution of rules is that individuals do not have the skills or information necessary to evaluate every particular action. That is as true for judges and arbitrators as it is for anyone else. Thus, people find it beneficial to develop and follow standard rules in similar situations. The rule may not be perfectly ideal for every circumstance, but the transaction costs of calculating the appropriate payment in each situation outweigh the costs of having a standard rule to follow. In other words, in true restitution-based systems, institutions evolve to prevent the victim hold-out problem. In modern Japan, for instance, restitution is an integral part of the criminal justice process, as explained below. It is determined through bargaining (generally with intermediaries or mediators) before prosecution occurs, rather than through the courts in the process of criminal prosecution. Hold-out problems do not appear to be significant, because if the victim demands too much, the criminal can refuse to pay. The victim has no coercive power to impose a settlement, so if he is to receive restitution, it cannot be excessive (incentives for paying this restitution are discussed below).

The justification for restitution may appear to be in conflict with the typical libertarian justification. For instance, Rothbard (1982: 85–95) logically derives the right to restitution from the right to punish, which in turn derives from the right to self-defense in a libertarian world. He contends that the fundamental right of the victim is to exact proportional punishment, so restitution arises only if the victim is willing to accept payment in lieu of punishment. Here, on the other hand, it is contended that the fundamental right is for the victim to be restored. Rothbard's arguments apply in a theoretical libertarian world wherein only the victim and the offender are involved in a legal dispute; the issue addressed here is how to move toward that world from a very different one.

Furthermore, consider that, in all likelihood, every restitution-based system that has existed probably evolved from a situation such as the one Rothbard envisioned, in which individuals exacted punishment and perhaps some were willing to forgo punishment in exchange for a sufficient economic payment. Individuals also found, however, that there were situations in which such unilateral exactions of punishment were either very risky or impossible because of differences between the victim's and the offender's relative capacities for violence. Thus, reciprocal mutual support groups (or mutual insurance groups) evolved to assist members in their pursuit of justice, such as the Anglo-Saxon tithings and hundreds discussed in chapter 9. Under these circumstances, legal issues no longer involve only the victim and the offender, and since violent exaction of retribution (e.g., through a blood feud) can be quite costly to other members of such groups, rules evolved, which reordered the primacy of rights to punish and to receive restitution. In early medieval England, Ireland, and Iceland, and in the large number of primitive societies that anthropologists have studied, victims did not have the right to impose physical punishment *unless and until* the offender refused to pay fair restitution (Benson 1989b, 1990: 11–30; 1991a, 1992b, 1994a; Peden 1977; Friedman 1979; Pospisil 1971; Goldsmidt 1951; Barton 1967). Victims who exacted retributive punishment before giving the offender a chance to pay restitution were considered to be lawbreakers. Thus, the emphasis placed here on the primacy of a right to restoration rather than to punishment reflects a different institutional arrangement than the one envisioned by Rothbard: one in which individual victims call upon others to back their claims against offenders (either through participatory voluntary associations for pursuit and prosecution, or through the purchases of pursuit and/or prosecution services in a market for specialists), and therefore in which the interests of these others in minimizing the costs of violence come into play. In essence, potential victims are expected to willingly trade for: (a) a right to fair restitution and (b) support in the pursuit of justice, in exchange for promises to: (a) forgo proportional punishment if fair restitution is paid and (b) provide similar support for others.

The measurable part of damages is relatively straightforward, and modern courts, both public and private, have a great deal of experience in determining awards for measurable harms (e.g., in contract and tort cases). No legislator or planner had to tell these courts how to do this. The process has evolved over time and has become relatively standardized, at least for commonly observed harms.

More significant is the question of how to determine the so-called punitive damages, or unmeasurable damage, portion of restitution, since that reflects the nonmeasurable portion of the harms associated with the invasion of a person's property rights. Nonmeasurability means that setting such damages is an inexact exercise. Determining damages on a case-by-case basis would initially involve very high transactions costs, including those associated with "holding-out" on the part of victims. As suggested above, however, standardized rules that are generally perceived to be fair by members of the community would, in all likelihood, be established through precedent, allowing judgments to specify payments that are reasonably appropriate for most criminal offenses. As determination of damages for crimes became a regular part of the dispute resolution process, standard rules for damages would tend to evolve so that both victims and criminals would be able to predict the payments (implying

that mediation and negotiation would probably be the dominant dispute resolution mechanisms); that certainly has occurred in various historical and
primitive societies where legal systems were restitutive.

History suggests that the restitution rule may be quite simple or quite complex. For example, the Hebrew Bible dictates that "[w]hen anyone, man or
woman, wrongs another . . . . that person has incurred guilt which demands
reparation. He shall confess the sin he has committed, make restitution in full
with the addition of one fifth, and give it to the man to whom compensation
is due" (Num. 5:6–7 New English Bible). Measurable damages plus one-fifth
to cover the unmeasurable part of the harm was apparently the rule of thumb
established among the ancient Jewish community. Other societies have developed other rules. In some legal systems, well-known rules evolved that detailed
the payment to be made for every type of offense (e.g., Peden 1977; Goldsmidt
1951; Benson 1996c, 1989b; Barton 1967). In some societies, including medieval Iceland (Friedman 1979), the payment that an offender was obliged to
pay also depended in part on whether the offender tried to hide or deny the
offense. If the offender admitted guilt, thereby lowering the costs of pursuit,
prosecution, and trial, the fine was lower. Repeat offenders were also treated
differently from first-time offenders in many restitution-based systems. In
Anglo-Saxon England, an offender could "buy back the peace" on a first offense, but a second offense would not be forgiven. Such an offender was an
outlaw with no protection (no property rights): fair game for anyone who
wanted to attack him. In other societies capital punishment has been applied
for repeat offenders. Restitution-based systems also have recognized the problem of collection from potentially "judgment-proof" offenders. Offenders in
Anglo-Saxon England had up to a year to pay large fines, and if they were unable to that, they could become indentured servants until the fine was worked
off (Benson 1990: 25; 1992b, 1994a). Payments do not necessarily have to be
monetary; labor services or other goods have often served as restitution. Frequently an indentureship contract was purchased by someone else so the victim received immediate financial compensation and the offender was obliged
to work off the debt under the supervision of someone other than the victim.
As with the hold-out problem discussed above, victim supervision of an indentured laborer could involve more work and/or physical retribution than
was actually required for restoration. Similarly, in many primitive and medieval societies where restitution was the primary goal of the justice process,
fines have been a function of the status of both the victim and the offender.
The harm imposed on a wealthy person who loses one of his cars to a thief is
obviously less significant than the harm done to a poor person who loses his

only car. Thus, restitution may require a relatively large payment to the poor person. But if a person is diverted from earning income, whether because of the need to pursue and prosecute an offender or because of injuries incurred, the value of lost time will be much higher for the high-income person than for the low-income person. Therefore, restitution payments for a particular offense may be higher for the well-to-do. The schedule of payments in the *wergeld* system in Anglo-Saxon England discussed in chapter 9 reflected the status of the parties involved, for instance: the wealthy and powerful were required to pay more as offenders and also received more as victims. The man-price system in medieval Ireland (Peden 1977) and the customary payments in various primitive systems (e.g., Barton 1967) also reflected wealth and social status. The point is that the rules regarding restitution can be as complex and fine-tuned as the society wants them to be, and the precise rules that might evolve in a modern restitution-based system would naturally depend on the norms of the citizens of that society.

A restitution-like system can have multiple objectives, just as the current system is presumably intended to punish, deter, incapacitate, and rehabilitate criminals (although it probably does not do any of them very well). It is doubtful that any restitution system has ever been established for the sole purpose of restoring victims. Other objectives were also determining factors, just as multiple objectives always influence collective actions. Fines for restitution can have a deterrent effect if the fine is high, for instance. Of course, if restitution is to serve as a deterrent as well as a restorative device, then fines may have to be a function of the wealth of the individuals involved. When pursuit and prosecution are left up to victims and their voluntary support groups, a restitution-based law system may involve greater payments for a particular offense made *to* a wealthy victim than to a poor victim in order to induce the wealthy person to pursue offenders, thereby deterring intentional offenses more effectively. Otherwise, because a wealthy person is harmed relatively less by a theft of a particular monetary magnitude than a poor person is, the wealthy person has weaker incentives to pursue the offender for a specific magnitude of restitution than a poor person does. Therefore, if the fine paid for a particular offense is the same for both rich and poor victims, there will be greater incentives to steal from the rich than from the poor.

A fine that is an extreme hardship for a poor person may be trivial for a wealthy one, so effective deterrence may require higher fines for the same offense as wealth increases (e.g., as in the Anglo-Saxon system). The potential loss of reputation may be a sufficient punishment for such individuals, though. Depending on how valuable reputation (honor, prestige) is in a community, relatively heavy punishments may not be necessary for deterrence (Lott 1987). Certainly, there is a great deal of empirical evidence suggesting that the propensity to commit crimes falls as wealth increases, but it does not follow that poverty causes crime. Rather, at least part of the reason those who have more wealth do not choose to commit crimes as often as those with less wealth is the risk they face in terms of lost reputation and wealth (serving time in prison is much more costly for someone who could be earning one hundred thousand dollars a year than for someone who earns ten thousand dollars a year). Furthermore, those low-income people who choose to invest their time and energy in criminal activity are likely to remain poor because they may never accumulate the knowledge and skills necessary for pulling them out of poverty (Bidinotto 1994a: 12–14). The point is that, as history demonstrates, a restitution system can have a very complex set of goals and of fines.

There are other options that also have an inherent logic, besides those that have existed historically. Rothbard (1982: 88) offers a compelling alternative; Since a criminal should be punished to *"the extent that he deprives the victim,"* Rothbard proposes that he should pay *more than twice* the amount that would restore the victim's measurable harms. For instance, if the criminal steals $15,000 then he should pay back the $15,000 and also be punished to the same extent, thus being deprived of an additional $15,000 of his own. But as Rothbard notes, the criminal did more than take the $15,000: he also put the victim in a state of fear and uncertainty, and the victim should be compensated for these aspects of the ordeal as well. How much, Rothbard suggests, is unclear, but a rational system should work out the problem, as implied by the standardized rules discussed above.

Yet another alternative is that restitution fines be set to cover all measurable costs to the victim plus the full cost of bringing the offender to justice (costs that may or may not be borne by the victim, depending on the implementation of policies discussed below), all divided by the probability that the offender will be brought to justice (Becker 1969: 191–93; Stigler 1970: 531; Lester 1996). For example, the fine for stealing a car would be the value of the loss plus the cost of pursuit, court time, and so on, associated with solving and prosecuting the offense, all divided by the probability of successful solution and prosecution. If half the car thefts are solved, then the long list of costs would be divided by .5, or, in effect, multiplied by two (today, of course, the probability of solving a car theft is substantially lower than this, so the fine would be substantially higher, but with changes outlined below, the probability of solution should rise). The fine would be double the measurable damages. Lester agrees with this principle:

> When one imposes a cost on another the full cost to him need not, despite superficial appearances, be merely the damage done by the act itself (including indignity, anxiety, etc.). The full cost must also take account of the likelihood that the criminal might get away with the crime. If a thief steals ten pounds with a one in ten chance of capture, then that is to impose a cost in excess of ten pounds, even neglecting indignity, anxiety, etc., in the sense that it would not pay the average victim to agree beforehand to such a risk unless he were sure of at least one hundred pounds if the thief were caught. So the real imposition, in monetary terms, is probably in excess of one hundred pounds (and the damages for the indignity, etc., has also to be multiplied). (1996: 7)

Another multiplier might be added to reflect the criminal history of the offender, so that repeat offenders face stiffer fines than first-time offenders because presumably they learn by doing and lower their chances of getting caught with practice.

Such fines should function as a deterrent as well as serving the cause of justice. The benefit to the offender is probably substantially less than the market value of stolen property, for instance. The expected cost is the probability of being brought to justice multiplied by the resulting fine, or, given that the offender and the judge perceive the same probability, the measurable cost to the victim plus the cost of bringing the offender to justice. The expected cost of the crime for the potential criminal is therefore clearly greater than the expected benefit. The justification here for establishing a high cost is not that it is a deterrent, however, or that it is punitive, for that matter, although it obviously can be. Rather, it is still justified as being restorative, as Lester's logic illustrates. The fact that it may achieve some other goals that people in a community desire (deterrence or punishment) is certainly worth noting but of secondary importance given the normative perspective taken here.

Some might argue that restitution awards determined as described above are too punitive even though they are not determined by the victim. Certainly, if the rights of the criminal are at issue, there may be some optimal fine that does not "over-tax" the criminal. Or if efficiency in deterring crimes is the goal, there may be some optimal fine that just balances the marginal cost of another crime with the marginal benefits of preventing it. Of course, although a criminal may pay a restitution fine that is several times the measurable (but not the total risk-adjusted) costs to the victim in one particular case, that same criminal may well have committed several other crimes without being caught, given the probability used to calculate the multiplier (Lester 1996), so even a large multiple may not be "too punitive." In any case, the goal here is justice for victims, not for criminals. Therefore, it may be better to err on the side of overcompensating the victim even if it means overtaxing the criminal. But there are some counterarguments that should be recognized.

If damage awards are set too high, there are incentives to falsely accuse and to falsify evidence in order to collect the damages. Such incentives always exist, however, for anyone who expects to benefit from successful criminal (or tort) prosecution. Thus, we see increasingly frequent examples of police officials falsifying evidence in order to gain successful arrests and convictions and of informers, paid by police and prosecutors, falsifying evidence, as noted in chapter 8. (Informers may be provided monetary payments and/or forgiveness of crimes committed by them.) The problem is a relative one, then, and there are at least two issues involved. First, do modern police officers or prosecutors have more incentives to falsify evidence (e.g., to gain promotions, reputations for being tough on crime in order to run for higher political office, etc.) than an individual would under a restitution system? And second, is the capacity to falsify evidence greater (e.g., is the cost of doing so lower) for modern public police officers or prosecutors, with their control over evidence and knowledge of evidentiary procedures, than it would be for an alleged victim seeking damage awards? Though the answer to the first question is not obvious one way or the other, the answer to the second appears to clearly favor a restitution system. As explained in chapter 9, the problem of false evidence arose in England long after restitution was abolished, when public rewards for successful *prosecutions* were initiated and when publicly employed justices of the peace acting as prosecutors were allowed increasing discretion in deciding whom to prosecute (that led to the crown witness program, an exchange of immunity from prosecution for testimony against other criminals that would enable successful prosecution), and it appears to continue to be a problem as prosecutors grant freedom from prosecution to criminals who provide testimony against other criminals (Benson 1990: 65–66; Rasmussen and Benson 1994: 165–66; Cotts 1992). Rules of evidence evolved to protect the accused from the public-sector criminal justice process (bounty hunters seeking public rewards, criminals trading evidence for freedom or lesser charges, police and prosecutors manipulating evidence to achieve prosecutions), not to protect them from false victims.

A second argument against restitution fines that are multiples of measurable damages has to do with marginal deterrence. Specifically, if the fine for, say, a robbery is so high that a criminal will be able to pay it only with great difficulty (e.g., by working for the rest of his life) if at all, then there is no incentive to avoid committing another crime against the same victim. In fact, there may be incentives to commit an additional crime: if killing the robbery victim reduces the chances of getting caught, and the restitution for robbery is greater than or equal to what the robber can conceivably pay, then the robber might rationally also commit murder. This could be a significant problem, but it should be recognized that the same argument applies to any kind of punishment that is not appropriately adjusted to create marginal deterrence. For instance, if dealing crack is punishable by death, then the dealer may have few misgivings about killing a police officer who tries to arrest him. Similarly, if the maximum punishment for both murder and rape is twenty-five years (perhaps with the possibility for parole after twelve), a rapist has incentives to murder his victim rather than allowing her to report the crime. The point is that for effective deterrence of relatively costly crimes, either the restitution required or the traditional physical punishments imposed today must be relatively severe.

The prime objective of the proposals made here is to restore victims, not to deter criminals, but anyone advocating restitution would probably have second thoughts if it appeared that a system of restitution would encourage more serious crimes against victims than the current system does. Whether it does or not depends on a number of related institutional developments. For instance, it is contended in chapter 11 that a restitution-based criminal justice system will be much more effective at deterring crime because the probabilities of reporting and cooperating to achieve successful pursuit and prosecution will be considerably greater. Thus, the multipliers that may appear to be ten or even one hundred under the current system are likely to be much smaller under restitution. Furthermore, although this appears to be a significant problem today because even small fines would mean that many of today's criminals are effectively judgment proof, the incentives to develop collection mechanisms under a restitution system, including an active competitive market for supervised labor services (e.g., as in a prisonlike environment, or some sort of halfway house, depending on the risks of flight), are likely to alleviate this problem to a considerable degree (see chapter 12). Beyond that, if individuals with no skills and no wealth are effectively judgment proof in a restitution system, even with markets for prison labor (but see chapter 12 in this regard, where it is contended that this is not likely to be the case), they are apparently largely judgment proof today, too. Prison does not appear to impose very high costs on them since they are rarely punished enough to alter their behavior. Even for criminals sent to prison, the recidivism rate appears to be at least 60 to 75 percent within two or three years of release (see chapter 4), suggesting that the punishment did not impose a sufficient cost to serve as an effective deterrent. Frequently the criticisms of restitution systems (and of privatization) arise because the critic recognizes a problem with the current system and wants to know how the alternative would solve it. There is no perfect system, but the failures that are anticipated by looking at current institutionalized problems may not occur under an alternative set of institutions.

Once a restitution system is in place, these potential problems can be assessed, and victims, potential victims, insurance companies, arbitrators, and mediators (or judges and legislators, depending on the degree of privatization) will search for solutions and set reasonable fines accordingly. Falsification of evidence is itself a crime as defined above, for instance, and given the multiplier effect, the size of a potential payment would have to be larger than the actual payments obtained through a successful false accusation. Through experimentation, appropriate levels of restitution can evolve that diminish the incentives to falsely accuse. Courts presumably do this in tort law, and they have been able to do so for offenses we now consider to be crimes in many primitive and medieval societies, so such damage awards should be determinable today for crimes. Furthermore, to the degree that marginal deterrence becomes a potential problem, community standards (customs) can be expected to adjust. Effective marginal deterrence is much more likely to be achieved in a privatized system where more costs and benefits are internalized than in the current common-pool political environment, where policy objectives are determined through interest group politics and bureaucratic discretion.

Some of the issues just addressed regarding how to implement a restitution system, such as what levels of fines to impose, are of a technical nature, and though they deserve attention, they are relatively trivial compared to the question of how to actually develop a criminal justice system to impose *and* collect restitution judgments. If the normative perspective outlined above is accepted, restitution for the victim should be the overriding goal of the criminal justice process (even if that normative perspective is rejected, a focus on restitution should not necessarily be rejected; other reasons to support restitution are explained in chapters 11 and 12). Thus, refocusing the system away from its current emphasis on social control toward an emphasis on individual rights and responsibilities, including a right to restitution for victims and a responsibility to pay for offenders, is the most important recommendation made here.[3] Even though we may not be able to predict precisely what the rules would be if such a system were to be put in place, theory and history tell us that rules and institutions would evolve to mitigate major abuses. The hard question is, How can restitutive justice be raised to the level advocated here, so that it is the primary focus of criminal justice. To see why this is a difficult question, let us consider the status of victim restitution in criminal justice today.

Restitution in American Criminal Justice Today

Over the last eighteen to twenty years, much of the political rhetoric and re-sulting statutes regarding restitution appear, on the surface, to be moving in the direction suggested above.[4] For instance, President Reagan's Task Force on Victims of Crime (President's Task Force 1982: 17–18) recommended that statutes should be enacted by Congress and state legislatures that would re-quire courts to order restitution for victims "in all cases" unless the court gives specific "compelling reasons" for not ordering it. This recommendation was made, not for some punitive or rehabilitative reason, but in the name of jus-tice for victims. Congress passed the Victim Witness Protection Act in Octo-ber of 1982, authorizing restitution "to any victim of the offense . . . in addi-tion to or in lieu of any other penalty authorized by the law." Furthermore, if a federal court does not order restitution, it must say why, on the record. Al-most every state has also enacted or amended restitution statutes since 1977, and particularly during the four years following the President's Task Force re-port in 1982 (Evers 1994: 14). California and Rhode Island even have consti-tutional provisions that presumably mandate a right to compensation for any victim losses or injuries.[5]

Unfortunately, the perception created by such statutes and constitutional amendments is very misleading. Although the victim's "right to restitution" is supposedly recognized, the statutes generally do not specify when or under what conditions state courts must order restitution (Hillenbrand 1990: 193). Despite the fact that statutes and constitutional provisions in some thirty-five states appear to actually dictate victim restitution, the supposed goal of restor-ing victims is, at best, "an ancillary goal" for most of the restitution programs that exist (Hillenbrand 1990: 195; also see Evers 1994 and Harland 1983: 195). This is true, in part at least, because the actual criminal law process is dominated by lawyers, including judges and prosecutors; and among members of the legal profession, restitution is generally viewed as an alternative *punish-ment,* an "intermediate sanction" between the extremes of probation and prison, rather than as a mechanism for restoring victims. The American Bar Association's 1988 "Guidelines Governing Restitution to Victims of Criminal Conduct" states that "it should be remembered that victim restitution is not the primary goal of the criminal process; it is only a desirable and proper com-ponent of that process" (quoted in Evers 1994: 14). Moreover, when courts rule on restitution orders, they generally deny "victim's rights" arguments as a basis for restitution, seeing them as "offender oriented: rehabilitation, alterna-tives to more restrictive sentences, work experience, and strengthening community ties" (Hillenbrand 1990: 195; also see Harland 1983: 195–96). For instance, the U.S. Supreme Court ruled that restitution orders are not debts like other debts that can be discharged under Chapter 7 of the Federal Bankruptcy Act:

> Although restitution does resemble a judgement "for the benefit of" the victim, the context in which it is imposed undermines that conclusion. The victim has no control over the amount of restitution awarded or over the decision to award restitution. Moreover, the decision to impose restitution generally does not turn on the victim's injury, but on the penal goals of the State and the situation of the defendant. . . . Because criminal proceedings focus on the State's interests in rehabilitation and punishment, rather than the victim's desire for compensation, we conclude that restitution orders . . . operate "for the benefit of" the state. (*Kelly v. Robinson,* 479 U.S. 36 [1986] at 52–53)

The orientation of the government's criminal justice system is still toward the criminal and various social engineering goals associated with punishment and/or rehabilitation, not toward the victim and a goal of justice.

Not surprisingly, victims find existing court-ordered restitution programs to be inadequate in terms of obtaining payments from offenders (Smith, Davis, and Hillenbrand 1989: 27–28). For instance, state courts ordered only 16 percent of convicted felons to pay restitution in 1990 (this included only 26 percent of the property felons), and only 14 percent of nonprobationary felony convictions included restitution (Reynolds 1994b: 29). But more significantly, even when restitution is ordered, the criminal justice system has been either inefficient or impotent at enforcing the orders (Pudlow 1993: 1E). Prosecutors, who see their concern as "punishing" offenders rather than making victims whole, readily admit that restitution orders are not likely to be fulfilled. They may be under mandate to obtain a restitution order, but they do nothing to see that the criminal actually pays (Evers 1994: 15).

Restitution orders are currently enforced by officials in the public-sector criminal justice system. No one has clear responsibility for seeing that restitution is collected, and since collection of restitution generally adds to workloads without the addition of bureaucratic resources or any benefits for the public officials charged with collections, bureaucrats have no incentives to actively pursue restitution. The reality of punishment is that there is virtually no hope of collecting restitution if a criminal goes to prison, because most criminals have little wealth; and because of the historical constraints on prison work programs (an issue discussed in chapter 12), prisoners can generate very little income at all to pay restitution (Benson 1990: 337–39). Furthermore, probation officers who may be charged with collecting restitution are generally unable to do so even if they want to, in part because of their large caseloads and in part because there is no way to investigate probationers' claims regarding their inability to pay.

Implementing a Restitution-Based System

With attitudes leading to legal doctrine such as that expressed by the Supreme Court in the above quotation from *Kelly v. Robinson,* the potential for developing a victim-oriented, rights-based system of criminal justice in the current institutional environment is unlikely if not impossible. The focus of criminal justice must change from social engineering through punishment and rehabilitation to justice for victims. How can such a transformation be achieved?

Neither statutes nor state constitutional amendments seem to be enough. The fact is that, as Elias explains:

> [V]ictims regularly clash with criminal justice's internal organizational politics. They symbolize official failures, and represent outsiders whose participation will more than likely interfere in official routines. Contrary to our adversarial ideals, criminal justice personnel usually form cooperative "work-groups," which seek rapid case disposals, usually through plea bargaining, free from outside participants and surprises. Personal objectives bolster these organizational goals, making it especially difficult for victims to become institutionalized into a process that already routinely considers crimes as victimization of society, not individual victims. (1986: 237; also see Rasmussen and Benson 1994: 161–64)

Vague and imprecise statutes and constitutional amendments will not change these fundamental incentives. They allow too much discretion for those in the criminal justice process whose incentives are to bend restitution programs to serve the goals of the entrenched criminal justice interest groups, dominated by prosecutors, police, and other bureaucrats (Evers 1994: 17; Rasmussen and Benson 1994: 151–74). Unless legislation can somehow elevate "restitution to primary importance in sentencing" (Shapiro 1990) by creating a different incentive structure for criminal justice personnel, justice for victims will not become a product of the government's criminal justice system. This would require a huge array of changes. In particular, there would have to be a major reorientation of legislation and court rulings from their current social engineering agendas focusing on rehabilitation, deterrence, and incapacitation, toward a goal of justice for victims. Then there would have to be changes in the focus of punishment toward the collection of restitution. Those changes would have to include the development of prison work programs that are capable of generating substantial income, the allocation of sufficient budgets for probation officers to actually investigate claims made by offenders and to actively pursue restitution, and the creation of an incentive structure for corrections and probation officials that induces them to actively pursue restitution.

It is difficult to imagine this happening in the context of the government-run, bureaucrat-dominated criminal justice system of the United States. Consider the victim-offender mediation (VOM) programs, community dispute resolution centers, and other similar alternatives that have been developing in the United States over the last twenty years, for instance (see chapter 6 for descriptions and chapter 12 for additional discussion). Many of these alternatives are advocated based on "the restorative justice paradigm," which also defines crime as a violation of one person by another rather than a violation of state interests and focuses on "restitution as a means of restoring both parties; reconciliation of the parties is the goal" (Umbreit 1995; Umbreit and Stacey 1996). As explained in chapter 12, focusing criminal justice on establishing and enforcing victims' rights to restitution actually creates an environment conducive to "restoring" the offender as well, so this "restorative justice paradigm" is quite complementary to the normative objective advocated here.

VOM programs appear to have considerable potential for achieving satisfactory resolution of crime for victims, as Umbreit explains in summarizing the results of the research, including a large-scale survey of victims and offenders:

> Victims who participated in mediation were far more likely to feel the justice system had treated them fairly than were similar victims who went through the normal court process. Over 90 percent of the mediation sessions produced a negotiated restitution plan to compensate the victim, and more than four out of five offenders complied with their restitution obligations. . . . Victims who engaged in mediation were far more likely to receive the agreed upon restitution than were similar victims assigned restitution as a result of a court order only. (1995: 272)

Why? Because "the mediation process had a strong effect on humanizing the justice system response to the crime for both victims and offenders" (272). Both victims and offenders feel a high degree of satisfaction with the process. The offender learns about the impact of the crime on the victim and often feels remorse. Apparently this increases the likelihood of payment. It would appear that the foundation for the refocusing of criminal justice is already being established! Yet programs of this kind have been developing for at least two decades now, and their role in the resolution of crimes remains extremely minor relative to both private justice and public prosecution through plea bargaining and trials. The fact is that these programs generally must rely upon referrals from the criminal justice system, so prosecutors and/or judges tend to dominate the decision-making process that determines their use.

Although some criminal justice officials may share the same vision of VOM as these programs' advocates do, most apparently do not take the programs seriously. When prosecutors and judges consider them to be valuable, they tend to view them as one of an array of "alternative punishments" like community service, fines, and so on, or as one of the diversionary programs to be used for controlling their caseloads. For instance, they may refer "minor" property crimes (e.g., crimes that result in small monetary losses and therefore are likely to have occurred in low-income and minority neighborhoods) to mediation, either because the alternative punishment they expect to get through plea bargaining is trivial (or unlikely—they may refer cases that they do not think they can win [Umbreit 1995: 272]), or because diverting cases considered to be unimportant and "inappropriate for adjudication" reduces their caseload. Some of the programs are even sponsored, financed, and run by bureaucracies, often as a mere adjuncts of the existing judicial system (Auerbach 1983: 131; Benson 1990: 217; 1998d; forthcoming, b). For example,

> The law reformers who founded the urban court [in Dorchester] were committed to active community participation in dispute-settlement processes that would heal and reconcile, not isolate and punish. But the presiding judge of the district court, expressing strong reservations about involving lay citizens in dispute settlement preferred mediation to serve the efficiency needs of his own tribunal. By controlling the diversion of cases to mediation, and deterring self-generated cases, district court personnel deprived the mediation tribunal of an independent existence. "Community" mediation was absorbed by [government] adjudication. . . . With the presiding district court judge apprehensive lest judicial control be compromised by deflections from his own court, mediation slipped into the institutional cracks between the "community" proclaimed by the reformers and the adjudicatory power of the local judge. (Auerbach 1983: 131)

Such programs have relatively little chance of making a major impact because they are simply part of the government-controlled institutional arrangement of law enforcement dominated by people who are interested in maintaining their power and influence or pursuing their perception of the "public interest," rather than in actually achieving justice in the interest of individual victims. Thus, the programs tend to get the cases that prosecutors or judges do not want to be bothered with. Because many programs are eager to get referrals of any kind, they accept such "garbage cases" (Umbreit 1995: 272), and in doing so, they reinforce the opinion that criminal justice officials have of them and become increasingly marginalized.

In order to achieve the objectives supported here, or the largely complementary objectives of "restorative justice" advocated by supporters of VOM and similar programs, a dramatically different criminal justice system is required: one that instills a different set of objectives and incentives in criminal justice officials. Consider how different the criminal justice system is in Japan, for instance, where victim-offender mediation and restitution are integral parts of the process for almost all crimes.

Restitution and Responsibility in Japan

In contrast to the generally ineffective restitution programs that exist in the United States, (perhaps with some experimental exceptions noted in chapters 5, 6, and 12), the Japanese take restitution very seriously, and it appears to work (Evers 1994: 22).[6] A key feature of Japanese culture that apparently underlies the success of restitution is that there is no acceptable excuse for criminal activity. Criminals are expected to acknowledge their guilt, repent, and seek absolution from their victims, and this is the dominant focus of each stage of the criminal justice process (Haley 1989: 204; Evers 1994: 22). The vast majority of all criminals do admit their responsibility, show repentance, and bargain for forgiveness from their victims. They then ask for mercy from the public-sector criminal authorities, and given admission of guilt, repentance, and a successful bargain with the victim, the punishments imposed by the state tend to be lenient compared with punishment in other modern countries. All of this occurs despite the fact that the accused in Japan have constitutional protections similar to those in the United States.

Importantly, most Japanese criminals admit guilt not only to the authorities but also through an intermediary (e.g., family member or friend) to the victim. The admission to the victim occurs before public prosecution occurs. Then the criminal bargains with the victim through an intermediary (mediator), offering restitution in an effort to convince the victim to write a letter to the prosecutor or judge stating that the victim has been restored and no further punishment is necessary. Without such a letter, punishment can be harsh. Thus, the victim generally receives restitution before prosecution occurs; in addition, the victim typically has an advisory role (although not control or veto power) at each stage of the prosecutory process, as decisions regarding charges, prosecution, and sentencing are made. Evers explains:

> The emphasis on restitution and pardon by the victim in the Japanese approach tends to satisfy the victim's desire that justice be done. After the criminal's contrition and on top of the restitution the criminal agrees to, the authorities usually impose only a small additional punishment. That punishment is probably enough to make crime unattractive (in terms of costs and benefits) and to satisfy the natural desire of victims for retribution. In Japan, in order to obtain a pardon from the victim, the criminal has usually bargained (through intermediaries) with the victim to establish an acceptable level of restitution. Therefore, both the criminal and the victim tend to view the restitution as reasonable and any supplemental court-imposed small fine or short prison term as acceptable. (1994: 25)

Thus, in contrast to plea bargaining in the United States between prosecutors and criminals, the bargain struck in Japan is between victims and criminals. Rather than satisfying a prosecutor with a guilty plea, the criminal must satisfy the victim with sufficient restitution. Of course, the victim might be in a position to hold up the criminal by demanding a large restitution in exchange for a letter to the judge or prosecutor. The victim's ability to do so is clearly constrained, however, both by the moral standards of the society and by the fact that the criminal can refuse. The victim cannot really force payment because the criminal has a choice. Presumably the choice is between making such a payment or facing what should be a harsher punishment if he is prosecuted without a victim's pardon. If the victim attempts to hold up the offender, it is likely that confessing to the prosecutor/judge, expressing sincere remorse, and explaining the unreasonable demands of the victim will mitigate the punishment, so victims' incentives are to not demand what would be considered excessive restitution.

The importance of confessions in the Japanese system might suggest that there are strong incentives to extract confessions through force. But the bargain between the victim and the offender takes place outside the official channels of coercion. The victim is not likely to benefit from a coerced confession. Furthermore, confessions alone are not sufficient for convictions in the Japanese courts. There is no guilty plea (e.g., as through plea bargaining) in the Japanese process, although many proceedings are summary in nature. Every case that is prosecuted (not all cases are, as explained below) must involve a hearing on the evidence, and even when a confession exists, the burden of proof remains with the prosecutor, who must show that the confession was freely given and must also provide corroborative evidence. The underlying focus on admission of responsibility and remorse also has a great moral force in Japan. In contrast to prosecutors and judges in the United States, who appear to be more concerned with getting large numbers of convictions, the officials in Japan apparently desire to obtain confessions that are sincere and expressions of remorse that are genuine. Thus, as Evers explains,

> The rectification of crime, leniency of punishment, and rehabilitation of criminals in Japan have a moral basis that would be undermined by false confessions.
>
> Honest, uncoerced confession and genuine remorse put the criminal on the path of rehabilitation and provide the moral motivation for restitution. Restitution and future good behavior are discernable evidence of rehabilitation. The criminal's likely rehabilitation and restitutive effort justify punishing leniently. This integrated, balanced system of criminal justice will not work if false confessions are extracted from the accused. (1994: 24)

What does the focus on confession, remorse, and an exchange of restitution for forgiveness produce in terms of the relative effectiveness of the criminal justice system? In Japan, the clearance rate is very high compared to the U.S. rate: Evers (1994) cites sample figures that exceed 52 percent, well over twice what they are in the United States. Why? Perhaps because victims, who can anticipate restitution as well as a good deal of influence on the criminal justice process, are much more likely to cooperate with policing.

Now consider the level of public-sector involvement in trials and punishment, recognizing that in the United States very large expenditures on prisons have been and are being made. In Japan over 21 percent of the criminals who could be referred for prosecution are released by the police without additional criminal proceedings. They have the power to do this for simple cases in which they and the victims are satisfied that the offender is sufficiently remorseful. The vast majority of the cases that are prosecuted are settled in a summary procedure based on documented evidence, for which the maximum public penalty (on top of the privately negotiated restitution) is a fine. For example, in 1983, 85.8 percent of the adult criminal cases that were prosecuted were through summary procedures; only 5.1 percent involved ordinary criminal trials (prosecution was suspended for 9 percent of the adult accused). Summary proceedings are not allowed for serious offenses like murder, fraud, and extortion, for which fines are not statutory options for punishment (although prosecution can be suspended in such cases). Nonetheless, although conviction rates are very high (almost 99.5 percent), few offenders receive government-imposed penalties on top of their restitution other than small fines or short prison terms (generally less than a year).

In the absence of harsh punishment by imprisonment, how successful is this criminal justice process, which substitutes holding criminals responsible to their victims (restitution) for harsh punishment? The number of offenses and the numbers of criminals are substantially lower in every crime category than they are in any other modern, industrialized country in the world. Moreover, among the industrialized countries of the world, only Japan's crime rates have fallen continuously since World War II (Haley 1989: 204). Finally, there is at least some evidence that recidivism is very low in Japan (Evers 1994: 25). This should not be surprising, since the Japanese system breeds a very different attitude among criminals. Recall the quotation at the beginning of this chapter indicating that in the United States criminals see themselves as victims of society, and they rationalize their criminal behavior by convincing themselves that they are not responsible for their actions. In contrast, "the process of confession and restitution found in Japan discourages such self-indulgent self-forgiveness and develops honest attitudes and patterns of conduct by punishing in moderation only when criminals show remorse and pay restitution" (Evers 1994: 25).

Could such a system be implemented in the United States in the context of the existing system of public prosecution and corrections? Perhaps, but it is highly unlikely. It would take some significant changes in law, in procedures, and most significant, in public-sector attitudes. As Evers notes, trends appear to be running in the opposite direction: the government's influence in society is rising, while "[i]n Japan, society runs largely on its own; government officials do not figure importantly in making things work. Norms are mostly enforced through social pressure in the family, school, workplace, and local neighborhood. Face-to-face communities enforce conformity . . . [and] strive to curb criminal violence and to correct its practitioners. . . . In Japan, it is mostly society rather than government that is in charge of crime control" (1994: 25–26). What makes restitution work as well as it does in Japan, then, is the fact that by and large, private individuals and groups are much more responsible for controlling crime.

An Alternative to "Fixing" the Public-Sector Criminal Justice
Process: Privatization

Successful restitution programs appear to require much greater privatization than currently characterizes the U.S. criminal justice system. Perhaps more accurate, given the very large investment the private sector is making in crime prevention and protection, successful restitution programs appear to require a much smaller role for government in prosecution and punishment. Only by taking personal responsibility for active involvement in prosecution and collections, either through direct participation or contracting with specialists (e.g., private police, prosecutors, and collection agents), can victims expect to increase the chances of collecting adequate restitution. Such privatization is now severely hampered by legal barriers. Thus, instituting a restitution-based system of justice cannot be achieved without significant changes in the laws limiting the potential scope for private policing, prosecuting, and collection of court-ordered restitution. Nonetheless, these legal barriers to privatization are relatively easy to identify and change compared to the alternative: changing the incentives that underlie the operations of the existing public-sector criminal justice system. Therefore, the focus of chapters 11 and 12 is on lifting barriers to privatization. Although a major implication of the normative perspective adopted here is that criminals should be held responsible for their actions, this perspective, "premised on notions of free will, rights, duties, and justice, and not on theories regarding how best to structure a society or to shape the behavior of its members" (Logan 1995: 84), has other implications as well. In particular, free individuals must take responsibility for protecting themselves and their property, rather than expecting someone else (e.g., government officials paid by taxes) to provide those services.

Individuals reap the primary benefits of secure property rights, and therefore they should have primary responsibility for that security. They certainly may cooperate with others in fulfilling their responsibility, but the cooperation of others should come with a voluntarily agreed-upon price; it should not be expected to be provided free upon demand. That principle alone suggests that the criminal justice system should be privatized to a substantial degree, since free exchange is the best way to achieve efficient cooperative outcomes (Coase 1960). This normative perspective suggests, in fact, that no one should be forced to pay for helping to secure other peoples' property rights. Of course, if they do not contribute to the production of security for their own property rights by some cooperative arrangement, then they also should not be allowed to consume it. Thus, the normative perspective developed here implies a fully privatized criminal justice system. The discussion of policy options that follows in the next two chapters is much more pragmatic, though. Rather than simply advocating an imaginary system of private justice, as in Benson 1990: 349–78, an array of policy options, from the modest to the extreme, is discussed. All of them are intended to create incentives to develop varying degrees of additional private-sector involvement in the area of criminal justice. These policy options include both options that rely on a shift in emphasis for criminal justice to a victim-restitution system and options that do not involve such a shift. It is true that the key component of a fully implemented rights-based crime policy (a policy built on the foundation of liberty, justice, and individual responsibility) is full restitution for victims, as noted above, but I expect that the results of a rights-based approach to criminal law will in fact be a society with substantially less crime: that is, such a policy is both relatively just and relatively efficient compared to the current criminal justice system.

The efficiency of the rights-based system arises because of the strong incentives that are created to develop relatively effective private institutions for law enforcement. Recall (chapter 9) that Anglo-Saxon England's legal system was based to a large extent on the cooperative pursuit and prosecution of offenders *because* of the incentives created by the fact that victims had rights to restitution. Furthermore, the voluntary policing and prosecution functions generated by the rights to restitution were so vital to law enforcement, and the taking of this right altered behavior so significantly, that kings ultimately had to establish public institutions to take on many of those functions. Thus, a return to restitution should create strong incentives for victims and potential victims to get personally involved in all aspects of the criminal justice process, and this should make crime control more effective. Restitution, then, is a mechanism that leads toward privatization of the demand side of the criminal justice process. When victims cannot expect to collect restitution, their incentives to participate in or pay for investigation and pursuit, prosecution, and collection are very weak. When restitution becomes a realistic possibility, victims have much stronger incentives to demand such services. In other words, when victims have private property rights to restitution, they have incentives to invest more in claiming what is due to them (Benson 1994a).

Conclusions: Going beyond Property Rights to Restitution

The Norman Kings used force in order to claim the "right" to take other people's property. Indeed, when they took the private right to restitution away from Anglo-Saxons over nine centuries ago (see chapter 9), they simultaneously took many other property rights as well (e.g., they claimed ownership of all land in England and then granted parcels to their powerful supporters). Over the course of history, the struggle between individuals seeking freedom and their governments seeking power over individuals' property has ebbed and flowed, so that at times (e.g., the American Revolution) the power of the government to take was sharply limited and many private property rights were reestablished. The right to restitution was also implicitly established in America during the colonial period, as explained in chapter 6, but it was never made explicit and was soon undermined by the growing power of the state. Today, even though most states have statutes that require judges to consider restitution as an option, a relatively small portion of criminal convictions actually include restitution orders, and even if restitution is ordered, the victim has no right to collect it. Thus, restitution is far from a private property right. If restitution was truly established as a property right, the criminal justice system would become more effective and efficient, in part because it would have to be more privatized. As noted above, though, the primary normative objective of this proposal is to enhance liberty and justice, both of which require a system of private property rights. A right to restitution is only one cog in such a system, albeit an important one, and such a right may do relatively little to stem the crime problem as long as the organized taking of other people's property is condoned and accepted as part of the political process.

Policies focusing exclusively on criminal justice, including privatization and restoration of victims, actually probably have limited potential for success in dramatically reducing crime. A broader policy perspective is required that focuses on liberty and individual responsibility, but it too calls for privatization—privatization in a much broader sense (Benson 1995b). As Walter explains,

> If one is to understand the failure of government to check the crime wave, one must first recognize that government has taken to itself or been urged to assume many additional functions which are difficult to distinguish from outright criminality. Government, on all levels, is infringing upon the rights of individuals and taking their property by force. Government is increasingly seeking to control, without permission, those businessmen, entrepreneurs, and hard-working individuals who provide our high standard of living through the free market. If these same interventions were visited upon citizens by private persons, the actions would be clearly identified as crimes. But government, by "legalized" methods, now manages to deprive citizens of some 43 percent of their own earnings. And many persons condone this system; they see the similarity of actions, but feel that coercion for "the right reasons" (to benefit the collective) is permissible. (1994: 59–60)

The increasing attack on private property by government both reflects and reinforces (or causes) a significant change in the basic attitudes of citizens toward other people's property, including other people's lives and possessions: many people no longer feel obliged to respect property rights. If they want to take someone else's property and they have enough political power to influence government officials, they can do so by establishing taxes and/or regulatory policies that limit the ability of an owner to consume property, earn income from it, exclude others from using it, or alienate it. But "legalized" taking through government is completely analogous to "illegal" taking through crime (Tullock 1967; Walter 1994; Benson 1995b). The analogy includes the underlying attitude toward other people and their property: "[T]his change in the basic attitude toward private property . . . explains the rise in crime" (Walter 1994: 60).

People who are willing to use the coercive powers of government (taxation and transfer payments and regulation) to take from others are not content to play by the constitutional rules established when the country was founded: they do not believe that they have a responsibility to respect other people's property rights. They believe that they have the "right" to take property from others through political action. Thus, they speak of "rights" or "entitlements" to welfare, medical care, social security, disaster relief, farm subsidies, jobs protected from competition, and so on, all of which require taking property from someone else (e.g., taxing current income, borrowing against the income of future generations, and making regulations that limit competition).

The "right" to take from others no longer seems to a policy question. Rather, the questions debated today focus on how much to take, when to take it, and what the purpose for the taking is: "Labor unions, pressure groups, looter groups such as the Welfare 'Rights' Organization, political parties, . . . business organizations and industrial groups are all engaged in organized, sophisticated taking of other people's property" (Walter 1994: 61). Little wonder that others, who may not have the political power necessary to benefit from such takings, adopt a similar attitude toward property rights and turn to crime. As Walter explains, some people who are not "content to play by the political rules" simply take the same idea one step further: "Why, they ask, should they wait for some greedy bureaucrat to get around to giving them the money 'everyone' recognizes as having no rightful owner? . . . [T]hese people decide to 'take what is theirs by right' (or at the very least, belongs to no one except he who can take it and hold it)" (1994: 61).

The increasing power and scope of government both reflects and causes an undermining of individuals' responsibility to respect private property rights. Thereby it undermines liberty. It simultaneously reflects and fosters an attitude toward property rights that encourages crime. And then crime is used as an excuse to further limit liberty. As Logan notes, it is commonly claimed that "increasing freedom brings with it increasing crime. Liberals respond with proposals that would decrease *economic* freedom; conservatives respond with proposals that would decrease *social* freedom" (1995: 84). Both types of proposals tend to involve more government and less liberty. But in reality, crime is likely to decrease through greater emphasis on the tenets of individual liberty, because there is a "corollary of freedom: individual responsibility" (Logan 1995: 84) *when* liberty is conceived of in the way it was at the time this country was formed; it was believed to arise through the exercise of individual rights, which in turn are based on individuals' obligations or responsibilities toward others. Thus, in contrast to widely held beliefs, reductions in liberty (limits on people's ability to use private property in the pursuit of happiness while recognizing an obligation to respect others' private property) are associated with increased crime, because both reflect the same attitudes toward property rights. Therefore, while privatization *in criminal justice* is the focus of the next two chapters, truly significant reductions in crime may actually require much greater levels of privatization in the form of the reestablishment of the sanctity of private property rights, in part through the reestablishment of a real constitutional limit on government's powers to take property. Nonetheless, greater levels of privatization in criminal justice alone should induce noticeable reductions in crime, so it is a worthy goal in itself.

11

Encouraging Effective Privatization in Criminal Justice, Part I

Prevention and Pursuit

Restitution for victims is much more likely to be the focus of a privatized criminal justice system than of a system dominated by public policing, prosecution, and corrections personnel. Therefore, from the normative perspective of liberty and justice, privatization is desirable. Of course, making such changes will not be easy for politicians, even if they happen to accept the argument. As Fixler and Poole explain,

> perhaps the greatest political barrier to privatizing police services [and other aspects of the criminal justice system] is that of union opposition. As shown in the Reminderville and Oro Valley [and San Francisco and other] cases, public officers' associations will strongly react to any local jurisdiction which attempts to privatize police services. In light of today's budgetary constraints, it is shortsighted to permit special interest political pressures to override the public's interest in cost-effective public services. (1992: 38)

It takes political courage and farsighted leadership to stand up to the police unions, or it takes a strong lobbying effort by some other groups. Since victims' rights groups (discussed in chapter 4) are the only organized groups that are likely to be able to counter the political power of the entrenched criminal justice lobbies, at least at this time, one purpose of this book is to advise such groups about the kinds of changes that are needed to create a criminal justice system that truly will be responsive to the desires of crime victims. Unfortunately, the police and other public-sector interests have frequently positioned themselves as allies of victims by demanding harsher punishments, and so forth, and most victims' groups apparently do not realize that police actions to limit privatization actually work against victim interests.

Interest groups and politicians who do realize that police resistance to privatization is counterproductive may still be cowed by the fact that police will raise strong challenges to any privatization efforts. They should realize, however, that public employee unions are always going to resist any changes that might appear threatening to their security or discretion, including relatively small ones (Benson 1995c). It sometimes seems as though what civil servants produce most effectively is inertia. And since they are going to resist even marginal changes, why not go all the way? That does not mean that public institutions necessarily have to be eliminated. Lobbying for the elimination of the barriers to privatization and for recognition of private property rights to restitution is likely to be a more effective approach. One possible way to induce public police to change is to create a competitive environment, so allowing the option does not necessarily mean the end of public bureaucracies: if they can offer a competitive set of services at a competitive price, they certainly may survive. Public police departments in small towns and suburban areas often are very responsive to their constituencies (Sherman 1995), and they may be very competitive when compared to private alternatives. Perhaps even big-city police departments can change if the right incentives are created.

This presentation should not be viewed as a blanket condemnation of criminal justice bureaucrats. Even though criminal justice bureaucracies are one of the most influential lobbies in the area of crime policy (Berk, Brackman, and Lesser 1977; Benson 1995c; Benson, Rasmussen, and Sollars 1995; Rasmussen and Benson 1994: 127–41), other groups may also oppose privatization, and the reasons for their opposition will probably also have to be challenged if political changes are to be achieved (see chapter 12 in this regard). Furthermore, these bureaucrats are just people, responding to the incentives and constraints they face in an effort to maximize their own well-being. It is the institutional environment creating those incentives and constraints that leads to the undesirable results.[1] Some, and perhaps many, of these bureaucrats get personal satisfaction when justice for victims as they see it, or some other perception of justice (e.g., moral retribution), is achieved. Some do take victims seriously, whether out of a sense of justice or in recognition of the vital role victims must play in an effective criminal justice system. But, as Breton and Wintrobe explain, "[o]ne need not assume Machiavellian behavior, deceit, or dishonesty on the part of bureaucrats, because in all likelihood the pursuit of their own interest will be, as it is for everyone else, veiled in a self-perception of dedication and altruism" (1982: 152). And clearly, some (most?) people, including some (most?) criminal justice officials are frequently going to be explicitly motivated by self-interests; this must be recognized in judging their political demands and developing arguments to counter them. Thus, demonstrating that crime can actually be relatively effectively controlled through the interactions of private buyers and sellers and through various voluntary cooperative arrangements is a second function of this book. Justice for crime victims remains the primary objective of all of the recommendations made here, but the fact that achieving this objective through privatization and creation of private rights to restitution will also lead to a more efficient system, given goals of effective deterrence and/or rehabilitation, should broaden their appeal and provide more arguments to counter objections raised in the political arena.

In order to demonstrate the reasons for expecting a more efficient criminal justice system and a reduction in crime under greater degrees of privatization (including a rights-based restitution system), the recommendations for increasing privatization will focus on the "expected price of crime" introduced in chapter 4 and the potential for raising it in order to reduce criminal activity.[2] A wide range of policy options will be suggested, which, even in the absence of a refocus on victims' rights to restitution, should encourage greater levels of personal responsibility and private-sector involvement while reducing the severity of the crime problem. In each case, however, reasons will be presented for expecting that private property rights to restitution would enhance the crime reduction effects even more than other policies that only increase privatization.

Recall that the expected price of crime is not the actual sentence given to convicted criminals, or even the portion of that sentence served (e.g., time in prison before parole or early release). Rather, it is determined by the probabilities of (1) the crime or its consequences being observed; (2) either the observation being reported to someone in a position to investigate and/or apprehend (arrest) the wrongdoer (e.g., public police or private security), or the observer being in such a position; (3) the wrongdoer being apprehended; (4) the apprehended offender being charged and prosecuted after being apprehended (either through public or private justice procedures); (5) the prosecution being successful so that an appropriate sentence to one of a number of alternative punishments can be imposed; and (6) the sentence being actually carried out (criminals almost never serve the entire prison sentence that a judge hands down today, nor do they pay the restitution that judges often mandate). Greater private-sector involvement can increase the price of crime by raising the probability that all of these events will occur. Therefore, greater privatization can increase deterrence and reduce crime. The first three stages of this process, those involving prevention and pursuit, are considered in this chapter, and the last three, focusing on prosecution and punishment, are examined in chapter 12.

Encouraging Preventive Observation

The function of public police in the minds of most citizens is to fight crime. But how can voters, taxpayers, and/or elected representatives tell whether police are doing a good job? The number of arrests is a natural measure of effectiveness, and this, along with response times and reported levels of Index I crime, tends to be the primary statistic that police focus on in lobbying for expanded budgets (Sherman 1983: 156). Thus, incentives for police to watch or patrol in order to prevent crimes are relatively weak, and incentives to wait until crimes are committed in order to respond quickly and make arrests are relatively strong. It is not surprising, therefore, that after an extensive review of research on police performance, Lawrence W. Sherman, a highly respected and long-time researcher for the Police Foundation (and now an academic criminologist), concludes that "[i]nstead of *watching to prevent crime,* motorized police patrol [is] a process of merely *waiting to respond* to crime" (149). There is also a growing body of evidence that implies that as policing has become more capital intensive, it has become less effective at crime deterrence. That is, additional police resources, and particularly additional policing capital, will not necessarily reduce reported crime rates (Benson, Kim, and Rasmussen 1998). Capital (e.g., cars, radios, etc.) may be relatively effective at producing arrests but relatively ineffective at observation. As Sherman laments: "In general, as the level of *crime prevention watching* has declined, the level of crime has risen" (1983: 149).[3]

Police incentives may actually be even more "perverted" than suggested so far: there are incentives to allocate resources in order to avoid deterring Index I crime. After all, though arrest statistics may be the primary indicators of police performance used in the budget bargaining process, they are not the only important statistics used. As Milakovich and Weis note, police have a vested interest in keeping crime rates relatively high: if crime rates drop too much, then support for more police and larger budgets declines, and "like all bureaucracies, criminal justice agencies can hardly be expected to implement policies that would diminish their importance" (1975: 10).

As an example, consider that much of the information emanating from police bureaucrats about the relationship between drugs and crime has been false or misleading, as noted in chapter 7. This information has been used to justify political demands for the criminal justice system to "do something" about the "drug/crime problem," demands that largely emanate from the police lobbies; it has also been used to justify an emphasis on control of illicit drug traffic as a means of general crime prevention. State and federal legislators have been passing increasingly strict sentences for drug offenders, police have reallocated resources to make more drug arrests, and judges have sentenced increasingly large numbers of drug offenders to prison. Through this focus on drug enforcement, however, police have actually caused crime rates to rise as non-drug-related crimes are less effectively deterred (see chapter 7 as well as Benson and Rasmussen 1991; Benson et al. 1992; Sollars, Benson, and Rasmussen 1994); police are making large numbers of arrests, but many of them are drug arrests rather than arrests for property crimes. Furthermore, the large seizures are developing into another indicator of "effectiveness" that police like to advertise (drug seizures are always reported in terms of "street value" whether the drug has been processed, cut with additives to make it consumable, packaged, and shipped to the market or not; it is much like reporting that two cents worth of wheat in the field is worth a dollar since that is what the bread sells for after the wheat is processed, mixed with other ingredients, and baked, packaged, and delivered to a grocery store). Whether police are actually this calculating or not may be questionable (although some clearly are—see Stutmann and Esposito 1992 and the discussion of the Volusia County Sheriff and others in chapter 8), but the drug war has certainly tended to increase the indicators of need for and effectiveness of policing.[4] In light of such perverse incentives of police, how might we change the probability of successful watching to observe crimes? There are several possibilities.

Make Public Police Act like Private Security

A number of experiments in "community policing" are now under way. They involve taking police officers out of patrol cars and out of the "emergency response system" so they can focus on risk control by creating more effective proactive crime prevention, often by patrolling neighborhoods on foot (Skolnick and Bayley 1988). Such activities require a personal service orientation (Sherman 1995: 339) in order to create more trust between an officer and the citizens in the community and to allow the officer to gather better information about the problems and people of the neighborhood (Trojanowicz and Moore 1988). The measurable impact of experimental community policing projects on crime is somewhat limited, since only a few experiments have been examined. However, these programs appear to be effective (Blackstone and Hakim 1995). In Madison, Wisconsin, for instance, an Experimental Policing District was created in April of 1988, and after three years citizens and police officers were surveyed to determine their perceptions. There was a general perception that crime was less of a problem in the community, although it is not clear that this was actually true since the results came from a survey (Blackstone and Hakim 1995: 33).

The Ranier Valley section of Seattle also started a community policing project in 1988, at the insistence of the Ranier Chamber of Commerce, which even offered to fund the project if the police department would not. The crime rate in the area began dropping almost immediately (the crime rate in the rest of the city also has dropped, but other portions of Seattle did not experience falling crime rates until a year after the Ranier section did [Blackstone and Hakim 1995: 35]). Furthermore, willingness on the part of citizens to cooperate with the police apparently increased, because calls for services rose in the Ranier Valley area while they were declining in the rest of the community (the issue of reporting is discussed in more detail below).

Private security personnel and voluntary patrols essentially do community policing. Indeed, Sherman defines community policing as police acting like security guards, explaining that "[w]hat security guards do is to *control risk factors*. They do not roam far and wide looking for action, as many young police officers do" (1995: 338). And they do not sit and wait for crimes to occur, as many other police officers do. The payments to security personnel and the benefits of voluntary watchers arise from the prevention of crimes against persons and property rather than from making arrests after such crimes are committed. Thus, a major part of private security involves visible patrolling and watching to deter crime. That is, private security already provides the kind of policing services that community policing advocates suggest that public police should be providing. Therefore, the evidence of the effectiveness of private security cited in chapter 7 can be added to recent public experiments in community policing to support the development of such programs. Community policing, or more accurately, policing based on the private security model, works: visible and obvious watching, such as that provided by public police on foot beats, private security, and voluntary patrols, deters crime.

Community policing is likely to result in fewer arrests, but the reduction in arrests in areas that enjoy the services of community police, private security, or active voluntary associations does not imply a reduction in the probability of arrest for criminals. Rather, there are fewer arrests because there are fewer crimes, because more criminals are deterred. They recognize that because they are more likely to be observed, *the probability of punishment (either through arrest, prosecution, and sentencing, or through immediate and violent response by the security or police officer) is higher.*

Unfortunately, public police in major cities are well aware that community policing requires them to act like security guards, and as Sherman notes, they tend to be insulted by the idea that they should do so. Sherman (1995: 338) contends that police should not be insulted (many small town and suburban police departments probably have been practicing community policing since before it was called community policing), noting that security-guard-type service is what the people they are suppose to serve apparently want; he points out that "[i]n the past two decades, people have voted with their wallets, increasing spending far more rapidly on security guards than on public police" (335). Nonetheless, the fact is that in many major policing jurisdictions where crime problems are the most significant, police resist adoption of the community policing mode of operation (if they do act like private security, people who believe that effective police must be public employees may recognize that private security can effectively provide quality policing and change their minds). Despite growing recognition that traditional approaches (rapid response, random patrol, etc.) do not work (Chicago Police Department 1993), police unions in particular resist changes. "Policing is an occupational culture driven by rapid responses to short-term problems, unaccustomed to judgments about success or failure" (Sherman 1995: 344) of longer-term problem-oriented or risk-control-oriented activities. Thus, the potential for a rapid and widespread transformation to a community policing approach by public police is relatively remote, even though cities such as Chicago are trying it over the objection of their police unions.

Replace Public Police with Private Security

The probability of observation actually can be increased either by creating incentives for public police to act like private security *or by* increasing the use of private security. Moreover, since private security already has a service-oriented, risk-control approach to crime such as that which community policing requires, and since public police personnel strongly resist efforts to adopt such an approach, it makes more sense to create an environment that is conducive to greater use of private security alternatives than to try to force community policing on public police personnel (sufficient competition from private security may induce public police to adopt better procedures without efforts to mandate it). Not surprisingly, public police are also frequent critics of private security and active opponents to actions that may encourage greater use of such services (Sherman 1995; Cunningham and Taylor 1985: 43; Fixler and Poole 1992: 36). For instance, a Chicago police union representative speaking at a conference entitled "Privatization in Criminal Justice," sponsored by the Office of International Criminal Justice at the University of Illinois at Chicago in March 1995, said (paraphrasing) that the union resists privatization on every front that they can, using all of the political power that they have. And as suggested above, these police unions and other organizations of public police (e.g., police benevolent associations, sheriffs' associations, etc.) are very influential political pressure groups. They often effectively prevent or at least delay any programs that might reduce their members' wages, job security, numbers of positions, or discretionary powers. Even if they are not able to force a ban on private security alternatives, they often can influence and have influenced the regulatory environment in order to restrict the potential uses of private security and/or limit its competitiveness. Therefore, in order to encourage the further development of private security alternatives, groups such as the victims' rights organizations that are seeking improved crime control should lobby against police demands and for the elimination of various politically erected barriers to such privatization. One of the strongest barriers to competition tends to be professional licensing.

Eliminate Licensing Restrictions on Competition in Private Security Markets

The political rhetoric about professional licensing and regulatory restrictions is that they are mechanisms for protecting citizens. For instance, it is often suggested that unscrupulous firms might provide inferior services by unqualified personnel if licensing is not required. This argument is used to justify the licensing of everything from cab drivers to barbers to doctors to private security. The fact is, however, that licensing serves as a barrier to entry that prevents competition (Stigler 1971), and competition is often a much more effective regulator than government is. This is as true for private security as it is for grocery stores. As Alberto Benegas Lynch points out, "[w]hile the professional auditing of corporations is important, the most relevant audit is carried out by consumers through competition. This concept seems to be well understood when it refers to goods and services in general, but not when it comes to the provision of the services of protection and justice" (1995: 6).

Limiting competition (along with serving as a source of revenue for the state or local government) actually is licensing's only real function in many situations, since once licensed, the license holders are rarely inspected or monitored by the licensing authority (recall the discussion of complaints against private security firms in chapter 8, where it was noted that many agencies do not even keep records of complaints). Furthermore, even if the licensing agency requires an initial license holder to meet certain requirements (often political connections is the relevant requirement rather than any particular expertise), licenses often can be sold at very high prices (because of the profits that can be earned in the market subject to such restrictions on competition) to people who are not subject to the same requirements. This is not surprising since most licensing boards are dominated by the firms holding licenses, either explicitly through appointment, or indirectly through political influence. A survey of managers of existing security firms suggests that, by-and-large, they favor state licensing, probably in large part because it can limit competitive entry to challenge these established firms. Existing firms naturally prefer not to have to compete with new entrants, just as police unions prefer not to have to compete with private security alternatives (given the mistaken belief that licensing is intended to protect consumers, even competitive firms may also want licensing because it provides a signal of reliability to uninformed consumers—a "catch 22" problem). Thus, security managers also recognize that licensing and regulatory boards dominated by industry representatives "lead to a limitation on competition, through the enactment of provisions that only certain firms could meet" (Cunningham and Taylor 1985: 28).

Since private security firms are also increasingly being seen as a threat to police budgets and/or job security, licensing policies controlled by public police imply the same incentives to limit competition. Of the 35 states requiring guard and patrol firms to be licensed in 1985, regulation in 15 was provided by the state police or the Department of Public Safety, but there clearly are alternatives: 7 states did their regulating through a department of commerce or occupational licensing agency, and 5 did so through the Department of State (Cunningham and Taylor 1985: 28). Furthermore, 15 obviously did not require such licenses, suggesting that a real option may be laissez-faire (local governments also may require licenses, of course). Not surprisingly, "[o]f these [regulatory] mechanisms, the regulation by law enforcement agencies appears to be the least popular. . . . security firms generally oppose the practice. . . . [which] has led to unfair and counterproductive controls, such as an overemphasis on police training in the curriculum for security guards," as well as other problems, including long processing delays (28–29). When police, who clearly have a vital stake in limiting the effectiveness of their competition, are in charge of regulating that competition, the predictable result is severe limits on competition through unnecessarily strict regulations and licensing requirements. Thus, if regulation and licensing is desirable (and it generally is not), it clearly should be done by some agency other than the police (or the security industry).

One excuse for licensing requirements and one cause of regulatory delays, as well as other problems that arise with such licensing, is that private security firms themselves are generally denied access to criminal records, even for job applicants. Thus, without public-sector "supervision," private security firms could end up employing criminals and placing them in positions where they can easily commit crimes. Both the 1985 (Cunningham and Taylor 1985: 65) and 1991 (Cunningham, Strauchs, and Van Meter 1991: 4) reports to the NIJ recommend that all security employers be given access to criminal history records in order to screen their own applicants. This would reduce processing delays and lighten the regulatory "burden" of the state (perhaps even freeing up some scarce policing resources to fight crime).

Interestingly in this regard, the federal government is turning over a substantial part of its security checks to the private sector by creating an employee-owned private company out of the former Office of Federal Investigations of the Office of Personnel Management ("Security Checks" 1996). This bureaucracy had been conducting about 40 percent of the federal government's background and security checks. The FBI does such checks for the White House and for cabinet level appointments, and the Defense Department has its own investigative service. This privatization process is far from ideal, since it does not involve a competitive market, an option that clearly is viable; given the recent scandal over large numbers of FBI files on Republicans turning up in the Clinton White House, perhaps it should be considered on a much broader scale. The point is, however, that while many private security firms are unable to legally perform complete background checks for their own potential employees, the federal government is privatizing a substantial part of its own security check business. If it is good enough for Uncle Sam, why is not appropriate for private security firms? The answer appears to be that limiting authority to perform background checks is a mechanism for limiting entry and effective competition. After all, because the private firms are generally liable for the actions of their employees, they have stronger incentives to do a more careful screening of applicants than public officials do (recall the discussion in chapter 8 of the lack of liability for government officials who make a mistake in hiring their own employees, and recognize that the incentive to effectively screen applicants for potential competitors has to be much weaker). Private security firms often even attempt to obtain access to criminal records "illegally" in order to check applicants now, so giving them access to such information would simply legalize a process that many firms currently feel compelled to undertake in an effort to screen applicants and provide quality services.

Encourage Private Watching and Privatize Streets

Watching does not have to be performed by either professional security personnel or police. It can also be done by private citizens. In fact, evidence suggests that volunteer and paid private security patrols are both more effective watchers than public police (Sherman 1983), implying that for cost-effectiveness reasons public police should *not* be the primary providers of crime prevention through watching. Sherman (1983: 158) concludes that the organization and use of both private voluntary watch groups *and* private police should be encouraged and public police should focus on other tasks. But private watching can be encouraged in a number of different ways, some of which are much less desirable than others.

An undesirable way to encourage more private watching is to limit citizens' options through constraints on private security markets, forcing citizens to fend for themselves when public police fail them. Public police may actually cooperate in the formation of crime watch and other programs of this type even as they attempt to discourage the use of private security. Even with police encouragement, though, the incentives to perform watching functions are relatively weak if private citizens do not have the power to take actions that can actually prevent crimes when they perceive a risk, as for example, when a stranger is observed to be acting in a suspicious manner on the public streets in a neighborhood. Citizens can call the police, of course, and *if* the police have the manpower and inclination to respond, the stranger might be harassed enough that he or she moves on. A superior way to encourage private involvement in watching is through a general privatization movement that reduces the perceived dependence on the public sector, gives citizens more powers and incentives to act, either on their own or in conjunction with other security input, and opens up options that may cause citizens to weigh the personal costs and benefits of an array of alternatives.

One example of such a general privatization policy that would encourage greater participation in watching is private streets. Private citizens do have the power to take action when they own the streets. They can approach the stranger and inquire about his or her purpose; if they are not satisfied with the answer, they can demand that the stranger leave, because they have the right to exclude anyone from their private property. As noted in chapter 7, there is strong evidence that private streets create much stronger incentives for neighbors to cooperate in watching to prevent crime (Newman 1980; Gage 1981). Private streets are common in new residential developments, but the potential gains from privatization of streets should also be allowed in areas where public streets have been established. Thus, experiments with privatization of public streets, such as those that have taken place in Saint Louis, should be encouraged. In many places, however, the opposite appears to be the case. Developers are offered incentives by local governments to accept annexation and deed their streets to the government, because the government officials want to capture more taxpayers and purchasers of various services that they supply on a fee basis (e.g., sewer and water, perhaps garbage collection, and even cable TV and electric and gas utilities). Similarly, zoning laws requiring that residential lots outside the "urban area" (e.g., outside the jurisdiction of a city government) be larger than those inside discourage the development of middle- and low-income private communities by pushing up the size and cost of lots and increasing commuting distances and simultaneously increasing the demand for and the price of (and therefore potential property tax revenues from) the limited number of smaller lots within the city. Such government controls on and ability to manipulate land use probably will have to be substantially curtailed before the private street option can spread to most lower- and middle-income residents. But there is another privatization option to consider as well.

Create Benefits from Reporting a Crime

In general, the primary benefit from effective watching is that crimes are deterred. Although fewer crimes occur, some crimes still are carried out, of course. Effective watching programs such as private security, neighborhood and building watch groups (Crime Watch), and private street associations should also increase the probability that those crimes will be observed. The relatively powerful eyewitness evidence will also increase the probability of arrest and conviction *if* the crime is reported. Thus, to capture the full benefits of improved watching, changes that encourage more reporting should also be instigated. There are a number of policy adjustments that can accomplish this objective, at least to a degree (Cary 1994: 263–66), as suggested below, but the most powerful is likely to be creation of private property rights to restitution for victims (Benson 1996c).

Encouraging More Reporting

There are two ways to increase the probability of victim (and/or witness) reporting of crime: (1) lower the costs of cooperating with apprehension and prosecution, and (2) raise the expected benefits of cooperating (the expected benefits of victim cooperation might be raised by increasing the probabilities of apprehension, prosecution, conviction, and punishment, assuming that the resulting punishment is something like restitution or revenge that the victim obtains satisfaction from; these issues are discussed below). Policymakers in the criminal justice system, including legislators, have not taken many self-initiated steps to do either. As indicated in chapter 4, though, the growing political importance of the victims' rights movement has forced legislators in many states to produce statutory changes that may either lower the costs of or increase the benefits from cooperation. Those changes are occurring not because legislators are trying to increase the propensity of victims to cooperate but because victims have organized into effective political pressure groups.

The demand for tougher sentencing laws, victim compensation or restitution, the right of victims to testify prior to sentencing about the effect of crime on their lives, and numerous other reforms is being expressed by a number of similar victims' organizations all over the country. They are having increasing levels of success, at least in influencing elected representatives and the laws that they pass. Nevertheless, the experience of the Society's League Against Molestation (S.L.A.M.) emphasizes that enhancement of victims' rights is not something that policymakers are likely to initiate themselves without prodding by well-organized interest groups. S.L.A.M. was organized in California following the sexual torture and murder of a two-year-old child by a pedophile with a twenty-year history of violent sexual abuse. S.L.A.M.'s initial efforts in Sacramento were ineffective. They were too small and politically inconsequential to attract notice (despite the fact that in 1985 responses to earlier political pressures led California to establish the first victim assistance program). S.L.A.M. returned the next year with five hundred people and sixty thousand signatures on a petition (Satchell 1985: 16). This attracted the attention of lawmakers, and a number of new laws that S.L.A.M advocated were passed, including mandatory prison terms for repeat molesters or violent first offenders, elimination of the hospital treatment program that freed the murderer whose crime led to the group's formation, and access by organizations to criminal records of anyone seeking a job that brings them into close contact with children. S.L.A.M. members learned quickly: political action requires organization and effective lobbying; legislators rarely give much attention to issues simply because they happen to be good ideas, or just ideas. By 1989 S.L.A.M. had seventy-five chapters in forty-three states lobbying for legislative change, as well as actively monitoring court cases and providing counseling for victims and information for parents.

Crime rates have been falling modestly since 1990 (Benson and Rasmussen 1994a), while political expressions of concern over crime have been skyrocketing. This widespread expression of concern over crime issues by elected politicians probably reflects political pressure from increasingly numerous and effective victims' groups as much as anything else. Law enforcement lobbies also advocate more spending on crime control, so in this regard these groups' demands are complementary: both interest groups want politicians to be concerned about crime. Law enforcement groups probably have even convinced many victims' groups that they are allies in the fight against crime, as suggested above. It is contended here that victims' groups should be very cautious in accepting such an alliance. To see why, recognize that legislation mandating more spending, tougher sentences, and so on, is not enough. A significant problem faced by the victims' rights movement is that victims have no real remedy when criminal justice officials ignore the statutes that they have managed to get passed, while still capturing their direct benefits in the form of larger budgets and more discretion because of the increased political importance of crime.

Alchian and Allen define personal property rights to be "the expectations a person has that his decision about the use of certain resources will be effective" (1969: 158). This definition is very revealing because it reflects the fact that rights or expectations are variables related to the direct efforts to protect or enforce them. Thus, the alleged "victims' rights" are not true property rights because victims cannot be confident that they will be enforced. Some victims groups have recognized this, at least to a degree. S.L.A.M. members monitor criminal courts, for instance, because they recognize that judges and prosecutors may not respond to their demands the way legislators do unless they also put pressure on them directly. But even monitoring courts is not enough. Recall the discussion in chapter 10 regarding the problem that even when restitution is mandated and ordered by judges, it is not likely to be collected by probation officers.

Pressure has also been brought to bear directly on prosecutors, and some local jurisdictions are experimenting with various ways to reduce the cost of victim cooperation. In one New York jurisdiction, a single prosecutor now works with a victim of a sex crime for the entire prosecution process, thus lowering the cost of cooperation (see chapter 4 for a discussion of these costs). Furthermore, by focusing on such cases, these prosecutors become more personally involved with the victim and therefore more concerned about the victim's perspective on the process and its outcome. To the degree that such measures are successful, increased reporting might be anticipated. But their success depends, to a large degree, on monitoring and pressuring local officials directly in order to limit their discretion.

Some victims' groups advocate constitutional amendments in an effort to give victims' rights more force (Cary 1994: 264). Such amendments in one form or another have been passed in several states, including Florida, Kansas, Michigan, Rhode Island, and California; they vary considerably in their content and scope. If a "victims' bill of rights" could give victims greater control over criminal justice officials, such an amendment might be quite beneficial, but it is not clear that bureaucrats would view it much differently than statutes. The point is that although political action by victims' groups may ultimately lead to lower costs and/or greater benefits for victims who cooperate with public police and prosecutors, victims' groups should not count on such results. Statutes and amendments, and even monitoring of courts and/or prosecutors, may mean very little, given the discretion that remains in the hands of various criminal justice system officials. Victims' organizations might attempt to monitor every stage of the public criminal justice process, including legislators, judges, prosecutors, police, corrections officials, parole boards, probation officers, and various other criminal justice decision makers, but an alternative investment of their time and effort may have greater payoff: advocating elimination of political barriers to greater privatization (some of which are discussed above, and others considered below), so that they can deal with people who have much less discretion (a private firm that does not do what it is paid to do does not remain in business for long). Before considering these options, however, one specific program, public compensation for innocent victims of crime, deserves explicit mention, in part to distinguish it from restitution, since that program may appear to be very similar and equally desirable.

Victim compensation programs have been developing in many states. Unfortunately, victim compensation is like so many other publicly administered programs of the criminal justice system. It appears to be desirable, but "in reality, victim compensation threatens to emerge as another tentacle of leviathan, encompassing far more in territory and dollars than ever envisioned" (Meiners 1977: 328–29). It is turning out to be another example of a largely symbolic policy (Elias 1983, 1986: 239) that benefits politicians who are seeking support in reelection, bureaucrats who can expand their power and scope by administering the programs, lawyers who are often paid even when victims do not win claims against compensation funds, and other political interests, while doing relatively little for victims. Consider, for instance, that the American Bar Association has actively pursued such programs, even at the federal level. Why? Perhaps out of a desire for justice, but the fact is that most federal bills, as proposed, included a payment of the victim's lawyer by the compensation board *whether the victim's claim is successful or not.* Similarly, several state victim compensation programs mandate a 15 percent legal fee from a victim's award (these fees produced enough revenues to support about one thousand full-time lawyers in 1975 [Meiners 1977: 314]).

Lawyers are not the only nonvictim advocates of victim compensation. The International Association of Chiefs of Police has supported such legislation since 1966, for instance, probably because it can trade this support for victim groups' support of its own initiatives. In the attempt to produce the political compromise necessary to pass federal compensation legislation, for instance, such bills have been joined with proposals for federal payments to policemen and firemen killed in the line of duty (Meiners 1977: 314–15). Police may support victim compensation out of concern for victims or out of recognition that victims would then have greater incentives to cooperate in generating arrests and convictions, but the linkage of the two pieces of legislation suggests strong self-interest motives as well.

Other advocates have included bureaucrats expecting to administer the program. The Department of Justice, anticipating serving as the bureaucratic home of the federal compensation commission and the program funds, issued the "LEAA study, which pushed for adoption of the program, claiming that the cost would be trivial" (Meiners 1977: 314–16). The LEAA study estimated annual compensation of about $25 million, allowing roughly a one-thousand-dollar payment per victim to perhaps 2 percent of the victims of reported crime with injury in the mid-1970s. Meiners (316) points out that upon passage of such bills, the relevant government ends up being forced to cover much larger costs for the program, because legislators find it very difficult to vote for reduced benefits to innocent crime victims, particularly in the face of demands for increased expenditures by both victims' groups and law enforcement bureaucracies. Therefore, he suggests that by underestimating costs, bureaucracies such as the Department of Justice are attempting to achieve passage so that they will be in a position to expand budget and power after the fact. Indeed, no victim compensation program has ever been funded at a level that can fully compensate even a majority of crime victims, even for measurable harms, but many of them have become quite costly because they pay increasing amounts of money to lawyers and require large numbers of bureaucrats to administer them.

An even more fundamental objection to victim compensation programs is that they do not make the criminal accountable, and even when some collections from criminals are made, they are not directly accountable *to their own victims*. The collections from a criminal need not even go to his or her victim and need not be tied closely to the damages done. Furthermore, taxes are likely to be at least a supplemental source of funding, and generally the primary source, thus shifting the cost of crime onto taxpayers rather than criminals. As Evers (1994: 12) explains, "A government compensation fund that does not rely for its revenues on contributions from reparations-paying convicts is simply another welfare-state benefits program. It cannot teach the criminal anything about the meanings of justice and personal responsibility. It is a form of debtors' relief for the criminal class" (1994: 12). To the degree that the victim is compensated out of taxpayer funds, the demand for holding the criminal accountable is mitigated, pressure for more severe punishment is reduced, and crime may well increase as a result.

In reality, victim compensation programs probably provide only slightly greater incentives for victim reporting, since no compensation program has ever received the large budget that would be necessary to actually compensate many crime victims at anything close to a level that would greatly increase the expected benefits of cooperating in pursuit and prosecution. A superior option is victim restitution, in part for reasons given in chapter 10; but unfortunately, restitution programs as they are currently administered by probation agencies are often no more effective than compensation programs. Restitution has been one of the programs demanded by victims' groups, and government has responded, at least in a half-hearted way, as suggested in chapter 10. Restitution orders are certainly being made by judges in increasing numbers of cases. They are just not being collected by the public officials charged with collections.

If restitution were to become the primary goal of the criminal justice system, as suggested in chapter 10, much stronger incentives for greater victim reporting and cooperation in prosecution would obviously arise, thus increasing the certainty of punishment and generating greater deterrence. But in the United States restitution is not treated as a private right to a debt owed by the criminal; rather, it is seen as one among many sanctions to be used by the social engineers in the criminal justice system. If there was a right to negotiate and arrange to collect restitution in conjunction with or *before* criminal prosecution takes place, or even in the absence of criminal prosecution, as in Japan (see chapter 10) and France (see chapter 12), incentives for victims to cooperate in policing and prosecution could be much stronger.

Restitution can actually be arranged through private justice, as a substitute for public prosecution, and it frequently is (Cunningham and Taylor 1985; Ellickson 1991). The Hallcrest survey (Cunningham and Taylor 1985) finds that restitution agreements are one method of resolving employee crimes that arise within firms. Such private justice, however, is a substitute for cooperating in public pursuit and prosecution. Thus, the failure of the criminal justice system to make restitution a true right creates incentives for those who want restitution to avoid cooperation with public police and prosecutors, thereby reducing "formal" crime-reporting incentives (at least, for reporting to public police, although informal reporting to private security or to neighborhood groups may increase, resulting in more private justice). In Japan, where victims have a recognized right to collect restitution through private channels (mediation), there are no strong disincentives to cooperate with public officials in pursuit and prosecution (victims also have much more input into the public prosecution and sentencing process than they do in the United States).

Increasing the Probability of Arrest

Public police currently perform many duties beyond crime control. Criminologist Abraham Blumberg suggests that approximately 80 percent of police resources are used up in what he refers to as "social-worker, caretaker, baby-sitter, errand-boy" activities (1970: 185). A 1990 Bureau of Justice Statistics survey of state and local police departments (Reaves 1992a: 4) bears this out, reporting that police have responsibility for many activities that may not deter any crimes or produce any arrests: 96 percent of the surveyed departments were responsible for accident investigation, over half performed the community's telephone and radio emergency communications and dispatch services (e.g., 911 services) for all emergency response agencies (fire, ambulance, search and rescue, etc.), 43 percent had animal control duties, 33 percent did search and rescue, 18 percent had emergency medical services, 18 percent provided court security, 14 percent did civil defense, 10 percent provided civil process serving, and so on. A similar survey of sheriffs' departments (Reaves 1992b) notes that these agencies are even more likely to have non-law-enforcement functions to perform.

With so many duties to perform, scarce public policing resources are simply unable to respond to many of the calls for assistance that come in. Donovan and Walsh (1986: 49) found, for instance, that New York City police responded to only 30.6 percent of the requests for assistance that they received. Indeed, police in some cities decide that for large categories of crimes, particular larcenies and burglaries, they will not send an officer in response to calls. One way to increase the police's ability to respond to crimes might be to contract out many of the non–criminal-law-enforcement functions the public police have taken on. Nonsecurity services, such as accident investigation, funeral escorts, animal control, telephone and radio emergency communications and dispatch services, search and rescue, emergency medical services, civil defense, and civil process serving are frequently cited as candidates for contracting out. The expectation of significant benefits from such contracting out, however, requires an assumption that police would then actually allocate the freed up resources to effective crime control, and police discretion in how resources are allocated means that this clearly cannot be guaranteed (see chapter 7). If police allocate these resources to control of consensual crimes, for instance, or simply expand their motorized rapid response system, rather than increasing their watching efforts as suggested above, relieving public police departments of certain non-crime-related duties is not likely to go very far toward reducing crime.

Contracting Out by Communities for Full Police Services

As explained in chapter 2, some local community governments and some government entities that might be characterized as "communities" (e.g., the Kennedy Space Center and the Energy Research and Development Administration's Nevada nuclear testing site complexes) have contracted with private firms for full police services, and as noted in chapters 5 and 7, many private communities (e.g., private residential and business developments such as Starrett City, neighborhoods, malls, business groups) have contracted with security firms for all security services that the law allows (when states do not give private security the power to make arrests, etc., the private security firms are forced to call in the public police on occasion). The studies of contracting out for full police services are few, but the evidence suggests that it can be a very effective means for a community to lower the cost of its policing services while increasing the quality of services provided, because of the differences in incentives that exist for private firms and public bureaucracies. Whether this would be true in general is a question that is unlikely to be tested in the current political environment, however, because many states have significant barriers to such contracting out (many of the same barriers as those discussed above, applying to private security in general).

Contracting out, whether for support services or for all police services, is also an obvious threat to public-sector job security, wages, and positions, so in Fitch's (1974) words, "once a public employee union has gotten a firm hold on a government function, any attempt to escape by resorting to private contracts will be considered union-busting and dealt with accordingly" (508). Public-sector unions, including police unions, have "argued against contracting out since the idea's inception" (Freeman 1992: 136). Local experimentation with contract policing is also severely limited by the explicit or implicit threat of lawsuits filed by public police organizations. Recall from chapter 2 that the Arizona Law Enforcement Advisory Council filed a suit challenging the Oro Valley contract with Rural/Metro Fire Department for police services, and though Rural/Metro may have won in court had they pursued the case (similar allegations in Ohio and North Carolina have been decided in favor of private security, [Fixler and Poole 1992: 38]), they dropped it and gave up the contract because they could not afford the court/legal costs. The bases for such lawsuits include the issue discussed below: private police and citizens in general do not have recognized police powers, so they cannot take people into custody, gather evidence for trial, or cite suspects in court. These powers are often explicitly monopolized by public police through statute; if not, they may be implicitly monopolized through threatened litigation and uncertainty about how courts might rule on such issues. As long as such barriers to private policing are maintained, the potential uses of private police to increase the probability of arrest will be limited.

This raises an important point. Unfortunately, even if the power to regulate private security was taken away from public police at the local and state levels, as advocated above, and even if public police's lobbying powers were curtailed or successful countered by another powerful group, they still have a litigation option that can severely limit the ability of private security to replace public police in production of either community policing or investigation and pursuit. As Fixler and Poole (1992: 38) suggest, "it is more the political fight or potential legal costs that constitute the barrier" than any real legal restrictions, since laws can be changed if a political battle or court case is successful. Clearly, overcoming the power and financial resources of "entrenched bureaucracies" is likely to be the biggest problem in a privatization effort (Benson 1990: 331–47). Therefore, rather than focusing political efforts on fighting police over directly replacing them through contracting out, a superior option is to fight for changes that will simply encourage the development of more private provision of investigation and pursuit (in addition to the private provision of watching discussed above). These changes also threaten police, but the threat is less direct and obvious, so resistance may be weaker. Such changes include reductions in legally established barriers to entry, such as licensing, but other factors become important as well when more extensive uses of private policing are the goal.

Lowering the Legal Barriers to Privatization in Policing

Statutes in many states mandate that private security personnel and citizens in general not have police powers. Essentially, that means that they cannot take people into custody, let alone gather evidence for trial or cite suspects in court. Some states have granted limited numbers of private security personnel either full or partial police powers, but typically only within confined areas, such as plants, stores, campuses, or retail malls. In a survey of private security managers, 29 percent of the respondents reported that they had some special police powers (Cunningham and Taylor 1985: 16). A survey of medium-to-large police departments found that about 25 percent of them "deputize" special private security officers to give them special police powers, although most of these private deputies are proprietary security personnel (i.e., in-house employees of a large firm or development), rather than contract agencies (i.e., independent security firms) (40). In New York, for instance, retail security personnel can act as agents of their employers and apprehend a suspect, cite the suspect in court, and preserve evidence, if they have completed an approved course of training. Private security personnel in Washington, D.C., also can be awarded certain powers of arrest if they meet the qualifications for being licensed as "special police officers"; in Maryland the governor has the power to appoint "special policemen" with full police powers when they work on the premises of certain businesses; North Carolina has a similar law, and Las Vegas security guards can be appointed as special deputy sheriffs (Fixler and Poole 1992: 35–36). Other states have similar laws that allow private security to obtain special police powers under specific circumstances and/or in specific places. Oregon's governor can appoint "special policemen" in the railroad and steamboat industries, and the Texas Department of Public Safety can commission certain people who work for private employers as "Special Rangers" with the full arrest and firearms powers of public police. Around forty states have passed legislation giving varying degrees of police authority to campus security personnel on public university campuses, and some states have extended these powers to private university security departments (a survey in the 1970s found seven such states); others allow governors, courts, law enforcement agencies, or city governments to grant such powers to private university police (36). Railroad police, discussed in chapter 7, originally received powers from the federal government to work on interstate problems of railroad crime, but since then many states have also given full police powers to these private police.

The point is that the ability for private citizens, and for private security in particular, to obtain police powers varies from state to state and locality to locality in reflection of a hodge-podge of federal, state, and local rules and regulations. In some places the barriers to effective privatization are very high, and in others they are not. These legal barriers should be relaxed in order to encourage greater use of cost-effective private security for "community policing" and for investigation and pursuit as well. The private police beats in San Francisco and the experience of the railroad police and the Starrett City Security services, as well as other arrangements discussed in more detail in chapters 5 and 7, illustrate that private police can be very effective.

As suggested above, police unions and other law enforcement organizations are likely to resist the elimination of such legal barriers to effective competition from the private security market. In fact, and unfortunately, the political battle in many states is not over weakening regulatory barriers to allow for more privatization; rather, it is a battle to prevent additional barriers from being raised. The Patrol Specials in San Francisco have had to wage an ongoing political fight against local police lobbying in an effort to retain their powers. With the strong political support of the neighborhoods they protect, they have managed to beat back nine attempts to impose additional restrictions on what the Patrol Specials can do (OICJ 1995). They have also been forced to file a lawsuit against California's Police Officer Standards and Training Commission in order to maintain their certification (Fixler and Poole 1992: 37). Similar police efforts to restrict the potential scope of private alternatives (e.g., create monopoly powers for public police) have been successful in other places, however. For instance, "in North Carolina, recent legislation has ended the citizen arrest. Only government commissioned law enforcement officers are empowered to effect an arrest—even if . . . [a witness or a victim is] capable of effecting an arrest" (McLaughlin 1994: 9).

Should There Be Changes in the Regulatory Jurisdiction?

Even if complete deregulation of private security and policing is not politically possible (at least currently), Cunningham, Strauchs, and Van Meter suggest, in their report to the NIJ (1991), that a fallback alternative in some states may be attractive. In particular, although state licensing and regulations can limit competition, particularly when state policing agencies are in control of the regulatory apparatus, they suggest that local ordinances and licensing of security firms are even more troubling. In part they are clearly cor-

rect: differing requirements across jurisdictions can create barriers to successful interjurisdictional security operations, raising the costs for firms serving
regional clients, preventing the pursuit of suspects across jurisdictions, and
preventing testimony, and so forth, by security personnel licensed in some jurisdictions and not others. Furthermore, these local regulations may be more
likely to be in the control of or easily manipulated by police interests than
state-level regulations are, so they tend to either add to or even conflict with
state-level regulations (Cunningham and Taylor 1985: 28). About one-third
of the law enforcement agencies surveyed by Hallcrest (Cunningham and
Taylor 1985) have the power to suspend or revoke private security licenses,
for instance, and law enforcement executives strongly advocate even more
widespread use of city and county ordinances granting them such powers,
whereas about two-thirds of the state licensing agencies and an overwhelming majority of private security managers oppose such ordinances. Therefore,
Cunningham, Strauchs, and Van Meter (1991: 4) recommend that licensing
and regulation of private security should be done through state, not local authority.

A counterargument should be considered as well, however. Although local
politicians are probably more responsive to police interests than state-level
politicians are, they are also more responsive to effective political pressures by
organized groups of citizens (Rasmussen and Benson 1994: 180–84; Benson
and Rasmussen 1994b). Furthermore, if some local experiments with deregulation and privatization can be instituted, they can have a dramatic demonstration effect and spread to other jurisdictions. For instance, contracting out
for police support services was virtually unheard of three decades ago, but it
is widely practiced at the local level today, as explained in chapter 2. Other
innovative local law enforcement experiments such as the Miami Drug Court
program have also been copied and even improved upon by several other
local jurisdictions in Florida and other states (Benson and Rasmussen
1994b). The likelihood of statewide experiments is much lower. Thus, a
more long-term or "dynamic" perspective than Cunningham, Strauchs, and
Van Meter (1991) take suggests that all aspects of law enforcement should be
decentralized to the greatest degree possible. Their NIJ report also recom-
mends "regulation and licensing reciprocity between states," however, in
order to overcome the barriers to serving multistate clients and avoid other
costs that arise because of varying requirements and limitations on powers
across regulatory jurisdiction including states, and this recommendation is
much more attractive.

Restitution and Private Pursuit of Criminals

The potential for private policing depends on the function of the criminal justice system. Under the current system, private security is relatively effective at protecting property. However, investigation of crimes already committed still tends to be dominated by the public police. There is a private investigator market, but much of its work focuses on noncriminal investigations (e.g., search for evidence to be used in a divorce or some other civil litigation). Insurance investigators do provide investigative services under some circumstances (e.g., when the losses are large enough to warrant the cost of investigating), and many private organizations and businesses (e.g., in the railroad industry, banking, and the hotel-motel business, as discussed in chapters 5 and 7) also rely on private investigative services because they do not get satisfactory results from public police. Furthermore, internal security organizations investigate most employee crimes for many business enterprises, partly in reflection of the very low priority public police put on such crime (Cunningham and Taylor 1985). But incentives can be created to expand such private investigative services.

Historically, rewards offered by private citizens have led to private pursuit of criminals, including investigative services, although, in contrast to public rewards, private rewards are probably more likely to be offered for the return of stolen goods than for successful prosecution.[5] The private bail bonding system relies on private bounty hunters today. If the focus was on restitution for victims, however, the potential scope for private investigation and pursuit of criminals would expand considerably. As with any true private property right, a private right to restitution should be transferable. Victims could then offer bounties or rewards, but a more likely scenario in modern America would be, in effect, the sale of the right to collect a particular fine. If the right to restitution is a marketable claim for a victim, such as it was in medieval Iceland (Friedman 1979), for instance, then it can be sold to someone willing to pursue the offender. Specialized firms (thief-takers and bounty hunters) could arise to pursue criminals and collect fines, but the more likely alternative is that individuals would contract with "protection firms," and those contracts would include insurance that pays clients who are victimized, thereby giving the right to collect restitution to the firm, creating incentives for firms to pursue offenders in order to recover their insurance payments (Molinari 1849; Rothbard 1973: chap. 11; Friedman 1973: chap. 29; Benson 1990: chap. 14; Benegas Lynch 1995: 8).

Conclusions

By now it should be clear that the criminal justice *system* is truly an interrelated system (Rasmussen and Benson 1994; Benson and Rasmussen 1994a, 1994b, 1995). Actions taken that attempt to increase the probabilities of arrest (e.g., more police) or the severity of punishment (e.g., more prison beds) can increase the incentives to report crimes, for instance, and with increased reporting the probability of arrest and the severity of punishment will tend to fall again, particularly if the new resources are simply added to the public-sector common pools. Furthermore, actions to induce increased reporting, in the absence of actions taken to expand the capacity to respond by the policing and punishment parts of the system, will lower the probability and the severity of punishment (e.g., by crowding common-pool police files and prisons). Therefore, the most important changes that can be proposed are those that affect several or all levels of the system in the same way. That is, a relatively effective policy to increase the incentives to report is one that also increases the incentives to pursue, prosecute, and develop effective means of "punishment" (defined to include restitution). In recognition of this, policies that can simultaneously have systemwide positive impacts are being proposed and discussed in several of the stages of the criminal justice process; and significantly, the change that should have the greatest positive systemwide effect is the creation of effective property rights to restitution. The institutional developments that would accompany a restitution-based system should both increase deterrence by increasing incentives to observe, report, pursue, and prosecute *and* enhance the probability of rehabilitation by creating strong incentives for both victims and offenders to establish mechanisms through which convicted offenders can improve their legitimate earning abilities and speed up the restitution payments. Before offenders can be rehabilitated, however, they must be observed, reported, and apprehended. As suggested above, privatization and a restitution focus should increase the likelihood of those events occurring. Once arrested, they must be charged, prosecuted, and sentenced, and again, privatization and rights to restitution enhance the probability of those events occurring.

12

Encouraging Effective Privatization in Criminal Justice, Part II

Prosecution and Punishment

Recognition of the already massive private investments being made in crime prevention may be sufficient to convince many people that much of the burden of observation to prevent crimes can be handled by the private sector. Similarly, after one recognizes how reluctant victims and witnesses are to get involved with the criminal justice system, the contention that reporting can best be increased by encouraging more participation by that vital private-sector input may appear to be quite reasonable. Many people may also need very little convincing to accept the idea that at least some additional privatization can facilitate arrest (e.g., contracting out support services to allow public police to focus on crime and perhaps reducing some of the regulations that limit the numbers and scope of private security and private investigation activities). There may be considerable misgivings about complete privatization of these first three stages in the criminal justice process; but the private sector is already actively and vitally involved in all of them, so hopefully, the policy changes discussed in chapter 11 that can encourage at least some more involvement in stages one (observation), two (reporting), and three (arrest) seem quite plausible upon reflection. On the other hand, for many people private justice implies arbitrary justice and lynch-mob vigilantes (counterarguments in chapters 6, 9, and 10 notwithstanding); prosecution and punishment are therefore widely perceived to necessarily be products of the public sector (perhaps with some contracting out for corrections services). But the fact is that privatization can also increase the probability of effective and efficient prosecution, conviction, and punishment, whether the objective is crime deterrence or criminal rehabilitation or justice for victims. The potential benefits from and policy changes for encouraging more privatization in stages four (prosecution), five (conviction), and six (punishment) of the criminal justice process are considered here.[1]

Increasing the Probability of Prosecution

In order to prosecute accused criminals, those arrested obviously must be available for trial (or plea bargaining), but since jails and courts are crowded, many arrested criminals must be released until prosecution occurs. Once released, they do not have to return.

End Publicly Supervised Pretrial Release Programs

One way that the private sector is already affecting the probability of prosecution is through the private bail bonding system. As explained in chapter 4, this market institution is clearly much more effective at insuring the appearance of alleged criminals than its public counterpart, pretrial release (PTR) programs. Private bondsmen have much stronger incentives to monitor accused criminals under their bonds than PTR bureaucrats have. They also have much stronger incentives to pursue them if they fail to appear, relative to the public police who are responsible for pursuing those released through PTR programs who do not return. Therefore, replacing PTR with private bail bonding should increase the probability of successful prosecution and the expectation of punishment for criminals. Unfortunately, the trend is toward increased use of public PTR programs and reduced use of private bail bonding. Reynolds (1994b) suggests that the growth in the use of public PTR systems since the 1960s has been so substantial that it may help explain the much higher rates of crime that the country is now experiencing, since it dramatically lowers the probability of prosecution and turns many criminals back out on the street without effective supervision.

Dissatisfaction with public PTR programs is growing, however, and political opposition is mounting, as more and more serious crimes are committed by individuals released on the recommendations of pretrial release agencies. Some state legislatures have passed uniform bail acts in an effort to constrain PTR agencies' discretion (e.g., they may specify that no one can be released without a monetary bond who has a prior criminal record or who has "jumped" a previous free recognizance bond). Some judges are also refusing to deal with PTR agencies because they have almost no recourse against a person who fails to appear and has not paid a monetary bond up front. Therefore, as Reynolds (1994b: 19) concludes, taxpayer-funded PTR programs should be abolished, so that the private bail bonding system can take over full responsibility for supervision of accused criminals who are released pending prosecution. If a private bondsman is unwilling to provide a bond, that should serve as a signal that the criminal is too unreliable and/or dangerous to be released.

Encourage Private Prosecution

There is a more fundamental problem with public prosecution than the fact that criminals are released before trial and conviction and then fail to return. Every accused criminal is guaranteed counsel, but the same is not true for victims of crime. Public prosecutors supposedly represent victims, of course, but they clearly do not do so (Rasmussen and Benson 1994: 152–64; Bidinotto 1994b; Fine 1994a). For one thing, there are far too many victims for the limited number of prosecutors to effectively represent (Valentine 1992: 226), and for another, the incentives of prosecutors do not encourage high levels of concern for individual victims (Rasmussen and Benson 1994: 152–64). Prosecutors have become, in large part, political animals who pursue their own interests by responding to the demands of powerful interest groups, rather than pursuing the interests of crime victims.[2] Thus, to the despair of many victims, prosecutors dismiss or plea bargain away many of the crimes that caused their suffering, presumably in order to handle the huge number of accused criminals that pass through the system, discriminating among cases, at least in part, on the basis of the likely political clout of the victim. Why not privatize prosecution?

Other countries allow and even encourage some private prosecution. In England, prosecution remains a private duty, as explained in chapter 9, and despite the development of a legal fiction that allows public police to prosecute, some 3 percent of criminal prosecutions are still done by victims or their employed attorneys today (Cardenas 1986). Public prosecutors in Germany enjoy a monopoly on the right to prosecute, much as prosecutors in the United States do, but there are two exceptions that do not exist in the United States (Reynolds 1994b: 27). First, there is a class of misdemeanor offenses, including things like domestic trespass, that can be prosecuted by victims. Second, and perhaps more significant, a crime victim can demand that the public prosecutor pursue a case, and if the prosecutor refuses, the victim can appeal to the state appellate court. The court in turn can order the prosecutor to bring charges; under these circumstances the victim can join the prosecution as a "supplementary prosecutor" to ensure that the prosecutor does an adequate job in presenting the case (since the prosecutor has been ordered to prosecute against his will). The situations in France and Japan are even more supportive of private involvement in prosecution in order to pursue restitution, as explained below.

Private prosecution is possible in the United States too, in a limited way (Valentine 1992). Victims can employ attorneys to help insure that prosecution occurs. When a private attorney acts for a victim, though, he or she generally must obtain "the district attorney's approval and be, in effect, welcomed into the case by him" (226). Nonetheless, as Valentine explains, "the fact should be faced that the employment of private prosecution is in some cases and in some jurisdictions the only way for victims of crime to get justice. You either have a private attorney to assist the state in prosecuting [the accused] . . . or he just does not get prosecuted" (227). A private prosecutor does not take over a case in the United States. Rather, the victim's attorney works to help the public prosecutor and/or to badger the public prosecutor when he tries to postpone, dismiss, or plea bargain the case (226). A victim may even have to employ an attorney "just to get a straight answer as to a trial date" (227).

Why should a private prosecutor not be allowed to take over a case? Why should a victim not be allowed to pursue prosecution even when the district attorney does not want to? Why should district attorneys have monopoly powers over decisions to prosecute, particularly when they cannot adequately serve as representatives of all victims and when defendants are guaranteed legal representation? As Valentine states,

> [p]rivate prosecutors make sense to citizens who are concerned about the rights of both defendants and victims. Fairness and justice for crime victims should not be something for which one needs to apologize. Fair, aggressive, and timely prosecution of persons charged with crimes does not deprive them of any rights except in the eyes of those who think that defendants have all the rights. Does a defendant have the constitutional *right* to a sloppy, ill-prepared prosecution?
>
> Does a defendant, under any circumstances, have a fundamental right to the benefits which accrue to him as the result of a harried, overworked, understaffed district attorney's office? (1992: 227)

Widespread private prosecution in the current environment is unlikely because it adds to the victim's costs of crime. In chapter 4 it was pointed out that most victims do not want to invest the time and effort it takes to cooperate with police and prosecutors, so why would they want to invest their own money on top of that time and effort? One answer is that it can increase the probability of successful prosecution and the severity of the resulting sentence, so the publicly produced benefit of cooperation increases even as the cost does. Revenge may be a strong motive in some cases, and the fact that some private attorneys are occasionally employed to assist and prod public prosecutors suggests that it is a sufficient motive for some victims. But since the incentives to cooperate in pursuit and prosecution for most victims are actually quite weak, we should not anticipate large investments in private prosecution without either supplementing its costs or increasing its potential benefits for victims.

Restitution and Private Prosecution

One way to lower the cost of private prosecution would be through a voucher system such as the one suggested by Schulhofer and Friedman (1993) for privatizing indigent defense (that is, for eliminating the public defender bureaucracy). This shifts more of the costs of crime onto taxpayers rather than onto the criminals, who should be bearing them. A superior way to pay for private prosecution, which simultaneously creates incentives to pursue prosecution, is the refocusing of the criminal justice system on restitution. Restitution should include payments both for the costs that the crime has inflicted on victims and for the cost of collecting the restitution, including the cost of prosecution (and postprosecution supervision, as explained below). A restitution-based system could effectively turn crimes with victims into torts, wherein the victim has strong incentives to pursue prosecution in order to collect restitution (Benson 1990: 349–78).

This is not a far-fetched idea. In Japan mediated negotiation between the victim and the offender over the appropriate restitution actually occurs before criminal prosecution, and in a very significant way it substitutes for such prosecution, as explained in chapter 10. If the negotiation is successful, public prosecution may be waived entirely; and if not, it generally will involve a summary procedure resulting in only moderate additional punishment (plea bargaining with the prosecutor is not an option in Japan). The developing but still small-scale victim-offender mediation and family-group-conferencing processes in the United States and elsewhere also are substitutes for criminal prosecution, as explained in chapters 6 and 10, and offer a potential base upon which a large-scale process similar to Japan's might be built.

In France a crime victim has the right to file a civil claim against the accused, but this claim can be filed in a criminal court and considered at the same time as the criminal case is being prosecuted by a public prosecutor. Furthermore, the civil suit can be filed in the criminal court even *before* the public prosecutor files a criminal proceeding. As a result, "[p]rivate prosecution is very popular in France, since it enables the victim to collect damages quickly and inexpensively" (Cardenas 1986: 385). Some victims in the United States also have an option similar to this French system, although it is more limited, time consuming, and costly. The O. J. Simpson civil case of 1996–97 illustrates the process, but it is not the only example (Hoffman 1997). Victims can, under some circumstances, sue for civil damages in a separate civil trial after the criminal outcome (trial, plea bargain, or dismissal) has been achieved, and they are actually choosing to do so in growing numbers. Suits against drunk drivers, perpetrators of domestic violence and other assaults, and accused murderers are all being filed. Some defendants in these cases were acquitted in a criminal trial, as O. J. was, but some were found guilty either through trial or through plea bargaining, and some had their criminal charges dismissed. When prosecution of such civil cases is pursued, as Columbia law professor George Fletcher notes, "[t]he victim becomes the center of attention, not the police, and the victim can have more control of the action by choosing the lawyer" (quoted in Hoffman 1997). This is not an attractive option for most victims, though, given the costs of a civil trial. And unlike O. J., most criminals are probably judgment-proof, having no significant wealth and very limited legal income-earning options (a problem that can be alleviated, as explained below, given a focus on restitution). Furthermore, since most accused criminals are not able to employ a team of the best defense attorneys in the country, they are much more likely to be convicted (generally through plea bargaining). If the conviction results in a prison sentence, the potential for earning income to pay restitution is remote at best in the current institutional environment; if the sentence is probation, evidence from existing restitution programs suggests that criminals will probably be able to avoid payment by pleading hardship with their probation officers.

Encouraging private prosecution through establishment of a restitution-based program will substantially increase the probability of prosecution only if the probability of collections is high; therefore institutions to facilitate collections may also have to be developed, as explained below (as noted in chapter 10, however, restitution is much more likely to be paid if it arises through victim-offender mediation than if it arises from a court order, so it may be that fewer collection agencies will be needed than one might anticipate). If true private property rights in restitution are established (that is, if expectations of collection are high), victims will have much stronger incentives to pursue a case than public prosecutors do. Fewer cases will be dismissed, and fewer crimes will be forgiven through plea bargaining. That does not mean that bargains will not be struck to avoid the costs of a trial, though. Forgiveness of crimes might also arise, but it will be the victim who accepts the bargain and/or grants the pardon, not a public prosecutor or judge. A restitution system in which the

criminal anticipates having to pay the cost of prosecution if a guilty verdict is handed down creates strong incentives for the guilty criminal to bargain with the victim in order to avoid the higher restitution payments that will be required after a trial.[3] The bargain is much less likely to involve the forgiveness of some crimes or guarantees of light sentences in order to gain guilty pleas; instead, the focus will tend to be on the avoidance of additional costs that are anticipated to fall on the guilty.

The threat of private prosecution and accompanying litigation costs for the accused could mean that an accuser has a good deal of bargaining power. As noted in chapter 10, this could lead to collections from people who are falsely accused. Certainly, this is the case in tort law today, as many people (or their insurance companies) accused of a tort choose to bargain and pay something rather than go through an expensive and time-consuming trial, even if they are very likely to win. This does not have to be the case, however. In France a penalty is imposed on the accuser if the court decides that the accusation is either false or frivolous. The accuser then pays both the court costs for and damages to the accused, and if the accusation is believed to be intentionally false, criminal charges are brought as well (Cardenas 1986: 386). If such penalties were imposed, the potential to use a threat of criminal prosecution to extort money from innocent people or to just harass people that one does not like, as happens with threats of tort litigation today, would be significantly reduced. The results should be quite similar to those in Japan, where guilty criminals have strong incentives to bargain with victims in order to "buy" forgiveness. Failure to bargain results in a much harsher punishment through formal prosecution, but a letter of pardon from the victim indicating that the criminal has paid a satisfactory restitution (e.g., is remorseful and has been forgiven by the victim) means a much lighter public sanction. Those who are innocent and falsely accused will have incentives to go to trial and even to countersue for damages.

Increasing the Probability of Conviction

One of the problems that prosecutors often face in trying to convict a criminal is that police make errors in arrests and evidence gathering that lead to judicial exclusion of key elements of the prosecution (Neely 1992; Benson 1996b; Bidinotto 1994b; Nelson 1994; Fine 1994b). These errors reflect negligence both on the part of public police and on the part of courts, which often promulgate new evidentiary rules without providing sufficient guidelines for

obtaining admissible evidence. The result, as the National Advisory Commission on Criminal Justice Standards and Goals (1973: 206) explains, is that one major factor contributing to increases in serious crime is court application of more and more stringent standards for admitting evidence. Similarly, David Jones (1979: 83) reports that lower court judges and prosecutors generally complain that the extension of exclusionary rules has shackled their ability to bring the guilty to justice.

Privatization and Exclusionary Rules

The fact is that the intended goal of protecting civil liberties has not been effectively achieved by exclusionary rules, particularly where the rights of the *innocent* are concerned. For instance, if the police enter a person's home, destroy or damage his property, and find nothing incriminating, exclusionary rules do not protect the home owner. That person's only recourse is to file a damage suit with its accompanying costs to recover (Neely 1982: 144–45). Furthermore, such damage suits are frequently not successful, because many states require proof of vicious intent or prior knowledge of innocence before damages will be paid (see chapter 8 for more discussion). Thus, "there is little effective remedy against the police available to those who are not guilty," and "for every search that produces contraband there are untold scores that do not" (Barnett 1984: 54). The exclusionary rule protects criminals, not innocent victims.

"Every serious student of the exclusionary rule . . . agrees that the exclusionary rule is a limited deterrent to the most persistent forms of police bullying" (Neely 1982: 141). The exclusionary rule provides no direct sanction against police, and the only personal cost to a police officer for improperly obtaining evidence is very indirect. Should an officer consistently violate the rights of criminals so that convictions cannot be obtained, then he *might* expect a lower salary or loss of his job. Even these sanctions are extremely tenuous when an officer is protected by his union and when firing a civil servant is virtually impossible. At some point, the officer *may* be passed over for promotion, but such possibilities are so uncertain that they provide little perceived threat. Given its goals, the court system had little option but to establish exclusionary rules, however.

Rules of evidence are under the court system's control, but more efficient means of achieving the desired end are not. The courts do not actually require release of felons whose rights have been violated, after all; they simply

have dictated that release will be the solution until another means of protecting civil rights is established, and as Richard Neely (1982: 140), chief justice of the West Virginia Supreme Court, explains, a logical remedy is legislation requiring a civil fine on the offending officers or their government departments for violation of a person's rights (innocent and guilty alike). If sufficiently direct sanctions were applied, then police "bullying" would be significantly reduced *without* any exclusionary rule. There would be more direct incentives to perform properly if police departments and therefore governments were liable for full damages any time police violate a citizen's rights. As Nelson explains, "if the exclusionary rule were abolished in favor of a sensible mechanism for directly punishing offending policemen, the Court's present dilemma would be resolved" (1994: 109). Similarly, Neely contends that if a state legislature were to enact a comprehensive compensation system for all citizens, with reasonable money damages for *all* unconstitutional police intrusion, and simultaneously prohibit the exclusionary rule in the state's courts, the Supreme Court would be forced to reconsider its exclusionary rules (1982: 162). Essentially, what Nelson (1994) and Neely (1982) propose is that public police bear responsibility similar to that of private security. In particular, if public police were to face liability rules like those faced by private security firms (as evidenced by the fact that they spend a good deal of money on liability insurance [Blackstone and Hakim 1995]), the need for exclusionary rules would be undermined. This would enhance the probability of conviction by removing rules that are intended to protect the innocent but end up protecting the guilty. The result would be an increase in the probability of conviction.

Public police departments and even the city governments that would be liable for such damage awards will resist such legislation, of course. One way to achieve this goal is to contract out for public police services with private firms who are already liable for the misbehavior of their employees. As Cunningham and Taylor note, "cases brought by private security are usually well developed" (1985: 12), reflecting the fact that they have strong incentives to avoid violations of the rights of the accused, or of the suspected who are subsequently discovered to be innocent, for which they can be sued (see chapter 8).[4] Police resist such contracting out as well, so once again, the best approach may be to undermine the role of public police by opening up more avenues for the development of private alternatives (e.g., granting police powers to private security and allowing private communities like Starrett City and privatization of public streets with authority to employ private police).

Restitution and Private Courts

Court crowding is another major factor in limiting the deterrent effect of convictions. Prosecutors obtain large numbers of convictions through plea and charge bargaining, as a result, and these bargains almost inevitably involve reduced numbers and/or severity of the charges relative to the actual crimes committed. The private sector has responded to the impact of civil court crowding with a rapidly expanding system of private alternatives such as arbitration, mediation, and the new for-profit courts (see chapter 6). But the potential for private courts to relieve criminal court crowding is clearly limited under the existing criminal justice focus on punitive sanctions. Civil liberty concerns about private judges' mandating prison sentences and other forms of punishment will probably prevent the development of any formal private-sector criminal courts (despite the fact that, as noted in chapter 2, so-called public judges are also private citizens who happen to be employed by the state and who are given considerable power in the process). Informally, sanctions are being imposed within business firms and by various other groups of private citizens, as noted in chapter 6, but publicly visible arbitration would probably be more accurate and less likely to be abusive.

Formal private courts would probably move into criminal justice very quickly if the system was refocused on restitution. The issues of criminal law would be determination of damage payments that the criminal owes to the victim, at least for most crimes. Deciding damage awards is a frequent function of private arbitrators and mediators. In Japan, restitution awards are determined through mediation before criminals ever go to court, and if the mediation is successful, the criminal trial is a brief summary proceeding. The developing victim-offender mediation options in the United States illustrate that similar arrangements are clearly possible here. Furthermore, the traditional outcome of mediation is the establishment of a contract specifying obligations on the part of both parties; mediation (or arbitration, for that matter) between a victim and an offender can also produce a legally binding contract that specifies the amount of debt and how it should be paid. Contract issues are regularly handled by private mediators and arbitrators today (Benson 1989a, 1990, 1995a, 1997a, 1998a, 1998e). Thus, refocusing criminal justice toward restitution would open up a much wider avenue for privatization in order to increase the probability of conviction, because the number of courts available would expand dramatically, thereby reducing plea and charge bargaining as it is currently practiced. Bargaining still could be important, as noted above, but it would be between criminals and victims, generally facilitated by a mediator,

and not between prosecutors and criminals. Competitive entry into the private court market significantly lowers both the time and monetary costs of trials, however, so the incentives to bargain may well be reduced (and the potential for using a trial threat to extort unjust payments clearly would be reduced).

Implementing Just Punishment

One reason for the perception that the criminal justice system does not effectively implement sanctions is the fact that prison crowding reduces the portion of sentences criminals actually serve. The most popular political "solution" to crime seems to be building more prisons, presumably in order to alleviate crowding and early release programs such as parole, gain time, good time, and so on (this "build-our-way-out" strategy is not likely to have much impact on crime, however—see Benson and Rasmussen 1994a, 1995). Budgetary trade-offs have in turn forced many local, state, and federal administrators to consider contracting with private firms (Krajick 1984b: 20–21) in order to reduce the costs of meeting the political demands for increased uses of imprisonment.

The potential cost savings from contracting out clearly have not been exhausted. The relatively limited use of contract prisons reflects government barriers, however, rather than a lack of willing suppliers. For instance, Buchingham Security wanted to construct a 716-bed "interstate" jail in Lewisburg, Pennsylvania, for protective-custody prisoners from several government jurisdictions (Logan and Rausch 1985: 307). Negotiations to provide supervised prison space were under way with seventeen states, and by April 1984 the company had letters of intent for more prisoners than they had planned space for. The project was widely supported by the community, but it was abandoned following defeat of enabling legislation in the Pennsylvania legislature. Similarly, when Corrections Corporation of America proposed to take over the entire Tennessee prison system, state lawmakers turned down the offer despite substantial cost savings. Furthermore, various states put tighter restrictions on private prisons than on prisons built and operated by public agencies. In Florida a contract prison must save at least 7 percent before it can be considered as an alternative to a public facility. More significantly, twenty-five states are still without statutory authorization for contracting out (down from 50 in 1980, however). These kinds of legal barriers shelter state-run facilities from the forces of competition, thus undermining one of the potential benefits of privatization. They should be eliminated, although attempts to do so will face considerable political resistance.

The majority of the political activity and job actions by corrections unions involve demands for higher wages, earlier retirement, disability pay, sick leave, shorter hours, and so on; other factors can also play a role, but as Wynne reports, another major cause for strikes by correctional institution employees is "issues pertaining to safety and security, a matter made particularly complex by the presence of covert motives" (1978: 218). For instance, a prison employees' union may try to prevent community-based programs and deinstitutionalization (e.g., halfway houses) out of an expressed concern for public safety, but the fact is that such programs result in relatively reduced needs for prison facilities and institutional jobs. Perhaps all such demands represent true concerns for public safety; nonetheless, one has to at least recognize the potential self-interest motive. In this regard, contracting out in corrections is a recent threat to prison employees, but their unions expressed opposition as early as 1976 (Wynne 1978: 228), showing concern over the poor quality of services that the profit-seeking firms will allegedly deliver (but see chapter 3).

Corrections unions have actively opposed virtually any new program that reduces the traditional custodial role of public correctional institutions; thus, strong opposition to contracting out (particularly for existing facilities) can be anticipated. And *any* move toward eliminating public facilities in favor of a fully private system will run up against strong opposition, including illegal actions. For example, during the spring of 1975, New York State proposed to close one prison, transfer 380 prison inmates to another facility, and lay off a number of corrections employees. The union representative called a press conference and reported that "the announced closing, transfer of inmates, and the proposed layoffs of employees represent total fiscal irresponsibility and this union will not be a party to it" (quoted in Wynne 1978: 198). The union membership refused to do the work necessary for transferring the prisoners and threatened that if the employees were replaced by "scabs" the union would *prevent* the transfer. As a result, the facility was *not* closed. In 1975 illegally striking corrections officers in Ohio stopped delivery trucks from entering the prisons, forcing the state to use national guard helicopters to send in needed supplies. The power of corrections (and police) employee unions is often even more substantial because of cooperation with other unionized public employees. Massachusetts fired striking correctional officers in 1973, but the officers were reinstated after the president of the state's American Federation of State, County and Municipal Employees threatened to declare a strike of all state employees.

Contracting out is not likely to eliminate crowding anyway, however. As noted in chapter 7, crowded prisons reflect both supply (cost) and demand conditions, because the decisions made by local prosecutors and judges are often not integrated and coordinated in a way that adequately reflects state-level prison capacity. To the degree that private firms are successful at providing more prisons at lower costs, thereby perhaps making prisons relatively more cost-effective, prosecutors and judges will have incentives to turn even more to the use of prisons for punishment rather than alternatives (e.g., probation, intensive supervision programs, restitution). Thus, mechanisms for reducing the flow of criminals into prisons (e.g., sentencing guidelines and decentralization of corrections so that decisions on their use can be integrated locally—see Benson and Wollan 1989; Benson and Rasmussen 1994a, 1994b, 1995; Rasmussen and Benson 1994: 191–99) will have to accompany cost reductions through contracting out if prison crowding is to be eliminated. Nonetheless, more punishment can be obtained for any given level of expenditure if more contracting out for prisons is done and if the pitfalls inherent in the process (e.g., contracts awarded on the basis of political considerations and/or corruption rather than on the basis of price/quality competition—see chapter 3) can be avoided. Therefore, either more criminals can be imprisoned for terms similar to those that criminals typically serve now, or a given set of criminals can be held for longer periods, depending on what kinds of access controls are maintained.

Paying the Costs

There is a more fundamental issue that should also be considered in this context—an issue raised in chapter 10: who should pay the cost of crime? Corrections budgets clearly are part of that cost. From the rights-based normative approach taken here, the answer is quite simply that *criminals should pay as much of the cost as they possibly can.* With the right institutional arrangement, making criminals pay the costs may produce efficiency gains as well, through both increased deterrence and stronger rehabilitation effects.

Today, criminals presumably "pay" for their crimes by being incarcerated and/or supervised in some other correctional program. At best, however, this means that criminals pay only part of the costs of their crime, while other costs are added. The primary costs are still borne by victims, who are not compensated for their losses; but costs are also added for noncriminal taxpayers, who pay for probation and parole officers, prisons and corrections personnel, treatment and education programs, and so on. Beyond that there are costs for consumers of other public services that are curtailed in order to finance corrections. When a criminal is imprisoned, taxpayers cover the direct cost of running the corrections process, as well as such indirect costs as the maintenance of the families of many criminals by means of welfare programs because the criminals are not in a position to earn money for family support. There may be some deterrent effect that benefits taxpayers in general because everyone is a potential victim, but this effect is clearly modest. For instance, empirical evidence indicates that although a higher probability of punishment is likely to be a general deterrent, more severe punishment measured by longer prison terms is probably not (Elliot 1977; Silver 1974; Rasmussen and Benson 1994: 41–43). Furthermore, the high rate of recidivism for those who go to prison (somewhere in the 60 to 75 percent range [Beck 1987; Klein and Caggiano 1986; Illinois Criminal Justice Information Authority 1986]) implies that existing levels of imprisonment are also probably not very effective at specific deterrence (e.g., punished criminals generally resume committing crimes when released). And probation is an even less effective specific deterrence than prison (Kim et al. 1993). Thus, it appears that the only people who really gain are the criminal justice officials whose livelihood depends on the current focus on punishment (e.g., prison and probation workers) and those who can use the common-pool prisons to improve their political standing (e.g., prosecutors who want to look tough on crime and shift crime costs off their constituents onto statewide taxpayers). This high cost of crime for taxpayers and victims is not necessary. First consider alternatives for probation and parole, and then for prisons.[5]

SHIFTING THE COSTS OF PROBATION AND PAROLE ONTO CRIMINALS

Imprisonment is only one form of punishment, of course. More criminals are sentenced to probation than to prison, in fact, and large numbers of criminals are released from prison to be supervised by parole systems. "To say that there are problems with both the probation and parole systems is putting it mildly. A large amount of crime is committed by people on probation or parole" (Reynolds 1994b: 30). Parole and probation supervision have not been privatized (unless we broaden the definition of probation to include such relatively intensive supervision as halfway houses and some drug treatment programs), but they could quite easily be, by using the commercial bail system discussed above and in chapter 4 as a model (31).

Prisoners eligible for probation or parole could be required to post a financial bond against specific violations of their release program. As with a bail bond, the amount could be set by the courts or a parole board based on the criminal's history and prospects. These bonds might be obtained from family or friends, as bail is in some cases (or for parole, the money might be earned in a prison work program as discussed below), but in addition they could be obtained from private bondsmen for a fee. Upon successful completion of the period of supervised release, the bond would be returned to the bonding agent. Violating the terms of the release program would result in imprisonment, whereupon a prorated portion of the private bond could be returned to the bonding agent who successfully turns over a violator. A private bondsman would have strong incentives to ensure compliance with probation or parole requirements in order to obtain full repayment of the bond upon successful completion of the period of supervised release, and a bounty hunter arrangement could easily develop to pursue those who flee, in order to avoid loss of the entire bond, given that turning in such a fugitive results in repayment of a substantial portion of the bond. If a convicted felon is unable to obtain a private bond, that would imply that the individual is too high a risk in the eyes of both friends or relatives and private bondsmen; as Reynolds suggests, "why should the general public risk having that person on the street?" (1994b: 31). Such a private financial market would provide valuable information for the courts and parole boards in their attempts to sort out who should be released and who should not. It would also substantially reduce the need for public parole and probation officers since private bondsmen would provide close supervision in order to insure against loss of the bond.[6] If such privatization of probation and parole were to increase the effectiveness of selection and supervision, as private bail does relative to pretrial release, then the criminals released to these programs would pose less significant threats to citizens. Perhaps they would become less unpopular, relieving some of the pressure to put certain types of criminals (e.g., nonviolent felons) in prison and leave them there for long periods. The private sector can also relieve the costs of imprisonment, however.

MARKETING PRISONERS' LABOR

The huge prison population is an untapped resource that could be employed to substantially reduce the burden on taxpayers. It is time to give serious consideration to using this resource, thereby making prisoners pay for their own punishment (and rehabilitation, as well as restitution, as suggested below). Given the conclusion that criminals should pay at least a substantial portion of the costs of their crimes rather than placing the burden on victims, taxpayers, school children, college students, and so on, the next question is, What is the most effective way of extracting such payments? The answers proposed here, in increasing degrees of probable effectiveness, involve encouraging a market for criminals' labor services with competition among employers to obtain contracts from the state; giving prisoners property rights to their labor, rather than the state, so that competitive employers would compete directly for the labor services; and establishing private rights to victim restitution with a private and competitive collections market, including private supervision of criminals who are likely to flee, while they work off their debts.

When prisons were first developed, they were self-financing because they put prisoners to work. During the nineteenth century many state prisons actually were able to finance their own operations and turn over surplus funds to state treasuries. As late as 1885, 75 percent of all prison inmates were involved in some sort of productive endeavor, mostly in private contract and leasing systems. By 1935 the portion of prisoners working had fallen to 44 percent, and almost 90 percent of those worked in state-run programs rather than for private contractors (Reynolds 1994b: 33). Today, except for the newly emerging experimental programs discussed below, the prison population represents a huge pool of almost completely unused labor that drains state treasuries rather than contributing to them.

THE POLITICS OF PRISON LABOR

The prison work programs that existed in the nineteenth century are notorious for their abuses of prisoners, but they did not disappear because of concerns over prisoner abuse. Political concern for prisoners was not widespread (and it probably is not now). Instead, resistance to state-controlled but productive use of criminals' labor came first from firms producing products that were in competition with the outputs of the prison work programs and later from organized labor, who saw prison labor as a cheap source of competition. Such political pressure led to a number of legal barriers to prison work programs. In most states, laws or constitutional provisions were established that prevented the sale of all but a few prison-made items (e.g., license plates). New York passed the first of these laws in 1901 in the face of business pressure to eliminate competition from the then-self-supporting prisons. Under pressure from business and labor unions, Congress later passed the Hawes-Cooper Act of 1935, prohibiting interstate commerce in prison-made products when the receiving state had laws against the marketing of such goods. Private contractors were also prohibited from using prison labor to meet government contracts exceeding ten thousand dollars under the Walsh-Healy Act of 1936. Then in 1940 the Sumners-Ashurst Act made it a federal offense to transport prison-made goods across state borders, regardless of state laws.

The effect of all these [state and federal] statutes was virtually to wipe out the market for prisoner labor and for prisoner-made goods, [so that now] . . . in virtually every prison the only work opportunities are in the traditional prison industries—the making of license plates being, of course, the classic example—and in prison maintenance and custodial work. In almost every case these positions are low-paying, and in spite of that the industries involved are almost everywhere money losers. (Shedd 1982: 27–28)

Prison work programs were further undermined in the 1950s and 1960s "with the ascendancy of the correctional treatment model" (Auerbach et al. 1988: 1). Rehabilitation was thought to be more directly achievable through education, vocational training, and counseling programs than through actual work experience (evidence cited below denies this assumption).

In the face of soaring prison costs and the pressure on prison administration to reduce idleness among the increasing numbers of prisoners, both state and federal laws regarding prison labor and the marketing of prison-made goods have begun to change. The growing belief that the correctional treatment model of the 1950s and 1960s has failed and that life in prison is too "soft" has also added to the political support for prison work (Auerbach et al. 1988: 9). Congress removed the federal restrictions on the interstate sale of prison-made goods in 1979, on the conditions that (1) inmates working in private prison industries are paid at a rate equal to or greater than the rate paid locally for similar work; (2) local unions are consulted before the project is initiated; and (3) no employed workers outside the prison are displaced, the prison work does not involve an occupation for which there is a local surplus of labor, and existing contracts for services are not impaired (Auerbach et al. 1988: 10–11). This legislation also authorizes up to an 80 percent deduction of the participating workers' gross wages for taxes, room and board, family support, and state-run victim compensation programs. Between 1979 and 1988, more than half of the states also passed legislation authorizing prison work programs of some kind (11–13), and several more have done so since 1990 (between 1990 and 1996, thirty states passed legislation authorizing contracting prison labor to private firms [Walker 1996: 38]).

Political and bureaucratic resistance to prison work programs has continued, however, and in some cases their development has been stifled. Consider this example: in Montana, state officials looked long and hard for a prison industry that would not compete directly with any producer in the private economy. They chose to manufacture office furniture, which was to be produced and sold only to state agencies. There were no office furniture manufacturers in the state at the time. Nonetheless, resistance came from office furniture retailers (Cook 1984). A substantial political and publicity campaign was mounted to destroy this modest project that employed only twelve prisoners, who were paid thirty-one to fifty-eight cents an hour (above room and board, of course) in a small prison factory. The perceived low wage is part of the problem. One reason for resistance to prison industries in the past has been that they are seen as cheap labor pools that have unfair competitive advantage. A bookkeeping change showing that prisoners are paid the prevailing market wage for the type of work done, and then subtracting part to cover "room and board" and extra costs arising from the risks the prisoners pose, can overcome that excuse for political resistance, as several industry programs have recognized (examples are noted below). Furthermore, in Montana the state also "marketed" the product to itself, replacing real market forces. The program was not an example of market competition, then, but precisely the opposite. If they had, instead, marketed prison-produced goods through established wholesale and retail outlets, actually entering the market rather than withdrawing part of the market from potential competitors, they probably would have had the support of the state's retailers rather than their opposition. A number of other prison industry programs are apparently surviving, precisely because the potential for resistance has been recognized and the institution arrangements have been structured accordingly.

Several federal experimental programs are now under way, and several state and county programs also have been established. As a result, evidence is beginning to mount that prison work arrangements can be developed to the satisfaction of firms as well as prisoners, public officials, and political interest groups. These experimental programs have taken a number of forms. Some of the prison industry programs are run by state corrections bureaucracies that sell the product (as the Montana program was), some are run by quasi-independent not-for-profit organizations (e.g., Florida's program), some involve private employers of prison labor (e.g., Kansas's program), and some include several private firms offering prison labor employment opportunities (e.g., programs in Washington state). A 1989 NIJ survey identified more that seventy private manufacturing, service, and light assembly firms that employed prison labor in sixteen states (Stewart 1989), up from thirty-eight in fourteen states two years earlier (Auerbach et al. 1988: 16). Expansion has continued. South Carolina prisoners in the start-up phase of two private-sector programs had already earned $2.4 million in wages by the end of 1992, with about $500,000 going to taxes, $119,000 to victim compensation, $322,000 to room and board, $364,000 to family support, and $1.1 million to inmate savings accounts (Reynolds 1994b: 34).[7]

Despite considerable change in the political environment surrounding the prison labor issue, the vast majority of prisoners in the country are still not employed in productive activities. Some advocates and researchers suggest that one potential barrier to a rapid development of private markets for prison labor is simply the lack of willing private-sector participation (Auerbach et al. 1988). To the degree that this is true, it probably reflects, in part at least, a lack of information available to potential participants, perhaps because of the long period between the 1930s and the 1980s when private markets for prison labor were effectively outlawed. Businessmen may be generally unaware of the potential source of labor offered by prisoners. On top of that, there probably are "deeply embedded negative stereotypes of prisons and prisoners" (15). By definition, of course, most prisons inmates are "maladjusted" people: they have chosen crime over legal alternatives. That may imply that they do not share the work ethic that characterizes traditional labor forces. But many criminals may simply see crime as a relatively lucrative enterprise, perhaps because they do not have marketable skills that allow them to earn as much as they can through crime, or perhaps because they are relatively good at crime and therefore expect large returns relative to expected costs (i.e., the low probability of punishment).

Consider the evidence from a Rand Corporation study of drug dealers in Washington, D.C., for instance. The majority of the dealers have legitimate jobs that earn them, on average, about twice the minimum wage (Reuter, MacCoun, and Murphy 1990). Furthermore, the individuals making the most in their legal jobs also tend to be the ones who take in the most through drug dealing. In other words, ambitious, hard-working criminals also can be ambitious, hard-working employees in legitimate businesses. Just because a person has chosen to commit a criminal act does not mean that he or she will not respond to incentives and opportunities. Chances are that inmates have chosen criminal acts *as a response* to incentives and opportunities. The fact is that at least some prisoner labor can be effectively harnessed to legitimately produce quality products. This has been clearly demonstrated in a number of the experimental programs, and additional direct evidence is presented below, but it should not be surprising.

In order to rapidly overcome the lack of knowledge and the misinformation (stereotypes) about the potential for prison work programs, some advocates suggest that it may be necessary for the state to disseminate information and perhaps even provide start-up incentives to private firms in order to stimulate their interests in investing in projects that can employ prison labor. Since employing prison labor is relatively costly (e.g., because of the need for greater security and supervision), it is suggested that such incentives might even have to be permanent (Auerbach et al. 1988: 58). The states should be very cautious in providing incentives such as tax benefits or subsidies, however, because this could easily and justifiably result in the same kinds of political opposition that low wages for prisoners have produced in the past. Giving such advantages to firms employing prison labor amounts to "unfair" competitive advantages if the benefits exceed the actual additional costs associated with employing such labor. In addition, strong sources of political resistance remain. For instance, the Traffic Safety and Sign Manufacturing Association successfully lobbied for legislation, passed in 1987, mandating that the future production of highway signs by prison industries not exceed the dollar volume produced in 1996, and the Business and Institutional Furniture Manufacturing Association voted to exclude government agencies from its membership, essentially to limit prison industry programs' access to the association's information and connections (Grieser 1989: 19).

It may well be that the private sector will generate the necessary information without state involvement or subsidies, if the states change their laws. Private-sector advocates of prison work programs are already disseminating considerable information. One of the leading promoters of private-sector employment of prison labor, Fred Braum, Jr., is the president of the Workman Fund in Leavenworth, Kansas. This nonprofit foundation lends venture capital to private firms interested in training and employing on-site prison labor in "real world" enterprises. Braum also is president of Creative Enterprises, which has two plants (one making sheet metal products, and one making electric heating elements) that train and employ minimum-custody inmates at the Lansing East Unit in Leavenworth. The two plants employed 150 prisoners in 1990 (Miller, Sexton, and Jacobsen 1991; Criminal Justice Associates 1990). A more recent development is the Enterprise Prison Institute, a private research, information-disseminating, and advocacy organization located in Washington, D.C. As information spreads about successful programs, both through organized efforts such as the Enterprise Prison Institute and through word of mouth within the business community, misperceptions about the potential benefits of prison labor markets will be corrected. In Florida, the Federation of Independent Business originally opposed the state's prison industry program, but it is clearly reevaluating that position; it even cited "significant recent improvements" within the program (Enterprise Prison Institute 1996c: 2). It is possible that some of the businesses supporting prison industries are doing so because they expect to gain access to a source of cheap subsidized labor (a recent survey of Florida business leaders suggests that 65 percent feel that private firms should be provided with "incentives" to employ prison labor [Meese and Rostad 1996]), so the danger of such subsidization remains.

Organized labor is also coming around. Although the national offices of the AFL-CIO still tend to oppose prison industries, local union officials in Texas and Iowa are actively working with and even advocating their state's programs. The changing political environment is described by Knut Rostad, president of the recently created Enterprise Prison Institute:

> The landscape around prison industries in the states has fundamentally changed in the past three years. Three years ago prison industries was not a major interest of state policy makers and the general public; three years ago the impact of industries programs was relatively unknown; and three years ago business and labor were not partnering with industries as they are today. Today, support for industries is bipartisan, and includes liberals and conservatives alike. (Enterprise Prison Institute 1996c: 1)

ALTERNATIVE MODELS FOR PRISON INDUSTRIES

As indicated above, some current prison industry programs are run by state corrections bureaucracies that sell the product, often only to other government agencies; some are run by quasi-independent not-for-profit organizations; some involve a private for-profit employer of prison labor; some appear to encourage competition among potential employers; and some have a combination of one or more of these arrangements. These institutional arrangements are obviously not equivalent in terms of either their likely incentives and impacts or their potential scope.

One characteristic is common to all of the arrangements. Prison labor is essentially owned, at least in large part, by the state. The state's bureaucracy decides what laborers can work, either determines what the labor will produce and organizes the production or chooses which contract to accept and who to put to work, and determines the "tax rates" on the labor services (e.g., how much of the competitive wage goes to room and board, how much to victim compensation or restitution, how much to the prisoner's family, and how much to the prisoner). Essentially, this is slavery, and though it was contended in chapter 10 that criminals should lose their property rights when they violate someone else's rights, such slavery is not what was envisioned (indentured servitude differs from slavery, for instance, because the indentured individual generally chooses to contract himself into servitude with various conditions including a fixed period of time). Such slavery could lead to coercive practices as prisoners are forced to work under excessive "taxes" (room and board charges) in order to increase correction bureau budgets. The nineteenth- and early-twentieth-century prison work programs were also run by state correction authorities, and they were notorious for their inhumane treatment of prisoners. Other potential sources of abuse arise if corruption takes root or political factors come to dominate. Contracts with state institutions could be awarded on the basis of competition for the attention of politicians or corrupt officials. Private entrepreneurs would not be interested in paying market wages for labor that is being abused to the degree that workers' productivity is impaired, but corrupt officials conceivably could offer labor for lower wages and force prisoners to work without any personal compensation.

One way to avoid these potential sources of abuse may be to allow prisoners to refuse a work assignment. If participation is voluntary, abuse is less likely. And since current programs have more prisoner volunteers than they can employ, the potential for abuse has apparently not materialized. Of course, these programs tend to be pretty small relative to the prison population. If the programs expand so that larger and larger portions of the correctional bureaucracy's budget comes from the sale of prison labor, the coercive power that the state puts in the hands of a potentially corrupt or politically motivated official might be used to threaten mistreatment of prisoners who do not "volunteer." Therefore, state-run programs may be subject to abuse even with such mandated safeguards. Monitoring by civil libertarian and prison rights groups can mitigate this problem to a degree, but it does not necessarily go away.

Although the potential for corruption, abuse, and/or political maneuvering may be relatively low (but see Walker 1996 in this regard), the programs that are directly run by bureaucrats will probably be relatively inefficient for several reasons. If wages are not competitively determined, the actual value of prison labor cannot be effectively determined, and it is likely to be either undercompensated or overcompensated. Comparisons with the wages of nonprison labor doing similar work may not be valid, since the prison workers may have less education, the costs of training may be higher, labor turnover can be much higher (prison labor turns over upon release), the need for a security presence may raise production costs, and the prison labor may have to work with less efficient equipment than employees of private firms do (Grieser 1989). Furthermore, if the product is not marketed competitively (e.g., as when a state allows sales only to other state agencies), the value of the output cannot be effectively determined; as a result either too much or too little may be produced. Indeed, given the advantages to correctional personnel of reducing the level of idleness, "featherbedding" (the intentional overemployment of inmates in industry programs run by the correction authority itself) is very attractive (21). In all likelihood, bureaucratically managed programs will not generate enough revenue to cover the incarceration costs for the prisoners, let alone providing extra revenue for victim compensation or restitution or for prisoners' families.

In order for the states to maximize the returns on prison labor by allocating it to its highest-valued use, contracts between firms and the state could be awarded on a competitive basis. The production processes should be more efficient, and the full market value for the labor should be more accurately determined. Such competition is clearly possible. For instance, fourteen private firms were purchasing prison labor in Washington state during 1996 (Price 1996), despite the fact that only 3 percent of the state's prison population was employed by these firms (Meese and Rostad 1996). Three companies have assembly or production operations inside a single Texas prison, the Lockhart Correctional Facility, where 180 of the 500 inmates are employed full time to produce electronic circuit boards, control valves, and optical lenses. In this case, the companies also interview, hire, and train workers, just as they would in any other labor market, but the distribution of the wages is dictated by the state (about 40 percent of the incarceration costs are being recovered, with other funds directed to a victims' compensation fund, state and federal taxes, family support, court-ordered restitution, and a savings account available upon release). This suggests another alternative that might overcome the potential problems of bureaucratic inefficiencies and abuses: more complete privatization.

Rather than contracting with the state, firms could offer wages and working conditions directly to prisoners. An offender could choose between a specified prison term in a conventional "nonproductive" prison facility and contracting with one of several competitive firms offering work in or adjacent to secure facilities. The secure facilities might be run by the state, contracted out by the state, or run by the firms themselves, perhaps by contracting with specialists in security (more on this below). Since the labor contract would be voluntary and the market would be competitive, the prisoner would receive the prevailing wage for the type of work being done. In this case, the prisoner would retain much closer to full ownership of his labor (it would be heavily taxed, of course, as portions would be withheld for room and board, security, and so on). Friedman refers to such a competitive market for *voluntary* prison labor services when he explains that "[a]n arrangement which protects the convicted criminal against the most obvious abuses would be for the . . . criminal . . . [to] have the choice of . . . accepting bids for his services. The employer making such a bid would offer the criminal some specified working conditions" (1979: 415), as well as a specified wage rate and payment procedure and perhaps the distribution of those wages (but see the discussion of restitution below).

Would criminals voluntarily contract to work off their "debt to society"? There are a number of reasons to expect that they would. Consider the evidence from a very limited prison work experiment: At the Maine State Prison, inmates were given access to the prison's shop equipment to produce novelties. Other prisons have done the same thing, but Maine's program differed from others in some significant ways. First, there is a strong market for novelties because the prison is located on a major tourist route. Second, inmates were allowed to hire one another, thus allowing for specialization and the division of labor. The prisoners could not use dollars for these transactions, however (they could earn dollars from selling their novelties, and bank their income for use upon their release), so an alternative was needed. The currency used within the internal labor market was canteen coupons, which could be spent in the prison's canteen or banked in the prison's business office.

After Warden Richard Oliver was appointed in 1976, prisoners were allowed to "patent" their novelty designs; thus, they had incentives to innovate and expand their production. More significantly, Oliver lifted the limit on inmates' economic activity, and by 1978 the cap of five thousand dollars and five novelty patents that existed in 1976 was tripled (Shedd 1982: 25). A "miniature economy" quickly developed inside the prison, with two-thirds of the inmates *voluntarily* participating as employers, employees, or both.

Clearly, prisoners will work voluntarily if incentives to do so exist. Additional evidence comes from the fact that prisoners strongly support the developing prison work programs discussed above (Auerbach et al. 1988: 1). Prisoner support for the programs rises when they are paid wages based on productivity, when they are able to keep some of the payments, and when they are given an opportunity to develop marketable skills. Resistance to such programs does not come from the prisoners.[8]

The Maine program also had some significant effects on prisoners. Some entrepreneurs were extremely successful. One took over the prison's canteen and turned it into a profit-making operation. This individual also had thirty to fifty employees in novelty production and had diversified into other areas (e.g., he owned and rented to inmates about one hundred TV sets). One prison administrator considered him to be the "most brilliant businessman I've ever seen" (Shedd 1982: 26). This example suggests another potential source of competition for prison labor. As Walker advises, "prisoners should be able to work for themselves or for each other" (1996: 38). After his release from prison, the "brilliant businessman" from the Maine program started a novelty firm that employs former prisoners.

Reducing Crime: Rehabilitation in Prison Work Programs

Shedd concludes, "It wasn't called that, but Maine State Prison had a rehabilitation program that was *working*" (1982: 24).[9] Private markets for prison labor are advocated here from the normative position that criminals should pay the costs of crime; others have advocated such an arrangement from other normative perspectives. For instance, former chief justice of the U.S. Supreme Court Warren Burger (1992) sees prison work programs as a desirable and potentially effective mechanism for rehabilitation. Burger apparently is correct. Several recent studies indicate that prison industries can substantially reduce recidivism rates. Ohio's prison industry program was credited with reducing the state's overall recidivism rate by 18 percent in 1995, for instance. Prisoners who did not participate in Florida's prison industry program had recidivism rates that were 245 percent higher than those of prisoners who participated in the program. The Texas program produced even more dramatic results: the overall recidivism rate for the general prison population was estimated to be 700 percent of the rate among prisoners who participated in the program.[10] In Florida, only 11 percent of prisoners employed in the prison industry program for six months returned to prison during a four-year study, compared to the 60 to 70 percent recidivism rate that applies nationally (Yeomans 1995). This is not surprising. Productive use of inmates' time provides them with incentives to develop new marketable skills or to strengthen existing ones. That is likely to be particularly true if the employer is a private firm in a competitive market. Prison industry work also teaches inmates the discipline needed to hold a job in the marketplace after their release. An inmate who did a good job in prison could earn a position later in one of the same employer's plants employing nonprison labor (if training costs are high, developing both types of plants to reduce turnover would in fact be quite attractive for profit-seeking entrepreneurs). Bronson and coauthors ask and then answer: "Who benefits from a privatization experience inside a prison? The quick answer is that everyone does" (1992: 325). But even more benefits for criminals *and* for victims could be generated through establishment of true property rights to restitution *and* the right to turn to private organizations for collection of the restitution.

Recall that several states have passed laws urging judges to sentence criminals to restitution. In addition, victim-offender mediation (VOM) programs and several others with similar purposes (e.g., family group conferencing, community dispute resolution centers, and restitution centers) began developing in the United States in the 1970s with the expressed objective of obtaining reconciliation and restitution for victims (although the objectives of the criminal justice officials who refer cases to these programs may be quite different). Robert Poole describes such a victim restitution experiment with the following example:

> When "Fred Stone" broke into the Tucson house and stole the color TV, he had little idea that he would be caught. Still less did he expect to be confronted face-to-face by the victim, in the county prosecutor's office. In the course of the meeting, Stone learned that the TV set was the center of the elderly, invalid woman's life. With the approval of the Pima County, Arizona, prosecutor, he agreed not only to return the TV, but also to paint her house, mow her lawn, and drive her to the doctor for her weekly checkup. By doing so he avoided a jail sentence, and saved Tucson area taxpayers several thousand dollars.
>
> The Pima County program under which Fred Stone was handled is just one example of a promising *new concept in criminal justice:* restitution by offenders to victims. (1977: 1)

But this "promising new concept" is not new at all. As suggested in chapters 6, 9, 10, and 11, it has been a benchmark of law and order throughout most of history, and it remains an important part of criminal justice in at least some modern societies such as Japan and, perhaps to a lesser degree, France. Poole makes three important points here, however. First, some of the restitution programs, even though sanctioned by public prosecutors and courts, have found it desirable to produce private restitution contracts negotiated between the offender and the victim (Poole 1977: 1; Anderson 1983). In this particular case, the mediator is the prosecutor and/or the court, but that service clearly can be privatized, as in Japan and in some of the victim-offender mediation programs discussed in chapters 6 and 10. Indeed, private mediators appear to be much more widely used in these restitution programs than public prosecutors or other public officials.

The second point to be taken from Poole is one made in chapter 9: the payment of restitution need not be monetary. One criticism of monetary fines as a means of punishment is that criminals may not be able to pay a fine large enough to achieve the objective of the critic (e.g., to compensate the victim, to be an effective deterrent, or to achieve sufficient retribution). If the only option is an immediate monetary fine, criminals may indeed be judgment proof. Restitution arrangements should allow for working off the fine, either by working directly for the victim, as in Poole's example, *or* by selling labor to pay off the victim, perhaps in a prison environment. "Community service" sentences seem to be popular in many states today for various misdemeanors and minor felonies, and several states have recently reestablished "community service" for serious felons by authorizing the "road gangs" that disappeared decades ago. Why not "victim service" sentences instead?

The third point is that restitution can be a relatively efficient form of punishment (Friedman 1979: 408; Barnett 1977: 279; Benson 1996c). By comparison, imprisonment is very inefficient. It uses up social resources such as guards and other personnel, the capital and resources needed to build the prisons, *and* the prisoners' idle and therefore wasted time (in the absence of prison work programs). Restitution requires far fewer resources, in part because the criminals are no longer idle; if they can pay the required restitution, they are free to pursue employment in the open labor market (without the stigma of being labeled as a con), and if not, they are working to produce goods and services that can be sold to pay off their debts.

Under the current criminal justice system, the potential for capturing the benefits of a restitution-based system is almost nonexistent, as explained in chapters 10 and 11. In most states, if a criminal goes to prison, restitution cannot be paid because the criminal has no way to earn money (but that appears to be changing, as noted above). Similarly, although a probation sentence presumably can involve a requirement to pay restitution, such a sentence generally means that the overworked probation officer is responsible for supervising the restitution process; the result is that restitution is rarely collected. Restitution is much more likely to be collected when the payment is determined through victim-offender mediation (VOM) and several other similar programs, as explained in chapter 10.

RESTITUTION AND REHABILITATION

The primary purposes of programs like VOM are reconciliation and restitution rather than punishment, and though it may not be surprising to find that victims are much more satisfied with such a procedure than with public prosecution and punishment (Umbreit 1995: 263), it turns out that criminals are as well. As Umbreit explains, face-to-face mediated negotiation results include "humanizing the justice system response to the crime for both victims *and* offenders" (272, emphasis added). The offender learns about the impact of the crime on the victim and often feels remorse. Offenders who have participated in such negotiation often express remorse and regret, accepting responsibility. Apparently this dramatically increases the likelihood of payment, as noted in chapter 10, but it also has a direct rehabilitative impact:

"Considerably fewer and less serious crimes were committed within a one-year period by juvenile offenders who participated in a victim-offender mediation program than by similar offenders who did not participate in mediation" (272).

The same results are clearly present on a larger scale in Japan. Overall recidivism rates appear to be very low (Evers 1994: 25), and crime rates are much lower than in the United States. Japan is the only industrialized country in the world where crime rates have fallen every year since World War II. The fact is that when restitution is determined through mediation rather than litigation, as in the Japanese system and in programs like VOM, a very different attitude develops among criminals. Evers puts it well when he notes that in the United States

> [c]riminals all too often try to relieve their moral and psychological guilt for their crimes by portraying themselves in the forum of their own consciences as victims of society who are not responsible for their deeds. But the process of confession and restitution . . . discourages such self-indulgent self-forgiveness and develops honest attitudes and patterns of conduct by punishing in moderation only when criminals show remorse and pay restitution. (Evers 1994: 25)

When people are induced to admit responsibility for their actions that harm others, they are apparently much less likely to repeat those actions.

There are other reasons to expect that a restitution-based system will tend to be rehabilitative. For one thing, the restitution payment and process can be specified contractually. When a criminal is working off a predetermined restitution fine, even in a secure prisonlike environment, the sentence takes on a self-determinative nature: the harder a prisoner works, the faster he obtains release. "He would be master of his fate and would have to face the responsibility. This would encourage useful, productive activity and instill a conception of reward for good behavior and hard work" (Barnett 1977: 294). These incentives could have a significant rehabilitative impact, which may be much stronger than those envisioned by Burger (1992), Meese and Rostad (1996), and other advocates of prison industries in the current criminal justice system. As Poole stresses, "by integrating the offender into the work force and making him assume responsibility for his offense, restitution may just do more to rehabilitate offenders than all the fancy programs dreamed up by psychologists and sociologists over the past quarter century" (1977: 2–3). Thus, once again, a program intended to make criminals pay can also have benefits for the criminal and for society at large, since an increased level of rehabilitation reduces future crime.

There are a number of other reasons to expect rehabilitation to be relatively effective under such a system (Barnett 1977: 293). Violence and drug abuse, both significant problems in modern prisons, are not as likely to occur in a privatized labor market system. Under current arrangements an inmate sacrifices very little if he participates in violence or uses drugs; in a privatized system he sacrifices much more. Drugs may reduce productivity and delay release, and the risk of injury that significantly delays release is a substantial deterrent to violence. Even in the limited market experiment in Maine, inmates reacted to these deterrents. Novelty producers themselves avoided violence and drugs for fear of losing their market-participation privileges. Beyond that, the major novelty producers used their economic power to "counteract theft . . . and general thuggism" because it threatened their enterprises (Shedd 1982: 27). Private justice was brought to bear to reduce prison violence. But in a restitution system individuals' incentives to avoid violence are even more positive: "the convict will have a direct incentive to exhibit good behavior. The better risk he appears to the penal agency, the more likely he is to be allowed parole or other freedoms in the interest of increasing his productivity" (Sneed 1977: 123) and reducing the cost of supervision that he must cover.

PRIVATE COLLECTIONS

When restitution is determined through mediator-facilitated negotiation (or, should that fail, through face-to-face binding arbitration), both the payment and the collection process can be established contractually. If a victim perceives little risk that a debtor will renege, continuation of a current trade may be allowed so that the criminal can make periodic payments; alternatively, the contract may specify work to be done for the victim, as in the example from Poole cited above. Both may be rare, of course, depending on the perceived risk of flight (although they apparently are not rare in Japan). If a risk of reneging is perceived, the debt contract with the victim might specify that a criminal contract his labor services with a private firm that acts as "collection" agency for the victim. Such a collections firm might pay a bond to the victim equal to the discounted value of the anticipated restitution and then collect the payments itself in order to recover the bond plus the costs they bear in supervision and interest, by withholding an agreed-upon "service charge" from the offender's wages. The criminal may or may not require a high-security facility, so a range of environments with varying degrees of monitoring and security would develop to maximize the likelihood that payments are made at the lowest possible cost. Some offenders may require supervision in "restitution centers" where they may have to return each night and even wear an electronic monitor while they are at work. Others may require even closer supervision in prisonlike workplaces to ensure payment.

Variants of this idea actually can be observed: A restitution program called EARN-IT was established some time ago in Quincy County, Massachusetts (Anderson 1983; Umbreit 1995: 269). The program began with forty local businessmen providing jobs to offenders who were unable to find jobs elsewhere (Anderson 1983: 37). The employers supervised the offenders during work hours, and the offenders reported to probation officers. Bend, Oregon, has a similar program (Pranis 1996: 29). In other experimental programs, offenders work during the day and return to jail or a halfway house environment (or a restitution center) at night (recall that most halfway houses are contracted out to private firms, which clearly could also take on the role of collecting and distributing restitution payments). This model can be extended to include private firms employing labor in secure prisons.

Given competition in private markets for prison labor, where the prisoners themselves voluntarily accept or reject the contracts from private firms that provide varying degrees of secure production facilities, other significant benefits for prisoners can be generated as well. Under these circumstances, for instance, those who run the private collections firms have strong incentives to treat prisoners well because a firm with a reputation for mistreating prisoners and reducing their productivity will not be able to employ many prison laborers. Furthermore, a firm that violates contractual stipulations regarding treatment can be sued for breach of contract. Competitive forces and enforceable contracts work to preclude inhumane treatment of prisoners, then. A competitive market for such labor, in which the convict has the right to withdraw from the contract with a particular prison firm (but not from a contract with the victim unless the victim is personally abusive) if the prison firm does not live up to its agreement, means that the convict also is in a position to make the highest possible wage and earn his or her way out of prison as quickly as possible—a characteristic that should be attractive to the victim or bonding firm as well as the criminal. Furthermore, the criminal has incentives to gain marketable skills in order to increase earning power; "good behavior" is also likely to lead to relocation into a less secure environment, thereby reducing the cost of supervision for the collection firm and the criminal and increasing the speed at which the restitution payments can be made.

As with all of the other issues discussed in this chapter and the previous one (increasing the probability of effective observation, reporting, arrest, prosecution, and conviction), refocusing criminal justice on restitution for victims would create many more opportunities for cost-effective privatization in the imposition of punishment. The full potential for privatization cannot be achieved, or probably even envisioned, without a reorientation of criminal justice toward concern for the victim, and the full potential for victim restitution cannot be achieved, or probably even envisioned, without greater privatization.

Conclusions

In the context of an overriding objective of justice for victims of crime, one purpose of this book is to advise victims' advocacy groups on the kinds of changes that are needed to create a criminal justice system that truly will be responsive to the desires of individual crime victims. Considerable political resistance to such changes can be anticipated. Perhaps the most significant resistance will come from the entrenched criminal justice bureaucracies. Such opposition can be anticipated because the most effective means of obtaining justice for victims is through privatization of criminal justice functions, coupled with establishment of recognized and enforceable property rights to restitution for victims, which effectively turns crimes with victims into torts. Police and corrections unions and other criminal justice interests have frequently positioned themselves as allies of victims by demanding harsher punishments, of course, and most victims' groups apparently do not realize that these criminal justice interests' efforts to limit privatization are actually counter to victim interests. Therefore, demonstrating that the justifications for public control of criminal justice and the typical criticisms of privatization are not valid has been another major function of this book. In contrast to the claims of public police interests, crime can actually be relatively effectively controlled through the interactions of private buyers and sellers and through various voluntary cooperative arrangements.

Although criminal justice bureaucracies are probably the most influential lobbies in the crime policy determination process (Berk, Brackman, and Lesser 1997; Benson 1995c; Benson, Rasmussen, and Sollars 1995; Rasmussen and Benson 1994: 127–41), other groups also oppose privatization, and the reasons for their opposition also have to be challenged if political changes are to be achieved. For instance, opposition often arises out of mistaken beliefs about how competitive markets work, as suggested in chapter 8. Many civil libertarians oppose privatization in criminal justice because they believe that profit-seeking firms will cut quality and abuse those suspected of or convicted of crimes. Others believe that only the state should have police powers, perhaps for similar reasons. Such views are certainly understandable since, as chapter 3 explains, they can be quite valid when government is the buyer of services produced by private firms under contract. Furthermore, that kind of behavior can also be observed in firms protected from competition through government barriers to entry. The reason for such behavior is that political considerations, corruption, and/or bureaucratic self-interests prevent the price-quality competition that effectively regulates competitive markets, not that the markets themselves are inherently flawed. Of course, it is difficult for most people to imagine a fully privatized system of effective criminal law, so they naturally assume that government must be the buyer of at least some services and/or that government regulatory oversight will have to be considerable. Theoretical arguments and empirical evidence provided in chapters 7 and 8 indicate the fallacy of these beliefs, while illustrating that the very abuses that are expected from private firms are widely observed within public bureaucracies.

Others may object to privatization because they do not accept the normative perspective of liberty, responsibility, and justice for victims of crime as adopted and explained in chapter 9. Many are convinced that criminal justice can and should be used to pursue various social engineering objectives, whether they be deterrence or rehabilitation, or that crimes demand retribution rather than restitution, or that criminals are really victims who should be excused when they have suffered under some form of discrimination or abuse—therefore, neither retribution nor restitution is warranted. Arguments in chapter 10 suggest that retribution can be achieved through restitution, however, and an alternative justification for privatization and restitution based on other norms was emphasized in this chapter and chapter 11. In particular, a goal of deterrence can be more effectively achieved through privatization with rights to restitution (also see chapter 7 for discussion of evidence), because competitive private firms and voluntary groups are more efficient at preventing crimes than public police, and with rights to restitution victims have much stronger incentives to participate in or employ specialists for pursuit, prosecution, and effective collection of restitution debts. In addition, a fully privatized market for criminals' labor creates incentives that support more effective rehabilitation and better treatment of criminals. Therefore, almost any objective that might be widely seen as appropriate for crime policy is likely to be more effectively achieved through privatization and a restitution focus. There is one exception, however. Criminals would tend to be treated better than they are now because they would be paying their debt through restitution rather than being punished, but they would not be treated as victims of society and forgiven. The normative perspective of liberty, responsibility, and justice demands that they be held responsible for their actions. The relevant arguments in chapter 10 may not convince many in the "excuse-making industry" described by Bidinotto (1994b), which depends on turning criminals into victims for their livelihood, but these arguments should be powerful in the political arena, where they appeal to victims' groups, law enforcement groups, and conservatives in general, as well as to the growing libertarian segment of the population.

Criminal justice is not going to be privatized immediately upon the publication of this book. The hope is, however, that at least some of the analysis presented here will be sufficiently convincing that the already very rapid privatization trend can be accelerated, at least on some dimensions. That is why a large number of privatization options have been discussed, from more contracting out (recognizing its potentially serious flaws and shortcomings), to lifting legal barriers that limit the use of private security, all the way to a major reorientation of criminal justice into a restitution-based system that allows private courts (arbitrators or mediators) to determine restitution fines and private collection firms to supervise them.

What will happen if interest groups do not demand any of these recommendations, with the result that policymakers do not follow them but continue to listen to criminal justice interests? Privatization will occur to a large degree anyway. Note that the growth in private sector security, protection, and justice documented in chapters 5 and 6 has occurred in the face of the legal barriers that are the focus of several of the recommendations made in chapters 11 and 12. In 1985 Cunningham and Taylor (1985: 2) suggested that a shift of protection responsibility from the public to the private sector is clearly occurring; since then that shift has become increasingly obvious: as Cunningham, Strauchs, and Van Meter observe, "Private security is now clearly the Nations's primary protective resource" (1991: 1). Furthermore, the demand for such services continues to increase at a tremendous rate. Although the scope of private justice is impossible to delineate, some observers now believe that it already exerts far greater control over citizens than the criminal justice system does (Cunningham and Taylor 1985: 12). If local, state, and federal government policy advocates and policymakers continue to underestimate the potential benefits of these private developments while investing more in a public-sector criminal justice system that continues to fail, citizens will continue to invest in private alternatives (Benson 1990).

The choice policymakers face is not between privatization and no privatization. It is between encouraging and supporting the privatization trend and attempting to thwart it, thereby perhaps slowing its evolution and diverting its path, but not stopping it. Some cost-effective developments (e.g., private markets for criminal labor, private prosecution, and formal private courts) can certainly be prevented, but it is a mistake to believe that preventing them will force people to use the public system. There are other alternatives, but unfortunately, when the process is diverted from its most cost-effective path, some of the results can be quite undesirable. There are legitimate concerns about the fairness of the types of informal private justice that are developing inside firms and other organizations, for instance, but limitations on the use of private prosecution and the lack of development of formal private criminal courts available without prior referral from the public criminal justice system (e.g., such referrals are the source of disputes for the current victim-offender mediation programs) create stronger incentives to turn to private justice. Furthermore, when the state rules that private justice actions are illegal "vigilantism," many private citizens will continue to carry them out, but in secret, increasing the chances of abuse. Many other examples of undesirable developments arise when barriers to privatization are raised (e.g., efforts to slow the expansion of private security firms by not allowing them access to applicants' criminal records have forced some firms to illegally obtain criminal records in order to screen applicants), but the fact is that the continuing failure of the public sector's efforts to control crime means that privatization will not be stopped. Even diverting a massive amount of resources from other activities and completely trampling our economic and civil liberties is not likely to be effective, given the record of the criminal justice system's failures in controlling crime, especially consensual crimes such as the voluntary purchase of marijuana, liquor during prohibition, and guns for protection.

Notes

NOTES TO CHAPTER 1

1. This information is from a presentation by Sgt. Charles P. Duffy, APPL coordinator, during the Office of International Criminal Justice Conference "Privatizing Criminal Justice: Public Private Partnerships," held at the University of Illinois at Chicago, March 13–15, 1995.

NOTES TO CHAPTER 2

1. Parts of this chapter are drawn from Benson 1990: 180–84, 1994b, and 1996b; Benson 1996a, 1998b, and 1998d are based in part on material in this chapter.

2. See Benson 1990: 211–13; 1996b, and 1998b for more details.

3. "Operating Private Prisons" 1983; Corrections Corporation of America press release, July 26, 1988.

NOTES TO CHAPTER 3

1. Parts of this chapter draw upon Benson 1990: 184–96 and especially upon Benson 1994b; 1996a; and forthcoming, a. Parts of Benson 1998b and 1998d are in turn taken from this chapter.

2. Competition can actually come from other sources as well. Many local jurisdictions contract with other larger jurisdictions for police services when economies of scale are important, as noted above.

3. This point was made by Russell Clemens, representing the American Federation of State, County, and Municipal Employees, at a conference entitled "Privatizing Criminal Justice: Public and Private Partnerships" sponsored by the Office of International Criminal Justice and held at the University of Illinois at Chicago in March of 1995.

NOTES TO CHAPTER 4

1. Poor life experiences and economic opportunities should not be considered excuses for committing crimes, however. See chapter 10 in this regard, as well as Bidinotto 1994a and Barger 1994.

2. Parts of this chapter draw from and expand on Benson and Rasmussen 1994a, and Benson 1996b. Parts of Benson 1996c also draw from this chapter.

3. For reviews of the literature, see Elliot 1977; Silver 1974; or Rasmussen and Benson 1994: 41–43.

4. Fear of reprisal is another factor, but that also reflects victims' perceptions that the criminal justice system probably will not lock up and hold criminals (Wilson 1977: xv–xvi).

5. These data come from the Bureau of Justice Statistics, *Sourcebook of Criminal Justice Statistics, 1993* (Washington, D.C.: Bureau of Justice Statistics), tables 1.1., 1.3, and 4.24.

6. In some cases a limited deposit bail may actually be required, so that a defendant must put up 10 percent of the specified fine or forfeiture. Then if he or she does appear, the deposit bail bond is repaid (less a service fee for the court).

7. Fugitive rates may vary from year to year; they also depend on the time period examined. Reynolds (1994b: 17) reports rates of 3 percent for private bondsmen and 9.5 for public pretrial release after one year, whereas the estimates cited above of less than 1 percent for privately bonded defendants is a three-year fugitive rate.

8. See table 5.5 in the Bureau of Justice Statistics, *Sourcebook of Criminal Justice Statistics, 1993*. Note that "dismissals" include transfers and pretrial diversions.

9. Important among these statutes, from a rights-based perspective (explained and advocated in chapter 10), are laws eliminating various criminal defenses such as insanity and drug or alcohol use as mitigating circumstances in violent acts: there should be no excuses for criminals to avoid responsibility for the harms they do.

10. See the Bureau of Justice Statistics, *Sourcebook on Criminal Justice Statistics, 1993*, tables 5.18 and 5.55.

11. Estimates of rates of recidivism implied by rearrest of convicted criminals depend on a number of factors, of course. For instance, studies using inmate surveys produce evidence of higher recidivism rates than studies using official records because of the difficulty of tracking offenders over time in official records (Beck 1987: 9). In addition, the time frame of the study matters. An Illinois study found that 60 percent of a sample of released felons from all age groups had been rearrested within twenty-seven to twenty-nine months (Illinois Criminal Justice Information Authority 1986). A Rand Corporation study reported that 76 percent, 60 percent, and 53 percent of relapsed felons in California, Texas, and Michigan, respectively, had been rearrested within three years of their release (Klein and Caggiano 1986). A study for the Bureau of Justice Statistics (BJS) using a sample of young parolees from twenty-two states found that 69 percent had been rearrested within six years of release from prison (Beck 1987). The rearrest rate also varies by characteristics of the criminals. In the BJS study, 90 percent of those with a history of six or more arrests were rearrested again, whereas 59 percent of first-time offenders were rearrested and 79 percent of those charged as adults before the age of seventeen were rearrested during the six-year follow-up period. Time served in prison had no consistent impact on recidivism (e.g., a person who had

served two years was just as likely to recidivate as a person who had served six months). This result has been supported in sophisticated statistical studies that control for numerous characteristics of the felon (Kim et al. 1993).

NOTES TO CHAPTER 5

1. Parts of this chapter draw from Benson 1984a, 1986a, 1990: 201–13 and 1996b; Benson 1998b also draws upon this chapter.

2. This information was provided by Barbara Benson, a certified gemologist and jewelry appraiser for Molberg's.

3. Another group activity is the "sanctioning of wrongdoers" (e.g., drug addicts, pushers, drunks, prostitutes, and troublesome families) in an attempt to expel them from the community (Podolefsky and Dubow 1981: 64). See the discussion of private justice in chapter 6 for more details.

4. For a more detailed examination of the history of private streets in Saint Louis, see Beito 1988.

5. As explained in chapter 7, limited access alone is not enough. Experiments that have tried to create similar "safe" environments for public streets have failed to produce the same results that private streets generate.

6. There is also a growing business in providing more "exotic" equipment such as bullet-proof cars and vehicle security systems for those in positions of wealth or power who face high risks of assassination or kidnapping. In 1983 there were roughly a dozen U.S. firms specializing in armoring cars at prices ranging from $32,000 to $250,000, depending on the degree of safety required. Many other privately provided forms of protection equipment are available to those willing to pay (Dobson and Payne 1983: 34–41).

NOTES TO CHAPTER 6

1. See, for example, Gard 1949; Valentine 1956; Stewart 1964; McGrath 1984; Benson 1990: 312–23; 1991b; and Morriss 1997.

2. This section draws from Benson 1991b, and some subsections originated in Benson 1986b and 1990: 312–21.

3. See McGrath 1984: 201–27 for a more detailed review.

4. Some historians focus on vigilante activity as a source violence. Brown (1975) cites at least three hundred historical vigilante movements in the United States and its western territories. Those occurrences began as early as 1767 in South Carolina, but they were particularly prominent on the western frontier because private citizens had to enforce their own laws. The vigilante movements were frequently quite effective at establishing social order and deterring offenses, but in doing so they often resorted to capital or corporal punishment. Vigilante justice is discussed below.

5. Anderson and Hill explain that very similar situations also arose later in Colorado, Montana, and Idaho, where "in each case, the first to arrive were forced into a

situation where they had to write the rules of the game" (1979: 18). Morriss (1997: 43–51) adds the Black Hills of South Dakota to the list of gold rush areas with privately produced miners' law; in all likelihood, other gold rush areas (e.g., Alaska) can be similarly characterized.

6. As further evidence, consider the obvious confidence that miners had in their privately produced and protected property rights system. Umbeck lists several pieces of historical evidence of this confidence:

1. From 1849 to 1866 scarce resources were used by miners to agree upon and to enforce the contractual provisions. Any individual found guilty of a violation was punished immediately. [If the miners did not have faith in the system, why would they devote time, effort, and resources to promote it?]

2. By 1849 and throughout the 1850s and 1860s, it was observed that miners were devoting hundreds of thousands of dollars in developing their claims. . . . In other words, the miners behaved *as if* they had some expectation of continued use rights.

3. By 1850 most districts allowed miners to buy and sell claims and shortly thereafter this transfer of mining rights became a common occurrence. Some of the richer claims were exchanged for thousands of dollars. Had exclusive rights to the claim not existed, no one would have paid for them.

4. In 1866 the federal government passed an act allowing miners to acquire fee simple absolute in mineral lands. By 1867 only 4 claims had been patented and in 1869 and 1870 a total of 6 claims had been patented. This does not prove that miners already had property rights, but it does indicate that the additional benefits of federally recognized rights were not worth the patenting cost for most miners.

5. The mining act of 1866 legally recognized the rights of miners to the exclusive use of what was previously public land. Yet with this federal recognition and enforcement of property rights, there was no noticeable change in total gold yield. . . .

6. In his report of 1868, government agent J. Ross Browne gives a detailed report on the history and current operations of hundreds of mines in California. I can detect no systematic change in resource allocation after 1866. (1981a, pp. 96–97)

When property rights are not clearly assigned, resources tend to be used up more quickly than when clearly delineated private rights exist. Since no distinguishable change in the use of California's mineral lands occurred following governmental recognition of private rights to that land, we can assume that those rights actually existed prior to the government's action.

7. The following discussion draws from Valentine 1956; Stewart 1964; and Gard 1949; and parts originally appeared in Benson 1990: 315–21 and/or 1991b. For a more comprehensive examination of sources and evidence regarding the vigilante movements discussed here and others (but with a less favorable view of the San Fran-

cisco episodes), see Morriss 1997: 63–89. Also see McGrath 1984 for a very detailed examination of vigilante movements in two of the large California mining camps with conclusions that support the general conclusions proposed below.

8. See Morriss 1997: 79–89 for more detailed discussion and numerous references about the Montana vigilantes.

9. See Benson 1995a for a more detailed history of commercial arbitration in the United States. Also see Benson 1989a; 1990: 30–35, 60–62; 1998a; 1998d; and 1998e for discussion of the fact that arbitration often represents a "jurisdictional choice"— that is, a decision to use a different set of legal rules from the ones created and backed by the state.

10. Unlike some of its competitors (e.g., JAMS and EnDispute), Judicate has been facing financial difficulties, but in any free market, some firms will fail as others prosper.

11. Furthermore, unlike the Capital University–initiated program, some have not actually been voluntary private alternatives to the public courts, because the government has had substantial roles in their development, financing, and administration, and judges or prosecutors have controlled them for their own political purposes, deciding which case should go where without the voluntary consent of the disputants. If these programs fail when funding is withdrawn, as it has been over the past few years, some observers may conclude that the private sector is simply unable to provide neighborhood- or community-based conflict resolution services. Of course, any private industry is likely to have many firms that fail while others prosper, in part because some entrepreneurs lack the managerial skills that competitors have and consumers choose to take their business to those offering the best product at the lowest price. However, Auerbach (1983) and Benson (1990: 217; 1998d; forthcoming, b) emphasize that in all likelihood the failures of state-supported alternatives reflect the characteristics of those particular community-based systems that have been imposed by public officials.

12. This subsection draws from Carlson 1995b.

13. The threat of seizure is a very real one; property confiscation by the police is an increasingly important (and troubling) component of the criminal justice approach to illicit drug markets (Benson, Rasmussen, and Sollars 1995; Benson and Rasmussen 1996b; Rasmussen and Benson 1994: 132–41).

14. Other groups approach the problem of neighborhood crack houses by attacking owners first. Such groups, discussed by Carlson (1995b: 57–58), file civil suits against owners for creating a public nuisance. Indeed, "anti-drug groups frequently find civil law a more powerful ally than police departments in the fight against crack houses" (58). Civil procedures tend to be quicker, and they require only a "preponderance of proof" rather than "proof beyond a reasonable doubt."

15. In addition to the theft of money and property, "time theft" (e.g., conducting personal business on company time, abuse of sick leave, and general shirking) was estimated to cost employers $120 billion in 1981, and this kind of theft is "virtually im-

possible to prosecute" through formal criminal justice procedures (Cunningham and Taylor 1985: 8).

NOTES TO CHAPTER 7

1. Parts of this chapter draw from Benson 1984a; 1986a; 1990: 235–52, 271–328; 1994a; Benson and Rasmussen 1996b; Benson, Rasmussen, and Sollars 1995; and Rasmussen and Benson 1994. Benson 1998b and 1998d in turn draw upon the presentation in this chapter.

2. The situation reversed itself after 1989. The political backlash against the consequences of the early release of violent felons (which was largely due to the drug war) had begun to materialize. Drug arrests fell by 17.3 percent in Florida between then and 1992, and property crime rates fell by 7.4 percent. Drug enforcement efforts remain very high relative to what was going on in the early 1980s, however, and further cutbacks would allow for even greater reductions in property crime. The number of drug offenders sentenced to Florida prisons fell from 4,014 in the second quarter of 1989 to 2,304 in the last quarter of 1992, and the legislature revoked or reduced several of its minimum mandatory sentences for drug offenders in 1993. Prisoners in general were serving 43 percent of their sentences by mid-1993, but drug admissions still accounted for 25 percent of total admissions, so considerably more could have been done. Unfortunately, however, the cutback in drug enforcement does not appear to be long-lived. The drop in drug arrests appears to have ended in 1991, and the trend has been flat to upward since then. This probably reflects the fact that the Florida legislature, rather than focusing on capacity-based sentencing guidelines and/or diverting drug criminals (reducing the demand for prison space), embarked on a massive prison building program (increasing the supply) to alleviate crowding (at the expense of other potential uses of state revenues such as education or tax relief), and this short-run solution (short-run because crowding is inevitable in the longer term, given the common-pool environment that characterizes sentencing decisions) has allowed the police to continue their focus on drugs.

3. In fact, while drug arrests relative to arrests for reported crimes against persons and property (Index I offenses of murder, manslaughter, sexual assault, assault, robbery, burglary, larceny, and auto theft) remained fairly constant at a one-to-four ratio from 1970 to 1984, the *relative* effort against drugs increased by roughly 45 percent over the next five years. By 1989 criminal justice resources were being used to make only about 2.2 Index I arrests for each drug arrest.

4. Many states mandated that confiscated assets be turned over to a general government authority; others required that some or all seized assets be used for specific purposes, such as drug treatment or education. Various states also limited the kinds of assets that could be seized. For instance, in 1984 only seven states allowed seizure of real estate used for illegal drug activities. The federal statute had no such limitation.

5. Local interbureau competition for resources may lead government decision

makers (bureau sponsors) to treat confiscations as a substitute for ordinary appropriations. For that reason Benson, Rasmussen, and Sollars (1995) explored the budgetary impact of local police confiscation from the drug war. The findings are consistent with the hypothesis that confiscation legislation creates significant incentives to change the allocation of police resources: a 1 percent increase in seizures leads to about a 0.7 percent increase in the discretionary component of police budgets.

6. Products are priced and purchased individually unless some bundling of complementary goods is desirable, perhaps because of the reduction in production and/or transaction costs that results in a lower full price for the bundle than the items would cost if purchased separately (e.g., a consumer presumably could buy a car without a radio or tires and then purchase those items separately, but it would clearly cost more in time and effort [transaction costs] as well as in dollars).

7. Some suggest that this difference in fees explains both police hostility toward the Patrol Specials and the series of proposed restrictions on Patrol Specials that police have advocated (see chapter 10 for additional discussion of this issue).

8. Efficiency is not necessarily the only norm that should be applied to criminal justice, of course (see chapter 10 in this regard). There may be an equity issue, for instance, since the poor may be excluded while the wealthy command all the best private security services (Freeman 1992: 137)—this issue is examined in chapter 8.

9. There is another possibility as well, however. If private security is being substituted for public policing, then communities with relatively small investments in police resources may have relatively large investments in private alternatives. Then if the private alternatives generate roughly the same level of deterrence as the public police for which they have been substituted, the failure of deterrence studies to control for private security means that the deterrent effect of public police will not be detected.

10. See note 9, above, in this regard, because these results do not support the alternative hypothesis posed there.

NOTES TO CHAPTER 8

1. In this regard, Samuelson's delineation of the domain of public goods is much broader than the one employed above: "A public good is one that enters two or more persons' utility. What are we left with? . . . With a knife-edge pole of the private good case, and with all the rest of the world in the public good domain by virtue of involving some consumption externality" (1969: 108). In other words, a public good is any good that, in production or consumption, generates some benefits for which the producer cannot charge.

2. Parts of this chapter draw from Benson 1984a, 1984b, 1990: 271–328; 1992a, and 1994a; Benson 1998b and 1998d draw upon materials in this chapter.

3. An interesting example, the nonabusive characteristics of the very large private security operation at Disney World, is described in Shearing and Stenning 1987b.

4. For a few of the many other examples, see Hoebel 1967; Peden 1977; Benson 1990: 11–41; 1991a, 1992b, and 1994a; and chapter 9 of this volume.

5. For discussion and rejection of other arguments against privatization in crime control, see Osterfeld 1989; Benson 1990: 271–328; and Friedman 1984; for more detailed analysis of the causes and consequences of government failure in criminal justice, see Sherman 1983; Neely 1982; Benson 1990: 43–175; and Rasmussen and Benson 1994, among others.

6. Restitution still plays a major role in some societies. For instance, see the discussion of Japan in chapter 10.

7. Osterfeld (1989) also rejects the characterization of law as a public good, but by making a slightly different argument: essentially, he demonstrates that security as evidenced by laws, policing, and court services, is actually divisible so it can be broken down and either sold in a free market or provided in a nonmonopolized, noncoercive way (also see Benson 1990 for a similar point). His argument is complementary to the one made here, if not theoretically identical to it.

NOTES TO CHAPTER 9

1. This chapter draws heavily from Benson 1992b and 1994a, which in turn drew from portions of Benson 1990: 21–30, 46–60, 62–76. A substantially expanded version of both the theoretical and the historical analysis presented here is in preparation for publication as a book tentatively titled *The Evolution of Property Rights, Law, and Moral Behavior: Economics versus Politics in the Face of Scarcity,* which is under contract with the Independent Institute. The book and related research leading to a large number of published or forthcoming articles have been undertaken with the generous support of the Earhart Foundation and the Institute for Humane Studies and under contract with the Independent Institute.

2. For a sampling of other literature exploring historical and modern examples of legal systems that define large numbers of offenses against persons and property as illegal, but with institutions that are radically different than the current public-sector criminal justice system in the United States, see Benson 1986b, 1989b, 1991a, 1991b, 1996c; Cardenas 1986; Demsetz 1967; Goldsmidt 1951; Hoebel 1967; Laster 1970; Liggio 1977; Peden 1977; and Pospisil 1971.

3. See Peden 1977 regarding a similar Irish honor price system.

4. See also Peden 1977; Friedman 1979; Solvason 1992, 1993; Benson 1986b; 1990: 15–21; 1989b, 1991a; Goldsmidt 1951; and Pospisil 1971 for similar arrangements in other societies.

5. It has been suggested that as kingdoms grew, kings needed a way to organize local government, so they supplemented "the duties of the kindred in protection and policing by introducing . . . the tithing" (Lyon 1980: 84). Also see Hume 1983–85: vol.1, 75–77 and Yandle 1991: 231. However, this interpretation "mistake[s] the nature of Anglo-Saxon legal codes which were . . . concerned with . . . codification of es-

tablished custom. There is little doubt that the hundred [and the tithing] was functioning as a unit" long before kings developed legal roles (Blair 1956: 235).

6. Evidence of the nature of Anglo-Saxon law comes primarily from a few "codes" compiled by kings from the late Anglo-Saxon period and a number of tracts or custumals written after the Norman conquest to compile the customary law of the time, much of which was Anglo-Saxon in origin (Pollock and Maitland 1959: vol. 1, 10–27). Stephen notes that "the general impression . . . is that [Anglo-Saxons] had an abundance of customs and laws sufficiently well established for practical purposes" (1883: 52).

7. A Dane, Canute, took the throne in 1016. He appeased the Anglo-Saxons by confirming their customary laws, establishing a close rapport with the Anglo-Saxon aristocracy, and supporting their church (Lyon 1980: 32). Although Canute's reign (1016–1035) was a peaceful one, his sons viewed England as a foreign source of revenues. In 1042 the crown fell to Edward the Confessor, who surrounded himself with Norman advisors and appointed Normans to rich ecclesiastic positions. The most powerful earls actually controlled England. In 1066 when Edward died, Harold, the dominant member of the aristocracy, was chosen as his successor, despite stronger hereditary claims to the throne. Harold was killed on September 28, 1066, at the Battle of Hastings.

8. For a different view, see Lyon 1980: 85.

9. A very different view of the desirability and effectiveness of these arrangements is presented by Hogue (1985: 137) and Yandle (1991: 232).

10. See Benson 1990: 51–62 for a brief discussion of noncriminal law developments in English law (i.e., Magna Carta, parliament, and writs) explained in a fashion that is consistent with this presentation of criminal law's evolution (these developments will be explained in much greater detail in the book described in note 1, above). For instance, through their chancellors, kings had been issuing writs for some time at the request of a complainant, directing an adversary to appear before a court. By developing new writs, new civil trial procedures were inaugurated *and* pleas were established that could be tried only in the royal courts (Lyon 1980: 288). All the various writs were "exposed for sale; perhaps some of them may already be had for a fixed price, for others a bargain must be struck. As yet the king is no mere vendor, he is a manufacturer and can make goods to order" (Pollock and Maitland 1959: vol. l, 151). Thus, many developments in civil law also trace to the revenue-seeking efforts of kings.

11. See Laster 1970: 76 for discussion of the following laws.

12. The "evolution of the class [of legal advisors] has been slow, for it has been withstood by certain ancient principles" (Pollock and Maitland 1959: vol. 1, 216). Individuals who were not skilled in pleading were less likely to be able to conceal their guilt. Furthermore, one litigant might be unable to hire a skilled spokesman, whereas another could. Thus, rather than give one litigant an unfair advantage, custom developed whereby professional counselors and pleaders were not allowed. By the early thirteenth century, however, pleaders had begun to appear in civil cases. The earliest

records of a pleader was on behalf of Henry II, and Richard had a permanent contingency of pleaders. Thus, the legal profession was developed to give additional advantages to the king.

By 1268 Henry III had a number of men under permanent retainer to act for him in his cases. The king gained an advantage in his own suits, and he was able to sell the same privilege to others. Edward I had a very large number of "servants or sergeants at law" under retainer and a large number of "apprentices" who were their pupils. In 1292 Edward ordered his justices to provide for a sufficient number of attorneys and apprentices in each county so that the king and the powerful might be well served.

London began to license two groups of legal professionals—attorneys and pleaders—in 1280, but the king's justices took control of the licensing function in 1292 and severely limited entry into both branches of the profession: "apparently a monopoly was secured for those who had been thus appointed" (Lyon 1980: 447). Attorneys and counters quickly evolved into an organized professional group. They had an almost immediate effect: "It is hardly necessary to say that [lawyers] prolonged justice almost endlessly" (438). (Note that some observers see great virtue in the development and consequences of a professional class of lawyers—e.g., Hogue [1985: 246]). Unlike civil case litigants, however, criminal defendants were not permitted legal representation, so criminal procedure was much less complex.

13. Other reasons for plea bargaining are discussed in chapters 4 and 12. It can reduce prosecutors' and judges' workloads while guaranteeing a conviction, for instance.

14. Other aspects of the process of undermining capital punishment such as the "Benefit of Clergy" are not discussed here since the basic point can be made without them, but see Green 1985 in this regard. These issues will also be examined in the book in progress that is described in note 1 above.

15. "Houses of correction" were first established to punish and reform able-bodied poor persons who refused to work (Beattie 1986: 492). A "widespread concern for the habits and behavior of the poor" is often cited as the reason for the laws regarding vagrancy and the establishment of facilities to "reform" the idle poor by confining them and forcing them to work at hard labor (e.g., Beattie 1986: 497). But "there is little question but that these statutes were designed for one express purpose: to force laborers (whether personally free or unfree) to accept employment at a low wage in order to insure the landowner an adequate supply of labor at a price he could afford to pay" (Chambliss 1964: 69). This clearly reflected the transfer function of government and paved the way for the use of prisons as punishment.

16. Gradually, central government officials also expanded their power in prosecution of "political" crimes, and by the late nineteenth century a "limited system of governmental prosecution" was in place (Cardenas 1986: 362). The Prosecution of Offenses Act of 1879 established the Office of Director of Public Prosecutions, but that office prosecutes only a small portion of criminal cases.

NOTES TO CHAPTER 10

1. This chapter provided the basis for Benson 1996c and is therefore closely related to it. Part of the chapter is drawn from Benson 1995b.

2. Many awards of so-called punitive damages in tort cases today are not "legitimate," however (Benson 1996d). They do not punish for intentional acts that lead to harms, but rather they serve as transfer mechanisms with wealth being taken from firms that jurors and judges believe have "deep pockets." Thus, they reflect the kinds of breakdown in private property rights that encourage greater takings, whether through litigation, legislation, or theft, an issue raised in the concluding section of this chapter.

3. However, redirecting criminal justice by establishing a restitution-based system would create numerous beneficial side effects that will be noted in the following two chapters.

4. Parts of this section draw heavily on Evers 1994.

5. Other states have elevated the status of victims to the "constitutional level" as well, although not necessarily the status of victim restitution or compensation. The "victims' bills of rights" in Florida and Kansas do not even mention a right to restitution; Michigan simply lists it among a long list of other "rights." See chapter 11 for additional discussion of these constitutional provisions.

6. This subsection draws from Evers 1994: 22–26.

NOTES TO CHAPTER 11

1. I have an intimate understanding of such an environment, since I work in a bureaucracy that creates strong incentives to produce measurable output like numbers of publications and numbers of student FTEs [full-time equivalents] that can be counted rather than numbers of arrests and convictions; the quality of education suffers greatly as a consequence, just as the quality of crime control does—higher education should be privatized too!

2. Parts of this chapter draw from and expand on Benson 1996b.

3. The economics of crime literature provides a considerable amount of support for the hypothesis that a higher probability of arrest for a particular crime reduces the *level* of that crime (deters that crime). See chapter 7 for references and related discussion (in particular, note that increases in police resources generally do not affect the probability of arrest). The argument made here is not inconsistent with this empirical result; rather, it suggests that waiting to arrest may not be the most effective way to deter crime, and furthermore, that *too much* capital may be employed relative to the level that would maximize crime deterrence for a particular level of fixed input to crime deterrence not controlled by police (e.g., community characteristics). This suggests that the focus in many simultaneous-equation empirical models on production of arrests as the only deterrent is both inappropriate and misleading.

4. Breton and Wintrobe (1982: 150–51) also offer other arguments that can be used to explain why bureaucrats advocate policies like alcohol prohibition and the criminalization and prohibition of various drugs after 1914 and 1937; these arguments also explain the increased emphasis on drug control in the mid-1960s and then again in the mid-1980s. These changes were all advocated by law enforcement bureaucrats to reduce crime, even though such policies have a history of failure, because they can be claimed to be "a source of blame" for a problem such as crime that they cannot effectively solve. The fact that these polices of direct control also fail does not make them unattractive, because there is always opposition to such policies; therefore when they fail, opponents can be blamed for not allocating sufficient resources to combat the problem. Furthermore, because policy outcomes depend jointly on the input of several different groups and bureaus, and the set of possible control methods is very large, when the subset selected fails, the bureaucrats can argue that (1) although they advocated a control policy, they favored a different subset of control tools (e.g., more severe punishment of drug offenders or greater spending on supply interdiction efforts), so they are not responsible for the failure, and/or (2) the other groups whose contributions were necessary to make the effort successful (e.g., witnesses, judges, legislators who approve prison budgets, or other law enforcement agencies) did not do their share. Indeed, a policy can fail completely while at the same time entrepreneurial bureaucrats expand their reputations and end up being substantially better off.

5. Note that the criticisms of reward systems are generally valid when applied to rewards tied to prosecution, but not when applied to rewards tied to recovery of losses. In particular, when rewards are payable upon successful prosecution, incentives are created for the bounty hunter to falsify evidence, falsely accuse, and so on. As noted in chapter 9, this was a serious problem with public rewards from their inception, and it appears to continue to be a problem today as prosecutors trade monetary reward and/or freedom from prosecution for testimony leading to convictions (Benson 1990: 65–66; Rasmussen and Benson 1994: 165–66; Cotts 1992).

NOTES TO CHAPTER 12

1. Parts of this chapter draw from and expand on Benson 1996b.

2. For an overview of the substantial literature supporting this claim, see Rasmussen and Benson 1994: 152–64.

3. Courts are already overwhelmed with some kinds of tort litigation, of course, but these are generally in areas of rapidly changing law (Benson 1996d; Hensler et al. 1987). Where the law is clear, as in auto accident torts, the vast majority of cases are settled out of court.

4. The rights-based approach to criminal justice advocated in chapter 10 would also increase the probability of prosecution and conviction because it would do away with many of the "excuse"-based defenses that are now used by criminals. See Bidinotto 1994b; Coleman 1994; and Logan and DiIulio 1994.

5. There are numerous "intermediate sanctions" between probation and imprisonment that may provide cost-effective alternatives to the prison/probation dichotomy. Many are contracted out (e.g., halfway houses and intensive-supervision treatment programs). However, in the political/institutional environment that characterizes the public-sector criminal justice system, these alternatives tend to be underfunded and ineffectively utilized (Benson and Rasmussen 1994b).

6. Similar arrangements might be developed for more-intensive-supervision intermediate sanction programs as well. Many programs of this kind are actually contracted out now, as noted above, including halfway houses and drug treatment programs, so a ready market for such a bonding arrangement may be at least partly in place.

7. See Auerbach et al. 1988: 25–39 for discussion of a number of other examples.

8. Despite the Maine novelties program's significant successes, on April 16, 1980, a lockdown of the Maine State Prison began. Inmates were confined to their cells twenty-four hours a day for ten weeks. An extensive search and seizure operation destroyed the prisoners' businesses. After the lockdown, substantial reductions in economic incentives were implemented, which destroyed any potential for reviving the program. Why? One explanation may be political. For several years the Maine Corrections Bureau had tried unsuccessfully to obtain larger budgets and to have the bureau elevated to cabinet level. Following the dramatic lockdown, budget increases were approved, and the Bureau of Corrections was elevated to cabinet-level status. Key legislators switched their position on both issues because of the lockdown. Another explanation may simply be bureaucratic rigidity and resistance to change. Corrections officers and prison authorities wanted complete control over prisoners, not a miniature economy, evolving and changing as "ambitious and talented individuals [were] finding . . . [out how to stretch and avoid] bureaucratic restrictions on their activities" (Shedd 1982: 9).

9. Other potential rehabilitation effects of the program, such as its impact on the level of prison violence, are discussed below.

10. For details on these studies, contact The Enterprise Prison Institute, 1899 L Street, NW, Suite 500, Washington, D.C. 20036 (202-466-7001).

Bibliography

The following abbreviations are employed in the text and the notes:

NACCJSG: National Advisory Commission on Criminal Justice Standards and Goals

NIJ: National Institute of Justice

OICJ: Office of International Criminal Justice

Alchian, A. Armen, and William R. Allen. 1969. *Exchange and Production, Theory in Use.* Delmont, NY: Wadsworth Publishing.

Allison, John P. 1972. "Economic Factors and the Crime Rate." *Land Economics* 48:193–96.

Anderson, Annelise. 1979. *The Business of Organized Crime.* Stanford, CA: Hoover Institute Press.

Anderson, David C. 1983. "EARN-IT: A Key to the Prison Dilemma." *Across the Board* 20 (November): 34–42.

Anderson, Terry, and P. J. Hill. 1979. "An American Experiment in Anarcho-Capitalism: The *Not* So Wild, Wild West." *Journal of Libertarian Studies* 3:9–29.

Anderson, Terry, and Fred McChesney. 1994. "Raid or Trade: An Economic Model of Indian-White Relations." *Journal of Law and Economics* 37 (April): 39–74.

Archambeault, William G., and Donald R. Deis, Jr. 1996. *Executive Summary: Cost Effectiveness Comparisons of Private versus Public Prisons in Louisiana: A Comprehensive Analysis of Allen, Avoyelles, and Winn Correctional Centers.* Baton Rouge: Louisiana State University.

Auerbach, Barbara J., George E. Sexton, C. Franklin Farrow, and Robert H. Lawson. 1988. *Work in American Prisons: The Private Sector Gets Involved.* Washington, DC: U.S. Department of Justice, National Institute of Justice.

Auerbach, Jerold S. 1983. *Justice without Law?* New York: Oxford University Press.

Axelrod, Robert. 1984. *The Evolution of Cooperation.* New York: Basic Books.

Ayoob, Massad F. 1981. *The Experts Speak Out: The Police View of Gun Control.* Bellevue, WA: Second Amendment Foundation.

Ayres, Ian, and Steven D. Levitt. 1996. "Measuring Positive Externalities from Unobservable Victim Precaution: An Empirical Analysis of Lojack." No. 197, John M.

Olin Center for Law, Economics, and Business Discussion Paper Series, Harvard University, September.

Baker, J. H. 1971. *An Introduction to English Legal History.* London: Butterworths.

Barger, Melvin D. 1994. "Crime: The Unsolved Problem." In *Criminal Justice? The Legal System vs. Individual Responsibility,* ed. Robert J. Bidinotto, 26–33. Irvington-on-Hudson, NY: Foundation for Economic Education.

Barnett, Randy E. 1977. "Restitution: A New Paradigm of Criminal Justice." *Ethics* 87 (July): 279–301.

———. 1979. "Justice Entrepreneurship in a Free Market: Comment." *Journal of Libertarian Studies* 3 (Winter): 439–451.

———. 1984. "Public Decisions and Private Rights." *Criminal Justice Ethics* 3 (summer/fall): 50–62.

———. 1985. "Pursuing Justice in a Free Society, Part Two: Crime Prevention and the Legal Order." *Criminal Justice Ethics* 4 (summer/fall): 50–72.

Barton, R. F. 1967. "Procedure among the Ifugao." In *Law and Warfare,* ed. Paul Bohannan, 161–181. Garden City, NY: Natural History Press.

Beattie, J. M. 1986. *Crime and the Courts in England, 1660–1800.* Oxford: Clarendon Press.

Beck, Allen J. 1987. "Recidivism of Young Parolees." *Special Report.* Washington, DC: U.S. Department of Justice, Bureau of Justice Statistics, May.

Becker, Gary S. 1969. "Crime and Punishment: An Economic Approach." *Journal of Political Economy* 76 (March/April).

Beito, David T. 1988. "The Private Places of St. Louis: The Formation of Urban Infrastructure through Non-Governmental Planning, 1869–1920." Working Paper, Institute for Humane Studies, Fairfax, VA. May 20.

Benegas Lynch, Alberto, Jr. 1995. "Toward a Theory of Autogovernment." University of Buenos Aires, April. Mimeographed.

Bennett, James T., and Thomas J. DiLorenzo. 1992. *Official Lies: How Washington Misleads Us.* Alexandria, VA: Groom Books.

Benson, Bruce L. 1981. "A Note on Corruption of Public Officials: The Black Market for Property Rights." *Journal of Libertarian Studies* 5 (summer): 305–11.

———. 1984a. "Guns for Protection and Other Private Sector Responses to the Fear of Rising Crime." In *Firearms and Violence: Issues of Regulation,* ed. Don Kates, Jr., 329–56. Cambridge, MA: Ballinger Press.

———. 1984b. "Rent Seeking from a Property Rights Perspective." *Southern Economic Journal* 51 (October): 388-400.

———. 1986a. "Guns for Protection and Other Private Sector Responses to Government's Failure to Control Increasing Violent Crime." *Journal of Libertarian Studies* 8 (winter): 75-109.

———. 1986b. "The Lost Victim and Other Failures of the Public Law Experiment." *Harvard Journal of Law and Public Policy* 9 (spring): 399-427.

―――. 1988a. "Corruption in Law Enforcement: One Consequence of 'The Tragedy of the Commons' Arising with Public Allocation Processes." *International Review of Law and Economics* 8 (June): 73-84.

―――. 1988b. "An Institutional Explanation for Corruption of Criminal Justice Officials." *Cato Journal* 8 (spring/summer): 139-63.

―――. 1989a. "The Spontaneous Evolution of Commercial Law." *Southern Economic Journal* 55 (January): 644–61.

―――. 1989b. "Enforcement of Private Property Rights in Primitive Societies: Law without Government." *Journal of Libertarian Studies* 9 (Winter): 1–26.

―――. 1990. *The Enterprise of Law: Justice without the State.* San Francisco: Pacific Research Institute for Public Policy.

―――. 1991a. "An Evolutionary Contractarian View of Primitive Law: The Institutions and Incentives Arising under Customary American Indian Law." *Review of Austrian Economics* 5:65–89.

―――. 1991b. "Reciprocal Exchange as the Basis for Recognition of Law: Examples from American History." *Journal of Libertarian Studies* 10 (fall): 53–82.

―――. 1992a. "Market Failure versus Government Failure in the Production of Adjudication." In *Privatizing the United States Justice System: Police, Adjudication, and Corrections Services from the Private Sector,* ed. Gary W. Bowman, Simon Hakim, and Paul Seidenstat, 159–79. Jefferson, NC: McFarland.

―――. 1992b. "The Development of Criminal Law and Its Enforcement: Public Interest or Political Transfers." *Journal des Economistes et des Etudes Humaines* 3 (March): 79–108.

―――. 1994a. "Are Public Goods Really Common Pools: Considerations of the Evolution of Policing and Highways in England." *Economic Inquiry* 32 (April): 249–71.

―――. 1994b. "Third Thoughts on Contracting Out." *Journal of Libertarian Studies* 11 (fall): 44–78.

―――. 1994c. "Emerging from the Hobbesian Jungle: Might Takes and Makes Rights." *Constitutional Political Economy* 5 (spring/summer): 129–58.

―――. 1995a. "An Exploration of the Impact of Modern Arbitration Statutes on the Development of Arbitration in the United States." *Journal of Law, Economics & Organization* 11 (October): 479–501.

―――. 1995b. "Rights, Entitlements, and Individual Responsibility in the Welfare State." In *Can the Present Problems of Mature Welfare States Such as Sweden Be Solved?* ed. Nils Karlson, 88–98. Stockholm: City University Press.

―――. 1995c. "Understanding Bureaucratic Behavior: Implications from the Public Choice Literature." *Journal of Public Finance and Public Choice* 8 (December): 89–117.

―――. 1996a. "Are There Tradeoffs between Costs and Quality in the Privatization of Criminal Justice?" *Journal of Security Administration* 19 (December): 15–51.

———. 1996b. "Privatization in Criminal Justice." An *Independent Policy Report* prepared for the William I. Koch Commission on Crime Reduction and Prevention for the State of Kansas.

———. 1996c. "Restitution in Theory and in Practice." *Journal of Libertarian Studies* 12 (spring): 75–98.

———. 1996d. "Uncertainty, the Race for Property Rights, and Rent Dissipation Due to Judicial Changes in Product Liability Tort Law." *Cultural Dynamics* 8 (November): 333–51.

———. 1997a. "Arbitration." In *Encyclopedia of Law and Economics,* ed. Boudewijn Bouckaert and Gerrit De Geest. London: Edward Elgar.

———. 1997b. "Institutions and the Spontaneous Evolution of Morality." In *Values and the Social Order,* vol. 3, ed. Gerard Radnitzky, 245–82. Aldershot, Eng.: Avebury.

———. 1997c. "Privatizing Crime Fighting." *Madison Review* 2 (winter): 31–34.

———. 1998a. "Arbitration in the Shadow of the Law." In *The New Palgrave Dictionary of Economics and the Law,* ed. Peter Newman. London: Macmillan, forthcoming.

———. 1998b. "Crime Control through Private Enterprise." *Independent Review* 2 (winter): 341–71.

———. 1998c. "Evolution of Commercial Law." In *The New Palgrave Dictionary of Economics and the Law,* ed. Peter Newman. London: Macmillan, forthcoming.

———. 1998d. "Jurisdiction: Privatization of Legal and Administrative Services." In *The Merits of Markets—Critical Issues of the Open Society.* Keil, Germany: Egon-Sohmen Foundation, forthcoming.

———. 1998e. "Law Merchant." In *The New Palgrave Dictionary of Economics and the Law,* ed. Peter Newman. London: Macmillan, forthcoming.

———. 1998f. "Toxic Torts by Government." In *Harmful to Your Health: Toxics, Torts, and the Environmental Bureaucracy,* ed. Richard Stroup and Roger Meiners. Oakland, CA: Independent Institute, forthcoming.

———. Forthcoming, a. "Do We Want the Production of Prison Services to be More Efficient?" In *Private Corrections: Penal Reform, Justice, and Society,* ed. Jan Brakel. Oakland, CA.: Independent Institute.

———. Forthcoming, b. "Law without the State: The Merchant Courts of Medieval Europe." In *The Voluntary City: New Directions for Urban America,* ed. David T. Beito. Oakland, CA.: Independent Institute.

Benson, Bruce L., and John Baden. 1985. "The Political Economy of Government Corruption: The Logic of Underground Government." *Journal of Legal Studies* 14 (June): 391-410.

Benson, Bruce L., Iljoong Kim, and David W. Rasmussen. 1994. "Estimating Deterrence Effects: A Public Choice Prospective on the Economics of Crime Literature." *Southern Economic Journal* 61 (July): 161–68.

———. 1998. "Deterrence and Public Policy: Tradeoffs in the Allocation of Police Resources." *International Review of Law and Economics* 18 (March): 77–100.

Benson, Bruce L., Iljoong Kim, David W. Rasmussen, and Thomas W. Zuehlke. 1992. "Is Property Crime Caused by Drug Use or Drug Enforcement Policy?" *Applied Economics* 24 (July): 679–92.

Benson, Bruce L., and David W. Rasmussen. 1991. "The Relationship between Illicit Drug Enforcement Policy and Property Crimes." *Contemporary Policy Issues* 9 (October): 106–15.

———. 1994a. "Crime in Florida." Report to the Florida Chamber of Commerce, Tallahassee, FL, March.

———. 1994b. "Intermediate Sanctions: A Policy Analysis Based on Program Evaluations." Report to the Florida Task Force for the Review of the Criminal Justice and Corrections Systems, Tallahassee, FL, September.

———. 1995. "Tragedy of the Commons: Origins of Failed Innovations in Criminal Justice Policy." Working Paper, Florida State University, March.

———. 1996a. "Illicit Drugs and Crime." An *Independent Policy Report* prepared for the William I. Koch Commission on Crime Reduction and Prevention for the State of Kansas.

———. 1996b. "Predatory Public Finance and the Origins of the War on Drugs: 1984–1989." *Independent Review* 1 (fall): 163–89. [Also in *Taxing Choice: The Predatory Politics of Fiscal Discrimination,* ed. William F. Shughart II (New Brunswick, NJ: Transaction, 1997)].

Benson, Bruce L., David W. Rasmussen, and David L. Sollars. 1995. "Police Bureaucrats, Their Incentives, and the War on Drugs." *Public Choice* 83:21–45.

Benson, Bruce L., and Laurin A. Wollan, Jr. 1989. "Prison Crowding and Judicial Incentives." *Madison Paper Series* (May): 1–21.

Berk, Richard, Harold Brackman, and Selma Lesser. 1977. *A Measure of Justice: An Empirical Study of Changes in the California Penal Code, 1955–1971.* New York: Academic Press.

Berman, Harold J. 1983. *Law and Revolution: The Formation of the Western Legal Tradition.* Cambridge, MA: Harvard University Press.

Bidinotto, Robert J. 1994a. "Criminal Responsibility." In *Criminal Justice? The Legal System vs. Individual Responsibility,* ed. Robert J. Bidinotto, 5–25. Irvington-on-Hudson, NY: Foundation for Economic Education.

———. 1994b. "Subverting Justice." In *Criminal Justice? The Legal System vs. Individual Responsibility,* ed. Robert J. Bidinotto, 65–83. Irvington-on-Hudson, NY: Foundation for Economic Education.

———. 1994c. "Crime and Moral Retribution." In *Criminal Justice? The Legal System vs. Individual Responsibility,* ed. Robert J. Bidinotto, 181–200. Irvington-on-Hudson, NY: Foundation for Economic Education.

———. 1994d. "Restoring Responsibility." In *Criminal Justice? The Legal System vs. Individual Responsibility,* ed. Robert J. Bidinotto, 276–96. Irvington-on-Hudson, NY: Foundation for Economic Education.

Billington, Ray Allen. 1956. *The Far Western Frontier, 1830–1860.* New York: Harper.

Binzen, Peter. 1984. "Free Enterprise: Private Concerns Begin Delivering Public Services." *Philadelphia Inquirer,* August 12, 10C.

Blackstone, Erwin A., and Simon Hakim. 1995. *Police Services.* Oakland, CA: Independent Institute Report prepared for the William I. Koch Commission on Crime Reduction and Prevention for the State of Kansas, January (published as an *Independent Policy Report* in 1996 under the same title).

Blair, Peter Hunter. 1956. *An Introduction to Anglo-Saxon England.* Cambridge: Cambridge University Press.

Blumberg, Abraham. 1967. "The Practice of Law as a Confidence Game: Organizational Co-option of a Profession." *Law and Society Review* 1 (June): 15–39.

———. 1970. *Criminal Justice.* Chicago: Quadrangle Books.

Blumenthal, Ralph. 1993. "Private Guards Cooperate in Public Policing." *New York Times,* July 13, B1–B2.

Boaz, David. 1997. *Libertarianism: A Primer.* New York: Free Press.

Boostrom, Ronald L., and Corina A. Draper. 1992. "Community Policing, Problem-Oriented Policing, Police-Citizen Coproduction of Public Safety, and the Privatization of Crime Control." In *Privatizing the United States Justice System: Police, Adjudication, and Corrections Services from the Private Sector,* ed. Gary W. Bowman, Simon Hakim, and Paul Seidenstat, 56–66. Jefferson, NC: McFarland.

Bornman, Gary W. 1995. "We Hunt Down Animals That Attacked People." *Tallahassee Democrat,* February 24, 10A.

Bottom, Norman K., and John Kostanoski. 1983. *Security and Loss Control.* New York: Macmillan.

Bowman, Gary W., Simon Hakim, and Paul Seidenstat, eds. 1993. *Privatizing Correctional Institutions.* New Brunswick, NJ: Transaction Publishers.

Boyce, Joseph N. 1996. "Landlords Turn to Commando Patrol." *Wall Street Journal,* September 18, B1–B2.

Brakel, Samuel J. 1992. "Private Corrections." In *Privatizing the United States Justice System: Police, Adjudication, and Corrections Services from the Private Sector,* ed. Gary W. Bowman, Simon Hakim, and Paul Seidenstat, 254–74. Jefferson, NC: McFarland.

Breton, Albert, and Ronald Wintrobe. 1982. *The Logic of Bureaucratic Control.* Cambridge: Cambridge University Press.

Bronson, George D., Claire J. Bronson, Michael J. Wynne, and Richard F. Olson. 1992. "Barriers to Entry of Private-Sector Industry into a Prison Environment." In *Privatizing the United States Justice System: Police, Adjudication, and Corrections Services from the Private Sector,* ed. Gary W. Bowman, Simon Hakim, and Paul Seidenstat, 325–29. Jefferson, NC: McFarland.

Brown, Richard Maxwell. 1975. *Strain of Violence: Historical Studies of American Violence and Vigilantism.* New York: Oxford University Press.

Buchanan, James. 1975. *The Limits of Liberty.* Chicago: University of Chicago Press.

Buchanan, James, and Gordon Tullock. 1962. *The Calculus of Consent.* Ann Arbor: University of Michigan Press.

Buck, Andrew J., Meir Gross, Simon Hakim, and J. J. Weinblatt. 1983. "The Deterrence Hypothesis Revisited." *Regional Science and Urban Economics* 13:471–86.

Bureau of Census. *County Business Patterns.* Washington, DC: U.S. Department of Commerce, Bureau of Census, 1965–92.

Bureau of Justice Statistics. 1990. *Pretrial Release of Felony Defendants.* Washington, DC: U.S. Department of Justice, Bureau of Justice Statistics.

———. 1993. *Highlights from 20 Years of Surveying Crime Victims: The National Victimization Survey, 1973–1992.* Washington, DC: U.S. Department of Justice, Office of Justice Programs, October.

Burger, Warren E. 1992. "More Warehouses, or Factories with Fences?" In *Privatizing the United States Justice System: Police, Adjudication, and Corrections Services from the Private Sector,* ed. Gary W. Bowman, Simon Hakim, and Paul Seidenstat, 330–35. Jefferson, NC: McFarland.

Burns, Walter N. 1926. *The Saga of Billy the Kid.* Garden City, NY: Doubleday.

California Department of Justice. 1981. *Homicide in California, 1981.* Sacramento, CA: Bureau of Criminal Statistics and Special Services.

Cameron, Samuel. 1988. "The Economics of Crime Deterrence: A Survey of Theory and Evidence." *Kyklos* 41:301–23.

Camp, G. M. 1968. "Nothing to Lose: A Study of Bank Robbery in America." Ph.D. diss., Yale University.

Canlis, Michael N. 1961. "The Evolution of Law Enforcement in California." *Far Westerner* 2 (July).

Cardenas, Juan. 1986. "The Crime Victim in the Prosecutional Process." *Harvard Journal of Law and Public Policy* 9 (spring): 357–98.

Carlisle, John. 1992. "Criminal Welfare: A Jail Reduction Failure." *Policy Insights* (April): 1–2.

Carlson, Tucker. 1995a. "Safety Inc." *Policy Review* (summer): 66–72.

———. 1995b. "Smoking Them Out: How to Close Down a Crack House in Your Neighborhood." *Policy Review* (winter): 56–65.

Carr-Hill, Roy A., and Nicholas H. Stern. 1973. "An Econometric Model of the Supply and Control of Recorded Offenses in England and Wales." *Journal of Public Economics* 2:289–318.

Cary, Mary K. 1994. "How States Can Fight Violent Crime." In *Criminal Justice? The Legal System vs. Individual Responsibility,* ed. Robert J. Bidinotto, 250-69. Irvington-on-Hudson, NY: Foundation for Economic Education.

Chaiken, Marcia, and Jan Chaiken. 1987. *Public Policing—Privately Provided.* Washington, DC: U.S. Department of Justice, National Institute of Justice.

Chambliss, William. 1964. "A Sociological Analysis of the Law of Vagrancy." *Social Problems* 12 (summer): 67–77.

Chambliss, William, and Robert Seidman. 1960. *Crime and the Legal Process.* New York: McGraw-Hill.

———. 1971. *Law, Order, and Power.* Reading, MA: Addison-Wesley.

Chicago Police Department. 1993. *Together We Can: A Strategic Plan for Reinventing the Chicago Police Department.* Chicago: Chicago Police Department, October.

Clinnard, Marshall. 1978. *Cities with Little Crime: The Case of Switzerland.* Cambridge: Cambridge University Press.

Clotfelter, Charles T. 1977. "Public Services, Private Substitutes, and the Demand for Protection against Crime." *American Economic Review* 67 (December): 867–77.

Coase, Ronald H. 1960. "The Problem of Social Cost." *Journal of Law and Economics* 3:1–44.

———. 1974. "The Lighthouse in Economics." *Journal of Law and Economics* 17 (October): 357–76.

Cockburn, James S. 1985. *Calendar of Assize Records: Home Circuit Indictments, Elizabeth I and James I.* London: Her Majesty's Stationary Office.

Cole, John S. 1995. "Crime Stats Fall, with Thanks to You." *Tallahassee Democrat,* February 27.

Coleman, Lee. 1994. "The Insanity Defense." In *Criminal Justice? The Legal System vs. Individual Responsibility,* ed. Robert J. Bidinotto, 138–55. Irvington-on-Hudson, NY: Foundation for Economic Education.

Connelley, William E. 1933. *Wild Bill and His Era.* New York: Press of the Pioneers.

Cook, Philip. 1979. "The Effect of Gun Availability on Robbery and Robbery Murder: A Cross-Section Study of 50 Cities." In *Policy Studies Review Annual,* 743–81.

Cook, Tom. 1984. "Retailers See Prison Made Products as a Threat." *Billings Gazette,* August 12, 1.

Corrections Today. 1992. (December): 14.

Cotts, Cynthia. 1992. "The Year of the Rat: New Drug Laws Are Creating a Cadre of Unreliable and Unsavory Witnesses." *Reason* (May): 36–41.

Cowen, Tyler. 1988. "Introduction. Public Goods and Externalities: Old and New Perspectives." In *The Theory of Market Failure,* ed. Tyler Cowen, 1 –25. Fairfax, VA: George Mason University Press.

"Crime Pays." 1984. In *60 Minutes,* vol. 14, no. 11, transcript of a CBS Television Network broadcast November 25.

Criminal Justice Associates. 1990. *Private Sector Prison Industries.* Philadelphia: Criminal Justice Associates.

Cunningham, William C., John J. Strauchs, and Clifford W. Van Meter. 1991. *Private Security: Patterns and Trends.* National Institute of Justice, Research in Brief.

Cunningham, William C., and Todd H. Taylor. 1985. *Crime and Protection in America: A Study of Private Security and Law Enforcement Resources and Relationships.* Washington, DC: U.S. Department of Justice, National Institute of Justice.

Darby, Henry C., ed. 1973. *A New Historical Geography of England.* Cambridge: Cambridge University Press.

Dart, Roland C., III. 1992. "Police Privatization Venture as Strategies to Maintain and Enhance Public Safety." In *Privatizing the United States Justice System: Police, Adjudication, and Corrections Services from the Private Sector,* ed. Gary W. Bowman, Simon Hakim, and Paul Seidenstat, 107–30. Jefferson, NC: McFarland.

Demsetz, Harold. 1967. "Toward a Theory of Property Rights." *American Economic Review* 57 (May): 347–59.

———. 1968. "Why Regulate Utilities?" *Journal of Law and Economics* 11 (April): 55–65.

———. 1970. "The Private Production of Public Goods." *Journal of Law and Economics* 13 (October): 293–306.

Denenberg, Tai Schneider, and R. V. Denenberg. 1981. *Dispute Resolution: Settling Conflicts without Legal Action.* Public Affairs Pamphlet No. 597. New York: Public Affairs Committee.

Dewhurst, H. S. 1955. *The Railroad Police.* Springfield, IL: Charles C. Thomas.

Dionne, E. J., Jr. 1994. "Libertarian Lure." *Washington Post,* December 6.

Dobson, Christopher, and Ronald Payne. 1983. "Private Enterprise Takes on Terrorism." *Reason* 14 (January).

Donovan, Edwin J., and William F. Walsh. 1986. *An Evaluation of Starrett City Security Services.* University Park, PA: Pennsylvania State University.

Dorffi, Christine. 1979. "San Francisco's Hired Guns." *Reason* 11 (August): 26–29, 33.

Downie, Leonard, Jr. 1971. *Justice Denied: The Case for Reform of the Courts.* New York: Praeger.

Drago, Henry S. 1970. *The Great Range Wars: Violence and the Grasslands.* New York: Dodd.

Dykstra, Robert R. 1968. *The Cattle Towns.* New York: Knopf.

Easterbrook, Frank H. 1983. "Criminal Procedure and the Market System." *Journal of Legal Studies* 12 (June): 289–332.

Ehrlich, Isaac. 1972. "The Deterrent Effect of Criminal Law Enforcement." *Journal of Legal Studies* 1:259–76.

———. 1973. "Participation in Illegitimate Activities: A Theoretical and Empirical Investigation." *Journal of Political Economy* 81:521–65.

Eisenstein, James. 1973. *Politics and the Legal Process.* New York: Harper and Row.

Elias, Robert. 1983. "The Symbolic Politics of Victim Compensation." *Victimology* 8:213–24.

———. 1986. *The Politics of Victimization: Victims, Victimology, and Human Rights.* New York: Oxford University Press.

Ellickson, Robert C. 1991. *Order without Law: How Neighbors Settle Disputes.* Cambridge, MA: Harvard University Press.

Elliot, Mabel A. 1944. "Crime on the Frontier Mores." *American Sociological Review* 9 (April): 185–92.

Elliot, Nicholas. 1977. "Economic Analysis of Crime and the Criminal Justice System." In *Public Law and Public Policy*, ed. John Gardiner, 68–89. New York: Praeger.

Enterprise Prison Institute. 1996a. "Former Attorney General Meese Calls Growing Support for Prison Industries from Business Inevitable." Press release, December 12.

———. 1996b. "Prison Group Headed by Former Attorney General Meese to Research Inmate Labor and Prison Management." Press release, April 16.

———. 1996c. "Research Shows Prison Industries Reduce Costs, Improve Public Safety; Business and Labor Partnering to Create Prisons for the Future." Press release, September 18.

Epstein, Aaron. 1997. "Court Decides Not to Give Extra Police Powers." *Tallahassee Democrat*, April 29, 3A.

Evers, Williamson M. 1994. *Victim's Rights, Restitution, and Retribution*. Oakland, CA: Independent Institute Report prepared for the William I. Koch Commission on Crime Reduction and Prevention for the State of Kansas, November (published as an *Independent Policy Report* in 1996 under the same title).

Fine, Ralph A. 1994a. "Plea Bargaining: An Unnecessary Evil." In *Criminal Justice? The Legal System vs. Individual Responsibility*, ed. Robert J. Bidinotto, 84–101. Irvington-on-Hudson, NY: Foundation for Economic Education.

———. 1994b. "The Urge to Confess." In *Criminal Justice? The Legal System vs. Individual Responsibility*, ed. Robert J. Bidinotto, 112–37. Irvington-on-Hudson, NY: Foundation for Economic Education.

Fisk, Donald, Herbert Kiesling, and Thomas Muller. 1978. *Private Provision of Public Services: An Overview*. Washington, DC: Urban Institute.

Fitch, Lyle C. 1974. "Increasing the Role of the Private Sector in Providing Public Services." In *Urban Affairs Annual Review*, vol. 8, *Improving the Quality of Urban Management*, ed. Willis D. Hawley and David Rogers, 501–99.

Fitzgerald, Randall. 1988. *When Government Goes Private: Successful Alternatives to Public Services*. New York: Universe Books.

Fixler, Philip E., Jr. 1984. "Can Privatization Solve the Prison Crisis?" *Fiscal Watchdog* 90 (April).

Fixler, Philip E., Jr., and Robert W. Poole, Jr. 1992. "Can Police Be Privatized?" In *Privatizing the United States Justice System: Police, Adjudication, and Corrections Services from the Private Sector*, ed. Gary W. Bowman, Simon Hakim, and Paul Seidenstat, 27–41. Jefferson, NC: McFarland.

Florestano, Patricia S., and Stephen B. Gordon. 1980. "Public vs. Private: Small Government Contracting with the Private Sector." *Public Administration Review* 40 (January/February): 29–34.

Foldvary, Fred. 1994. *Public Goods and Private Communities: The Market Provision of Social Services*. Aldershot, Eng.: Edward Elgar.

Frantz, Joe B. 1969. "The Frontier Tradition: An Invitation to Violence." In *The History of Violence in America*, ed. Hugh D. Graham and Ted R. Gurr, 127–54. New York: New York Times Books.

Freeman, Mike. 1992. "Contracting Out: The Most Viable Solution." In *Privatizing the United States Justice System: Police, Adjudication, and Corrections Services from the Private Sector*, ed. Gary W. Bowman, Simon Hakim, and Paul Seidenstat, 131–37. Jefferson, NC: McFarland.

Friedman, David. 1973. *The Machinery of Freedom: Guide to a Radical Capitalism*. New York: Harper and Row.

———. 1979. "Private Creation and Enforcement of Law: A Historical Case." *Journal of Legal Studies* 8 (March): 399–415.

———. 1984. "Efficient Institutions for the Private Enforcement of Law." *Journal of Legal Studies* 13 (June): 379–98.

———. 1994. "Law as a Private Good." *Economics and Philosophy* 10:319–27.

Fuller, Lon L. 1964. *The Morality of Law*. New Haven, CT: Yale University Press.

———. 1981. *The Principles of Social Order*. Durham, NC: Duke University Press.

Furlong, William J., and Steven L. Mehay. 1981. "Urban Law Enforcement in Canada: An Empirical Analysis." *Canadian Journal of Economics* 14:44–57.

Gage, Theodore J. 1981. "Getting Street-Wise in St. Louis." *Reason* 13 (August): 18–20.

———. 1982. "Cops, Inc." *Reason* 14 (March): 23–28.

Gard, Wayne. 1949. *Frontier Justice*. Norman, OK: University of Oklahoma Press.

Geis, Gilbert. 1967. "Violence in American Society." *Current History* 52 (June): 354–58.

Gille, Michael S. 1992. "Private Dispute Resolution." In *Privatizing the United States Justice System: Police, Adjudication, and Corrections Services from the Private Sector*, ed. Gary W. Bowman, Simon Hakim, and Paul Seidenstat, 229–37 Jefferson, NC: McFarland.

Glick, Henry R., and Kenneth N. Vines. 1973. *State Court Systems*. Englewood Cliffs, NJ: Prentice-Hall.

Goldin, Kenneth D. 1977. "Equal Access vs. Selective Access: A Critique of Public Goods Theory." *Public Choice* 29 (Spring): 53–71.

Goldsmidt, Walter. 1951. "Ethics and the Structure of Society: An Ethnological Contribution to the Sociology of Knowledge." *American Anthropologist* 53 (October/December): 506–24.

Granelli, James S. 1981. "Got a Spat? Go Rent a Judge." *National Law Journal* 3 (June 8): 1–2, 30–31.

Green, Thomas A. 1985. *Verdict according to Conscience: Perspectives on the English Criminal Trial Jury, 1200–1800*. Chicago: University of Chicago Press.

Grieser, Robert C. 1989. "Do Correctional Industries Adversely Impact the Private Sector? *Federal Probation* (March): 18–24.

Grosman, Brian. 1969. *The Prosecutor: An Inquiry into the Exercise of Discretion.* Toronto: University of Toronto Press.

Gunnison, Robert B. 1997. "Privately Run Prison Planned for Mojave: Firm Says It Can House Inmates Cheaper." *San Francisco Chronicle*, August 1, A22.

Hakim, Simon. 1980. "The Attraction of Property Crime to Suburban Localities: A Revised Economic Model." *Urban Studies* 17:265–76.

Haley, John O. 1989. "Confession, Repentance, and Absolution." In *Mediation and Criminal Justice: Victims, Offenders, and Community*, ed. Marian Wright and Burt Gallaway, 195–211. London: Sage.

Hannan, Timothy. 1982. "Bank Robberies and Bank Security Precautions." *Journal of Legal Studies* 11 (January).

Hannon, Kerry. 1986. "Turnstile Justice." *Forbes* (December 15): 174–75.

Hardin, Russell. 1982. *Collective Action.* Baltimore: Johns Hopkins University Press.

Harland, Alan T. 1983. "One Hundred Years of Restitution: An International Review and Prospectus for Research." *Victimology* 8: 190–203.

Hayek, Friedrich A. 1937. "Economics and Knowledge." *Economica* 4:33–54.

———. 1967. *Studies in Philosophy, Politics and Economics.* Chicago: University of Chicago Press.

———. 1973. *Law, Legislation and Liberty.* Vol. 1. Chicago: University of Chicago Press.

Henry, Stuart. 1987. "Private Justice and the Policing of Labor: The Dialectic of Industrial Discipline." In *Private Police,* ed. Clifford D. Shearing and Phillip C. Stenning. Newbury Park, CA: Sage.

Hensler, Deborah R., Mary E. Vaiana, James S. Kakalik, and Mark A. Peterson. 1987. *Trends in Tort Litigation: The Story behind the Statistics.* Santa Monica, CA: Rand Institute for Civil Justice.

Herbert, Bob. 1997. "Texas Executes a Man Who Was Probably Innocent." *Tallahassee Democrat,* July 31, 12A.

Hillenbrand, Susan W. 1990. "Restitution and Victim Rights in the 1980s." In *Sage Criminal Justice System Annals,* vol. 25, *Victims of Crime: Problems, Policies, and Programs,* ed. Arthur J. Lurigio, Wesley G. Shogan, and Robert C. Davis. Newbury Park, CA: Sage.

Hoebel, E. Adamson. 1967. "Law-Ways of the Comanche Indians." In *Law and Warfare,* ed. Paul Bohannan, 183–203. Garden City, NY: Natural History Press.

Hoffman, Jan. 1997. "American-Style Justice: Keep Trying Them." *Tallahassee Democrat,* February 9, 4A.

Hogue, Arthur R. 1985. *Origins of the Common Law.* 1966. Reprint, Indianapolis: Liberty Press.

Holden, William C. 1940. "Law and Lawlessness on the Texas Frontier 1875–1890." *Southwestern Historical Quarterly* 44 (October): 188–203.

"Holding Down Holdups." 1976. *Business Week* (March).

Hollon, W. Eugene. 1974. *Frontier Violence: Another Look.* New York: Oxford University Press.

Hume, David. 1983–85. *The History of England.* 1778. 6 vols. Reprint, Indianapolis: Liberty Press.

Illinois Criminal Justice Information Authority. 1986. "The Pace of Recidivism in Illinois." *Research Bulletin* no. 2, April.

Iwata, Edward. 1984. "Rent-a-Cops on Trial." *This World,* March 18, 10.

Joel, Dana C. 1993. "The Privatization of Secure Adult Prisons: Issues and Evidence." In *Privatizing Correctional Institutions,* ed. Gary W. Bowman, Simon Hakim, and Paul Seidenstat, 51–74. New Brunswick, NJ: Transactions.

John Jay College of Criminal Justice/CUNY. 1997a. "Do You Get What You Pay For? With CJ Efforts, Not Necessarily." *Law Enforcement News* 23 (May 15).

———. 1997b. "Gated Enclaves Are Not Just for the Well-Heeled." *Law Enforcement News* 23 (May 15): 5.

———. 1997c. "Hard-Boiled Yeggs Turn Their Focus to Softer Bank Targets." *Law Enforcement News* 23 (May 15): 8.

———. 1997d. "Right to Privacy versus Public's Right to Know: Wisconsin Newspapers Seek Access to Cops' Complaint Files." *Law Enforcement News* 23 (May 15): 7.

Johnson, Ronald N., and Gary D. Libecap. 1994. *The Federal Civil Service System and the Problem of Bureaucracy: The Economics and Politics of Institutional Change.* Chicago: University of Chicago Press.

Jones, David. 1979. *Crime without Punishment.* Lexington, MA: Lexington Books.

Jones, William C. 1956. "Three Centuries of Commercial Arbitration in New York: A Brief Survey." *Washington University Law Quarterly* (February): 193–221.

Jost, Kenneth. 1981. "Renting Judges in California." *Los Angeles Daily Journal,* July 12.

Kakalik, James S., and Sorrel Wildhorn. 1971. *Private Police in the United States: Findings and Recommendations.* Santa Monica, CA: Rand Corporation.

Kaplan, John. 1970. *Marijuana: The New Prohibition.* New York: World.

———. 1983. *The Hardest Drug: Heroin and Public Policy.* Chicago: University of Chicago Press.

Kelly, David. 1994. "Stalking the Criminal Mind." In *Criminal Justice? The Legal System vs. Individual Responsibility,* ed. Robert J. Bidinotto, 34–46. Irvington-on-Hudson, NY: Foundation for Economic Education.

Kim, Iljoong, Bruce L. Benson, David W. Rasmussen, and Thomas W. Zuehlke. 1993. "An Economic Analysis of Recidivism among Drug Offenders." *Southern Economic Journal* 60 (July): 169–83.

Kinsella, N. Stephan. 1992. "Estoppel: A New Justification for Individual Rights." *Reason Papers* 17 (fall): 61–74.

Kirzner, Israel M. 1997. "Entrepreneurial Discovery and the Competitive Market Process: An Austrian Approach." *Journal of Economic Literature* 35 (March): 60–85.

Kleck, Gary. 1991. *Point Blank: Guns and Violence in America.* New York: Aldine de Gruyter.

Kleck, Gary, and David Bordua. 1983. "The Factual Foundation for Certain Key Assumptions of Gun Control." *Law and Policy Quarterly* 5 (spring): 271–98.

Klein, Daniel B. 1990. "The Voluntary Provision of Public Goods? The Turnpike Companies of Early America." *Economic Inquiry* (October): 788–812.

Klein, Stephen P., and Michael N. Caggiano. 1986. *The Prevalence, Predictability, and Policy Implications of Recidivism.* Santa Monica, CA: Rand Corporation.

Koenig, Richard. 1984. "More Firms Turn to Private Courts to Avoid Expensive Legal Fights." *Wall Street Journal,* January 4.

Krajick, Kevin. 1984a. "Private, For-Profit Prisons Take Hold in Some States." *Christian Science Monitor,* April 11.

———. 1984b. "Punishment for Profit." *Across the Board* 21 (March): 20–27.

Laband, David, and John Sophocleus. 1992. "An Estimate of Resource Expenditures on Transfer Activities in the United States." *Quarterly Journal of Economics* 107:959–83.

Lake, Stuart N. 1931. *Wyatt Earp: Frontier Marshall.* Boston: Houghton Mifflin.

Landes, William M. 1974. "Legality and Reality: Some Evidence of Criminal Procedure." *Journal of Legal Studies* 3 (June): 287–337.

Landes, William M., and Richard A. Posner. 1979. "Adjudication as a Private Good." *Journal of Legal Studies* 8 (March): 235–84.

Langbein, John H. 1973. "The Origins of Public Prosecution at Common Law." *American Journal of Legal History* 17:313–35.

———. 1974. *Prosecuting Crime in the Renaissance: England, Germany, and France.* Cambridge, MA: Harvard University Press.

———. 1978. "The Criminal Trial before the Lawyers." *University of Chicago Law Review* 45 (winter): 236–316.

———. 1979. "Understanding the Short History of Plea Bargaining." *Law and Society Review* 13 (winter): 261–72.

———. 1983. "Shaping the Eighteenth-Century Criminal Trial: A View from the Ryder Sources." *University of Chicago Law Review* 50 (winter): 1–135.

Larson, Elizabeth. 1992. "Cops Out?" *Reason* 23 (January): 16.

Laster, Richard E. 1970. "Criminal Restitution: A Survey of Its Past History and an Analysis of Its Present Usefulness." *University of Richmond Law Review* (fall): 71–80.

Lavan, Rosemary M. 1995. "Modern Buildings Become Fortresses against Terror." *Tallahassee Democrat,* May 17, 3A.

Lawrence, Richard. 1991. "The Impact of Sentencing Guidelines on Corrections." Paper Presented at the Annual Meeting of the Academy of Criminal Justice Sciences.

Lazarus, Steven, John J. Bray, Jr., Larry L. Carter, Kent H. Collins, Bruce A. Giedt, Robert V. Holton, Jr., Phillip D. Matthews, and Gordon C. Willard. 1965. *Resolv-*

ing Business Disputes: The Potential for Commercial Arbitration. New York: American Management Association.

Lester, Jan C. 1996. "Libertarian Restitution and Retribution." Working Paper, Middlesex University, England.

Levitt, Steven D. 1997. "Why Do Increasing Arrest Rates Appear to Reduce Crime: Deterrence, Incapacitation, or Measurement Error?" *Economic Inquiry,* forthcoming.

Liggio, Leonard P. 1977. "The Transportation of Criminals: A Brief Political Economic History." In *Assessing the Criminal: Restitution, Retribution, and the Legal Process,* ed. Randy E. Barnett and John Hagel III, 274–94. Cambridge, MA: Ballinger Press.

Lindesmith, Alfred. 1965. *The Addict and the Law.* New York: Vintage Press.

Logan, Charles H. 1990. *Private Prisons: Cons and Pros.* New York: Oxford University Press.

———. 1992. "Well Kept: Comparing Quality of Confinement in Private and Public Prisons." *Journal of Criminal Law and Criminology* 83 (fall): 577–613.

———. 1995. "Crime Stories." *Public Interest* 119 (spring): 80–85.

Logan, Charles H., and John R. DiIulio, Jr. 1994. "Ten Deadly Myths about Crime and Punishment in the U.S." In *Criminal Justice? The Legal System vs. Individual Responsibility,* ed. Robert J. Bidinotto, 156–78. Irvington-on-Hudson, NY: Foundation for Economic Education.

Logan, Charles H., and Bill W. McGriff. 1989. *Comparing Costs of Public and Private Prisons: A Case Study.* National Institute of Justice: Research in Review.

Logan, Charles H., and Shardla P. Rausch. 1985. "Punish and Profit: The Emergence of Private Enterprise Prisons." *Justice Quarterly* 2 (September): 303–18.

Lott, John R., Jr. 1987. "Should the Wealthy Be Able to 'Buy Justice'?" *Journal of Political Economy* 95 (December): 1307–16.

Lott, John R., Jr., and David B. Mustard. 1997. "Crime, Deterrence, and Right-to-Carry Concealed Handguns." *Journal of Legal Studies* 26 (January): 1–68.

Luce, Duncan R., and Howard Raiffa. 1957. *Games and Decisions.* New York: Wiley.

Lyon, Bruce. 1980. *A Constitutional and Legal History of Medieval England.* 2d ed. New York: W. W. Norton.

Mabry, Rodney H., Holly H. Ulbrich, Hugh H. Macauley, and Michael T. Maloney. 1977. *An Economic Investigation of State and Local Judiciary Services.* Washington, DC: National Institute of Law Enforcement and Criminal Justice, Law Enforcement Assistance Administration, Department of Justice.

MacCallum, Spencer H. 1970. *The Art of Community.* Menlo Park, CA: Institute for Humane Studies.

Martin, Dolores T., and Robert M. Stein. 1992. "An Empirical Analysis of Contracting Out Local Government Services." In *Privatizing the United States Justice System: Police, Adjudication, and Corrections Services from the Private Sector,* ed. Gary W. Bowman, Simon Hakim, and Paul Seidenstat. Jefferson, NC: McFarland.

Marx, Gary T., and Dane Archer. 1971. "Citizen Involvement in the Law Enforcement

Process: The Case of Community Police Patrols." *American Behavioral Scientist* 15:52–72.

Mast, Brent L., Bruce L. Benson, and David W. Rasmussen. 1997. "Entrepreneurial Police and Drug Enforcement Policy." Working Paper, Florida State University.

Mathur, Vijay K. 1978. "Economics of Crime: An Investigation of the Deterrent Hypothesis in Urban Areas." *Review of Economics and Statistics* 60:459–66.

Mattice, Richard A. 1995. "Webber Seavey Award, Semifinalist." Kentwood, Michigan, Police Department (document provided by Clifford Van Meter).

McCrie, Robert D. 1992. "Three Centuries of Criminal Justice Privatization in the United States." In *Privatizing the United States Justice System: Police, Adjudication, and Corrections Services from the Private Sector,* ed. Gary W. Bowman, Simon Hakim, and Paul Seidenstat, 12–26. Jefferson, NC: McFarland.

McDonald, William F. 1977. "The Role of the Victim in America." In *Assessing the Criminal: Restitution, Retribution, and the Legal Process,* ed. Randy E. Barnett and John Hagel III, 295–307. Cambridge, MA: Ballinger.

McGrath, Roger D. 1984. *Gunfighters, Highwaymen and Vigilantes: Violence on the Frontier.* Berkeley: University of California Press.

McLaughlin, Scott E. 1994. "Protection Services in a Free Nation." In *Free Nation Foundation Proceedings: Security in a Free Nation.* Research Triangle Park, NC: Free Nation Foundation.

Meese, Edwin III, and Knut A. Rostad. 1996. "Let Prison Inmates Earn Their Keep." *Wall Street Journal,* May 1.

Meiners, Roger E. 1977. "Public Compensation of the Victims of Crime: How Much Would It Cost?" In *Assessing the Criminal: Restitution, Retribution, and the Legal Process,* ed. Randy E. Barnett and John Hagel III, 309–29. Cambridge, MA: Ballinger Press.

Meyer, Josh. 1987. "Judicate, Others Provide Novel Alternative." *Legal Intelligencer,* March 17.

Michaels, Robert J. 1987. "The Market for Heroin before and after Legalization." In *Dealing with Drugs,* ed. Robert Hamowy, 289–326. Lexington, MA: Lexington Books.

Milakovich, Michael, and Kurt Weis. 1975. "Politics and Measures of Success in the War on Crime." *Crime and Delinquency* 21 (January): 1–10.

Milgrom, Paul R., Douglas C. North, and Barry R. Weingast. 1990. "The Role of Institutions in the Revival of Trade: The Law Merchant, Private Judges, and the Champagne Fairs." *Economics and Politics* (March): 1–23.

Miller, Rod, George E. Sexton, and Victor J. Jacobsen. 1991. *Making Jails Productive.* Washington, DC: U.S. Department of Justice, National Institute of Justice, October.

Miron, Jeffrey A., and Jeffrey Zweibel. 1995. "The Economic Case against Drug Prohibition." *Journal of Economic Perspectives* 9 (fall): 175–92.

Molinari, Gustave de. 1849. "De la Production de la Securite." *Journal des Economistes* (February): 277–90. Trans. J. Huston McCullock under the title *The Production of Security* (New York: Center for Libertarian Studies, 1977) (page references are to the translated edition).

Mondy, R. W. 1943. "Analysis of Frontier Social Instability." *Southwestern Social Science Quarterly* 24 (September): 167–77.

Monks, Gerald P. 1986. "Public Bail—A National Disaster." In *Crime and Punishment in Modern America,* ed. Patrick B. McGuigan and Jon S. Pascale. Washington, DC: Institute for Government and Politics of the Free Congress Research and Education Foundation.

Moran, James. 1995. "Privatizing Criminal Justice." *CJ the Americas* 8 (February–March): 3–4.

Morn, Frank. 1982. *The Eye That Never Sleeps.* Bloomington: Indiana University Press.

Morriss, Andrew P. 1997. "Miners, Vigilantes, and Cattlemen." Working Paper, Case Western Reserve University, College of Law.

Mullen, Joan, Kent Chabotar, and Deborah Carrow. 1985. *The Privatization of Corrections.* ABT Associates report to the National Institute of Justice. Washington, DC: U.S. Department of Justice, February.

Murray, Charles. 1995. "The Physical Environment." In *Crime,* ed. James Q. Wilson and Joan Petersillia, 349–61. San Francisco: Institute for Contemporary Studies Press.

Nader, Laura, and Harry F. Todd, Jr. 1978. "Introduction: The Dispute Process." In *The Disputing Process—Law in Ten Societies,* ed. Laura Nader and Harry F. Todd, Jr., 1–40. New York: Columbia University Press.

National Advisory Commission on Criminal Justice Standards and Goals (NACCJSG). 1973. *Report on Police.* Washington, DC: Department of Justice, Law Enforcement Assistance Administration.

———. 1976. *Private Security: Report of the Task Force on Private Security.* Washington, DC: U.S. Department of Justice, Law Enforcement Assistance Administration.

———. 1977. *Private Security: Standards and Goals—From the Official Private Security Task Force Report.* Cincinnati, OH: Anderson.

National Institute of Justice. 1993. *Felony Defendants in Large Urban Counties, 1990.* Washington, DC: U.S. Department of Justice, National Institute of Justice, May.

Neely, Richard. 1982. *Why Courts Don't Work.* New York: McGraw-Hill.

———. 1992. "The Reasons for the Inefficient U.S. Justice System and Suggested Remedies." In *Privatizing the United States Justice System: Police, Adjudication, and Corrections Services from the Private Sector,* ed. Gary W. Bowman, Simon Hakim, and Paul Seidenstat, 182–88. Jefferson, NC: McFarland.

Nelson, Caleb. 1994. "The Paradox of the Exclusionary Rule." In *Criminal Justice? The Legal System vs. Individual Responsibility,* ed. Robert J. Bidinotto, 102–11. Irvington-on-Hudson, NY: Foundation for Economic Education.

Newman, Oscar. 1972. *Defensible Space: Crime Prevention through Urban Design.* New York: Macmillan.

———. 1980. *Community of Interest.* Garden City, NY: Anchor Press.

Niskanen, William A. 1975. "Bureaucrats and Politicians." *Journal of Law and Economics* 18 (December): 617–43.

———. 1995. "A Good Start on the Contract." *Cato Policy Report* 17 (March/April): 2.

Office of International Criminal Justice (OICJ). 1995. "Readings." Paper presented at the Ninth Annual Futures Conference on Privatization in Criminal Justice: Public and Private Partnerships, University of Illinois at Chicago, March 13–15.

Office of National Drug Control Strategy. 1990. *National Drug Control Strategy.* Washington, DC: Government Printing Office.

"Operating Private Prisons." 1983. *Venture,* August, 18.

"Operation Ident Seen Helpful in Reducing Burglary Chances." 1975. *Crime Control Digest* (September 29): 1.

Osterfeld, David. 1989. "Anarchism and the Public Goods Issue: Law, Courts, and Police." *Journal of Libertarian Studies* 9 (winter): 47–67.

Parks, Roger B., and Ronald J. Oakerson. 1988. *Metropolitan Organization: The St. Louis Case.* Washington, DC: Advisory Commission on Intergovernmental Relations.

Peden, Joseph R. 1977. "Property Rights in Celtic Irish Law." *Journal of Libertarian Studies* 1:81–95.

Perrigo, Lynn I. 1941. "Law and Order in Early Colorado Mining Camps." *Mississippi Valley Historical Review* 28:41–62.

Person, Carl. 1978. "Justice, Inc." *Juris Doctor* 8 (March): 32–39.

Phalon, Richard. 1992. "Privatizing Justice." *Forbes* 150 (December 7): 126–27.

Pierce, Neal R. 1984. "Justice Demonstration Successful for Country." *Washington Post,* April 23.

Podolefsky, Aaron, and Fredric Dubow. 1981. *Strategies for Community Crime Prevention: Collective Responses to Crime in Urban America.* Springfield, IL: Charles C. Thomas.

Pollock, Frederick, and Frederick W. Maitland. 1959. *The History of English Law.* 2 vols. Washington, DC: Lawyers' Literary Club.

Poole, Robert W., Jr. 1977. "More Justice—For Less Money." *Fiscal Watchdog* (July).

———. 1978. *Cutting Back City Hall.* New York: Free Press.

———. 1980. "Can Justice Be Privatized?" *Fiscal Watchdog* 49 (November).

———. 1983a. "Rehabilitating the Correctional System." *Fiscal Watchdog* 81 (July).

———. 1983b. "Why Not Contract Policing?" *Reason* 14 (October).

Pospisil, Leopold. 1971. *Anthropology of Law: A Comparative Theory.* New York: Harper and Row.

Post, Richard S., and Arthur A. Kingsbury. 1970. *Security Administration.* Springfield, IL: Charles C. Thomas.

Pranis, Kay. 1996. "A Hometown Approach to Crime." *State Government News,* October.

Prassel, Frank R. 1972. *The Western Peace Officer.* Norman: University of Oklahoma Press.

Predicast, Inc. 1970. *Special Study 56.* Predicast, Inc.

President's Task Force on Victims of Crime. 1982. *Final Report.* Washington, DC: U.S. Government Printing Office.

Price, Joyce. 1996. "License Plates Not All That Inmates Make." *Washington Times,* April 17.

Priest, George L. 1977. "The Common Law Process and the Selection of Efficient Rules." *Journal of Legal Studies* 50 (January): 65–82.

"Prison Construction, Inmate Numbers Boom." 1997. *Tallahassee Democrat,* August 8, 6A.

Private Corrections Project. 1993. *Private Adult Correctional Facility Census.* 5th ed. Gainesville, FL: Private Corrections Project, University of Florida.

"Private Everything." 1980. *New York Times,* October 20, D3.

"Private Police Forces in Growing Demand." 1983. *U.S. News and World Report,* January 29, 54–56.

"Privatization Census Reveals Continued Expansion." 1995. *Corrections Alert* 1 (March 6): 1–2.

Pruitt, Gary. 1982. "California's Rent-a-Judge Justice." *Journal of Contemporary Studies* 5 (spring): 49–57.

Pudlow, Jan. 1993. "Without Restitution, Crime Really Does Pay." *Tallahassee Democrat,* January 3.

Rasmussen, David W., and Bruce L. Benson. 1994. *The Economic Anatomy of a Drug War: Criminal Justice in the Commons.* Lanham, MD: Rowman and Littlefield.

Rasmussen, David W., Bruce L. Benson, and David L. Sollars. 1993. "Spatial Competition in Illicit Drug Markets: The Consequences of Increased Drug Enforcement." *Review of Regional Studies* 23 (winter): 219–36.

Ray, Larry. 1992. "Privatization of Justice." in *Privatizing the United States Justice System: Police, Adjudication, and Corrections Services from the Private Sector,* ed. Gary W. Bowman, Simon Hakim, and Paul Seidenstat, 190–202. Jefferson, NC: McFarland.

Reaves, Brian A. 1992a. "State and Local Police Departments." *Bureau of Justice Statistics Bulletin* (February): 1–14.

———. 1992b. "Sheriff's Departments. 1990." *Bureau of Justice Statistics Bulletin* (February): 1–11.

Reed, Jane M., and Rhonda S. Stallings. 1992. *Bounty Hunting: The Alternative Justice System,* Houston, TX: Professional Bail Agents of the United States.

Reichman, Nancy. 1987. "The Widening Webs of Surveillance: Private Police Unraveling Deceptive Claims." In *Private Policing,* ed. Clifford D. Shearing and Philip C. Stenning, 247–65. Newbury Park, CA: Sage.

Reid, John Phillip. 1980. *Law for the Elephant: Property and Social Behavior on the Overland Trail.* Salt Lake City: Publishers Press.

"Rent-a-Narc." 1973. *Newsweek,* August 27, 25.

Research and Forecasts, Inc. 1983. *America Afraid: How Fear of Crime Changes the Way We Live, Based on the Widely Publicized Figgie Report.* New York: New America Library.

Reuter, Peter, Robert J. MacCoun, and Patrick J. Murphy. 1990. *Money from Crime: A Study of Drug Dealing in Washington, D.C.* Santa Monica, CA: Rand Corporation.

Reynolds, Morgan O. 1994a. "How to Reduce Crime." in *Criminal Justice? The Legal System vs. Individual Responsibility,* ed. Robert J. Bidinotto. Irvington-on-Hudson, NY: Foundation for Economic Education.

————. 1994b. *Using the Private Sector to Deter Crime.* Dallas: National Center for Policy Analysis.

Rhodes, Robert. 1977. *The Insoluble Problems of Crime.* New York: John Wiley.

Richards, David A. J. 1982. *Sex, Drugs, Death, and the Law: An Essay on Human Rights and Overcriminalization.* Ottawa, NJ: Rowman and Littlefield.

"Rich Towns Walling Themselves Off for Security, Privacy." 1983. *Daily Commerce,* July 4.

Ricks, Truett A., Bill G. Tillett, and Clifford W. Van Meter. 1981. *Principles of Security.* Cincinnati: Anderson.

Rommel, Bart. 1993. *Dirty Tricks Cops Use (and Why They Use Them).* Port Townsend, WA: Loompanics.

Rosa, Joseph G. 1968. *The Gunfighter: Man or Myth?* Norman: University of Oklahoma Press.

Rothbard, Murray. 1973. *For a New Liberty.* New York: Macmillan.

————. 1977. "Punishment and Proportionality." In *Assessing the Criminal: Restitution, Retribution, and the Legal Process,* ed. Randy E. Barnett and John Hagel III, 259–72. Cambridge, MA: Ballinger Press.

————. 1982. *The Ethics of Liberty.* Atlantic Highlands, NJ: Humanities Press.

Rubin, Paul H. 1977. "Why Is the Common Law Efficient?" *Journal of Legal Studies* 6 (January): 51–64.

————. 1979. "The Economic Theory of the Criminal Firm." In *The Economics of Crime and Punishment,* ed. Simon Rottenberg. Washington, DC: American Enterprise Institute.

————. 1983. *Business Firms and the Common Law: The Evolution of Efficient Rules.* New York: Praeger.

Rubinstein, Michael, Stevens H. Clarke, and Teresa T. White. 1980. *Alaska Bans Plea Bargaining.* Washington D.C.: National Institute of Justice.

Rummel, Rudolph J. 1994. *Death by Government.* New Brunswick, NJ: Transaction Publishing.

Rydell, C. Peter, and Susan S. Everingham. 1994. *Modeling the Demand for Cocaine.* Santa Monica, CA: Rand Corporation.

Samenow, Stanton E. 1994. "The Basic Myths about Criminals." In *Criminal Justice? The Legal System vs. Individual Responsibility,* ed. Robert J. Bidinotto, 47–58. Irvington-on-Hudson, NY: Foundation for Economic Education.

Samuelson, Paul A. 1969. "Pure Theory of Public Expenditures and Taxation." In *Public Economics: An Analysis of Public Production and Consumption and Their Relations to the Private Sectors: Proceedings of a Conference held by the International Economics Association,* ed. Julius Margolis and Henri Guitton, 98–123. London: Macmillan.

Samuelson, Paul A., and William D. Nordhaus. 1985. *Economics.* New York: McGraw Hill.

Sando, Bob de. 1986. "Rented Scales of Justice Ends Wait for Day in Court." *Asbury Park Press,* June 23, A2.

Satchell, Michael. 1985. "Victims Have Rights Too." *Parade,* March 17, 15–17.

Savas, E. S. 1974. "Municipal Monopolies versus Competition in Delivering Urban Services." In *Urban Affairs Annual Review,* vol. 8, *Improving the Quality of Urban Management,* ed. Willis D. Hawley and David Rogers, 473–500.

———. 1982. *Privatizing the Public Sector: How to Shrink Government.* Chatham, NJ: Chatham House.

Schmidtz, David. 1991. *The Limits of Government: An Essay on the Public Goods Argument.* Boulder, CO: Westview Press.

Schulhofer, Stephen J. 1988. "Criminal Justice Discretion as a Regulatory System." *Journal of Legal Studies* 17 (January): 43–82.

Schulhofer, Stephen J., and David D. Friedman. 1993. "Rethinking Indigent Defense: Promoting Effective Representation through Consumer Sovereignty and Freedom of Choice for All Criminals." *American Criminal Law Review* 31 (fall): 73–122.

"Security Checks Could Be Privatized." 1996. *Oakland Tribune,* July 2.

Shanahan, Michael G. 1992. "Private Sector Liaison with Police." In *Privatizing the United States Justice System: Police, Adjudication, and Corrections Services from the Private Sector,* ed. Gary W. Bowman, Simon Hakim, and Paul Seidenstat, 178–81. Jefferson, NC: McFarland.

Shapiro, Carol. 1990. "Is Restitution Legislation the Chameleon of the Victims' Movement." In *Criminal Justice, Restitution, and Reconciliation,* ed. Burt Galaway and Joe Hudson, 73–80. Monsey, NY: Criminal Justice Press.

Sharp, John. 1991. *Breaking the Mold: New Ways to Govern Texas.* Vol. 2, part 2. Austin: Texas Performance Review, Texas Comptroller of Public Accounts.

Shearing, Clifford D., and Phillip C. Stenning. 1987a. "Reframing Police." In *Private Policing,* ed. Clifford D. Shearing and Phillip C. Stenning. Newbury Park, CA: Sage.

————. 1987b. "Say Cheese! The Disney Order That Is Not So Mickey Mouse." In *Private Policing,* ed. Clifford D. Shearing and Phillip C. Stenning. Newbury Park, CA: Sage.

Shedd, Jeffrey. 1982. "Making Good[s] behind Bars." *Reason* 13 (March).

Shelling, Thomas. 1971. "What Is the Business of Organized Crime? *American Scholar* 40 (autumn): 643–52.

Sherman, Lawrence W. 1983. "Patrol Strategies for Police." In *Crime and Public Policy,* ed. James Q. Wilson, 145–64. San Francisco: Institute for Contemporary Studies.

————. 1995. "The Police." In *Crime,* ed. James Q. Wilson and Joan Petersillia, 325–48. San Francisco: Institute for Contemporary Studies Press.

Silver, Carol, and Don Kates, Jr. 1977. "Self-Defense, Handgun Ownership and the Independence of Women in a Violent, Sexist Society." In *Restricting Handguns: The Liberal Skeptics Speak Out,* ed. Don Kates, Jr., 139–69. New York: North River Press.

Silver, Marilyn. 1974. *Punishment, Deterrence, and Police Effectiveness: A Survey and Critical Interpretation of Recent Econometric Literature.* New York: Crime Deterrence and Offender Career Project.

Skogan, Wesley, and Michael Maxfield. 1979. *Coping with Crime: Victimization, Fear and Reaction to Crime in Three American Cities.* Evanston, IL: Center for Urban Studies, Northwestern University.

Skolnick, Jerome, and David H. Bayley. 1988. "Theme and Variation in Community Policing." In *Crime and Justice: A Review of Research,* vol. 10, ed. Michael Tonry and Norval Morris, 1–38. Chicago: University of Chicago Press.

Smith, Adam. 1976. *An Inquiry into the Nature and Causes of the Wealth of Nations.* 1776. Reprint, Oxford: Oxford University Press.

Smith, Barbara E., Robert C. Davis, and Susan W. Hillenbrand. 1989. *Improving Enforcement of Court-Ordered Restitution.* Chicago: American Bar Association.

Smith, George. 1979. "Justice Entrepreneurship in a Free Market." *Journal of Libertarian Studies* 3 (winter): 405–26.

Sneed, John. 1977. "Order without Law: Where will the Anarchists Keep the Madman?" *Journal of Libertarian Studies* 1 (spring): 117–24.

Sollars, David L., Bruce L. Benson, and David W. Rasmussen. 1994. "Drug Enforcement and Deterrence of Property Crime among Local Jurisdictions." *Public Finance Quarterly* 22 (January): 22–45.

Solvason, Birgir T. R. 1992. "Ordered Anarchy: Evolution of the Decentralized Legal Order in the Icelandic Commonwealth." *Journal des Economistes et des Etudes Humaines* 3 (June/September): 333–51.

————. 1993. "Institutional Evolution in the Icelandic Commonwealth." *Constitutional Political Economy* 4:97–125.

Sorin, Martin D. 1986. *Out on Bail.* Washington, DC: U.S. Department of Justice, National Institute of Justice.

Steckmesser, Kent Ladd. 1965. *The Western Hero in History and Legend.* Norman: University of Oklahoma Press.

Stephen, James. 1883. *A History of the Criminal Law of England.* Reprint, New York: Burt Franklin, 1963.

Stephenson, Frank. 1994. "War Crime: Legacy of a Lost Cause." *Research in Review* 5 (spring): 8–34.

Stewart, George R. 1964. *Committee of Vigilance: Revolution in San Francisco, 1851.* Boston: Houghton Mifflin.

Stewart, James K. 1989. Letter to the *Wall Street Journal,* July 26.

Stigler, George J. 1970. "The Optimum Enforcement of Laws." *Journal of Political Economy* 78 (May/June).

———. 1971. "The Theory of Economic Regulation," *Bell Journal of Economics and Management Science* 2 (spring): 3–21.

Stutmann, Robert M., and Richard Esposito. 1992. *Dead on Delivery: Inside the Drug Wars, Straight from the Street.* New York: Warner Books.

Swimmer, Eugene. 1974. "Measurement of the Effectiveness of Urban Law Enforcement—A Simultaneous Approach." *Southern Economic Journal* 40:618–30.

Thaler, Richard. 1977. "An Econometric Analysis of Property Crime." *Journal of Public Economics* 8: 37–51.

Thomas, Charles W. 1989. *The Background, Present Status, and Future Potential of Privatization in American Correction.* Gainesville, FL: Private Correctional Services Association.

Thornton, Mark. 1991. *The Economics of Prohibition.* Salt Lake City: University of Utah Press.

"To Catch a Thief: Antiburglar System Works in Iowa Town." 1970. *Wall Street Journal,* November 24.

Tolchin, Martin. 1985. "Private Courts with Binding Rulings Draw Interest and Some Challenges." *New York Times,* May 12, 38.

"Tough 'No-Plea-Bargain' Judge Shifted to Family-Court Division." 1994. *Tallahassee Democrat* (November 28): 3B.

Trojanowicz, Robert, and Mark H. Moore. 1988. *The Meaning of Community in Community Policing.* East Lansing, MI: National Neighborhood Foot Patrol Center.

Tullock, Gordon. 1967. "The Welfare Costs of Tariffs, Monopolies, and Theft." *Western Economic Journal* 5:224–32.

———. 1970. *Private Wants, Public Means: An Economic Analysis of the Desirable Scope of Government.* New York: Basic Books.

Umbeck, John R. 1981a. *A Theory of Property Rights with Application to the California Gold Rush.* Ames: Iowa State University Press.

———. 1981b. "Might Makes Rights: A Theory of the Formation and Initial Distribution of Property Rights." *Economic Inquiry* 19:38–59.

Umbreit, Mark S. 1995. "The Development and Impact of Victim-Offender Mediation in the United States." *Mediation Quarterly* 12 (spring): 263–76.

Umbreit, Mark S., and Susan L. Stacey. 1996. "Family Group Conferencing Comes to the U.S.: A Comparison with Victim-Offender Mediation." *Juvenile and Family Court Journal* 47 (spring): 29–38.

Valentine, Alan. 1956. *Vigilante Justice.* New York: Reynal.

Valentine, Tim. 1992. "Private Prosecution." In *Privatizing the United States Justice System: Police, Adjudication, and Corrections Services from the Private Sector,* ed. Gary W. Bowman, Simon Hakim, and Paul Seidenstat, 226–28. Jefferson, NC: McFarland.

Van Caenegem, R. C. 1973. *The Birth of English Common Law.* Cambridge: Cambridge University Press.

Wahlroos, Bjorn. 1981. "On Finnish Property Criminality: An Empirical Analysis of the Post-War Era Using an Ehrlich Model." *Scandinavian Journal of Economics* 83:555–62.

Walker, Jesse. 1996. "Behind These Bars. *Liberty* 9 (July).

Walsh, William, Edwin J. Donovan, and James F. McNicholas. 1992. "The Starrett Protective Service: Private Policing in an Urban Community." In *Privatizing the United States Justice System: Police, Adjudication, and Corrections Services from the Private Sector,* ed. Gary W. Bowman, Simon Hakim, and Paul Seidenstat, 157–77. Jefferson, NC: McFarland.

Walter, David. 1994. "Crime in the Welfare State." In *Criminal Justice? The Legal System vs. Individual Responsibility,* ed. Robert J. Bidinotto, 59–62. Irvington-on-Hudson, NY: Foundation for Economic Education.

Waters, Frank. 1960. *The Earp Brothers of Tombstone.* New York.

Williamson, Oliver E. 1983. "Credible Commitments: Using Hostages to Support Exchange." *American Economic Review* 83 (September): 519–40.

Wilson, James Q. 1977. "Preface: Thinking Practically about Crime." In *Assessing the Criminal: Restitution, Retribution, and the Legal Process,* ed. Randy E. Barnett and John Hagel III, viii–xxv. Cambridge, MA: Ballinger Press.

Wilson, James Q., and Joan Petersillia, eds. 1995. *Crime.* San Francisco: Institute for Contemporary Studies Press.

Wilson, Richard J. 1982. *Contract Bid Program: A Threat to Quality Indigent Care.* Washington, DC: National Legal Aid and Defender Association.

Wisotsky, Steven. 1991. "Zero Tolerance/Zero Freedom." Paper presented at the Seventh Annual Critical Issues Symposium, Florida State University, Tallahassee.

Wooldridge, William C. 1970. *Uncle Sam, the Monopoly Man.* New Rochelle, NY: Arlington House.

Wynne, John M., Jr. 1978. *Prison Employee Unionism: The Impact on Correctional Administration and Programs.* Washington, DC: National Institute of Law Enforcement and Criminal Justice, January.

Yandle, Bruce. 1991. "Organic Constitutions and Common Law." *Constitutional Political Economy* 2 (spring/summer): 225–41.

Yeoman, Adam. 1995. "Cars Are Prisons' Newest Product." *Tallahassee Democrat* (October 18): 4B.

Yin, Robert K., Mary E. Vogel, Jan N. Chaiken, and Deborah R. Both. 1977. *Citizen Patrol Projects.* Washington, DC: National Institute of Law Enforcement and Criminal Justice, Law Enforcement Assistance Administration, U.S. Department of Justice.

Zedlewski, Edwin W. 1992. "Private Security and Controlling Crime." In *Privatizing the United States Justice System: Police, Adjudication, and Corrections Services from the Private Sector,* ed. Gary W. Bowman, Simon Hakim, and Paul Seidenstat, 42–55. Jefferson, NC: McFarland.

Index

About the Author

Bruce L. Benson, DeVoe Moore Professor and Distinguished Research Professor at Florida State University, and Senior Fellow of the Independent Institute, is also an Associate of the Political Economy Research Center, an Adjunct Fellow of the Enterprise Prisons Institute, an Adjunct Scholar of the Ludwig von Mises Institute, and a Research Advisory Council Member of the James Madison Institute for Policy Studies. He serves as an Associate Editor of the *Journal of Regional Science,* a Contributing Editor for *The Independent Review: A Journal of Political Economy,* an Associate Editor of the *Quarterly Journal of Austrian Economics,* and and was an invited guest editor of the September 1998 issue of the *Journal of Drug Issues.* Professor Benson has published widely in academic journals and books on the economics of law and crime, public choice, and spatial economics. Along with more than ninety academic articles in a variety of journals, he has contributed more than thirty chapters to edited volumes. His books include *Antitrust Law in Theory and Practice* (1989, with M. L. Greenhut), *The Enterprise of Law: Justice without the State* (1990), and *The Economic Anatomy of a Drug War: Criminal Justice in the Commons* (1994, with David W. Rasmussen). Professor Benson has received the Georgescu-Roegen Prize in Economics for the best article in the *Southern Economic Journal* (1989), a Ludwig von Mises prize for Scholarship in "Austrian School Economics" (1992), an F. Leroy Hill Fellowship from the Institute for Humane Studies (1986), and three Earhart Research Fellowships from the Earhart Foundation (1991, 1992, and 1995). The Scaife Foundation, the Carthage Foundation, the Institute for Humane Studies, the Florida Legislature, the National Institute for Alcohol Abuse and Alcoholism, and several other private and public organizations have supported his work with research grants. His *Enterprise of Law* was an honorable mention runner-up for the 1991 Free Press Association's H. L. Mencken National Book Award. He has been an elected member of the Board of Trustees of the Southern Economic Association (1995 through 1997) and was a Salvatori Fellow of the Salvatori Center for Academic Leadership at the Heritage Foundation (1992–94).